The Evolutionary Emergence of Language

Language has no counterpart in the animal world. Unique to *Homo sapiens,* it appears inseparable from human nature. But how, when and why did it emerge? The contributors to this volume – linguists, anthropologists, cognitive scientists and others – adopt a modern Darwinian perspective to offer a bold synthesis of the human and natural sciences. As a feature of human social intelligence, language evolution is driven by biologically anomalous levels of social cooperation. Phonetic competence correspondingly reflects social pressures for vocal imitation, learning and other forms of social transmission. Distinctively human social and cultural strategies gave rise to the complex syntactic structure of speech. This book, presenting language as a remarkable social adaptation, testifies to the growing influence of evolutionary thinking in contemporary linguistics. It will be welcomed by all those interested in human evolution, evolutionary psychology, linguistic anthropology and general linguistics.

Chris Knight is Reader in Anthropology at the University of East London. His highly acclaimed and widely debated first book, *Blood Relations: Menstruation and the Origins of Culture* (1991), outlined a new theory of human origins. He has also authored many book chapters and journal articles on human cognitive and linguistic evolution and was coeditor of *Approaches to the Evolution of Language* (1998).

Michael Studdert-Kennedy is past President of Haskins Laboratories and Professor Emeritus of Psychology at the University of Connecticut and of Communications at the City University of New York. He has published numerous articles on speech perception and speech development and edited or coedited several books, including *Psychobiology of Language* (1983) and *Approaches to the Evolution of Language* (1998).

James R. Hurford has been Professor of General Linguistics at the University of Edinburgh since 1979. He is the author of many books, including *Language and Number: The Emergence of a Cognitive System* (1987), and was coeditor of *Approaches to the Evolution of Language* (1998). He is perhaps best known for his computer simulations of various aspects of the evolution of language.

The Evolutionary Emergence of Language

Social Function and the Origins of Linguistic Form

Edited by

CHRIS KNIGHT

University of East London

MICHAEL STUDDERT-KENNEDY

Haskins Laboratories
University of Connecticut
City University of New York

JAMES R. HURFORD

University of Edinburgh

CAMBRIDGE
UNIVERSITY PRESS

PUBLISHED BY THE PRESS SYNDICATE OF THE UNIVERSITY OF CAMBRIDGE
The Pitt Building, Trumpington Street, Cambridge, United Kingdom

CAMBRIDGE UNIVERSITY PRESS
The Edinburgh Building, Cambridge CB2 2RU, UK
40 West 20th Street, New York, NY 10011-4211, USA
10 Stamford Road, Oakleigh, VIC 3166, Australia
Ruiz de Alarcón 13, 28014 Madrid, Spain
Dock House, The Waterfront, Cape Town 8001, South Africa

http://www.cambridge.org

First published 2000

Printed in the United States of America

Typeface Times Roman 10/13 pt.   *System* LaTeX 2_ε [TB]

A catalog record for this book is available from the British Library.

Library of Congress Cataloging in Publication Data
The Evolutionary emergence of language : social function and the origins of linguistic
form / [edited by] Chris Knight, Michael Studdert-Kennedy, James R. Hurford.
        p.   cm.
    Includes bibliographical references and index.
    ISBN 0-521-78157-4
    1. Language and languages – Origin.   2. Linguistic anthropology.   3. Human evolution.
I. Knight, Chris, 1942–   II. Studdert-Kennedy, Michael.   III. Hurford, James R.
    P116.E93   2000
    401 – dc21   00–020471

ISBN 0 521 78157 4 hardback
ISBN 0 521 78696 7 paperback

Contents

Part II   The Emergence of Phonetic Structure

Part III   The Emergence of Syntax

Contributors

Derek Bickerton, Department of Linguistics, University of Hawaii, Honolulu, Hawaii 96822, USA. <derek@hawaii.edu>

Bart de Boer, Laboratory for Artificial Intelligence, Vrije Universiteit Brussel, Pleinlaan 2, 1050 Brussels, Belgium. <bartb@arti.vub.ac.be>

Robbins Burling, Department of Anthropology, University of Michigan, 1020 LSA Building, Ann Arbor, Michigan 48109, USA. <rburling@umich.edu>

Andrew Carstairs-McCarthy, Department of Linguistics, University of Canterbury, Private Bag 4800, Christchurch, New Zealand.
<a.c-mcc@ling.canterbury.ac.nz>

Barbara L. Davis, Speech and Hearing Center, University of Texas, Austin, Texas 78712, USA. <babs@mail.utexas.edu>

Rory A. DePaolis, Department of Communication Sciences and Disorders, James Madison University, Harrisonburg, Virginia 22807, USA.
<depaolra@jmu.edu>

Jean-Louis Dessalles, Modèles Informatiques pour le Langage et la Cognition, Département Informatique, E.N.S.T., 46 rue Barrault, 75013 Paris, France.
<dessalles@enst.fr>

Colin Fyfe, Department of Computing and Information Systems, University of Paisley, High St Paisley, Renfrewshire PA1 2BE, UK.
<colin.fyfe@paisley.ac.uk>

James R. Hurford, Department of Linguistics, University of Edinburgh, Adam Ferguson Building, George Square, Edinburgh EH8 9LL, UK.
<jim@ling.ed.ac.uk>

Simon Kirby, Department of Linguistics, University of Edinburgh, Adam Ferguson Building, George Square, Edinburgh EH8 9LL, UK.
<simon@ling.ed.ac.uk>

Chris Knight, Department of Sociology and Anthropology, University of East London, Longbridge Road, Dagenham, Essex RM8 2AS, UK. <c.knight@uel.ac.uk>

David Lightfoot, Linguistics Department, University of Maryland, College Park, Maryland 20742-7515, USA. <dlight@deans.umd.edu>

Daniel Livingstone, Department of Computing and Information Systems, University of Paisley, High St Paisley, Renfrewshire PA1 2BE, UK. <livi-ci0@paisley.ac.uk>

Peter F. MacNeilage, Department of Psychology, University of Texas, Austin, Texas 78712, USA. <macneilage@mail.utexas.edu>

Frederick J. Newmeyer, Department of Linguistics, University of Washington, Seattle, Washington 98195, USA. <fjn@u.washington.edu>

Jason Noble, Center for Adaptive Behavior and Cognition, Max-Planck-Institut für Bildungsforschung, Lentzeallee 94, D-14195 Berlin, Germany. <noble@canetoad.mpib-berlin.mpg.de>

Mark Pagel, School of Animal and Microbial Sciences, University of Reading, Whiteknights, Reading RG6 6AJ, UK. <m.pagel@reading.ac.uk>

Camilla Power, Department of Anthropology, University College London, Gower Street, London WC1E 6BT, UK. <ucsaccp@ucl.ac.uk>

Michael Studdert-Kennedy, Haskins Laboratories, 270 Crown Street, New Haven, Connecticut 06511-6695, USA. <msk@haskins.yale.edu>

Marilyn M. Vihman, School of Psychology, University of Wales Bangor, Gwynedd LL56 2DG, UK. <m.vihman@bangor.ac.uk>

Robert P. Worden, Charteris Ltd., 6 Kinghorn Street, London EC1A 7HT, UK. <rpw@charteris.com>

Alison Wray, Centre for Applied Language Studies, University of Wales, Swansea Singleton Park, Swansea SA2 8PP, UK. <a.m.wray@swansea.ac.uk>

Acknowledgements

This volume grew out of the Second International Conference on the Evolution of Language, held at the University of East London in April 1998. We gratefully acknowledge support from the British Academy, the Royal Anthropological Institute and the Linguistics Association of Great Britain. Chris Knight thanks the Department of Sociology and Anthropology, University of East London, and, in particular, acknowledges the dedication of his research assistant, Catherine Arthur. Michael Studdert-Kennedy thanks Haskins Laboratories for their support.

Language: A Darwinian Adaptation?

CHRIS KNIGHT, MICHAEL STUDDERT-KENNEDY
AND JAMES R. HURFORD

> Let me just ask a question which everyone else who has been faithfully attending
> these sessions is surely burning to ask. If some rules you have described consti-
> tute universal constraints on all languages, yet they are not learned, nor are they
> somehow logically necessary *a priori*, how did language get that way?
>
> Stevan Harnad, in a conference question to Noam Chomsky
> (Harnad, Steklis and Lancaster 1976: 57)

As a feature of life on earth, language is one of science's great remaining mysteries. A central difficulty is that it appears so radically incommensurate with nonhuman systems of communication as to cast doubt on standard neo-Darwinian
accounts of its evolution by natural selection. Yet scientific (as opposed to religious or philosophical) arguments for a discontinuity between human and
animal communication have come into prominence only over the past 40 years.
As long as behaviourism dominated anglophone psychology and linguistics, the
transition from animal calls to human speech seemed to offer no particular difficulty (see, for example, Mowrer 1960; Skinner 1957). But the generative revolution in linguistics, begun with the publication of Noam Chomsky's *Syntactic
Structures* in 1957 and developed in many subsequent works (e.g. Chomsky
1965, 1966, 1972, 1975, 1986; Chomsky and Halle 1968) radically altered our
conception of language, and posed a challenge to evolutionary theory that we
are still striving to meet.

The central goal of Chomsky's work has been to formalise, with mathematical rigour and precision, the properties of a successful grammar, that is, of a
device for producing all possible sentences, and no impossible sentences, of
a particular language. Such a grammar, or syntax, is autonomous with respect
to both the meaning of a sentence and the physical structures (sounds, script,
manual signs) that convey it; it is a purely formal system for arranging words

(or morphemes) into a pattern that a native speaker would judge to be grammatically correct, or at least acceptable. Chomsky has demonstrated that the logical structure of such a grammar is very much more complex and difficult to formulate than we might suppose, and that its descriptive predicates (syntactic categories, phonological classes) are not commensurate with those of any other known system in the world, or in the mind. Moreover, the underlying principle, or logic, of a syntactic rule system is not immediately given on the surface of the utterances that it determines (Lightfoot, this volume), but must somehow be inferred from that surface – a task that may defeat even professional linguists and logicians. Yet every normal child learns its native language, without special guidance or reinforcement from adult companions, over the first few years of life, when other seemingly simpler analytic tasks are well beyond its reach.

To account for this remarkable feat, Chomsky (1965, 1972) proposed an innate 'language acquisition device', including a schema of the 'universal grammar' (UG) to which, by hypothesis, every language must conform. The schema, a small set of principles, and of parameters that take different values in different languages, is highly restrictive, so that the child's search for the grammar of the language it is learning will not be impossibly long. Specifying the parameters of UG, and their values in different languages, both spoken and signed, remains an ongoing task for the generative enterprise.

By placing language in the individual mind / brain rather than in the social group to which the individual belongs, Chomsky broke with the Saussurean and behaviouristic approaches that had prevailed in anglophone linguistics and psychology during the first half of the twentieth century. At the same time, by returning language to its Cartesian status as a property of mind (or reason) and a defining property of human nature (Chomsky 1966), Chomsky reopened language to psychological and evolutionary study, largely dormant since *The Descent of Man* (Darwin 1871).

We have no reason to suppose that Chomsky actually intended to revive such studies. For although he views linguistics as a branch of psychology, and psychology as a branch of biology, he sees their goals as quite distinct. The task of the linguist is to describe the structure of language much as an anatomist might describe that of a biological organ such as the heart; indeed, Chomsky has conceptualised language as in essence the output of a unitary organ or 'module', hard-wired in the human brain. The complementary role of the psychologist is to elucidate language function and its development in the individual, while physiologists, neurologists and psychoneurologists chart its underlying structures and mechanisms. As for the evolutionary debate, Chomsky has had little to offer other than his doubts concerning the likely role of natural selection in shaping the structure of language. This scepticism evidently stems, in part, from the belief (shared with many other linguists, e.g. Bickerton 1990 and Jackendoff 1994) that language is not so much a system of communication, on which social selection pressures might indeed have come to bear, as it is a system for mental representation and thought. In any event, Chomsky has conspicuously left to others the social, psychological and biological issues that his work has raised.

The first to take up the challenge was Eric Lenneberg (1967). His book (to which Chomsky contributed an appendix on 'The formal nature of language') is still among the most biologically sophisticated, thoughtful and stimulating introductions to the biology of language. Lenneberg drew on a mass of clinical, comparative and evolutionary data to construct a theory of epigenetic development, according to a relatively fixed maturational schedule, with 'critical periods' for the development of speech and language. Lenneberg saw language as a self-contained biological system, with characteristic perceptual, motoric and cognitive modes of action; for its evolution he proposed a discontinuity theory, intended to be compatible both with developmental biology and with the newly recognised unique structure of language.

Other researchers were less willing to accept a gap in the evolutionary record. Indeed, it was apparently concern with the discontinuity implicit in the new linguistics that prompted the New York Academy of Sciences in 1976 to sponsor a multidisciplinary, international conference entitled 'Origins and Evolution of Language and Speech'. In his opening remarks at the conference, Stevan Harnad observed:

Virtually all aspects of our relevant knowledge have changed radically since the nineteenth century. Our concept of language is totally altered and has become both more profound and more complex. The revolution in linguistics due to Noam Chomsky has provided a very different idea of what the nature of the 'target' for the evolutionary process might actually be. (Harnad, Steklis and Lancaster 1976: 1)

While assembling many diverse and often still useful contributions on virtually every topic that might conceivably bear on the evolution of language, the conference did little to meet the challenge it had undertaken to address. In fact, its main achievement was to reveal the fierce recalcitrance of the problem, and the need for a more sharply focused attack on the evolution of linguistic form.

Such an attack came first from Derek Bickerton (1981, 1990, 1995, 1998), a linguist and an expert on pidgins and creoles. Bickerton has been at the controversial center of discussions on language evolution for nearly twenty years, and several aspects of his work deserve comment. First is his contribution to the continuity/discontinuity debate. Our difficulties arise, according to Bickerton, because we have focused too heavily on communication instead of on more basic systems of underlying representation. Natural selection favours increasingly complex systems of perceiving and representing the world. This is because enhanced sensitivity to aspects of the environment predictably affords an animal advantages over its fellows (cf. Ulbaek 1998). Eventually, however, curiosity, attention and long-term memory reach a point of development such that any further gain in knowledge of the world can come only from more complex representation, and this is what language provides. 'Language ... is not even primarily a means of communication. Rather it is a system of representation, a means for sorting and manipulating the plethora of information that deluges us throughout our waking life' (Bickerton 1990: 5).

How and when did the new representational system arise? According to Bickerton, the first step was taken by *Homo erectus* somewhere between 1.5 million and five hundred thousand years ago. This was the step from primate-style vocalizing into 'protolanguage', a system of arbitrary vocal reference that called only 'for some kind of label to be attached to a small number of preexisting concepts' (Bickerton 1990: 128). Bickerton's protolanguage is a phylogenetic precursor of true language that is recapitulated in the child (cf. Lamendella 1976), and can be elicited by training from the chimpanzee. Speakers (or signers) of a protolanguage have a referential lexicon, but essentially no grammatical items and no syntax. Bickerton justifies the concept of protolanguage as a unitary mode of representation, peculiar to our species, because it emerges, naturally and in essentially identical forms, through mere exposure to words. This happens not only in children under age two, but also in older children deprived of language during the 'critical period,' and even in adults obliged to communicate in a second language of which they know only a few words. The pidgins of the Caribbean and the Pacific, and of Russian and Scandinavian sailors in the Norwegian Sea, are adult forms of protolanguage.

The final step, the emergence of syntax in anatomically modern *Homo sapiens*, is more problematic. In his first book, *Roots of Language* (1981), Bickerton argued for the gradual evolution of a syntactic 'bioprogram', a dynamic, epigenetic process according to which language unfolds in the child, guided by the ambient language. He stressed that 'evolution has advanced not by leaps and bounds, but by infinitesimal gradations' (Bickerton 1981: 221). In his second book, however, Bickerton (1990: 177ff.) was troubled by logical difficulties in conceiving an 'interlanguage' that might have mediated between protolanguage and full language. He abandoned his gradualist bioprogram in favor of Chomskyan UG, and proposed a saltationist account of its origin. To support this account he drew on three main lines of evidence. First was fossil evidence for a sudden increase in the hominid 'tool kit' (bladed tools, cave paintings, stone figurines, lunar calendars and other artefacts) at the '*erectus-sapiens* interface', without any corresponding increase in brain size. Second were studies of child development, including the emergence of syntactically structured creole languages out of structureless pidgins in a single generation. Third was evidence, from the distribution of mitochondrial DNA in modern populations, that all modern humans descend from one female who lived in Africa about 220,000 (± 70,000) years ago (Cann, Stoneking and Wilson 1987). Bickerton proposed this female as the carrier of a single 'crucial mutation' that, in a catastrophic cascade of sequelae, reshaped the skull, altered the form of the vocal tract and rewired the brain (1990: 196).

Prominent archaeological contributors to debates on the evolution of 'modern' behaviour (e.g. Klein 1995; Mellars 1991, 1998) endorsed the notion of some such genetically based cognitive leap. But among evolutionary biologists Bickerton's syntax-generating macromutation met with incredulity and a barrage of forceful criticism. In response Bickerton (this volume) has moderated his position to allow for a slower, though still rapid, process of genetic assimilation through cumulative 'Baldwin effects' (Baldwin 1896). On this account, syntax emerged by cognitive exaptation of thematic roles (Agent, Theme, Goal) that had already evolved in the service of a social calculus of reciprocal altruism.

Criticism of Bickerton's saltationist Darwinism doubtless owed much of its vigour and confidence to a change in intellectual climate precipitated by the 'selfish gene' revolution in the life sciences (Hamilton 1964; Trivers 1971; Dawkins 1976). Notice of the impact of this revolution on linguistics was served by Steven Pinker and Paul Bloom, who broke the barrier between generative linguistics and language evolution with a widely discussed article entitled 'Natural language and natural selection' (Pinker and Bloom 1990). In this article, they portrayed the human language faculty (specifically, the capacity for generative grammar) as a biological adaptation that could be explained in standard neo-Darwinian terms (see also Newmeyer 1991). Appearing in a respected and widely read interdisciplinary journal, *Behavioral and Brain Sciences*, the article situated language evolution for the first time as a legitimate topic within the natural science mainstream, prompting a debate that has continued to this day.

In championing gradualist Darwinian adaptationism against the scepticism of Chomsky and others, Pinker and Bloom in fact set themselves a modest agenda. They attributed the language module to unspecified selection pressures whose onset they traced to the Australopithecine stage. They exempted themselves from having to offer a more precise or testable theory by arguing that Darwinians need not address the emergence of novelty, being required only to provide evidence that a novel adaptation – once it has emerged – confers fitness. The two authors therefore by their own admission said 'virtually nothing' (Pinker and Bloom 1990: 765) about language origins. They were satisfied with having established language as a biological adaptation, its evolution falling within the remit of standard Darwinian theory.

We may easily suppose that the evolution of language is unproblematic since it seems so beneficial to all. Indeed, as Nettle (1999a: 216) has pointed out, Pinker and Bloom in their seminal paper clearly take this view:

[There is] an obvious advantage to being able to acquire information second-hand: by tapping into the vast reservoir of knowledge accumulated by other individuals, one can avoid having to duplicate the possibly time-consuming and dangerous trial-and-error process that won that knowledge. (1990: 712)

For a strategy to evolve, however, it must not only increase fitness, but also be *evolutionarily stable*. That is, there must be no alternative strategy which gives competitors higher fitness. In the case of information exchange, there are such strategies: individuals who deceive others in order to further their own interests, or who 'freeload' – enjoying the benefits of cooperation without paying the costs – will, under most circumstances, have higher fitness than those abiding by the social contract (Nettle 1999a: 216). In the light of what we know about the 'Machiavellian' manipulative and deceptive strategies of the great apes (Byrne and Whiten 1988), it is far from self-evident that reliance on *second-hand information* would have been a viable strategy for early hominids. Or rather, unless there were additional mechanisms to ensure against *cheating on contractual understandings*, it would seem that language could not have been adaptive (Nettle 1999a; Knight 1998; Power 1998, this volume). We return to this point.

Pinker and Bloom dated language to some two to four million years ago, arguing that it allowed hominids to share memories, agree on joint plans and pool knowledge concerning, say, the whereabouts of food. Built into this model was the assumption that something resembling the lifestyle of extant hunter-gatherers was already being established during the Plio-Pleistocene. Such an approach has one clear advantage: it apparently allows sufficient time for slow, gradualist evolution of the posited complex module. However, palaeolithic ar-chaeologists have been unable to confirm claimed evidence for hunter-gatherer levels of cooperation among Australopithecine or other early hominids. Even as brain size exceeded the ape range, corresponding lifestyles seem to have re-mained essentially primate-like: *Homo erectus* males may have been relatively competent hunters and scavengers, but they were not provisioning dependents with hunted meat carried back to base camps (O'Connell et al. 1999). If these hominids had 'language', then it seems remarkable how little its effects show up in the archaeological record, which affords no evidence for home bases, logistically planned hunting, personal ornamentation, art or ritually enforced social contracts until late in the Pleistocene (Bickerton 1990; Binford 1989; Knight 1991; Mithen 1996, 1999; Stringer and Gamble 1993).

While these debates were under way, primatologist Robin Dunbar (1993, 1996) intervened with a substantially novel methodology and explanatory framework. In work conducted jointly with palaeontologist Leslie Aiello (Aiello and Dunbar 1993), he correlated language evolution with the fossil record for rapid neocortical expansion in *Homo sapiens*, dating key developments to between 400,000 and 250,000 years ago. For the first time, this work specified concrete Darwinian selection pressures driving language evolution. The outcome was a model consistent with primatological theory and testable in the light of palaeontological and archaeological data.

Dunbar (1993) set out from the observation that primates maintain social bonds by manual grooming. Besides being energetically costly, this allows only one individual to be addressed at a time; it also occupies both hands, precluding other activities such as foraging or feeding. As group size in humans increased, multiplying the number of relationships each individual had to monitor, this method of servicing relationships became increasingly difficult to afford. According to Dunbar (1993), the cheaper method of 'vocal grooming' was the solution. Reliance on vocalisation not only freed the hands, allowing simultaneous foraging and other activities, but also enabled multiple partners to be 'groomed' at once.

For Dunbar, the switch from manual to vocal grooming began with the appearance of *Homo erectus*, around two million years ago. At this early stage, vocalisations were not meaningful in any linguistic sense but were experienced as intrinsically rewarding, much like the contact-calls of geladas and other primates. Then from around four hundred thousand years ago, with the emergence of archaic *Homo sapiens* in Africa, 'vocalisations began to acquire meaning' (Dunbar 1996: 115). Once meaning had arrived, the human species possessed language. But it was not yet 'symbolic language'. It could enable gossip, but still fell short of allowing reference to 'abstract concepts' (Dunbar 1996: 116). Language in its modern sense – as a system for communicating abstract thought – emerged only later, in association with anatomically modern humans. According to Dunbar, this late refinement served novel functions connected with complex symbolic culture including ritual and religion.

Dunbar's account left many questions unanswered. Darwinians have recently come to understand that the discernible costliness of animal signals underscores their reliability (Zahavi 1987, 1993; Zahavi and Zahavi 1997). This requires us to build into Dunbar's model some way of explaining how the low-cost vocalisations which we term 'words' could have replaced costly manual grooming in signalling commitment to alliance partners (Power 1998). We also need to explain language's most remarkable, distinctive and unprecedented feature – its dual hierarchical structure of phonology and syntax. Instead of highlighting such challenges, Dunbar sought to minimise them by suggesting continuity with primate vocal communication. For example, he pictured the vocal signalling of vervet monkeys as 'an archetypal protolanguage', already incipiently speechlike. These monkeys, in Dunbar's view, are almost speaking when they emit 'quite arbitrary' sounds in referring to 'specific objects'. Grammar, argues Dunbar, is present long before human language, being central to primate cognition including social intelligence (cf. Bickerton, this volume). Dunbar has not addressed the problem of how 'meanings' came to be attached to previously content-free vocalisations; he glosses this development as a 'small step' not requiring special explanation (1996: 141). Nor does he see any theoretical difficulty in his scenario of premodern humans 'gossiping' in the absence of 'symbolism', their vocalisations counting as 'language' even though not permitting 'reference to abstract concepts'.

For psychologist Merlin Donald (1991, 1998) and for neuroscientist Terrence Deacon (1997), by contrast, the question of how humans, given their non-symbolic primate heritage, came to represent their knowledge in symbolic form is the central issue in the evolution of language. The emergence of words as carriers of symbolic reference – without which syntax would be neither possible nor necessary – is the threshold of language. Establishment of this basic speech system, with its high-speed phonetic machinery, specialised memory system and capacity for vocal imitation – all unique to humans – then becomes 'a necessary step in the evolution of human linguistic capacity' (Donald 1991: 236; cf. Deacon 1997: ch. 8).

What selective pressures drove the evolution of the speech system? Donald (1991) starts from the assumption that the modern human mind is a hybrid of its past embodiments, still bearing 'the indelible stamp of [its] lowly origin' (Darwin 1871: 920). Much as Bickerton takes the structureless word strings of modern pidgins as evidence for a protolanguage, Donald finds evidence for a prelinguistic mode of communication in the gestures, facial expressions, pantomimes and inarticulate vocalisations to which modern humans may have recourse when deprived of speech. 'Mimesis' is Donald's term for this analog, largely iconic, mode of communication and thought. The mode requires a conscious, intentional control of emotionally expressive behaviours, including vocalisation, that is beyond the capacity of other primates. We are justified in regarding mimesis, like Bickerton's protolanguage, as a unitary mode of representation, peculiar to our species, not only because it emerges naturally, independent of and dissociable from language, in deaf and aphasic humans unable to speak, but also because it still forms the basis for expressive arts such as dance, theatre, pantomime and ritual display. The dissociability of mimesis from language also justifies the assumption that it evolved as an independent mode before language came into existence.

Despite the current dominance of speech-based communication, we should not underestimate the continuing power of mimesis. Donald builds a strong argument for the necessity of a culture intermediate between apes and *Homo sapiens*, and for the value of a prelinguistic, mimetic mode of communication as a force for social cohesion. *Homo erectus* was relatively stable as a species for well over a million years, and spread out over the entire Eurasian land mass, its tools, traces of butchery and use of fire affording evidence of a complexity of social organization well beyond the reach of apes. Of particular importance for the evolution of language would have been the change in habits of thought and communication that a mimetic culture must have brought in its train. Mimesis, Donald argues, established the fundamentals of intentional expression in hominids, and laid the basis on which natural selection could act to engender the cognitive demand and neuroanatomical machinery essential to the emergence of words and of a combinatorial syntax as vehicles of symbolic thought and communication.

Can we specify more precisely the symbolic function fulfilled by words and syntax? As we have seen, many linguists insist that the primary function of language is conceptual representation, not communication. If we were to accept this argument, we would have no a priori grounds for attributing language to the evolutionary emergence of novel strategies of social cooperation. Most chapters in this book, however, take a different view. Language – including its distinctive representational level – is intrinsically social, and can only have evolved under fundamentally social selection pressures. Perhaps the most sophisticated, ambitious and elaborate presentation of this case was made by Terrence Deacon (1997) in his extraordinary book, *The Symbolic Species*, a work unique in its subtle meshing of ideas from the behavioural and brain sciences. Here, Deacon argues that language emerged concurrently with the emergence of *social contracts*. A contract, he observes, has no location in space, no shape or color, no physical form of any kind. It exists only as an idea shared among those committed to honouring and enforcing it. It is compulsory – one is not allowed to violate it – yet wholly nonphysical. How, then, might information about such a thing be communicated?

Deacon's insight was that nonhuman primates are under no pressure to evolve symbolic communication because they never have to confront the problem of social contracts. As long as communication concerns only current, perceptible reality, a signaller can always display or draw attention to some feature as an index or likeness of the intended referent. But once evolving humans had begun to establish contracts, reliance on indices and resemblances no longer sufficed. Where in the physical world is a 'promise'? What does such a thing look like? Where is the evidence that it exists at all? Since it exists only for those who believe in it, there is no alternative but to settle on a conventionally agreed symbol. In Deacon's scenario, such a symbol would originally have been an aspect of the ritual involved in cementing the contract. Selection pressures associated with such novel deployment of ritual symbolism led to the progressive re-engineering and enlargement of the primate brain.

Deacon argues that the key contracts whose symbolic representation pre-adapted humans for linguistic competence were those through which human females, increasingly burdened by child care, managed to secure long-term commitment from males. This argument ties in closely with recent Darwinian theory premised upon potential male/female sexual conflict, and brings speculation about the origins of language into the domain of anthropology in its widest sense – including current debates in sexual selection and mate choice theory, palaeoanthropology, evolutionary psychology, human palaeontology, archaeology and social anthropology. If Deacon is right, then his argument would add force to a growing contemporary awareness that language evolution must have been driven by strategies not just of cooperative males, but crucially of females (cf. Dunbar 1996; Key and Aiello 1999; Knight 1991, 1998, 1999, this volume; Knight et al. 1995; Power and Aiello 1997; Power 1998, this volume). In any event, regardless of the fate of Deacon's detailed anthropological scenario, his work in 'putting it all together' has raised our collective sights, lifting us decisively to a new plane.

The present book is the second published outcome of a series of international conferences on the evolution of language. Like its predecessor (Hurford et al. 1998), it addresses the need for a sharply focused attack on the evolution of language from a post-Chomskyan perspective. We have limited it to papers that deal directly with some aspect of form or function *unique to language* – points at which continuity with lower primate cognition and communication seems most difficult to establish.

In the introduction to the previous volume, we remarked on 'the interactive evolutionary spiral through which both individual language capacity and a communal system of symbolic communication must have more or less simultaneously emerged' (Hurford et al. 1998: 4). Yet few of the chapters in that volume in fact discussed that interactive spiral. By contrast, roughly half the chapters in the present volume are concerned directly or indirectly with language transmission across generations. One reason for this is their concern with social function. For only its early social function, whatever that may have been, can have launched language on its evolutionary path.

General recognition of this simple fact has perhaps been hindered by Chomsky's (1986) proscription of externalised language (E-language), the Saussurean language of the community, as a coherent object of linguistic and psychological study. Students of language evolution have instead chosen as their proper object of study Chomsky's internalised language (I-language), a structural property of an individual mind/brain. For Darwinians, an attraction of this focus is that the individual (or the gene), not the group, is the unit of natural selection in any adaptively complex system. But we have yet to work through the implications of the fact that it is only through exposure to fragments of E-language, to the utterance-meaning pairs of daily conversation, that a child learns its I-language. It is through others' performance – in other words, through language as embodied in social life – that speakers internalise (and, in turn, contribute to) the language in which they are immersed.

Theoretical models of such social processes are necessarily speculative, top-heavy with questionable assumptions, even when they draw on hard facts, such as the energetic costs of brain growth or fossil evidence of neuroanatomy. Mathematical modelling is often then the best method we have for objective testing of our assumptions. The following chapters illustrate several modes of mathematical modelling. Jason Noble, for example, applies game theory to test the Krebs-Dawkins predictions of the cooperative or competitive social conditions under which communication systems might arise (Krebs and Dawkins 1984). He assesses, within the limits of his own assumptions, a powerful, hitherto untested, verbal argument that has had wide impact on theories of animal communication. At the other end of the volume, Mark Pagel pursues the analogy between languages and species (Darwin 1871: ch. 3). He draws on methods from mathematical statistics, previously used to gauge past species diversity and rates of speciation, to estimate prehistorical language diversity and rates of change. He also estimates mathematically the role of both intrinsic ('glottochronological') and extrinsic (ecological and cultural) factors in language change.

Perhaps most remarkable among the modelling chapters are those that simulate social interaction between speakers and learners (Bart de Boer, Simon Kirby, James Hurford and others). Here, aspects of linguistic structure are shown to arise by self-organisation from the process of interaction itself without benefit of standard selection pressures. These papers might be read as an unexpected, if only partial, vindication of Chomsky's scepticism concerning the relevance of Darwinian evolution. Certainly, they promise a sharp reduction in the amount of linguistic structure that has to be attributed to natural selection. Computer simulations of birth, social engagement in linguistic action, and death, within a group of individuals, promote a novel view of language as an emergent, self-organising system, a view as unfamiliar to biologists and psychologists as to linguists.

Yet to explain the emergence of group phenomena from the premises of Darwinian individualism is certainly not a new idea. We have long recognised that biological processes involve complex hierarchies, with structure manifested on more than one level. The need to distinguish between analytic levels, and the possibility of modelling major evolutionary transitions between them, have indeed become central to modern Darwinism (Maynard Smith and Szathmáry 1995). Genes as such are never altruistic; yet few today would dispute that it is precisely gene-level 'selfishness' which drives the emergence of altruism and cooperation at higher levels. Many of the contributors to this book argue that linguistic communication emerges and varies as an expression of distinctively human coalitionary strategies. Such models acknowledge no incompatibility between the methodological individualism of modern Darwinism and the group-level focus of much social, cognitive and linguistic science (Dunbar, Knight and Power 1999; Nettle 1999b).

Linking all the following chapters is the idea that language is no ordinary adaptation, but will require 'special' Darwinian explanation (cf. Maynard Smith and Szathmáry 1995). This is explicit in Part I, which isolates biologically anomalous levels of social cooperation as central to the evolutionary emergence of language. It remains a theme in Part II, in which emerging phonetic competence is attributed to unique evolutionary pressures for vocal imitation, social learning and other forms of social transmission. Finally, it is central to Part III, where the emergence of syntax is acknowledged to be entangled in complex ways with novel social and cultural strategies. Language, in short, is remarkable – as will be any adequate Darwinian explanation of its evolution.

References

Aiello, L. C. and R. I. M. Dunbar. 1993. Neocortex size, group size and the evolution of language. *Current Anthropology* **34**: 184–193.
Baldwin, J. M. 1896. A new factor in evolution. *American Naturalist* **30**: 441–451.
Bickerton, D. 1981. *The Roots of Language*. Ann Arbor, MI: Karoma.
Bickerton, D. 1990. *Language and Species*. Chicago: University of Chicago Press.
Bickerton, D. 1995. *Language and Human Behavior*. Seattle, WA: University of Washington Press.
Bickerton, D. 1998. Catastrophic evolution: the case for a single step from protolanguage to full human language. In J. R. Hurford, M. Studdert-Kennedy and C. Knight (eds), *Approaches to the Evolution of Language: Social and cognitive bases*. Cambridge: Cambridge University Press, pp. 341–358.
Binford, L. R. 1989. Isolating the transition to cultural adaptations: an organizational approach. In E. Trinkaus (ed), *The Emergence of Modern Humans: Biocultural adaptations in the later Pleistocene*. Cambridge: Cambridge University Press, pp. 18–41.

Byrne, R. and A. Whiten (eds). 1988. *Machiavellian Intelligence: Social expertise and the evolution of intellect in monkeys, apes, and humans.* Oxford: Clarendon.

Cann, R. L., M. Stoneking and A. C. Wilson. 1987. Mitochondrial DNA and human evolution. *Nature* **325**: 31–36.

Chomsky, N. 1957. *Syntactic Structures.* The Hague: Mouton.

Chomsky, N. 1965. *Aspects of the Theory of Syntax.* Cambridge, MA: MIT Press.

Chomsky, N. 1966. *Cartesian Linguistics.* New York: Harper and Row.

Chomsky, N. 1972. *Language and Mind.* New York: Harcourt, Brace and World (revised edition).

Chomsky, N. 1975. *Reflections on Language.* New York: Pantheon.

Chomsky, N. 1986. *Knowledge of Language: Its nature, origin, and use.* New York: Praeger.

Chomsky, N. and M. Halle. 1968. *The Sound Pattern of English.* New York: Harper and Row.

Darwin, C. 1871. *The Descent of Man.* London: John Murray.

Dawkins, R. 1976. *The Selfish Gene.* Oxford: Oxford University Press.

Deacon, T. W. 1997. *The Symbolic Species.* New York: Norton.

Donald, M. 1991. *Origins of the Modern Mind.* Cambridge, MA: Harvard University Press.

Donald, M. 1998. Mimesis and the Executive Suite: missing links in language evolution. In J. R. Hurford, M. Studdert-Kennedy and C. Knight (eds), *Approaches to the Evolution of Language: Social and cognitive bases.* Cambridge: Cambridge University Press, pp. 44–67.

Dunbar, R. I. M. 1993. Coevolution of neocortical size, group size and language in humans. *Behavioral and Brain Sciences* **16**: 681–735.

Dunbar, R. I. M. 1996. *Grooming Gossip and the Evolution of Language.* London: Faber & Faber.

Dunbar, R. I. M., C. Knight and C. Power (eds). 1999. *The Evolution of Culture.* Edinburgh: Edinburgh University Press.

Hamilton, W. D. 1964. The genetical evolution of social behaviour. *Journal of Theoretical Biology* **7**: 1–52.

Harnad, S. R., H. D. Steklis and J. Lancaster (eds). 1976. *Origins and Evolution of Language and Speech.* New York: Annals of the New York Academy of Sciences, Volume 280.

Hurford, J. R., M. Studdert-Kennedy and C. Knight (eds). 1998. *Approaches to the Evolution of Language.* Cambridge: Cambridge University Press.

Jackendoff, R. 1994. *Patterns in the Mind.* New York: Basic Books.

Key, C. A. and L. C. Aiello. 1999. The evolution of social organisation. In R. I. M. Dunbar, C. Knight and C. Power (eds), *The Evolution of Culture.* Edinburgh: Edinburgh University Press, pp. 15–33.

Klein, R. G. 1995. Anatomy, behaviour, and modern human origins. *Journal of World Prehistory* **9**: 167–198.

Knight, C. 1991. *Blood Relations: Menstruation and the origins of culture.* New Haven, CT, and London: Yale University Press.

Knight, C. 1998. Ritual/speech coevolution: a solution to the problem of deception. In J. R. Hurford, M. Studdert-Kennedy and C. Knight (eds), *Approaches to the Evolution of Language: Social and cognitive bases.* Cambridge: Cambridge University Press, pp. 68–91.

Knight, C. 1999. Sex and language as pretend-play. In R. I. M. Dunbar, C. Knight and
    C. Power (eds), *The Evolution of Culture*. Edinburgh: Edinburgh University Press,
    pp. 228–247.
Knight, C., C. Power and I. Watts. 1995. The human symbolic revolution: a Darwinian
    account. *Cambridge Archaeological Journal.* **5**: 75–114.
Krebs, J. R. and R. Dawkins. 1984. Animal signals: mind-reading and manipulation. In
    J. R. Krebs and N. B. Davies (eds), *Behavioural Ecology: An evolutionary approach*.
    Oxford: Blackwell, pp. 380–402.
Lamendella, J. T. 1976. Relations between the ontogeny and phylogeny of language:
    a neorecapitulationist view. In S. R. Harnad, H. D. Steklis and J. Lancaster (eds),
    Origins and Evolution of Language and Speech. New York: Annals of the New York
    Academy of Sciences, Volume 280, pp. 396–412.
Lenneberg, E. H. 1967. *Biological Foundations of Language*. New York: Wiley.
Maynard Smith, J. and E. Szathmáry. 1995. *The Major Transitions in Evolution*. Oxford:
    Freeman.
Mellars, P. A. 1991. Cognitive changes and the emergence of modern humans in Europe.
    Cambridge Archaeological Journal **1**: 63–76.
Mellars, P. A. 1998. Neanderthals, modern humans and the archaeological evidence for
    language. In N. G. Jablonski and L. C. Aiello (eds), *The Origin and Diversification
    of Language*. Wattis Symposium Series in Anthropology. Memoirs of the California
    Academy of Sciences, No. 24. San Francisco: California Academy of Sciences, pp.
    89–115.
Mithen, S. J. 1996. *A Prehistory of the Mind*. London: Thames and Hudson.
Mithen, S. J. 1999. Symbolism and the supernatural. In R. I. M. Dunbar, C. Knight and
    C. Power (eds), *The Evolution of Culture*. Edinburgh: Edinburgh University Press,
    pp. 147–169.
Mowrer, O. H. 1960. *Learning Theory and the Learning Process*. New York: Wiley.
Nettle, D. 1999a. Language variation and the evolution of societies. In R. I. M.
    Dunbar, C. Knight and C. Power (eds), *The Evolution of Culture*. Edinburgh: Ed-
    inburgh University Press, pp. 214–227.
Nettle, D. 1999b. *Linguistic Diversity*. Oxford: Oxford University Press.
Newmeyer, F. J. 1991. Functional explanation in linguistics and the origin of language.
    Language and Communication **11**: 1–28.
O'Connell, J. F., K. Hawkes and N. G. Blurton Jones. 1999. Grandmothering and the
    evolution of *Homo erectus. Journal of Human Evolution* **36**: 461–485.
Pinker, S. and P. Bloom. 1990. Natural language and natural selection. *Behavioral and
    Brain Sciences* **13**: 707–784.
Power, C. 1998. Old wives' tales: the gossip hypothesis and the reliability of cheap
    signals. In J. R. Hurford, M. Studdert-Kennedy and C. Knight (eds), *Approaches
    to the Evolution of Language: Social and cognitive bases*. Cambridge: Cambridge
    University Press, pp. 111–129.
Power, C. and L. C. Aiello. 1997. Female proto-symbolic strategies. In L. D. Hager (ed),
    Women in Human Evolution. New York and London: Routledge, pp. 153–171.
Skinner, B. F. 1957. *Verbal Behavior*. New York: Appleton-Century Crafts.
Stringer, C. and C. Gamble. 1993. *In Search of the Neanderthals: Solving the puzzle of
    human origins*. London: Thames and Hudson.

Trivers, R. L. 1971. The evolution of reciprocal altruism. *Quarterly Review of Biology* **46**: 35–57.

Ulbaek, I. 1998. The origin of language and cognition. In J. R. Hurford, M. Studdert-Kennedy and C. Knight (eds), *Approaches to the Evolution of Language: Social and cognitive bases*. Cambridge: Cambridge University Press, pp. 30–43.

Zahavi, A. 1987. The theory of signal selection and some of its implications. In U. P. Delfino (ed), *International Symposium on Biological Evolution*. Bari: Adriatic Editrice, pp. 305–327.

Zahavi, A. 1993. The fallacy of conventional signalling. *Philosophical Transactions of the Royal Society of London* **340**: 227–230.

Zahavi, A. and A. Zahavi. 1997. *The Handicap Principle: A missing piece in Darwin's puzzle*. New York and Oxford: Oxford University Press.

PART I

THE EVOLUTION OF COOPERATIVE COMMUNICATION

1

Introduction: The Evolution of Cooperative Communication

CHRIS KNIGHT

'Selfish gene' Darwinism differs from earlier versions of evolutionary theory in its focus on one key question: Why cooperate? The faculty of speech which distinguishes *Homo sapiens* from other species is an aspect of human social competence. By inference, it evolved in the context of uniquely human strategies of social cooperation. In these chapters, therefore, Darwinism in its modern, socially aware form provides our theoretical point of departure.

Where, previously, attention has focused on speech as the biological competence of individuals, here our themes are social. To study communication is inevitably to study social structure, social conflict, social strategies, social intelligence. Communication, as Robbins Burling observes in the next chapter, 'does not begin when someone makes a sign, but when someone interprets another's behaviour as a sign'. Reminding us of this elementary principle, Burling spells out the logical corollary: where the evolution of language is concerned, it is comprehension, not production, which sets the pace. Even a purely instrumental action, after all, may be read by others as a signal. Where this has evolutionary significance, instrumental behaviour may then undergo modification in the service of novel, socially conferred, signalling functions. Chomsky's focus upon the innate creativity of the speaker has been enormously productive. But over evolutionary time, Burling points out, 'the only innovations in production that can be successful, and thus consolidated by natural selection, are those that conform to the already available *receptive* competence of conspecifics'. If Burling is correct, then that syntactical structure which so radically distinguishes speech from nonhuman primate signalling must have become progressively elicited and then consolidated by generations of comprehending listeners. First, conceptual complexity is 'read into' signalling by the attentive mind reader; subsequently, the signaller – given such encouragement – may succeed in externalising aspects of that complexity in the signal itself.

19

Consistent with this scenario, one possible speculation is that speech emerged in the human lineage thanks to novel levels of care, solicitude and understanding shown by mothers toward immature offspring. Drawing on Tomasello's work, Burling cites the infant chimpanzee 'nursing poke' – a conventionalised begging gesture suggestive of a human speech act. To this might be added the 'head nod', 'head shake', 'wrist flap' and 'tap/poke' – cognitively expressive gestures, each with its own meaning, used by immature apes in playful interaction with each other or with mothers (Blount 1990: 429). Poignantly, however, such incipiently symbolic signs do not survive into adulthood. As potential 'memes', therefore, they lack any prospect of being passed on. Each mother-infant dyad or immature peer group is condemned within each generation to 'reinvent the wheel'.

Associated with this is a social fact: whereas the human infant may anticipate long-term kin-based solicitude, benefiting from social provisioning well beyond infancy, the young chimp, from around age five, must fend for itself. Deprived of the prospect of caring support, it abandons the now irrelevant nursing poke along with any other subtle indications of need. Given the competitive exigencies of impending adulthood, the best preparatory training for the ape youngster may in fact be to *avoid* excessive reliance on cooperative understanding from others. From this perspective, elaboration of symbolic potential as young apes mature appears constrained less by cognitive deficits than by a decisive *social* one – the obvious absence, in the wild, of any unconditionally supportive or caring audience. Why bother to elucidate one's aims or interests to others who may at best show indifference – or at worst exploit such intelligence for their own ends?

Jason Noble takes up the theme of cooperation versus competition to ask whether a 'pure' state of competition is consistent with any kind of signal evolution at all. He sets out to test a theory first proposed by John Krebs and Richard Dawkins (1978), according to whom conflict in the animal world leads to costly, manipulative signalling. Noble's simulations suggest that contrary to these authors' expectations, intensification of competition does not culminate in maximally manipulative, inefficient signals. Rather, the outcome is simply a breakdown in all communication. If empirically confirmed, this would endorse the more traditional standpoint of theoretical linguistics, linking communication with shared interests. However, we need not assume generalised social harmony. According to Zahavi and Zahavi (1997), even violent antagonists may communicate on the basis of interests which they share. Predator and prey, for example, may share an interest in avoiding a chase if the potential victim is able to demonstrate that pursuing it would be a waste of time. Likewise, human military combatants may seek to retain at least certain honest channels of communication to avoid costly misunderstandings.

From all this, it would appear that there is no ultimate incompatibility between Noble's findings, Zahavi's and the tenets of Krebs and Dawkins. In the real world, both competition and cooperation may prevail simultaneously, albeit on different levels. Babblers collectively 'mobbing' a predator, for example, are on one level cooperating. Yet on another, they are competing in advertising to one another their ability to afford taking such risks (Zahavi and Zahavi 1997).

Dessalles (1998) roots speech evolution in a comparable dynamic, in which status-seeking individuals compete to emit signals perceived as relevant by their peers. Dissolving simplistic dichotomies, such behaviour might be termed 'competition to cooperate'. Consistent with Krebs and Dawkins, however, is the finding – confirmed from all sides – that fast, cheap, efficient communication presupposes at least *some level* on which interests converge. Signals become costly and inefficient – culminating eventually in physical violence – in proportion as mutual conflict on that level intensifies.

In his contribution to this volume, Dessalles sets out to delineate more precisely the cooperative social matrix in which speech must therefore have evolved. With Dunbar (1996), Deacon (1997) and many others, he posits an evolutionary background in which increasingly large, stable coalitions engage in group-on-group competition and local conflict. The decisive selection pressure is status-linked social inducement to provide information relevant to the concerns of one's own group. Dessalles accepts that such coalitional activity amounts to cooperation, driven by strategies of reciprocal altruism which are a precondition for the evolution of speech. In his view, however, speaking as such is *not* reciprocal altruism.

A speaker, according to Dessalles, does not donate valuable information on a tit-for-tat basis, checking to ensure repayment in kind. Rather, it is listeners – not speakers – who are left to pay the costs of checking up on cheats. This is because, whether honestly or dishonestly, speakers are always striving to persuade their audience to reward them with status. Those coalitions which can award such status, according to Dessalles, are 'groups of individuals showing solidarity in action, i.e. being able to take collective decisions'. In competing against the out-group, each coalition seeks to allocate *internal* status exclusively in return for relevance. Rather than displaying altruism, therefore, conversationalists – like contestants in any competitive board game – strive to win through linguistic 'moves' capable of earning status while diminishing the relative significance of rival contributions.

Why is it that within human coalitions, status is earned this way – whereas in ape society it may be earned more effectively by manipulation or concealment of relevant information? In suggesting an answer, Dessalles points to the intrinsic dynamic of group-on-group conflict, whose effect may be to progressively exclude physical aggression and/or manipulative signalling from the sphere of *in-group* communication. 'In primate societies, the company of strong individuals is much sought after. From the perspective we propose, relevant information may have replaced physical strength as a determining factor in the decision to join a coalition and remain in it'. As threats and correspondingly exploitative signals become reserved for outsiders, internal status – emancipated from determination by such factors – becomes allocated on quite different grounds. Internally, signallers may now avail themselves of a novel opportunity – to compete in producing messages valued by other members of their group. As Dessalles concludes: 'Social status among humans is not extorted by brute force. It emerges from others' willingness to establish social bonds with you. The decision to become closer to somebody is taken according to definite criteria. Linguistic relevance may be an essential component of this choice'.

Adopting the same perspective with respect to coalitionary dynamics, status and relevance, Camilla Power reminds us of the evolutionary centrality of sexual and reproductive strategies. In Power's model as in those of Dunbar (1996) and Knight (1991), the stable coalitions responsible for speech arise out of long-term strategies of reciprocal altruism between *females*. A key area of potential conflict between females is the issue of differential male sexual attention and associated provisioning. In particular, according to Power, pregnant and nursing mothers may experience younger and/or imminently fertilisable local females as a sexual threat. In Power's model, they respond by coercively controlling and bonding with pubescent females from the moment of menstrual onset. Signals of imminent fertility, which might potentially incite males to differentially target menstruants, are now deliberately scrambled.

On this basis, Power explains the ethnographic pattern in which first menstrual onset in pubescent girls triggers coercive initiation into a ritual group. Although the subjects of such treatment surrender freedom of movement and incur numerous immediate costs, in the longer term these should be outweighed by benefits. Each menstruant will one day be a nursing mother herself, whereupon she will reap the benefits of a coalitionary strategy aimed at preventing younger or more attractive female rivals from gaining disproportionate provisioning and attention. Moreover, the costly and often painful process of initiation has intrinsic value, acting as a demonstration of personal commitment. Here is Power's answer to Dessalles's question about how listeners can check up on 'cheats' – speakers who falsely gain status by faking the relevance of their utterances. In Power's model, nobody even listens to speakers who have not already paid the costs of initiation into the secret society or coalition. Gossip depends on the relationships of trust that are established as commitment to the sisterhood is signalled via hard-to-fake, costly display. Relevance-based in-group status allocation operates only within such a framework.

Power demonstrates the precision with which this model's expectations match details of the ethnography of women's 'secret' language use in the context of African initiation rites. In her case studies, however, in-group solidarity is neither uniform nor unconditional. Instead, ritually bounded coalitions do show internal status differentials. Depending on their status, speakers can control or determine the relevance and availability of vital social information – such as who has been having sex with whom, or who has fathered a given child. 'Gossip' is the exchange of *social* information; inevitably, it is manipulated to serve sectional interests. The relevance or irrelevance of an utterance, according to Power, depends less on any objective informational content than on *prior* ritually established relationships linking the speaker with her audience.

Power observes that during an actual ritual performance, or when deployed to signal ritual status, an utterance may be accepted as relevant despite lack of propositional meaning or content. Theoretically, even a nonsense rhyme learned during initiation might appear relevant. This recalls Maurice Bloch's (1975) ethnographic study, in which Merina political elders display ritual status through verbose speeches almost devoid of creativity, syntactical combinatoriality or any novel content. At first sight, all this might seem in conflict with Dessalles's expectation that status should depend on linguistic relevance. Ethnography indeed suggests the reverse possibility: where the purpose of signalling is to display evidence of ritually conferred status, the most relevant strategy may be to produce propositionally meaningless, repetitive verbiage.

If this is accepted, then to retain consistency with Dessalles, we must distinguish between two contrasting settings in which 'authorised language' (Bourdieu 1991) is used. Where internal status differentials are in the process of being established by *ritual* as opposed to verbal means, we expect displays or negotiations of such status to violate Dessalles's 'relevance' maxims. In such contexts – as Power shows – signalling may be relevant without informational content and without making any contribution to collective decision making or problem solving.

'Relevance' in Dessalles's terms, however, cannot be a property of nonsense rhymes or ritualistic, repetitive verbiage. Neither can it be a feature of simple ritual marks such as bodily scars, cosmetic designs or tattoos. Where group members demand information relevant to cooperative decision making, the necessary vehicle is syntactical speech. Here, the social matrix is one in which preordained status can be ignored, for the simple reason that in principle, everyone shares the same such status. In this democratic setting, the ground is cleared for a quite different contest, in which communicators make no prior assumptions about status differentials dividing them. Conversationalists set out with a level playing field, in which the contest is to provide information of value to the group. Power has outlined a persuasive, ethnographically testable model to explain how such status-conferring groups in the human case came to be established.

Knight turns from an examination of costly ritual signals to an examination of low-cost symbolic communication. Young primates frequently engage in play behaviour, whose make-believe creativity often seems suggestive of human cultural symbolism. In contrast to primate vocal signalling, the playful gestures of young apes may be rich in cognitive expressivity and complexity. Whereas ape vocal calls are analog indices of physical and/or emotional condition, the distinction between a play bite and its functional prototype is cognitive and categorical. Whereas ape vocal calls, when delivered in sequence, can yield only a blended compromise between meanings, a gesture indicating 'This is play!' may systematically reverse the significance of subsequent 'chases' or 'bites'. If we are seeking a primate precursor for speech creativity and combinatoriality, Knight suggests that the most convincing candidate is primate play.

But if conversational speech including humour in the human case extends and develops the creative, combinatorial potential of immature primate play, then we must ask how the conditions for such creativity came to be extended into adulthood during the course of human evolution. For Knight, the key factor acting to deny animals freedom to play is reproductive competition and conflict. The onset of sexual maturity brings with it the Darwinian imperative to engage in potentially lethal sexual competition. In the primate case, this impinges upon life concurrently with sexual maturity, setting up anxieties, divisions and status differentials which permeate and effectively constitute adult sociality. If imaginative playfulness diminishes in frequency, it is because autonomous, freely creative expressivity is simply not compatible with a situation in which individuals feel anxious or externally threatened. Admittedly, adult primates – most notably bonobos – do sometimes play with one another. But as competitive stresses intensify, the dominant tendency is for play fights to give way to real ones. On a more general level, by the same token, involvement in shared make-believe yields to a more narrow preoccupation with the serious competitive imperatives of adult life.

Among humans, however, the transition to adulthood takes a different form. Human offspring go through an extended period of childhood followed by adolescence (Bogin 1997). During this extended period, the young are enabled to rely to a considerable extent on social as opposed to 'fend-for-yourself' provisioning. Hunter-gatherer ethnography demonstrates in addition that at a certain point, young adolescents become coercively incorporated into ritual coalitions. Rites of initiation – central to intergenerational transmission of human symbolic culture – may be viewed as a modality of animal play. In fact, they are spectacular 'pretend-play' performances, drawing on hallucinatory techniques such as trance, dance, rhythm, face painting and so forth. Whether or not genital mutilation is involved, the declared aim is to curb individualistic pursuit of sexual advantage. Bonds of coalitionary solidarity, typically modelled on sibling solidarity, are accorded primacy over sexual bonds.

How did such coalitions and associated rituals become established? Power's model of reciprocal altruism within female coalitions suggests a route through which the playfulness of infancy and childhood might have been preserved into adult life. If young fertile females are simply *prohibited* from presenting themselves as objects of male competitive attention, being instead retained under control by siblings and other protective kin, then such kin-based coalitionary solidarity might reduce sexual conflict and so establish extended opportunities for adults to engage in 'play'. Knight argues that with the emergence of *Homo sapiens*, the childhood significance of kinship indeed became preserved within adult sociality, overriding sexual bonds and thereby opening up a new social space within which language – an extension of the creativity of primate play – could now for the first time flower.

What is clear from all these contributions is the extent to which they dovetail and support one another. Burling sets the scene by reminding us that speakers could not effectively innovate in the absence of prior understanding on the part of listeners. The ensuing chapters in their different ways explore the evolutionary roots of such creative and rewarding acts of cooperative understanding. All are agreed that speech evolved to enable thoughts to be shared, its emergence inseparable from distinctively human strategies of social cooperation.

References

Bloch, M. 1975. *Political Language and Oratory in Traditional Society.* London: Academic.

Blount, B. G. 1990. Spatial expression of social relationships among captive *Pan paniscus:* ontogenetic and phylogenetic implications. In S. T. Parker and K. R. Gibson (eds), *'Language' and Intelligence in Monkeys and Apes: Comparative developmental perspectives.* Cambridge: Cambridge University Press, pp. 420–432.

Bogin, H. 1997. Evolutionary hypotheses for human childhood. *Yearbook of Physical Anthropology* **40**: 63–89.

Bourdieu, P. 1991. *Language and Symbolic Power.* Cambridge: Polity.

Deacon, T. 1997. *The Symbolic Species: The co-evolution of language and the human brain.* London: Penguin.

Dessalles, J.-L. 1998. Altruism, status and the origin of relevance. In J. R. Hurford, M. Studdert-Kennedy and C. Knight (eds), *Approaches to the Evolution of Language: Social and cognitive bases.* Cambridge: Cambridge University Press, pp. 130–147.

Dunbar, R. I. M. 1996. *Grooming, Gossip and the Evolution of Language.* London: Faber and Faber.

Knight, C. 1991. *Blood Relations: Menstruation and the origins of culture*. New Haven, CT, and London: Yale University Press.

Krebs, J. R. and Dawkins, R. 1978. Animal signals: information or manipulation? In J. R. Krebs and N. B. Davies (eds), *Behavioural Ecology: An evolutionary approach*. Oxford: Blackwell, pp. 282–309.

Zahavi, A. and Zahavi, A. 1997. *The Handicap Principle: A missing piece in Darwin's puzzle*. New York and Oxford: Oxford University Press.

2

Comprehension, Production and Conventionalisation in the Origins of Language

ROBBINS BURLING

The Priority of Comprehension

This chapter explores the implications of two observations that should be reasonably obvious, or at least familiar, but when they are considered together, they lead to an unfamiliar but interesting way of thinking about the early stages of language. The first of the two observations is simply that all of us, humans and animals alike, are always able to understand more than we can say. Comprehension runs consistently ahead of production. The second observation extends the first: both humans and animals are sometimes able to interpret another's instrumental behavior even when that other individual had no intention at all to communicate. In the first part of this chapter I seek to justify these two observations. I will then consider their implications for our understanding of the origins of language.

Children, who appear to learn their first language with such magical ease, give us the most familiar example of the priority of comprehension. Parents are always convinced that their children understand far more than they can say. Linguists have occasionally been sceptical of the superior comprehension of children, partly because a vaguely behaviourist bias makes the 'behaviour' of speaking seem more important than mere 'passive' comprehension, but also for the much better reason that it really is very difficult to study comprehension. How do we know whether or not a child understands, and how do we know how he understands? Hold out a cookie to a child and ask "Do you want a cookie?" When he responds enthusiastically, how do we know whether he understands the words, or simply interprets the situation correctly? It is difficult to prove to the satisfaction of a linguist, let alone some kinds of hard-nosed experimental psychologists, that children always understand more than they can say, but parents are rarely in doubt. At the time when one of my grandsons had a total productive vocabulary of exactly three words, one of which was a loud repeated grunt meaning 'Give it to me', he could point appropriately not only in response to a request to show his eye, nose or mouth, but also to show his elbow, knee or shoulder. He could point not only to a window or door, but to the wall, ceiling or floor. He appeared to have a receptive vocabulary of hundreds of words at a time when he articulated only three. Comprehension is so consistently ahead of production that we ought to recognize that much that is essential about language learning happens silently as children learn to understand. Speaking should be seen as merely the final step in a long process, the point at which language that is already under firm passive control is finally made active.

Even as adults, we understand more than we can say. We all understand dialects that we cannot produce. English speakers from opposite sides of the Atlantic and from the southern extremities of the globe can generally understand each other with no more than an occasional hitch, but few of them would ever try to speak another's dialect. We all understand words that we would not use. We understand some of the slang of ethnic groups or generations other than our own, even if we would not risk using it ourselves. We understand some technical terminology from fields with which we are only partially familiar. We understand, and even admire, rhetorical styles that we cannot, ourselves, duplicate. In New Guinea people have a nice way of distinguishing receptive and productive skill. They may say 'I can hear that language but I cannot speak it', recognising that it is possible to have a skilled ability to understand a language without the ability to speak.

If we had been clearer about the ability of human beings, both young and old, to understand more than they produce, we might not have waited so long to ask how much spoken human language nonhuman primates can learn to understand. Even if an ape is incapable of uttering a single spoken word, an ability to comprehend would demonstrate some genuine knowledge of a language. Anecdotal reports have suggested that captive chimps have sometimes learned to understand a good deal of spoken language even though they said nothing at all. These reports have sometimes been met with some scepticism for the same reasons that parental claims for their children's ability to comprehend have been doubted, partly because production seems more real than passive comprehension, but also because it so difficult to measure skill in comprehension. Like people, apes can infer a great deal from the context in which language is used. It is always difficult to know how much any listener, even an ape, depends upon context, and how much upon the language. Hayes and Nissen suggest that Viki learned to understand a considerable amount of spoken English, but they were so eager to teach her to articulate words that they did not systematically study her comprehension (1971). As a result, Viki is remembered for her failure to speak, rather than for her success at understanding.

With the help of Savage-Rumbaugh and her colleagues, Kanzi, the famous bonobo, has now dramatically confirmed the ability of apes to learn to comprehend a significant amount of spoken language (Savage-Rumbaugh et al. 1993). At the age of eight, Kanzi was compared to a two-year-old human girl, and their ability to understand English was remarkably similar. Kanzi, like the girl, was able to respond correctly to a large number of different words and to a considerable variety of spoken sentences. Kanzi's receptive skills give far better evidence of linguistic ability than has ever been shown by any nonhuman primate who has been trained to produce language or language-like signals, whether by articulating spoken words, signing, manipulating plastic chips or pressing buttons. Indeed, Kanzi's ability to comprehend a human language seems sufficiently extensive that he should be credited with a degree of linguistic competence that linguists have most often presumed to be exclusively human. No one need fear that a bonobo or any other ape is about to give serious competition to human children in their speed or thoroughness of language learning, but I do not doubt that Kanzi has learned a good deal of English. The pattern is consistent. Not only humans of all ages, but apes as well, are always able to understand more than they can say.

Ritualisation

Comprehension plays a crucial role in the origin of animal signals, for signals become communicative not when they are first produced, but only when they are first understood. The gestures and vocalisations by which animals communicate with one another develop from acts that were originally purely instrumental (Tinbergen 1952). Instrumental acts are the movements or noises that form a part of the ordinary business of living – moving around, eating, scratching, yawning. Although instrumental behavior is produced with no communicative intent whatsoever, conspecifics may still be able to interpret it. Only after such behavior has come to convey some sort of meaning to another animal can it develop into a specifically communicative signal. A classic example is a dog's snarl.

Snarls began as simple instrumental gestures, nothing more than a part of getting ready to bite. The lip had to be moved out of the way of the teeth, but at first, the gesture had no communicative intent and probably no communicative result. Eventually, however, potential victims came to recognize the retracted lip as a signal that a bite was imminent. Those clever enough to read the signs would then be encouraged to flee, and so they could avoid the bite and live to reproduce. Comprehension, in other words, came before any communication was intended by the snarler. Comprehension was the first step but once the victims were able to understand, the aggressor was presented with a new opportunity. By retracting his lip as if to bite, he might manage to frighten off his enemy but avoid the much riskier activity of really biting. It might even help to move the lip in a stereotyped or exaggerated manner and so reduce the sign's ambiguity. As production and comprehension of the signal evolved together, the sign can be said to have become 'ritualised', modified from a purely instrumental act into a stereotypic communicative signal.

The instrumental lip movement evolved into a communicative snarl, transmitting information that was useful both to the aggressor and to his potential victim. All this happened, of course, under the slow but relentless pressures of natural selection, and it required no individual learning. The term 'phylogenetic ritualisation' is sometimes used for this process so as to emphasise that signals like the snarl develop by slow evolution, not by rapid learning, but the point that I want to stress here is that the process has to start with comprehension. The ritualisation of the lip movement could not even begin until it was understood. Other animal signs probably began much as did the snarl. Some sort of instrumental gesture or noise that was already being made for purposes other than communication was understood by other animals. Only then could it be ritualised into a specifically communicative signal.

By recognising that comprehension has priority over production, both in our own language and in the origin of animal signals, we can start to solve a puzzle that has hovered over the first appearance of language: what could the first speaker have hoped to accomplish with her first words if no one else was around with the skills to understand her? The puzzle disappears as soon as we recognize that communication does not begin when someone makes a sign, but when someone interprets another's behaviour as a sign. Comprehension must have been ahead from the very beginning. The original behaviour that was understood in a language-like way could not have been intended as a sign at all. A lonely producer who tries out a new kind of sign will almost certainly fail to communicate. A lonely comprehender, on the other hand, may gain considerable advantage by being able to interpret another's actions even when no communication at all had been intended. At every stage of evolution, the selective pressures favouring skill at comprehension are likely to have been considerably more insistent than the selective pressures favouring skill at production. Producers often benefit by *not* giving themselves away. Comprehenders have little to lose and much to gain by understanding more.

The precocity of comprehension implies that at every point along the evolutionary path toward language, understanders needed to be ready before another complexity could be added to production. More accurately: The only innovations in production that can be successful, and so consolidated by natural selection, are those that conform to the already available receptive competence of conspecifics. At every point, production would have been limited by and directed by the ability to comprehend that was already found in the population. Only when others were able to understand would a speaker be able to use new linguistic tricks. This disposes of any mystery about the communicative usefulness of the first wordlike signs. They would not even have been produced with communicative intent. Their communicative value came from the skill of the receiver, not from the intent of the producer.

The question that we should ask, therefore, is not 'Why did the first speaker try to communicate if no one was around who shared his talents?' The answer to this is very simple: 'He didn't. It would have been useless'. A much better question is 'Why would anyone make wordlike signs in the absence of any intention to communicate?' A plausible answer to this question is that the first interpretable language-like signs were instrumental acts. Once these instrumental acts could be interpreted by conspecifics, it became possible to conventionalise them as deliberate communicative signals. This implies that wordlike signs could have had an origin that is quite similar to that of animal signals like the snarl, but there is one crucial difference. Almost all animal signals have been ritualised by the long process of natural selection. Early wordlike signs, on the other hand, could have been conventionalised within the lifetime of a single individual.

The process that I am calling 'conventionalisation' is sometimes referred to as 'ontogenetic ritualisation' (Tomasello and Call 1997: 299–302). By using the word 'ritualisation', this phrase acknowledges the parallels between the origin of animal signals such as the dog's snarl (phylogenetic ritualisation) and the origin of signals that depend upon individual learning (ontogenetic ritualisation). I prefer to keep the jargon under at least partial control by calling the latter process 'conventionalisation' (or, when I want to be very explicit 'ontogentic conventionalisation') but, whatever it is called, it must be distinguished from the ritualisation that is phylogenetic. If we are to find examples of conventionalisation today, we should look for instrumental acts that can be interpreted by conspecifics, but that then become conventionalised as communicative signals. Such instrumental acts can be found among both humans and apes. Indeed, conventionalisation can take place so easily that we hardly realise that it is happening.

Conventionalisation

Consider, for example, the simple and familiar 'arms-up' gesture by which toddlers ask to be picked up. This begins instrumentally. It is simply one part of a baby's adaptation to the impinging world, in this case a part of his interaction with bigger people. After being lifted often enough by adult hands that have been placed under his arms, a baby learns to spread and then raise his arms in anticipation. Adults, in turn, learn to recognize the gesture, and it quickly becomes conventionalised into a stylised request. The arms-up gesture is so common that we might almost suppose it to be an innate and species-wide signal, but it is more dependent upon learning than, for example, our facial expressions of anger or joy. Unlike the words of a language and unlike our 'quotable gestures' such as the bye-bye wave, the arms-up gesture is ordinarily learned not by imitation or direct instruction, but rather through mutual adjustment to the actions of other people. It is conventionalised from an instrumental gesture, but it comes to act as a deliberate communicative signal.

The begging gesture – hand extended, palm upward with the fingers together – is learned in much the same way. Humans share this gesture with chimpanzees so it has deep roots, but it requires more learning by each infant than do the calls and gestures that form the inherited communicative repertory of each species.

A parallel example, this one audible rather than visible, is provided by the humble grunt. Lorraine McCune and her colleagues have studied grunting in human and nonhuman primate infants, and have followed the development of human grunting from a purely instrumental noise to a communicative signal (McCune et al. 1996; McCune 1999). They were able to distinguish three stages of grunting in the children they observed. First came *effort grunts* that occurred when babies exerted themselves, as when reaching for an object, when changing position or when crawling. Effort grunts occurred in the first month of life and, of course, we all still make them. Those observed by McCune were purely instrumental, a by-product of a baby's exertion. *Attention grunts* appeared a bit later and occurred when children were paying attention to something by looking at it or by touching it, but they were made without any indication of special effort or any sign of an intention to communicate. These attention grunts could still have been noticed and responded to by caretakers, however, and the children could have discovered that they could attract attention with a grunt. Finally, the children made *communicative grunts*. These occurred while the child looked at its mother, reached toward her or tugged at her when trying to attract, or be certain of, her attention. Communicative grunts appeared during the second year, close to the time when words began to be used. Like words, the communicative grunts were deliberate communicative signals.

Examples of conventionalised instrumental acts that I find even more interesting than those of human children come from the observations of Michael Tomasello and his co-workers who have studied the communication of young chimpanzees who were growing up in a semi-naturalistic situation at the Yerkes Primate Center Field Station in Georgia, USA (1985, 1989, 1994). These young chimpanzees use a wide variety of gestures to communicate with each other and with adults. For example, infants develop idiosyncratic ways to let their mothers know that they want to nurse. These gestures begin when a baby simply pushes his mother's arm aside so that it can reach the nipple. Mothers learn to recognize this instrumental act and this, in turn, permits the gesture to be conventionalised until the infant needs only to touch its mother in a characteristic way, and she will understand that it wants to nurse. The interesting point is that the gestures are quite idiosyncratic. Each infant uses them only with its own mother, never with another individual, so each pair is free to develop its own convention.

Young chimps also learn to use a considerable number of other idiosyncratic gestures. Some slap the ground, stamp their feet or throw things as an invitation to play. They direct an adult's hand or point to their side when they want to be tickled. They present their back when they would like to be groomed. They beg with an extended hand. Many of these gestures vary from one individual to another, and many are never made to a young chimp by an older animal, making it impossible to learn them by imitation. Nevertheless, these communicative gestures of young chimps are under far less tight genetic control than a dog's snarl. They have to be learned by each individual, conventionalised in the course of ontogeny.

Signal Types

Table 2.1 places conventionalised instrumental acts in the context of other forms of animal and human communication. Examples of human and animal signals are listed on the left, and their most relevant properties are shown at the right. The two sets of rows at the top are all examples of signals that I like to call 'gesture-calls'. This term is simply a way to recognise the unity of the auditory and visible aspects of mammalian signaling and, at the same time, to acknowledge the similarity of one component of human communication to the communication of other mammals. We do not usually think of human beings as having 'calls' but our laughter, screams and sobs join with our bodily postures and facial expressions to form a thoroughly primate system of communication. This is the gesture-call system of the human primate, unique to our species in its details, just as the details of each gesture-call system are unique to its species, but consisting of signals very much like those of other primates, both in the way they are produced and in the kinds of messages they convey (Burling 1993). Our gesture-calls have been built into each of us by the long process of phylogenetic ritualisation. Like the gesture-calls of other primates, they need, at most, to be

Table 2.1. *Human and animal signs*

	Phylo-genetic Ritual-isation	Onto-genetic Conventional-isation	Imita-tion	Analog vs. Discrete Digital
Mammalian gesture-calls				
Vervet alarms	x			D
Dog's snarl, growl, bark, tail wag	x			A/D
Most ape calls	x			A
Ape play face	x			A
Angry and submissive postures	x			A
Human gesture-calls				
Laughs, cries, sighs	x			A
Facial expressions: joy, fear				
anger, sorrow	x			A
Angry and submissive postures	x			A
Conventionalised gesture and noises				
Arms-up, begging		x		D
Young chimpanzee gestures		x		D
Grunts		x		D
Quotable gestures and noises				
Thumbs up, head screw			x	D
Oh-oh, tsk-tsk			x	D
Words of spoken languages			x	D
Signs of signed languages			x	D

triggered by the experiences that come to each individual in the normal course of maturation. They are narrowly determined by our genetic inheritance.

Toward the bottom of the table are the most language-like parts of human communication. These include language itself, both the spoken languages of hearing people and the signed languages of the deaf, and also the gestures that Kendon has aptly called 'quotable' (1993). These include hand signals such as the V-for-victory sign, the thumbs-up gesture, the head screw to suggest that someone is crazy, and a great many more. Like the words of a language, these quotable gestures have to be learned. They differ much more from one community to another than do our gesture-calls, and they form a part of the community's cultural tradition. In addition to these wordlike gestures, wc also use a number wordlike noises, such as *oh-oh* and *tsk-tsk*. These noises are not quite words because they neither conform to the phonological system of a language (which is why they are difficult to spell) nor fit into its syntax. Like true words and like quotable gestures, however, these not-quite-words have to be learned, are passed down by tradition and vary from one community to another. By analogy with 'quotable gestures' they might be called 'quotable noises'.

Between the gesture-calls and the language-like signs in the table are the conventionalised gestures and noises that have already been discussed. They share some properties with gesture-calls and other properties with language.

These three types of communicative signals differ most sharply in the way they are acquired. Both gesture-calls and conventionalised gestures or noises begin as instrumental acts, but snarls and other gesture-calls have become communicative by being ritualised through the long process of natural selection. The arms-up gesture, communicative grunts and nursing pokes have to be learned, or in a sense invented, by each individual while interacting with others. Like language and like quotable gestures and noises, the conventionalised signals have to be learned by each individual, but only the language-like signals are learned by imitation. Only they can be perpetuated as a part of the cultural tradition of a community.

In addition to being learned, conventionalised gestures share one other important characteristic with language: instead of grading into one another they are in contrast. There are no half-way signals between two conventionalised gestures any more than there are half-way signals between two contrasting words. A different way of making this point is to say that the conventionalised gestures belong to a digital system, while our gesture-calls form an analog system. Giggles, laughs and guffaws are connected by a continuum of signals that are intermediate both in the way they are formed and in the meaning they convey. Many of our facial expressions, such as those that show our anger, joy and fear, also grade into each other. So, apparently, do many or most of the gesture-calls of the great apes (Marler 1976). The conventionalised gesture by which a chimpanzee infant shows that it wants to nurse, on the other hand, does not grade into anything else. Unlike a laugh, it does not occur in a range of slightly varied forms with related but slightly varied meanings. An arms-up gesture is unambiguously a request to be picked up. No intermediate gestures connect it to the equally unambiguous begging gesture. These signals are as discrete as human quotable gestures, and this makes them considerably more language-like than are gesture-calls. It is true, of course, that some animal signals are discrete.

The famous vervet alarm calls, for example, appear to be safely distinct from one another, but if ape and human gesture-calls are predominantly graded, the discreteness of vervet alarms is hardly relevant to the phylogeny of language.

Words and Conventionalised Gestures

Ontogenetically conventionalised acts are more wordlike than are gesture-calls but they are by no means words, and once we have isolated them as a special type of signal we can see both the ways in which they resemble words and the ways in which they differ.

One difference is the greater degree of iconicity of the conventionalised gestures and noises. It is true that the sign languages of the deaf have considerably greater iconicity than does spoken language, but as linguists like to insist, most spoken words have no resemblance at all to the things they stand for. Linguists illustrate this by such obvious examples as the words for *head*. The French say *tête* and the Germans say *Kopf*, and any other form would do equally well so long as it is accepted by the community. Many, though not all, of the gesture-calls of both humans and animals might also be regarded as arbitrary. A dog's wagging tail tells us that he is happy, while the wagging tail of a cat conveys a very different emotion. The relationship between the form and the meaning of a tail wag may seem to be every bit as arbitrary as the relation between the form and meaning of a spoken word. However, unlike words, but like other animal signals, tail wags are firmly set by the genetic inheritance of the species. This gives the ritualised arbitrariness of gesture-calls an utterly different basis than the conventional arbitrariness of words.

Conventionalised instrumental gestures are far from arbitrary, for they reflect the instrumental origin of the gestures or noises from which they were derived. In spite of their conventionalisation, for example, the arms-up and begging gestures retain a good deal of the iconicity of their instrumental origins. Comparing the iconicity and arbitrariness of various types of signs is difficult because most varieties of signs, even words, show a mixture of arbitrariness and iconicity so the differences are far from sharp. Nevertheless, the relatively high degree of iconicity of conventionalised signs seems clear.

Another difference between the conventionalised signs and language is that none of the conventional signs are used symmetrically between two individuals. A parent and child can use the same words with one another, but parents do not use the arms-up gesture to their children as a request to be picked up. If a parent uses the arms-up gesture it is in playful imitation of the child, not a serious request. Chimpanzee infants make nursing gestures to their mothers, but mothers do not make the same gesture to their offspring. Moreover, unlike most words, none of the conventionalised gestures are names for things. They are, instead, imperatives – requests or commands for an action by another individual. Even the attention grunt is a request for attention.

Finally, it must be emphasised once more that the conventionalised signs are not learned by imitation. Without imitation, it is impossible for an entire community to share the same sign, or for signs to be passed down from one generation to the next. There is no indication that chimpanzee nursing gestures, infant grunts or the arms-up gesture are learned by imitation. In the absence of imitation, individuals or pairs of communicating individuals are free to differ in the forms of their signals. Ontogenetically conventionalised gestures do not lead a species across the boundaries of culture.

In spite of their asymmetrical use and imperative function, the absence of imitation and their relatively high degree of iconicity, conventionalised signs resemble words in important ways. Like language, but unlike gesture-calls, the conventionalised signs are learned, conventional and discrete. These character-istics make them a much more promising source for early language than is any part of a gesture-call system.

Conclusions

As soon as we recognise that comprehension had to come first in the phylogeny of language, just as it came first in the history of animal calls and gestures and just as it comes first for each individual child, we are led to ask some new ques-tions about the first stages of human language. We should ask about the kinds of selective pressures that might have driven our prehuman and early human ancestors toward an increasingly skilled ability to interpret the instrumental acts of others. We should also ask how, at later stages, they could have begun to understand the acts of others in increasingly wordlike and then sentence-like ways. The origins of comprehension should, after all, be less mysterious than the origins of production. Producers may have excellent reasons not to give themselves away, so it is often highly advantageous *not* to communicate. On the other hand, any animal, including a human animal, has little to lose and potentially a great deal to gain by understanding as much as possible from the behaviour of conspecifics: What is that fellow likely to do? What does she want? Why is she moving off in that direction? What does that grunt mean? The more one animal can infer from the actions of others, the more skillfully it can plan its own behavior. As mutual comprehension improves, of course, a time will come when it will be advantageous for individuals to exploit the comprehension of others. Then they can adapt their own production to the comprehension skills of their conspecifics. They can act in deliberately informative ways. Then, and only then, does the coevolutionary development of productive and receptive skills begin.

A focus on improved comprehension might give us a different picture of the sequence by which new features enter language than does a focus on production. It is not at all obvious that we would expect the same sequence if we ask how people might have built up their understanding as we would expect if we ask how they would come to produce an increasingly complex language. If, for example, we assume that our forebears used single words before joining them together into orderly sequences, we will want to ask how the joining could have begun. A focus on comprehension should lead us to ask how understanders could start to make inferences from the sequence of the words they hear, even when the producer had made no effort to arrange them in orderly ways. The first step, quite plausibly, could have been nothing more than a gradual increase in the frequency of individual words. As more and more words were used, they would begin to bump up against each other. They would emerge in more rapid succession, but without any deliberate structure having been imposed upon them. Even without intending to do so, however, speakers might use words in consistent ways. If they thought chronologically, for example, they might utter their words in a sequence that iconically reflected the chronology of events. Once comprehenders began to perceive the chronological significance of the word order that they heard from others, producers might find it advantageous to exploit that understanding in order to communicate more precisely. A rudimentary iconic syntax would then become possible. As soon as we recognise that it becomes useful for speakers to use a new form of communication only after their interlocutors have the ability to understand it, we should ask, for every feature that must enter a language, why producers would have begun to use it without any intention of communicating. How could understanding develop even before speakers began to exploit it?

The questions that I have raised in this concluding section of the chapter are different from those that have most often been asked by those of us who are interested in the origin of language, but they arise naturally as soon as we recognise the central role of comprehension. I believe these questions deserve careful thought and debate.

References

Burling, R. 1993. Primate calls, human language, and nonverbal communication. *Current Anthropology* **34**: 25–53.

Hayes, K. J. and C. H. Nissen. 1971. Higher mental functions of a home-raised chimpanzee. In A. M. Schrier and F. Stollnitz (eds), *Behavior of Nonhuman Primates*. New York: Academic, pp. 59–115.

Kendon, A. 1993. Human gesture. In K. R. Gibson and T. Ingold (eds), *Tools, Language and Cognition in Human Evolution*. Cambridge: Cambridge University Press, pp. 43–62.

Marler, P. 1976. Social organization, communication and graded signals: The chimpanzee and the gorilla. In P. P. Bateson and R. A. Hinde (eds), *Growing points in ethology*. Cambridge: Cambridge University Press, pp. 239–80.

McCune, L. 1999. Children's transition to language: a human model for development of vocal repertoire in extant and ancestral primate species? In B. J. King (ed), *The Origins of Language: What nonhuman primates can tell us*. Santa Fe, NM: School of American Research Press.

McCune, L., M. M. Vihman, L. Roug-Hellichius, D. B. Delery and L. Gogate. 1996. Grunt communication in human infants (*Homo sapiens*). *Journal of Comparative Psychology* **110**: 27–37.

Savage-Rumbaugh, E. S., J. Murphey, R. A. Sevik, K. E. Brakke, S. L. Williams and D. M. Rumbaugh. 1993. *Language Comprehension in Ape and Child*. Monographs of the Society for Research in Child Development. Serial No. 233, Vol. 58, Nos. 3–4.

Tinbergen, N. 1952. Derived activities: their causation, biological significance, origin and emancipation during evolution. *Quarterly Review of Biology* **27**: 1–32.

Tomasello, M. and J. Call. 1997. *Primate Cognition*. New York and Oxford: Oxford University Press.

Tomasello, M., J. Call, K. Nagell, R. Olguin and M. Carpenter. 1994. The learning and use of gestural signals by young chimpanzees: A transgenerational study. *Primates* **35**: 137–154.

Tomasello, M., B. L. George, A. C. Kruger, M. J. Farrar and A. Evans. 1985. The development of gestural communication in young chimpanzees. *Journal of Human Evolution* **14**: 175–186.

Tomasello, M., D. Gust and G. T. Frost. 1989. A longitudinal investigation of gestural communication in young chimpanzees. *Primates* **30**: 35–50.

3

Cooperation, Competition and the Evolution of Prelinguistic Communication

JASON NOBLE

1. Language Origins and Darwinian Thought

Theories of the origin of language are necessarily speculative. Calvin (1983) suggests that the development of language involved a transfer of the skills involved in stone throwing; Knight (1998) puts the roots of language in ritual; Bickerton (1998) argues that language arose from protolanguage in a single catastrophic mutation. Any one of these accounts might be true, but it is difficult or impossible to gather direct evidence that would allow us to decide between them. An unkind observer might conclude that anything goes, and that one foundation myth is as good as another.

However, such cynicism would be misplaced. In recent years the range of acceptable speculation has been greatly narrowed by the recognition that any account of language origins must be consistent with the principles of evolution by natural selection. For instance, modern Darwinism tells us that complex traits do not evolve without having some function, that all of the intermediate stages in the evolution of modern linguistic capacity must themselves have had adaptive value and that gradual development is more plausible than catastrophic change. These sorts of constraints immediately rule out many stories of language origin, such as the suggestion by Gould (1987) that language is a mere by-product of having a large and complex brain.

The chief problem for a Darwinian account of human speech, however, is the apparent level of altruism involved. The orthodox position in evolutionary biology (Dawkins 1976) suggests that organisms are best understood as products of their selfish genes: they do not do things for the good of the group or the species, but in order to propagate copies of their own genetic material. Given this perspective, speech (and many other forms of cooperative behaviour) can be difficult to account for. Why do speakers freely exchange valuable information when the theory of natural selection predicts selfishness? In a hypothetical protolinguistic community, what would prevent the rise of a selfish mutant strain that listened but did not speak? Speaking or signalling always costs something in terms of time and energy, and may involve more indirect costs such as exposing the signaller to greater predation risk. Why not reap the benefits of the informative signals of others, without paying the costs of signalling oneself? Or worse, why not use the communication system to lie, misinforming others for one's own benefit?

Possible answers to this dilemma are usually phrased in terms of kin selection (Hamilton 1964) or reciprocal altruism (Trivers 1971): speakers or signallers remain honest because they are helping their relatives or because they want others to do the same for them, respectively. There are alternative explanations. Dessalles (1998, this volume) presents the intriguing suggestion that honest information is given freely because it is a way of competing for status within the group. Knight (1998) argues that the cooperative exchange of information that characterises speech involves a great risk of deception, and therefore that speechlike communication could only be evolutionarily stable if there was some mechanism that made it strategically sound to trust other members of the group. Knight believes that this mechanism is ritual; group members demonstrate their allegiance to the common cause by performing a costly ritual act, and this allows the rest of the group to believe their potentially fakeable signals in future.

Knight's argument relies in part on a view of communication presented in the behavioural ecology literature by Krebs and Dawkins (1984). Krebs and Dawkins do not define animal communication in terms of information transmission but as a method whereby one animal exploits the muscle power of another. They outline two possibilities for the coevolution of signalling and response behaviour (see Section 3): one that leads to costly, manipulative signals and another that leads to quiet, efficient and honest communication. The latter – cooperative signalling – occurs when it is in the interest of both animals that the signaller successfully 'manipulate' the receiver. Knight argues that human speech is the sort of system that one would expect to have resulted from the second process, and this motivates his hypothesis that ritual was the key to creating the necessary cooperative context.

2. Simulating the Evolution of Communication

Interesting as Knight's work is, the goal of this chapter is to explore not his theory but that of Krebs and Dawkins (1984), using game theory and computer simulations of evolution. The sceptical reader may need convincing, however, that Krebs and Dawkins's ideas are relevant to the evolution of language. It is true that their work is most easily applied to simple animal signalling systems, and it is certainly true that the communication systems presented here (in simulation) will be much simpler than language. Nevertheless, Krebs and Dawkins's theory is important and relevant because it forces us to recognise the Darwinian truth that animals, including ourselves, must be expected to be manipulative rather than informative, all things being equal. This fact must be constantly borne in mind in trying to account for the anomalous levels of altruism in speech. Furthermore, modelling simple prelinguistic communication is useful because it puts further constraints on theories of how language itself evolved – as things stand there is room for far too many plausible possibilities.

Mathematical and simulation modelling are necessary steps if we are to go beyond an impasse in which the proponents of competing theories merely trade rhetoric. Formal models can produce counterintuitive results, and show, for instance, that of two apparently plausible theories only one is internally consistent. An excellent example of the value of a good model in theorising about communication is the story of the handicap principle. This idea was introduced by Zahavi (1975), who proposed that signallers sacrifice some of their fitness (i.e. impose a handicap on themselves) in order to produce signals that will be believed by receivers. When the handicap principle was first introduced, it was generally not accepted by theoretical biologists. Simple population-genetic models seemed to show that it could not be evolutionarily stable. However, an elaborate mathematical model developed by Grafen (1990) appears to have vindicated Zahavi's idea, and has made the handicap principle a respectable explanatory construct.

Simulation models of the evolution of communication have been put forward before, but have rarely considered the general case that is implied by Krebs and Dawkins's theory: the possibility that different kinds of communication may evolve under conditions of conflict and of cooperation. Earlier models have often been constructed such that honest signalling was always in the interests of both signallers and receivers. Thus, only cooperative communication systems could possibly emerge. For example, Werner and Dyer (1991) postulated blind, mobile males and sighted, immobile females: the evolution of a signalling system was in the interests of both parties as it allowed mating to take place at better-than-chance frequencies. In MacLennan and Burghardt's (1994) model, signallers and receivers were rewarded if and only if they engaged in successful communicative interactions.

Other models (Ackley and Littman 1994; Oliphant 1996) have considered the special case where communication would benefit receivers, but the potential signallers are indifferent. Oliphant argues that this is a good way to model the evolution of alarm calls, for example: if one bird in a flock spots an approaching hawk, it is clear that its conspecifics would benefit from an alarm call. However, why should the bird in question, considered as a product of its selfish genes, give the call?

Finally, some simulation models have considered the evolution of communication in situations where the two parties appear to have conflicting interests. Wheeler and de Bourcier (1995) modelled aggressive territorial signalling. Bullock (1997) constructed a general model in which signallers of varying degrees of quality solicited receivers for a favourable response; receivers were rewarded for responding positively only to high-quality signallers. A secondary goal of the current chapter is to try to position this earlier simulation work in an overarching theoretical context.

3. Expensive Hype and Conspiratorial Whispers

Krebs and Dawkins (1984) view signalling as a competitive affair involving mind reading and manipulation. Mind reading consists of one animal exploiting tell-tale predictors about the future behaviour of another, such as a dog noticing the bared teeth of an opponent, concluding that it is about to attack and fleeing in order to avoid injury. Manipulation is what happens when those being mind-read fight back, influencing the behaviour of the mind readers to their own advantage. For example, a dog could bare its teeth despite not having the strength or inclination to attack, and thereby scare off its mind-reading opponent. Krebs and Dawkins predict evolutionary arms races between manipulative signallers and sceptical receivers: 'selection will act simultaneously to increase the power of manipulators and to increase resistance to it' (1984: 390). The result will be increasingly costly, exaggerated signals; examples from nature include the roars of red deer stags and the elaborate tails of peacocks.

Krebs and Dawkins admit, however, that not all interactions are competitive in nature. There are some situations in which it is to the receiver's advantage to be manipulated by the signaller. For example, a pack-hunting predator may attempt to recruit a conspecific in order to bring down prey too large for either to tackle alone. Foraging bees, on returning to the hive, may indicate to their closely related hivemates the direction and distance to a source of nectar. In these cases the receiver's compliance is to the benefit of both parties, i.e. there exists the possibility of cooperation. Krebs and Dawkins argue that when the two parties share a common interest in this way, then a different kind of signal coevolution will result. Specifically, there will be selection for signals that are as energetically cheap as possible while still being detectable; Krebs and Dawkins suggest the phrase 'conspiratorial whispers' to describe these signals. Rather than signallers needing to be more and more extravagant in their attempts to persuade receivers, the opposite process occurs: receivers are eager to be persuaded, and selection will favour subtle signalling and low response thresholds.

Krebs and Dawkins's argument has been influential but no formal justification of it exists. The models presented here will test their prediction that evolved signals will necessarily be more costly when there is a conflict of interests than when the two parties have common interests. In order to do so, it will first be necessary to determine whether communication should be expected *at all* when signallers and receivers have a genuine conflict of interests.

4.   Conflicts of Interest

The first requirement in constructing a general model of communication is a classification scheme for determining when a conflict of interests exists between signallers and receivers – Figure 3.1 shows such a scheme, adapted from Hamilton (1964). Assume that a successful instance of communication in a particular scenario has fitness implications for both participants. The fitness effect on signallers, P_S, and the fitness effect on receivers, P_R, together define a point on the plane in Figure 3.1. For example, consider a hypothetical food call, by which one animal alerts another to the presence of a rich but limited food source. By calling and thus sharing the food, the signaller incurs a fitness cost; by responding to the call, the receiver benefits through obtaining food it might otherwise have missed. Thus, the call would be located in the 'altruism' quadrant. The situations modelled by Ackley and Littman (1994) and Oliphant (1996), where receivers benefit but signallers are ambivalent, can be thought of as points on the positive vertical axis, i.e. where $P_S = 0$ and $P_R > 0$.

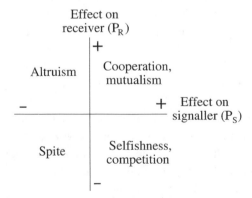

Figure 3.1. Possible communication scenarios classified by their effects on the fitness of each participant.

Conflicts of interest can be defined as interactions in which natural selection favours different outcomes for each participant (Trivers 1974) or in which participants place the possible outcomes in a different rank order (Maynard Smith and Harper 1995). Conflicts of interest therefore exist when P_S and P_R are of opposite sign, i.e. in the upper left and lower right quadrants. Selection will, by definition, favour actions that have positive fitness effects. In the upper left and lower right quadrants, one animal but not the other will be selected to participate in the communication system: their interests conflict. The 'spite' quadrant does not represent a conflict of interests because the two parties will each be selected not to communicate.

If the specified fitness effects of participating in a communicative interaction are truly net values, and already include such factors as the cost of signalling and the cost of making a response (as well as inclusive fitness considerations and costs due to exploitation of the signal by predators, etc.), then predicting the evolution of the communication system is trivial. Reliable communication requires, on average, honest signallers and trusting receivers, and thus will only develop when $P_S > 0$ and $P_R > 0$, i.e. when both participants are selected to participate. However, real animals sometimes communicate despite apparent conflicts of interest (Hinde 1981). Recent models (Grafen 1990; Bullock 1997) have established that, in certain situations where communication would otherwise be unstable, increasing the production costs of the signal can lead to a prediction of evolutionarily stable signalling. Therefore, in the current model, P_S and P_R refer to gross fitness effects before the specific costs of producing the signal, C_S, and making the response, C_R, have been taken into account.

5. A Simple Signalling Game

If the signalling interaction is to involve information transmission, and allow for the possibilities of deception and manipulation, it must be modelled as a game of imperfect information, in which the signaller knows something that the receiver does not. Figure 3.2 shows the extended form of a simple action-response game that fulfils this requirement. The game begins with a chance move (the central square) in which some state is randomly determined to be either 'high' or 'low'. The signaller has access to this state, and we can suppose that it represents some feature of the environment that only the signaller has detected, e.g. noticing an approaching predator. Based on this state, the signaller (Player I) must decide whether or not to send an arbitrary signal of cost C_S. The receiver (Player II) is ignorant of the hidden state and only knows whether or not a signal was sent – the dashed rectangles show the receiver's information sets. The receiver can respond either positively by performing some action appropriate to the high

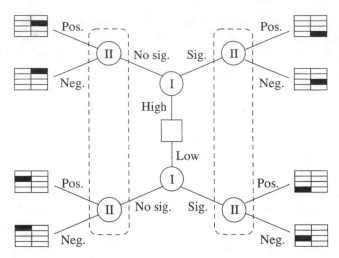

Figure 3.2. Extended form of the simple signalling game. The shaded cell in each chart icon indexes the relevant payoff value in Table 3.1.

state, or negatively by not responding at all. Positive responses incur a cost, C_R. If and only if the hidden state is high, a positive response results in the payoffs P_S and P_R to the signaller and receiver, respectively. Table 3.1 specifies the payoff matrix. Hurd (1995), Oliphant (1996) and Bullock (1997) used similar games with different payoff structures.

The game models a range of possible communicative interactions. For example, suppose that the high state represents the signaller's discovery of food. Sending a signal might involve emitting a characteristic sound, while not sending a signal is to remain silent. For the receiver, a positive response means approaching the signaller and sharing the food, whereas a negative response means doing nothing. Various possibilities exist besides honest signalling of the high state: the receiver might always approach the signaller in the hope of obtaining food, regardless of whether a signal was sent. The signaller might be uninformative and never signal, or only signal when food was not present. One important feature of the game is that the signaller is ambivalent about the receiver's response in the low state – in terms of the example, this represents the assumption that when no food has been discovered, the signalling animal does not care about whether the receiver approaches or not.

The strategies favoured at any one time will depend on the relative values of P_S, P_R, C_S and C_R, as well as on what the other members of the population are doing. (Another parameter of interest in the signalling game is the relative frequency of high and low states; in the models presented here each state occurs 50% of the time.) Allowing the base fitness effects P_S and P_R to vary across

Table 3.1. *Payoff matrix for the simple game*

	State of environment	
	Low	High
No signal		
Neg. response	0, 0	0, 0
Pos. response	0, -C_R	P_S, P_R - C_R
Signal		
Neg. response	-C_S, 0	-C_S, 0
Pos. response	-C_S, -C_R	P_S - C_S, P_R - C_R

Note: Entries in the table represent the payoff to the sender and receiver respectively.

positive and negative values will allow the payoff space of Figure 3.1 to be explored, and thus determine whether changes in signal and response cost can produce stable signalling in situations that would otherwise involve conflicts of interest. This will be a first step towards assessing Krebs and Dawkins's conspiratorial-whispers theory.

6.   Stable Strategies in the Simple Game

A signalling strategy in the simple game specifies whether to respond with no signal (NS) or with a signal (Sig) to low and high states, respectively. Likewise, a response strategy specifies whether to respond negatively (Neg) or positively (Pos) when faced with no signal or with a signal. A strategy pair is the conjunction of a signalling and a response strategy. For instance, the strategy pair (NS/Sig, Neg/Pos) specifies signalling only in the high state, and responding positively only to signals – call this the honest strategy.

It can be shown (Maynard Smith 1982) that honesty will be an evolutionarily stable strategy (ESS) if:

$$P_S > C_S > 0$$
$$P_R > C_R > 0.$$

That is, honest signalling is stable if the costs of signalling and responding are both positive and if the payoffs in each case outweigh the costs. The requirement that P_S and P_R must both be positive means that the honest strategy is only expected to be stable in cooperative contexts.

Of the 16 possible strategy pairs, there are three besides the honest strategy that involve the transmission of information in that the receiver responds differently to different hidden states. None of these three strategy pairs are ESSs if C_S and C_R are both positive; these two values represent energetic costs and so cannot sensibly be negative. If $C_S = 0$, i.e. if giving a signal is of negligible cost, then the reverse of the honesty strategy (Sig/NS, Pos/Neg) can be stable, although P_S and P_R must still be positive. It is also worth noting that any mixed strategy involving (NS/NS, Pos/Pos) and (NS/NS, Pos/Neg) – both nonsignalling strategies where the receiver always responds positively – can be an ESS if the payoff to the receiver is large enough, i.e. if:

$$C_S > 0$$
$$P_S > -C_S$$
$$P_R > 2C_R > 0.$$

The analysis indicates that while the cost of signalling plays some role in stabilising the honest strategy, there are no circumstances in which stable communication is predicted when a conflict of interests exists. This is true even though we have separated the costs of signalling and responding from the base fitness payoffs of a communicative interaction.

7. An Evolutionary Simulation Model

Game theory is limited to describing equilibria; an evolutionary simulation model of the simple game was also constructed in order to determine whether communicative behaviour might sometimes be found outside the range of identified ESSs.

A straightforward genetic algorithm (GA) was used; see Mitchell (1996) for an introduction to this technique. Each individual could play both signalling and receiving roles, and a strategy pair was specified by a four-bit genotype as shown in Table 3.2. The population size was 100, the mutation rate was 0.01 per locus, and crossover was not used. For each generation, 500 games were played between randomly selected opponents. An individual could therefore expect to play 5 games as a signaller and 5 as a receiver. The individual's fitness score was the total payoff from these games. For breeding purposes, the fitness scores were normalised by subtracting the minimum score from each, and proportionate selection was then applied to the normalised scores. The genetic algorithm was run in this manner for 500 generations. In the results presented below, the games played in the final, i.e. 500th, generation have been used as a snapshot of the evolved signalling strategies.

In order to see how communication might arise from a noncommunicative context, the initial population for the genetic algorithm was not randomly generated (as is usually done), but was constructed in such a way that no communication occurred. Populations underwent 100 generations of preliminary evolution in which their receiving strategies were free to evolve but their signalling strategies were clamped at '00', i.e. no signalling. A simulation run was performed for all combinations of integer values of P_S and P_R between -5 and $+5$, making 121 runs in all. Each run was repeated 25 times with different random seeds. The values of C_S and C_R were fixed at 1.

Communication was indexed by cross-tabulating the hidden state value with the receiver's response and calculating a chi-squared statistic. The receiver has no direct access to the hidden state, so any reliable correspondence between state and response indicates that information has been transmitted and acted upon. Values of the χ^2 statistic close to zero indicate no communication, and values close to the maximum (in this case $\chi^2_{\max} = 500$, given the 500 games played in the final, snapshot generation) indicate near-perfect communication.

Table 3.2. *Genetic specification of strategies*

	Bit value	
	0	1
If low state…	No signal	Signal
If high state…	No signal	Signal
Response to no signal	Negative	Positive
Response to signal	Negative	Positive

Communication

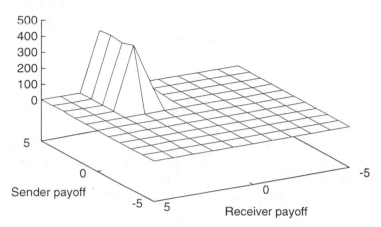

Figure 3.3. Mean communication index by P_S and P_R. Each point is a mean calculated over 25 runs.

Figure 3.3 shows the average values of the communication index over the repeated simulations; the cooperative quadrant is at the left rear of the graph. Clearly the conditions for the stability of the honest strategy, as established by the game-theoretic analysis in Section 6, are not the same as the conditions established here for the evolution of honest signalling from noncommunicative beginnings. If $P_S > 1$ and $P_R = 2$, communication develops but if $P_S > 1$ and $P_R > 2$ it does not. In the latter region $P_R > 2C_R$ and the population remains at the nonsignalling ESS described earlier: although communication would result in a higher average fitness, the high value of P_R keeps the receivers responding positively at all times, removing any incentive for the signallers to bother signalling. Note that under no circumstances does stable communication occur when there is any conflict of interest between the two parties, i.e. outside the cooperative quadrant.

8. A Game with Variable Signal Costs

In the simple signalling game, signallers can choose between a costly signal or no signal at all. The model does not allow for a range of possible signals with differing costs, and in this respect it is unrealistic. It may be that Krebs and Dawkins's implicit prediction, that signalling can occur when a conflict of interests exists, is in fact true, but can only be demonstrated in a more complex game with a range of signal costs. The simple signalling game (see Figure 3.2) was therefore extended to incorporate signals of differing costs.

In the extended game, the signalling player has three options: not signalling, which costs nothing; using the 'soft' signal, which costs C_S, and using the 'loud' signal, which costs $2C_S$. Strategies in the extended game require specifying the signal to give when the hidden state is low or high and the response to give to no signal, soft signal and loud signal. The two strategies representing conspiratorial whispers or cheap signalling are (NS/Soft, Neg/Pos/Pos) and (NS/Soft, Neg/Pos/Neg). Both strategies call for the soft signal to be used in the high state, and for positive responses to the soft signal; they differ only in the response to loud signals. Neither of these strategies can strictly be considered an ESS on its own (because neutral drift can take the population from one to the other) but it can be shown that the set of all mixed strategies involving these two is an ESS under the familiar conditions:

$$P_S > C_S > 0$$
$$P_R > C_R > 0.$$

Costly signalling would involve the use of the loud signal for the high state, and either the soft signal or no signal to denote the low state, with a corresponding response strategy. None of the four strategies in this category can be an ESS. For example, (NS/Loud, Neg/Pos/Pos) cannot be an ESS assuming positive costs of signalling and responding. The similar strategy (NS/Loud, Neg/Neg/Pos) is almost stable if $P_S > 2C_S$, but can drift back to the previous strategy, which can in turn be invaded by the cheap strategy (NS/Soft, Neg/Pos/Pos).

Analysis of the extended game indicates that if signalling is favoured at all, then at equilibrium the signallers will always use the cheapest and the second-cheapest signal available (i.e. no signal and the soft signal). Further extensions of the game, by adding ever more costly signalling options, do not alter this conclusion. None of the costly signalling strategies can even be an ESS, let alone support communication in the face of a conflict of interests. The possibility of expensive signalling arms races starts to look remote. However, it may be that the discrete signals used in the games presented so far have had an unwarranted effect on the results.

9.   Simulation Model with Continuous Signal Costs and Reception Threshold

A second evolutionary simulation was constructed, in which the cost of signalling was continuously variable. Signalling strategies were represented by two positive real numbers C_{low} and C_{high}: the cost of the signals given in the low state and in the high state, respectively. Response strategies were represented by a real-valued threshold T; positive responses were given to signals with costs greater than the receiver's threshold value. Note that threshold values could be negative, indicating a positive response to any signal.

A real-valued GA was used to simulate the evolution of strategies over time. Generally, the same parameters were used as in the previous simulation model, e.g. a population of 100. Mutation was necessarily a different matter: each real-valued gene in each newborn individual was always perturbed by a random Gaussian value, $\mu = 0$, $\sigma = 0.05$. If a perturbation resulted in a negative cost value the result was replaced by zero. In addition, 1% of the time (i.e. a mutation rate of 0.01) a gene would be randomly set to a value between 0 and 5 for signal costs, or between -5 and $+5$ for the threshold value. This two-part mutation regime ensured that offspring were always slightly different from their parent, and occasionally very different.

The C_S parameter was no longer relevant, but C_R, the cost of responding, remained fixed at 1. Nonsignalling initial conditions were implemented by setting T to a random Gaussian ($\mu = 0$, $\sigma = 1$) and then clamping $C_{low} = C_{high} = 0$ for 100 generations of preliminary evolution.

Figure 3.4 shows the average values of the communication index. The results are qualitatively similar to those for the discrete simulation model: communication occurs in a limited region of the cooperative quadrant, and never outside it.

The continuous model also allows investigation of the cost and threshold values over the payoff space. C_{low}, the cost of the signal given in response to the low state, always remained close to zero – this was unsurprising as signallers

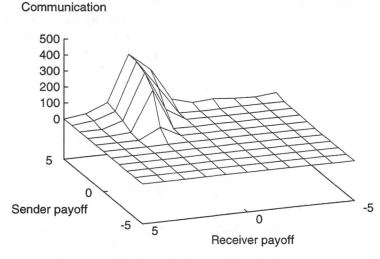

Figure 3.4. Mean communication index by P_S and P_R in the continuous simulation. Each point is a mean calculated over 25 runs.

Cost

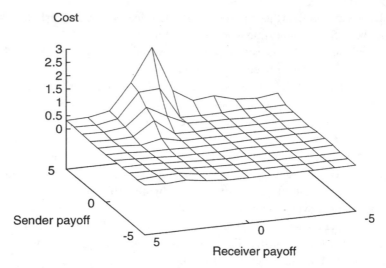

Figure 3.5. Mean cost of high-state signals by P_S and P_R. Each point is a mean calculated over 25 runs.

are ambivalent about the receiver's response to the low state. However, the value of C_{high} varied both inside and outside the region where communication was established: Figure 3.5 shows the mean values of C_{high}. The signals given in response to the high state are most costly when P_S, the payoff to the sender, is high and when the receiver's net payoff is marginal, i.e. $P_R \approx 1$. In order to study this effect more closely, additional simulation runs were performed, with P_S fixed at 5 and P_R varying between -5 and $+5$ in increments of 0.1. These runs can be thought of as exploring the cross section through $P_S = 5$ in Figure 3.5. Figure 3.6 shows the cross-sectional mean values of C_{high}. Note that the 'energy' devoted to signalling is at a maximum around $P_R = 1$ and drops off as P_R increases – it can be seen from Figure 3.4 that $P_R = 1$ is approximately the point where significant communication is established.

The threshold values showed corresponding variation. Figure 3.7 shows the mean value of T across the payoff space. The threshold values are typically very high (a 'never respond' strategy) or very low (an 'always respond' strategy), but in the region where communication evolved, receivers become progressively less demanding, i.e. T decreases as P_R increases. Figure 3.8 shows the cross-sectional results for $P_S = 5$.

Figure 3.9 plots the mean cost of high and low signals and the mean reception threshold on a single graph. This makes the relationship between costs and threshold clear: at approximately $P_R = 1$, the threshold falls to a level where the mean high-state signal generates a positive response. As P_R increases, i.e. as the

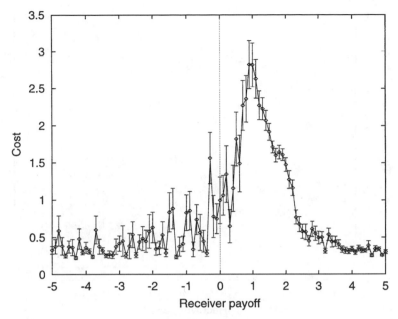

Figure 3.6. Cross-sectional means ($\pm$ 1 standard error) for high-state signal costs with $P_S = 5$. Each point is a mean calculated over 25 runs.

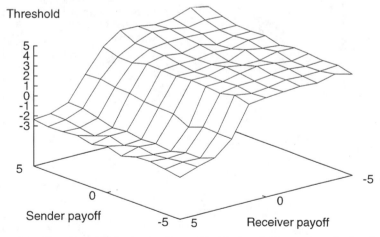

Figure 3.7. Mean threshold value by P_S and P_R. Each point is a mean calculated over 25 runs.

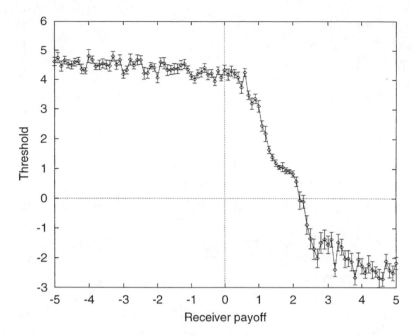

Figure 3.8. Cross-sectional mean threshold values (± 1 standard error) with $P_S = 5$. Each point is a mean calculated over 25 runs.

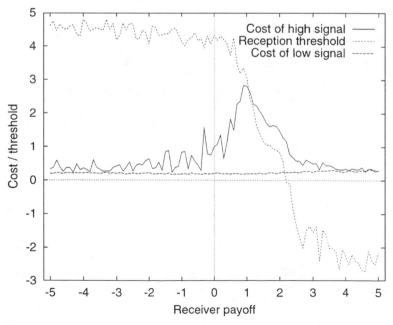

Figure 3.9. Cross-sectional means: cost of high and low signals, and reception threshold. $P_S = 5$. Each point is a mean calculated over 25 runs.

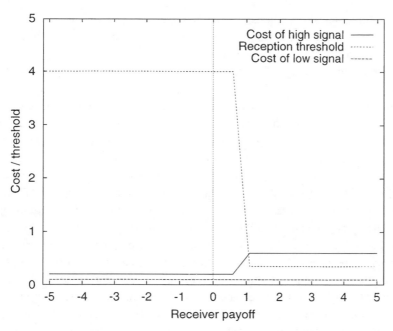

Figure 3.10. Approximate predicted results for Figure 3.9 according to discrete-cost game-theoretic model.

two players' payoffs approach each other, the signallers become less extravagant and the receivers less 'sceptical'. This contradicts the game-theoretic result of the previous section, which implies that when signals of varying costs are available, either the cheapest pair of signals will be used, or no signalling will occur. That is, something like Figure 3.10 would be expected if the soft-loud signalling game accurately modelled the continuous case.

10. Discussion of Results

In all of the models presented, communication evolved or was predicted to evolve only within the cooperative region of the signaller-receiver payoff space. This means that no signalling at all (costly or otherwise) was observed when the signaller and the receiver were experiencing a conflict of interests. The first game-theoretic model, in which discrete signals of varying costs are available, suggests that communication, if selected for, will use the cheapest pair of signals available. However, the second simulation model, incorporating the more realistic assumption that signals can vary continuously in cost, implies that cheap signals will only be used when both parties stand to gain a high payoff from effective communication. When the net payoff to the receiver is marginal, evolved signals will be more costly than strictly necessary to convey the information. The relationship is not symmetrical: when the net payoff to the signaller is marginal, a nonsignalling equilibrium, in which the receiver always responds positively, is likely to occur.

Krebs and Dawkins (1984) predicted that signalling would be costly if a conflict of interests existed, and strictly speaking, the results here neither support nor contradict their prediction, as no signalling occurred in the conflict-of-interest cases. However, although the results from the second simulation model do not confirm Krebs and Dawkins's conspiratorial-whispers theory, they definitely suggest a modification of it. As Figure 3.9 shows, when the net payoff to the receiver is marginal, receivers will be sceptical and express 'sales resistance' by responding only to costly signals; signallers in turn will be prepared to invest more energy in 'convincing' receivers to respond positively. When communication is unambiguously good for both parties, signals are cheaper and response thresholds lower. Therefore both costly manipulative signals and conspiratorial whispers are expected to evolve, but in a much smaller region of the payoff space than Krebs and Dawkins's theory suggests, i.e. within the cooperative region. Costly signals evolve when honest signalling is highly profitable to the signaller, but only marginally so to the receiver. For example, if a juvenile benefits by honestly signalling extreme hunger to its parent (because the parent responds by feeding it), but the net inclusive-fitness payoff to the parent is only slight, then costly signals by the juvenile are expected.

There are two qualifications that must be made concerning the results. Firstly, the signalling game used is not likely to be a universal model of all possible communicative interactions. In particular, and despite having the same basic structure with two signals potentially used to transmit information about a binary hidden state, the signalling game differs from those employed by Hurd (1995) and Oliphant (1996). Hurd's game models sexual signalling, and the male signaller is not ambivalent about the female receiver's response when the hidden state is low; the signaller always prefers a positive response. A low hidden state maps to low male quality, a positive response represents a copulative episode, and even low-quality males want mating opportunities. The current signalling game, in contrast, cannot model so-called handicap signalling, because low-state signallers do not care about what the receiver does. Furthermore, in both Hurd's and Oliphant's games, receivers are explicitly rewarded for accuracy in discerning the hidden state, but the game presented here allows the ecologically plausible outcome that receivers simply become disinterested in the signal. The current game is a reasonable model of situations such as alarm calls and food calls, in which potential signallers have no reason to care about what receivers do when no predator has been sighted or no food source has been found.

Secondly, it must be stressed that the simple games and simulations described here are in one sense an unfair way to test Krebs and Dawkins's (1984) conspiratorial-whispers hypothesis. Krebs and Dawkins were discussing the likely evolution of signals in complex real-world cases, and could therefore appeal to the effects of differing mutation rates in signallers and receivers, and the exploitation of behaviours that had originally been selected for other purposes. Communication in the predicted costly signalling arms races was not expected to be stable. For example, in a real-world situation where it was not in the interests of receivers to respond positively to a particular signal from a predator, they might nevertheless continue to do so for some time if the signal was structurally similar to a mating signal made by members of the same species. The manipulative signalling system would break down as soon as an appropriate sequence of mutations resulted in organisms that could distinguish between the predator's signal and the conspecific mating signal. In the simple signalling model all this complexity is abstracted into the base fitness payoffs for signallers and receivers, and there is no guarantee that any transient, unstable evolved communication systems will be detected.

11. Implications for Theories of Language Evolution

Where does all this leave Knight (1998) and others who wish to use Krebs and Dawkins's ideas as part of the foundations of a theory of language evolution? The simulations seem to show that the costly-arms-race/conspiratorial-whispers theory is simply not correct, at least not without modification. However, that is only to say that communication is not expected to evolve under conditions of conflicting interest in a simple action-response game. The suspicion that it would have evolved (of which the author is manifestly guilty) can now be put down to careless interpretation of Krebs and Dawkins's talk about the possibilities of 'manipulative signals'. Thus we are reminded of the value of formal modelling: when considering Krebs and Dawkins's verbal argument, it is easy to come away with the impression that communication will readily occur given a conflict of interests (and will involve high signal costs). The simulation models demonstrate the falsity of that impression.

Nothing has been established as to the success of Krebs and Dawkins's theory in more complex scenarios, however. For example, a single communication system may be subject to contemporaneous cooperative and competitive usage, e.g. when social animals use the same signal repertoire to communicate with both in-group and out-group conspecifics, as Knight (1998) has suggested. Dessalles (1998, this volume) describes a scenario in which competition for social status provides a new currency which can offset the costs of signal production. In such cases, costly signalling between agents with conflicting interests might well be evolutionarily stable – the issue is appropriate for further simulation modelling.

The immediate implications of the results presented should therefore not be overstated. Nevertheless, even such simple models start to put constraints on theories of protolanguage and language evolution. Given the results from the second simulation model, and supposing one suspects that language originated in the food and alarm calls of early hominids, then one has to establish that the balance of cooperative payoffs would have allowed communication to evolve. If one's theory of language evolution requires low-cost signalling, then the 'payoff window' will be even narrower. It is through exploring these sorts of constraints that our theories about the evolution of simple signalling systems will eventually connect up with our theories about language.

Acknowledgement

This work was conducted while at the University of Sussex, and I am grateful to the Association of Commonwealth Universities and the British Council for financial support. I would also like to thank Seth Bullock and Ezequiel Di Paolo for valuable discussions.

References

Ackley, D. H. and M. L. Littman. 1994. Altruism in the evolution of communication. In R. A. Brooks and P. Maes (eds), *Artificial Life IV*. Cambridge, MA: MIT Press.

Bickerton, D. 1998. Catastrophic evolution: the case for a single step from protolanguage to full human language. In J. R. Hurford, M. Studdert-Kennedy and C. Knight (eds), *Approaches to the Evolution of Language: Social and cognitive bases*. Cambridge: Cambridge University Press, pp. 341–358.

Bullock, S. 1997. An exploration of signalling behaviour by both analytic and simulation means for both discrete and continuous models. In P. Husbands and I. Harvey (eds), *Proceedings of the Fourth European Conference on Artificial Life (ECAL'97)*. Cambridge, MA: MIT Press.

Calvin, W. H. 1983. A stone's throw and its launch window: timing precision and its implications for language and hominid brains. *Journal of Theoretical Biology* **104**: 121–135.

Dawkins, R. 1976. *The Selfish Gene*. Oxford: Oxford University Press.

Dessalles, J.-L. 1998. Altruism, status, and the origin of relevance. In J. R. Hurford, M. Studdert-Kennedy and C. Knight (eds), *Approaches to the Evolution of Language: Social and cognitive bases*. Cambridge: Cambridge University Press, pp. 130–147.

Gould, S. J. 1987. The limits of adaptation: is language a spandrel of the human brain? Unpublished paper delivered to the Center for Cognitive Science, MIT.

Grafen, A. 1990. Biological signals as handicaps. *Journal of Theoretical Biology* **144**: 517–546.

Hamilton, W. D. 1964. The genetical evolution of social behaviour. *Journal of Theoretical Biology* **7**: 1–52.

Hinde, R. A. 1981. Animal signals: ethological and games-theory approaches are not incompatible. *Animal Behaviour* **29**: 535–542.

Hurd, P. L. 1995. Communication in discrete action-response games. *Journal of Theoretical Biology* **174**: 217–222.

Knight, C. 1998. Ritual/speech coevolution: a solution to the problem of deception. In J. R. Hurford, M. Studdert-Kennedy and C. Knight (eds), *Approaches to the Evolution of Language: Social and cognitive bases.* Cambridge: Cambridge University Press, pp. 68–91.

Krebs, J. R. and R. Dawkins. 1984. Animal signals: mind reading and manipulation. In J. R. Krebs and N. B. Davies (eds), *Behavioural Ecology: An evolutionary approach* Second edition. Oxford: Blackwell.

MacLennan, B. J. and G. M. Burghardt. 1994. Synthetic ethology and the evolution of cooperative communication. *Adaptive Behavior* **2**: 161–188.

Maynard Smith, J. 1982. *Evolution and the Theory of Games.* Cambridge: Cambridge University Press.

Maynard Smith, J. and D. G. C. Harper. 1995. Animal signals: models and terminology. *Journal of Theoretical Biology* **177**: 305–311.

Mitchell, M. 1996. *An Introduction to Genetic Algorithms.* Cambridge, MA: MIT Press.

Oliphant, M. 1996. The dilemma of Saussurean communication. *BioSystems* **37**: 31–38.

Trivers, R. L. 1971. The evolution of reciprocal altruism. *Quarterly Review of Biology* **46**: 35–57.

Trivers, R. L. 1974. Parent-offspring conflict. *American Zoologist* **14**: 249–264.

Werner, G. M. and M. G. Dyer. 1991. Evolution of communication in artificial organisms. In C. G. Langton, C. Taylor, J. D. Farmer and S. Rasmussen (eds), *Artificial Life II.* Redwood City, CA: Addison-Wesley.

Wheeler, M. and P. de Bourcier. 1995. How not to murder your neighbor: using synthetic behavioral ecology to study aggressive signaling. *Adaptive Behavior* **3**: 273–309.

Zahavi, A. 1975. Mate selection – a selection for a handicap. *Journal of Theoretical Biology* **53**: 205–214.

4

Language and Hominid Politics

JEAN-LOUIS DESSALLES

1. Introduction: The Language Gap

Language is the main distinctive feature of our species. Why do we feel the urge to communicate with our fellows, and why is this form of communication characterised by relevance – a feature unique in the animal kingdom? This chapter begins by stressing the specificity of human communication. We then challenge the claim that conversationalists are engaged in reciprocal altruism, arguing instead that the act of speaking must confer a selective advantage on the speaker. This advantage is elucidated by considering speech in its wider social and political context. Given what we know about 'chimpanzee politics' (de Waal 1982), it seems reasonable to suppose that ancestral humans were capable of forming large coalitions (cf. Dunbar 1996). We will suggest that relevant speech emerged in this context, as a way for individuals to select one another in forming alliances.

1.1. Uniqueness of Relevant Speech

The way we communicate is unique among animal species. Speech differs from nonhuman animal communication not only in its sophisticated syntax and complex semantics. An additional unique feature is that speech must be 'relevant'.

Relevance is a precise requirement which severely restricts what is acceptable in human conversation (Dessalles 1993, 1998). By human conversational standards, most messages exchanged in animal communication are 'boring'. Repetitive territorial signalling, individual identification, systematic threat displays – these cannot be considered genuine conversation. We expect human speakers to contribute novelty, to perform sound reasoning or to raise important issues. However, because we are immersed in relevant speech, we fail to recognise how peculiar the communicative behaviour of our species is. Human conversation can be seen as a game in which something is to be won or lost. Think of how easily one may appear ridiculous when uttering a dull remark, especially if there is a large audience. People who repeatedly fail to make relevant points will not gain high social esteem. Conversely, speakers able to make pertinent statements or interesting comments on certain subjects are likely to become the focal point of the conversational group. From such a perspective, language appears more as a kind of 'sport' than as a way of communicating information.

This is not, of course, the usual way to consider linguistic ability. Language confers extraordinary advantages upon human groups. Individuals are enabled to share information and knowledge. They may coordinate the group's actions more efficiently, keeping track of important events. Items of factual knowledge, innovations and memories become collective, extending social power well beyond the capabilities of single individuals. In this context, it might seem that the advantages of language are self-evident. Surely, every species would gain from possessing such an adaptation? In practice – according to this anthropocentric line of reasoning – only one species succeeded in developing language, but others started along the path leading to this remarkable achievement. Primates such as chimpanzees or gorillas appear to have remained at the gates of the Promised Linguistic Land. But their backwardness stems merely from quantitative limitations: they are not clever enough to manipulate abstract concepts, or their brain is not large enough to hold a sufficiently large vocabulary. This is not, however, the scenario we advocate.

Such accounts of language origin, which rely on quantitative factors, fail to explain the qualitative uniqueness of speech. Did other primate species lack sufficient time to evolve symbolic thinking and language? There is no support for such a hypothesis. On the contrary, descriptions of evolution as a punctuated process (Gould and Eldredge 1977; Dessalles 1996) suggest that evolution can be rapid. The underlying mechanism, which may be termed implicit parallelism (Holland 1975; Goldberg 1989) is used in computer optimisation for its rapidity. The fact that genes are selected in parallel is not considered by those evolutionary accounts which insist on evolutionary speed limits (Worden 1998). With evolutionary changes occurring rapidly, species stay in equilibrium most of the time, occupying different adaptive local optima and thus differing qualitatively. Following Monod (1970), we consider early language to have contributed to the qualitative distinction between humans and apes.

1.2. *Linguistic Relevance and Biological Relevance*

The kind of content exchanged during conversation is not mere information. As Wärneryd (1994: 407) states: 'If we encounter people walking around uttering arbitrary true statements about the state of the world for no particular reason other than telling the truth, we will probably think of them as being insane'. Elsewhere (Dessalles 1993), I have provided a definition of conversational relevance. In order to be accepted as relevant, a new topic must be either about an unusual state of affairs or present some issue at stake. Facts or events that can be recognised as improbable, paradoxical, undesirable or desirable may thus count as relevant. We say that they contribute conversational information. 'I damaged my neighbour's brand-new car with my ladder' may be said to friends, because they will worry about the consequences. In the utterance 'I found a tiny medallion I lost last year in the forest', friends may recognise a very unlikely, 'unbelievable' event and may be interested. However, one will not say 'Jack lost a pound coin last year' or tell stories such as 'I woke up this morning, I took a shower, I dressed; then I had breakfast and listened to the news'. Being neither unusual nor (un)desirable, such events are not acceptable as topics of conversation.

Whenever people are brought together, their attention is focused on finding something worth saying. If they fail, they would rather remain silent than utter a platitude. The task is far from trivial. Because most of us are experts at thinking up relevant utterances,[1] we fail to appreciate the true value of this skill. Finding some event in the environment or in recent memory that will contribute conversational information requires sophisticated cognitive abilities. The event must be perceived as unusual by addressees, or should appear as positive or negative. Such topics are, by definition, not easy to find. Admittedly, the relevance threshold varies according to the social context. Making an interesting statement is much easier when talking to one's best friend than when addressing a large audience. In the latter case, we devote all our attention to the task.

The knowledge we require in order to survive and prosper in human societies is learned mostly through conversation; only a minor portion comes through direct personal experience. We may recall the fate of deaf children who have no access to sign language. Deprived of the experience that other people offer in context during conversation, they may face difficulties in fitting into society (Kegl, Senghas and Coppola 1999: 199). What conversationalists make available is not simply information; it is relevant information. Relevant information is more likely to be useful (Dessalles 1998): biologically significant events are often unusual, or positive or negative, while events which are both common and neutral have no reason to attract attention. In short, conversational relevance is a good indicator of biological relevance.

If conversational information is so useful, we may wonder why speakers make every effort to offer it for free. Let us consider first the possibility that such behaviour is based on symmetrical cooperation between individuals.

2. Beyond Symmetrical Cooperation

The notion that human language relies on symmetrical cooperation between individuals seems at first glance self-evident. Conversation, which is the most common and universal use of language, involves participants who alternate between speaking and listening. Speakers give one another sufficient reliable, clear and relevant information for intended meanings to be understood (Grice 1975). Conversation, which relies on such solicitude, must be one of our most cooperative behaviours. Speakers express only the required amount of information to be clear and avoid being redundant. Then roles are reversed and the game continues.

However, I wish to offer a different, perhaps counterintuitive, picture of what is going on in linguistic exchange. I will suggest that there is no more cooperation between speaker and audience than between a figure skater and her judges. Both sides agree to play according to precise rules, but pursue quite different goals. One might then of course wonder why interlocutors exchange roles, if not to insure symmetrical cooperation. Besides the fact that such symmetry is far from systematic, I will consider an alternative explanation for such alternation.

2.1. *Evolution of Symmetrical Cooperation*

Cooperation is often claimed to be a prime cause of human sociality including language (Wilson 1978). A natural hypothesis is that language is based on reciprocation: A gives valuable information to B because B will give valuable information to A in return. This seems to be the obvious reason why conversation, this strange alternation of communicative moves, exists at all. Likewise, social bonds, friendship, the ability to coordinate collective action and altruistic acts would all result from the same ability to engage in inter-individual cooperative games (Wilson 1978). There are, however, several problems with symmetrical cooperation. One of them is that it may collapse in the presence of 'cheaters', who may benefit from the first move while failing to reciprocate. In the case of language, the presence of pure listeners is indeed a problem for the cooperation hypothesis. Relevant speech has a cost: those who provide information must spend time and energy finding interesting topics. If relevant conversational information is fruitlessly given to pure listeners, it is not only a waste of time and energy, but also a way of helping potential genetic competitors (Dessalles 1998). We should thus predict the disappearance of communicators.

A possible defence against pure listeners is for speakers to remember who cooperates and who does not, talking in future only to responsive individuals. This strategy is not absolutely safe, though. To illustrate the problem, let us

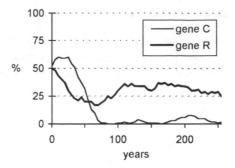

Figure 4.1. Basic simulation of cooperation.

consider the simulation presented in Figures 4.1–4.3. The simulation models the evolution of a population of five hundred individuals. They mate, reproduce and eventually die after a few 'years' or because their 'vitality' becomes too low. Following reproduction, ageing and random accidents decrease vitality and cause deaths until the population reverts to five hundred individuals. Two genes, C and R, are introduced in the population. These genes are at different positions on the genome, so that each individual may carry both, only one or neither. When an individual carries C, it chooses a fellow and gives it valuable information, which translates into vitality points. If this second individual carries R, it gives information back. Each of these behaviours has a cost, but both individuals eventually benefit from the cooperation. On the other hand, if the addressee is not an R-carrier, it remains unresponsive. It benefits from the information given while incurring no cost, and the speaker has lost its time. Under such conditions, R-carriers tend to be rare, causing C-carriers to die out (Figure 4.1).

   There have been many attempts to stabilise the evolution of cooperative strategies by introducing cheat detection (Axelrod 1984; Frean 1996; Ferriere and Michod 1996; Nakamaru, Matsuda and Iwasa 1997; Macy and Skvoretz

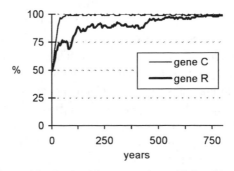

Figure 4.2. Favourable cooperation with 'marking'.

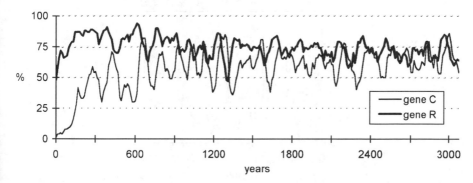

Figure 4.3. Typical cooperation with 'marking'.

1998). When no retaliation is possible in the case of cheating, the basic idea is to diminish the relative importance of the random first step, and thus to increase the reliability of subsequent moves by exclusively addressing responsive individuals. In Figures 4.2 and 4.3, individuals 'mark' responsive individuals so as to preferentially address them in subsequent trials. Evolution of the frequency of each strategy in the population over time is observed. Results crucially depend on the value of some parameters: the profit made when receiving information, the cost of producing information and the efficiency of 'marking' responsive individuals. For a very broad range of these parameters, we observe oscillations (Figure 4.3). These are due to the fact that in their first trial, speakers have no way to discriminate against unresponsive individuals. If speakers are numerous,[2] there is considerable advantage in remaining unresponsive and waiting to be randomly chosen. Consequently, the frequency of both respondents and speakers tends to decrease.[2] Conversely, when responsive individuals are rare, they take advantage of being repeatedly chosen for cooperation. They begin to increase in frequency, as do speakers. These conflicting effects explain why frequencies tend to fluctuate widely over time.

This simulation may help us to determine whether symmetrical cooperation can explain the evolution of human communication. The situation depicted in Figure 4.3 is not dynamically stable. It is not consistent with the evolution of complex faculties, because it creates no selection pressure. To verify this fact, we introduced two versions of each gene in the simulation. C1 and C2 are communication genes. Both induce their carrier to initiate communicative acts. With C1, however, the speaker gives only a fraction of the information it would have conveyed with C2. Similarly, R1-carriers return only a fraction of what R2-carriers return to the speaker. If the cooperative scenario were a sound explanation of the origin of communication, we would expect selection pressures

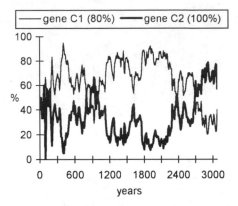

Figure 4.4. Relative proportions of two alleles of gene C. C1-carriers invest 80% of what C2-carriers invest in communication.

leading to a clear dominance of C2 and R2 over C1 and R1, respectively. The sophisticated features of language – the ability to process about ten phonemes per second, to use complex syntax including recursive structures, case marking and agreement, the existence of a complex conceptual semantics and the ability to control relevance – could not have evolved by accident. There must have been strong selective pressures driving the evolution of capacities for increased precision and expressive power. Can we reproduce such a selection pressure in our simple simulation? The answer is no. Figure 4.4 shows no clear dominance of either allele C1 and C2 over the other. Figure 4.5 shows a similar negative result for alleles R1 and R2. Comparable results have been obtained for iterated cooperation: when individuals can choose intermediate levels of cooperation, several strategies coexist (Frean 1996).

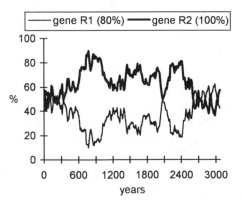

Figure 4.5. Relative proportions of two alleles of gene R. R1-carriers return 80% of what R2-carriers return to communicators.

The situation illustrated in Figure 4.2 seems more promising. It depends, however, on particular values of parameters: high payoffs, low costs and reliable cheater discrimination. These three favourable characteristics are needed to obtain dynamic stability and thus to enable selection pressures to arise. Unfortunately, human communication matches none of these three requirements. Most of the time, conversation provides no significant payoff. Even if acquiring information is profitable in the long run, immediate benefits are far from being guaranteed. Are the costs associated with language especially low? Talk is sometimes said to be 'cheap'. We stressed, however, the fact that being relevant requires all our cognitive resources and presupposes expenditure of time in acquiring information. This is not a negligible cost. Lastly, it is not the case that speakers perform work in checking up on cheats, as will now be shown.

2.2. Inverse Cheat Detection

Given a model of communication based on symmetrical cooperation, we would expect cheat detection to be performed by speakers attempting to ensure reciprocation by addressees. This prediction is not confirmed. Consider the following example:

Context: A and B have been having trouble with humidity in their house. The house was not heated over the weekend, and their clothes are still cold in the wardrobe.

A1: It's also wet in here! (in the wardrobe)
B1: It isn't wet. It's cold.

In A1, A draws attention to a very undesirable state of affairs: she (wrongly) believes that the clothes are wet. A1 contributes conversational information (cf. Section 2.1.) and is thus relevant. B's reply can be naturally understood as a cooperative act. B1 would help A to correctly assess the situation. Maybe this is B's subjective feeling. Face-to-face cooperation is generally understood as a symmetrical process: what A gives to B and what B returns to A are of the same nature. This is not, however, what happens here. Contrary to A1, B1 contributes no conversational information. The fact that the clothes are cold is neither unusual nor (un)desirable. Its relevance must be understood in relation to A1. If B's statement is true, then the situation described in A1 is no longer undesirable. In other words, the objective effect of B1 is to cancel the information contained in A1.

Conversation is inherently asymmetrical. It is not a mere succession of informative statements, as a model based on face-to-face cooperation would lead us to expect. When a relevant topic has been introduced, addressees' replies either reinforce or diminish the conversational information contributed by the speaker (Dessalles 1993). This is what we observed with B1. Conversational structure emerges from an alternation between information and evaluation (Dessalles 1993). To perform such evaluation, interlocutors often try to show that a previous utterance is inconsistent with what they know. Logical consistency is indeed an efficient test of reliability: it is very difficult to lie and remain consistent. A possible conjecture is that logical thinking evolved as part of the listener's ability to evaluate the quality of information.

The behaviour of addressees during conversation fails to match expectations of the symmetrical cooperation scenario. If cheat detection is occurring, it is being undertaken not by speakers – as the cooperative scenario would lead us to expect – but by listeners. This role reversal is totally mysterious if we see in conversation a cooperative game. The only viable strategy is for cooperative speakers to detect and penalise uncooperative addressees. The inverse situation, in which it is listeners who are 'choosy', is in this context inexplicable. It does make sense, however, if we depart from the model of symmetrical cooperation.

3.   Language and Coalition Formation

3.1.   A Social Role for Language

In his book *Chimpanzee Politics*, de Waal (1982) shows the importance of coalitions in the social organisation of our sister species. Humans are nevertheless unique in one respect: we form especially large coalitions. Dunbar (1966) suggests that language may have played a crucial role in organising these, arguing that linguistic exchanges perform social bonding functions and typically concern social affairs. People are brought together to gossip about the behaviour of others in the group. By denouncing uncooperative individuals, interlocutors reinforce their own solidarity.

Gossip seems to be a very common use of language. However, I do not agree that it can explain the emergence of language. First, information about social 'cheaters' is valuable. Why would people willingly give such information to one another? We are back to the difficulty highlighted in the preceding section: if gossip is a form of cooperation, how could it emerge through natural selection? It is precisely the efficiency of language for social bonding highlighted by Dunbar – the fact that speech reaches several individuals simultaneously – that is also an argument against the symmetrical cooperation scenario (Power 1998). Moreover, we do not see how the gossiping function could determine the specific way we communicate. Language can be used to convey any kind of information, provided it is relevant. We are not bound to talk about social facts, but we are bound to utter relevant messages. The need to exchange social information does not explain relevance. Relevance, however, does explain gossip. Social misbehaviour, when it is unusual or may have harmful consequences, matches our definition of relevance. Social relationships indeed prove to be an inexhaustible source of relevant information. Yet not all social facts are relevant. Certain forms of misbehaviour might not seem especially unusual or (un)desirable to the participants. In these cases, such behaviour could not be a topic of conversation.

Gossip is at best a secondary function of language; there is no evidence of any influence it could have had on the design of the language faculty. If there is a primary social function that constitutes a causal factor of language evolution, this function must still be determined.

3.2. Language as a Heterogeneous Exchange

We have seen that any plausible model of language based on cooperation leads to evolutionary instability. Moreover, while such models rely on cheat detection by speakers, observation suggests that such detection is performed instead by listeners. For these two reasons, symmetrical cooperation cannot be the causal factor in the evolution of language. A possible solution to the puzzle of language evolution is to consider that speakers have something to gain by using language to make relevant points, something different from mere reciprocation. We have suggested elsewhere that relevant information is exchanged for social status (Dessalles 1998). Such exchange is asymmetrical, and does not require face-to-face cooperation.

If relevant information were given to obtain social status, it would explain speakers' willingness to make their contributions as clear and interesting as possible (cf. Grice 1975). From a biological perspective, a communicative behaviour which would give access to social status would have a high selective value. Higher social status among primates is indeed correlated with enhanced reproductive success. Social status in human societies is a complex notion, which goes from esteem granted by friends to official social rank. Status is not always explicitly displayed in tangible form. It may be an emergent attribute resulting from a complex combination of attitudes adopted by other individuals – attitudes such as respect, esteem, deference, loyalty, allegiance, admiration, honour, homage or worship. For the purpose of this chapter, we will adopt a simplified notion of status, retaining only three features: (1) social status is correlated with biological fitness, (2) it emerges from others' appraisal of some definite quality Q, and (3) it is correlated with some form of influence or leadership within coalitions.

From characteristics (1) and (2), we understand how communicative ability can become biologically meaningful: if Q is competence in contributing relevant information, then relevant individuals will have a selective advantage. The high regard in which eloquent individuals are held has often been acknowledged (Locke 1998). As we will see, characteristic (3) is also an essential hypothesis of the model. It is what makes the model 'political'. By definition, coalitions are groups of individuals showing solidarity in action, i.e. being able to take collective decisions. Hypothesis (3) presupposes that higher status individuals are better able to influence others in taking collective action.

If we accept the assumptions of the model, we understand why cheat detection is performed by listeners (as observed earlier) and not by speakers (as cooperative scenarios wrongly predict). Because of its political significance, social status should not be attributed on unreliable grounds. If status is granted according to relevance, addressees must check the informational quality of what they hear, in order to avoid rewarding false or poor information. This explains the actual asymmetry of the conversational exchange at a given moment, with one individual contributing information while the others are checking for consistency and quality. The very existence of conversation as an alternation of argumentative moves is now exactly what one would expect. Conversation emerges from the wish of each participant to reach a correct appraisal of the information initially given. It is not an unstructured series of informative acts. What is at stake is whether the initial speaker's point is worth giving her a bit of status. We do not claim that this is a conscious goal pursued by interlocutors. It only appears as a likely reason why, from an evolutionary perspective, our communicative behaviour was selected.

This scenario presents human communication as based on a heterogeneous trade – relevant information in exchange for status. It promises to give us a satisfactory explanation for why language was originally selected and why it takes the form of recurrent speech moves. Yet from an evolutionary perspective, the behaviour of addressees who reward good speakers with status remains mysterious. In what follows, we will look for reasons why listeners might willingly give status in exchange for relevant and reliable information. Our third hypothesis about status, namely its correlation with some form of influence or leadership, will show its necessity.

3.3. *Hominid Politics*

Chimpanzees may form alliances in establishing leadership over the whole group (Goodall 1971; de Waal 1982). Typically, two or three subordinate male individuals may cooperate to defeat the group leader and take over power. As a result, they have privileged access to common resources and to mates. If we follow Dunbar's (1996) account of early hominid social organisation, our ancestors' coalitions were larger and more systematic than in other primate societies. Coalitions are associations based on solidarity. As such, they offer some security to their members. But coalitions are more than that. The power of single individuals is limited by comparison with what a sufficient number of allies can achieve. Leadership of a group cannot be exercised without support from at least some of its members. As a consequence, individual competition for leadership is replaced, when coalitions are established, by competition between coalitions. In this context, physical strength is far less important than the ability to enter a successful coalition. The analogy with politics as we know it in modern societies is quite close. We suggest that our remarkable communication system evolved in this context.

To understand the consequences of this new type of organisation with respect to the evolution of behaviour, we must consider the strategic options open to individuals. The best strategy would of course be to join a coalition which will accept the newcomer and which presents the best chances to succeed in the political competition. On which grounds should one take the decision to join? In primate societies, the company of strong individuals is much sought after. From the perspective we propose, relevant information may have replaced physical strength as a determining factor in the decision to join a coalition and remain in it. Coalition formation and maintenance would thus rely on the same mechanism. We suggest that others' ability to utter relevant messages is what individuals appraise before deciding to join a coalition or to remain in it. In the next subsection, we propose a simple simulation which shows that such an account is consistent: a behaviour like language can evolve as a reliable strategy in a context of political competition between coalitions.

3.4. A Simplified Account of Language Origin

The simulation used to illustrate the coevolution of status and communication was designed to offer a consistent account. It is of course oversimplified. The notions of coalition, information, status and leadership bear only little resemblance to their sociological counterparts. In particular, the fact that status increases the influence on collective decisions is implemented by considering one leader per coalition. The objective here is simply to arrive at a consistent scenario that can then be used as the basis for further refinements.

We consider again a population of several hundred individuals who carry two genes C and R. C-carriers (speakers) make the first step by choosing another individual to whom information is given. This is costly to the speaker. Speakers all

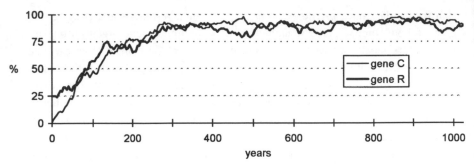

Figure 4.6. Simulation of the 'political' model.

differ in their ability to give information. Some random nongenetic coefficient P, given to them at birth, affects the quantity of information they are able to convey. R-carriers join the coalition of good speakers. To do so, they record the best information given to them in preceding interactions, and decide to follow new speakers on the basis of their relevance. At this point, the game is evolutionarily neutral: individuals exchange information and move between coalitions.

Periodically, coalitions confront each other in a contest. Coalitions are ranked according to the intrinsic value, i.e. the coefficient P of their 'leader'. When an individual joins the coalition of a speaker, the latter automatically receives 'status points'. The leader of a coalition is the individual with maximum status. After the contest, individuals are rewarded according to the relative performance of their coalition and according to their own status within the coalition. Figure 4.6 shows how both genes, C and R, are eventually carried by virtually all individuals in the population (if we exclude the residual noise due to mutations). We now explain the role of the different concepts introduced in the model.

Communicative competence. Individuals differ in their ability to communicate. Individuals who lack gene C remain silent. The communicative performance of individuals carrying C depends on their competence and on a random modulation affecting each communicative act. The competence, stored in coefficient P, is randomly determined at birth, and remains constant throughout life.

Political competition. The performance of a coalition depends on the competence of its leader. The core of the scenario is that this political competence is correlated with the ability to extract relevant information from the environment and to communicate it. This is a strong, fundamental feature of the model.

Status and coalition membership. Status is considered to be an emergent property. In our simplified model, status 'points' are objectively assigned by followers of successful speakers. Status thus results from several interwoven acts of allegiance. Real coalitions are often not materially defined. There is no union card to reify friendship, esteem or alliances. Individuals may manifest their adherence to a given coalition by showing interest in other members of that coalition. This is what we mean by an act of 'allegiance' or 'following'; coalition members with 'followers' gain status from such acts. Our interpretation of status is consistent with Dunbar's (1996) grooming metaphor: listeners in effect 'groom' relevant speakers.

Information. The intrinsic value of information as such is not so important in this model. We have stressed elsewhere (Dessalles 1998) the potential value of relevant information for listeners. Even if this remains a valid hypothesis, it is not necessary for the model. The potential significance of relevant information for listeners' survival may be a mere by-product of the relevance requirement. What is necessary for the emergence of communication in our model is rather the correlation between speakers' ability to produce relevant information and their capacity to exert a salutary influence on their coalition.

To continue the political metaphor, we may say that individuals are involved in an ongoing electoral process. Relevant information is used to advertise one's ability to lead the coalition. Our simulation indicates that language becomes a stable strategy in this context. It is a good strategy for speakers, because they obtain status. The more status, the more chances to be rewarded after the political competition. The strategy of followers, compared to those who lack gene R, is also profitable. The coalition they join is more likely to be successful, because (1) it already contains a competent speaker, (2) this speaker, or a still better one, is likely to achieve leadership and (3) the success of the coalition is correlated with the competence of its leader.

Could language evolve under such circumstances? This time, the answer is yes. In the experiment depicted in Figure 4.6, there were actually two alleles C1 and C2 of C. When C1 is present in the genome rather than C2, the individual utters only a fraction of the information that it would have conveyed with C2. Figure 4.7 shows that C2 wins decisively over C1. We conclude that there is a selection pressure leading to the expression of the best possible information. Still in the same experiment, there was an allele R' of R in the population. An individual who carries R' does not respond to speakers, instead randomly joining an individual, who thereby gains status. Figure 4.8 compares the frequencies of R, R' and non-R/non-R' as they evolve. We see that R wins over the two other alleles. The (responsive) follower's strategy appears to be evolutionary stable.

This simulation is of course a simplification. In human relationships, leadership is gradual and context-dependent. The model simplifies this relative and

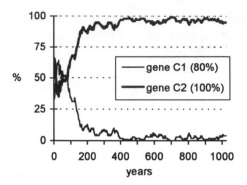

Figure 4.7. Relative proportions of two alleles of gene C. C1-carriers invest 80% of what C2-carriers invest in communication.

gradual influence by considering only the leader's role. Status, as understood in this model, represents a weight affecting the influence of individuals on collective decisions. The model nevertheless indicates that the coevolution of status and language is a sound scenario.

4. Discussion

It has been shown that language could have evolved in a context of political competition between coalitions. In this model, individuals use language to advertise their competence in producing relevant information. A central assumption is that individuals most competent in this respect are those best able to contribute to coalitionary success in political competition. If we look for qualities likely to give better chances to be politically effective, the ability to spot unusual events or to anticipate desirable or undesirable outcomes seems a good candidate. If

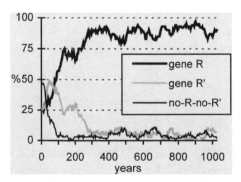

Figure 4.8. Proportions of R and its two alleles. R'-carriers follow a randomly chosen individual. Individuals carrying neither R nor R' show no response to communication.

we accept this, then the ability to be relevant is a reliable indicator of potential success and thus a good reason to be followed. This is enough for the communication of relevant information to emerge. The strategies leading to this emergence may be formulated as the following maxims: (1) be as relevant as you can, (2) check the consistency and relevance of information contributed by others and (3) try to establish friendship with genuinely relevant individuals.

Our status-based model of language evolution bears some resemblance to Zahavi's model of prestige. We have claimed that language is used to advertise some competence, namely 'political' competence. Its function may therefore be compared in certain respects to that of other forms of animal signalling. For instance, babblers seem to compete over apparently altruistic acts like food sharing and sentinel activities (Zahavi and Zahavi 1997). Such behaviour cannot result from symmetrical cooperation: 'If guarding were based on reciprocity, there would be no point in striving to do *more* guard duty than others' (Zahavi and Zahavi 1997: 135) (emphasis in original). The birds behave this way when they can be witnessed by other individuals, in order to gain 'prestige'. There is thus no need to invoke face-to-face cooperation to explain these apparently altruistic behaviours. Zahavi's theory of prestige provides no evolutionary account of status allocation, though. Our political model of language as a signalling behaviour is not only consistent with Zahavi's theory of prestige, but in addition explains why status should be given to relevant individuals. From Zahavi's perspective, on the other hand, there remains a problematic issue concerning language. Words are cheap, but only costly signals are reliable. Babblers do not hesitate to engage in costly signalling: they take real risks when serving as sentinel, and lose opportunities to feed when sharing food. Being costly, such behaviour is hard to fake. An overcautious sentinel is not a sentinel, and food sharing cannot be simulated. The case of language is thus enigmatic:

We don't know how symbolic word language evolved in humans. . . . The rub is that verbal language does not contain any component that ensures reliability. It is easy to lie with words. (Zahavi and Zahavi 1997: 222–223)

Since linguistic acts are so cheap, how can they be reliable indicators of a genuine competence? We suggested above that logic could have evolved as a powerful way to make lying very hard. If we accept this hypothesis, then relevance still appears difficult to achieve. Even if speech itself is not costly, relevance requires continuous effort and attention. Information gathering and processing needs much investment. This may explain why our species can be said to be 'information-oriented': some individuals spend part of their lives trying to collect original information on specific subjects and to become recognised specialists.

We dismissed symmetrical cooperation as a causal factor in language evolution. This does not preclude, however, the possibility that language generates phenomena that are altruistic or cooperative. Offering valuable information, like offering food, is genuinely altruistic, even if it is biologically motivated by the possibility of gaining status. Similarly, language can be seen as a form of emergent cooperation, which differs from face-to-face cooperation. When competing for relevance and for status, individuals behave for the good of the group. But this kind of emergent cooperation is an effect, not a cause, of our status-oriented social organisation.

We concluded earlier that face-to-face cooperation played no causal role in the evolution of language. This does not mean that this form of cooperation cannot exist. Axelrod (1984) showed that external policing, by deterring cheaters, can ensure reliable symmetrical cooperation. The problem is that policing itself is altruistic. In our 'political' model, the ability to perform efficient policing might emerge through being rewarded with status, as did the ability to communicate relevant information. The only requirement is that policing be correlated with coalitionary success. In a context in which policing exists, many forms of symmetrical cooperation become possible, including specific forms of language use. This conclusion is close to Knight's (1998) claim about the possibility of cooperative symbolic communication among individuals bound together by costly rituals. The risk of being excluded from the coalition by some form of policing is highly dissuasive, because it means losing the large investment necessary to become a member. The use of costly rituals as a means of guaranteeing solidarity and cooperation within the coalition may have led to the emergence of symbolic culture in our species (Knight 1991). However, costly membership does not prevent cheating if there is no form of policing. The point is that some individuals may benefit in terms of status through enforcing loyalty among coalition members.

The sketch of the evolutionary origin of language provided in this chapter is of course far from complete. It addresses the problem of the qualitative difference between speaking and nonspeaking species. In our account, conversational competence, i.e. the ability to make interesting, relevant points, is a way to advertise one's 'political' competence. Human societies, primitive or not, are complex webs of coalitions. Individual success crucially depends on the ability to form efficient coalitions and to acquire status. Social status among humans is not extorted by brute force. It emerges from others' willingness to establish social bonds with you. The decision to become closer to somebody is taken according to definite criteria. Linguistic relevance may be an essential component of this choice.

Notes

1. The notion of relevance is defined here as contributing 'conversational information'. It is a more restrictive definition than that proposed by Sperber and Wilson (1986). See Dessalles 1998 for a comparison.
2. What we call speaker and respondent here corresponds to a priori independent strategies. A given individual may adopt either strategy, or none, or both of them, depending on its genetic constitution.

References

Axelrod, R. 1984. *The Evolution of Cooperation*. New York: Basics Books.
de Waal, F. B. M. 1982. *Chimpanzee Politics: Power and sex among apes*. Baltimore: John Hopkins University Press.
Dessalles, J-L. 1993. Modèle Cognitif de la Communication Spontanée, Appliqué à l'Apprentissage des Concepts. Doctoral dissertation, E.N.S.T. (See http://www.infres.enst.fr/~jld/papiers/pap.conv/91111814.ps for a short English version.)
Dessalles, J-L. 1996. *L'ordinateur Génétique*. Paris: Hermès.
Dessalles, J-L. 1998. Altruism, status, and the origin of relevance. In J. R. Hurford, M. Studdert-Kennedy and C. Knight (eds), *Approaches to the Evolution of Language: Social and cognitive bases*. Cambridge: Cambridge University Press, pp. 130–147.
Dunbar, R. I. M. 1996. *Grooming, Gossip, and the Evolution of Language*. London: Faber and Faber.
Ferriere, R. and R. E. Michod. 1996. The evolution of cooperation in spatially heterogeneous populations. *The American Naturalist* **147**: 692–717.
Frean, M. 1996. The evolution of degrees of cooperation. *Journal of Theoretical Biology* **182**: 549–566.
Goldberg, D. E. 1989. *Genetic Algorithms in Search, Optimization and Machine Learning*. Reading, MA: Addison-Wesley.
Goodall, J. 1971. *In the Shadow of Man*. Boston: Houghton Mifflin.
Gould, S. J. and N. Eldredge. 1977. Punctuated equilibria: the tempo and mode of evolution reconsidered. *Paleobiology* **3**: 115–151.
Grice, H. P. 1975. Logic and conversation. In P. Cole and J. L. Morgan (eds), *Syntax and Semantics, Vol. III: Speech acts*. New York: Academic, pp. 41–58.
Holland, J. H. 1975. *Adaptation in Natural and Artificial Systems*. Ann Arbor, MI: University of Michigan Press.
Kegl, J., A. Senghas and M. Coppola. 1999. Creation through contact: sign language emergence and sign language change in Nicaragua. In M. DeGraff (ed), *Language Creation and Language Change*. Cambridge, MA: MIT Press, pp. 179–237.
Knight, C. 1991. *Blood Relations: Menstruation and the origins of culture*. New Haven, CT, and London: Yale University Press.
Knight, C. 1998. Ritual/speech coevolution: a solution to the problem of deception. In J. R. Hurford, M. Studdert-Kennedy and C. Knight (eds), *Approaches to the Evolution of Language: Social and cognitive bases*. Cambridge: Cambridge University Press, pp. 68–91.

Locke, J. 1998. Rank, reciprocity, and relationships in the evolution of language. In C. Knight (ed), *Abstracts of the Second International Conference on the Evolution of Language*. London: University of East London.

Macy, M. W. and J. Skvoretz. 1998. The evolution of trust and cooperation between strangers: a computational model. *American Sociological Review* **63**: 638–660.

Monod, J. 1970. *Le Hasard et la Nécessité*. Paris: Seuil.

Nakamaru, M., H. Matsuda and Y. Iwasa. 1997. The evolution of cooperation in a lattice-structured population. *Journal of Theoretical Biology* **184**: 65–81.

Power, C. 1998. Old wives' tales: the gossip hypothesis and the reliability of cheap signals. In J. R. Hurford, M. Studdert-Kennedy and C. Knight (eds), *Approaches to the Evolution of Language: Social and cognitive bases*. Cambridge: Cambridge University Press, pp. 111–129.

Sperber, D. and D. Wilson. 1986. *Relevance: Communication and cognition*. Cambridge, MA: MIT Press.

Wärneryd, K. 1994. Language, evolution and the theory of games. In J. L. Casti and A. Karlqvist (eds), *Cooperation and Conflict in General Evolutionary Processes*. New York: Wiley, pp. 405–421.

Wilson, E. O. 1978. *On Human Nature*. Cambridge, MA: Harvard University Press.

Worden, R. 1998. The evolution of language from social intelligence. In J. R. Hurford, M. Studdert-Kennedy and C. Knight (eds), *Approaches to the Evolution of Language: Social and cognitive bases*. Cambridge: Cambridge University Press, pp. 148–166.

Zahavi, A. and A. Zahavi. 1997. *The Handicap Principle*. New York: Oxford University Press.

5

Secret Language Use at Female Initiation: Bounding Gossiping Communities

CAMILLA POWER

The idea that 'gossip' or vocal exchange of social information was a vital mechanism for bonding early human groups appears plausible and concretely testable (Dunbar 1996, 1998; Dunbar, Duncan and Nettle 1995). The relatively rapid encephalisation seen in archaic-grade *Homo sapiens* is presumed to reflect the increasing size and complexity of these hominids' social groups (Aiello and Dunbar 1993). Vocal grooming in the first place and ultimately gossip offered alternative mechanisms for servicing such extensive social networks, because they saved valuable time compared with the traditional primate means of manual grooming.

This 'time-saving' argument leads to a serious problem for the gossip hypothesis of language origins, however. As our ancestors maximised brain size in response to the pressure for larger groups, they maximised their 'Machiavellian intelligence' (Byrne and Whiten 1988; Whiten and Byrne 1997). Humans appear to be selected for a capacity involving both social cooperation and alliance formation, but also manipulation and exploitation of their relationships. We cannot consider gossip as a mechanism of social bonding without factoring in this Machiavellian aspect of manipulating information for selfish purposes (cf. Kemmerer 1997). In the case of primate grooming, time becomes a currency (Byrne 1995: 200–202). The time an individual spends grooming an ally reliably quantifies its commitment to their relationship. Correspondingly, if vocal grooming and gossip mechanisms led to a reduction in time spent grooming per individual groomed, this implies a reduction in the level of commitment signalled to each individual (not necessarily equally distributed). Hence, while archaic *Homo sapiens* had larger numbers of allies than any previous hominid, those more numerous alliances would have been less intrinsically reliable.

This anomaly led Power (1998) to argue that for gossip to function as a means of social bonding, it necessarily coevolved with another independent mechanism for establishing commitment to alliances. Raising the costs, in terms of time and energy, of forming coalitions safeguards against exploitation by 'freeriders' – those who accept benefits of social cooperation without paying the costs (Enquist and Leimar 1993; Dunbar 1999). Knight (1998) posits costly ritual performance as the means for securing trustworthy long-term alliances and sealing the boundaries of speech communities. Deacon (1997: 403–410) similarly argues that ritual cements the contractual obligations which underlie symbolic communication.

In this chapter, I will investigate specific forms of initiation ritual, drawn predominantly from ethnographic accounts of Bantu groups. In recent history, these rituals may have functioned to demarcate communities within which gossip was assumed to be reliable. In particular, I will look at how forms of special or secret language are integrated with ritual acts to provide mechanisms that prevent freeriding. What factors lead to the elaboration of such mechanisms, and do these factors correlate with increased risk of freeriding or defection from gossiping alliances? Can these case studies of the interface between linguistic and ritual signals in complex modern societies shed light on the politics of communication among Machiavellian gossiping hominids? If gossip is a means of social bonding, should it be modelled as a reciprocal trade of information (Enquist and Leimar 1993) or as a trade of relevant information for status (Dessalles 1998)?

A Prototype for Ritual: Cosmetics and Female Coalitions

In Dunbar's model for the emergence of gossip, the process is driven by the need for living in larger groups, which compromised social time budgets. Can we model a coevolutionary process giving rise to costly ritual behaviour, resulting from the same selection pressure?

Among primates, the ability to monitor relationships and alliances appears to be limited by relative neocortex size (Dunbar 1992). Pressure for larger groups leads to a greater requirement for coalitionary alliances to act as buffers against the increasing stress of group living. Under the Machiavellian intelligence or social brain hypothesis, this in turn leads to selection for larger-brained individuals. The costs of encephalisation would drive changes in behaviour to alleviate the increasing reproductive stress on females (Power and Aiello 1997; Key and Aiello 1999). Time and energy budgets of female hominids would have been most severely compromised as they were selected to produce more encephalised offspring. This implies that it was females who initially developed more efficient means of servicing alliances, to reduce social time budgets as a direct result of the costs of encephalisation (cf. Dunbar 1996: 148ff., 1998: 99).

Larger group sizes also result in increased opportunities for freeriders. Factors such as size, mobility and dispersal of population affect the rate at which cheats will encounter naive individuals whom they may exploit (Enquist and Leimar 1993). Prisoner's dilemma simulations suggest that gossip (exchange of information about others' behaviour) can function as an effective countermeasure against social cheats (Enquist and Leimar 1993, Dunbar 1999). But these models generally assume without question the uniform reliability of such gossip. In real life, that reliability will be affected by many factors including kin relatedness, rank, age and sexual strategies.

The high energetic costs of encephalisation for females imply that a key area where cheating – and exchange of information about cheats – will critically affect reproductive success is in contexts of mating. Early desertion by a mate and subsequent loss of parental investment could compromise offspring survival, or simply lengthen female interbirth intervals. The trade-offs between pursuing mating opportunities and channelling resources into current offspring will not be the same for both sexes (Hill and Kaplan 1988).

It is the asymmetry of the services exchanged between males and females that makes it so difficult to establish reciprocity. Key and Aiello (1999) use prisoner's dilemma models to investigate the evolution of cooperation as the energetic costs of reproduction rise. Female-female cooperation is the easiest to establish, since females share common goals and can exchange similar altruistic acts, such exchange being easy to monitor. By contrast, 'cooperation between males and females is much more difficult to establish and is likely to be much less common than intra-female cooperation since the currencies of exchange are usually very different' (Key and Aiello 1999: 21). However, in certain conditions, according to Key's simulations, males will cooperate with females even where females do not reciprocate. Such unconditional cooperation implies that a male may offer food or other services to a female and her offspring without guarantee of paternity or even of sexual access. But this strategy depends on two factors. Firstly, female energetic costs of reproduction must be much higher than male energetic costs. Secondly, females must develop strategies whereby males who fail to cooperate unconditionally are severely punished by long-term refusal to cooperate. Key and Aiello (1999: 25) suggest that such factors would have become operative during the late Middle Pleistocene (500,000–100,000 B.P.) period of encephalisation in late archaic to early modern *Homo sapiens*.

Crucially, in these models a form of male investment emerges without any requirement of paternity certainty. One specific model of female coalitionary strategies compelling male unconditional cooperation is the 'sham menstruation/sex strike' hypothesis (Power 1998; Power and Watts 1996; Power and Aiello 1997; Knight, Power and Watts 1995). Costly ritual behaviour and symbolism arise as a result of reciprocal altruistic strategies between cycling and non-cycling female members of coalitions. From the viewpoint of a pregnant or lactating female, cycling females represent a threat, capable of diverting male investment away from the current partner. Male philanderers will be most interested in targeting cycling females, and specifically in locating menstruating females since this is a reliable indicator of *imminent* fertility. The menstrual signal is economically valuable: males should compete in providing mating effort for chances of access to a female who is soon to be fertile. In other words, males will be unconditionally cooperative with reproductively valuable menstrual females. A possible strategy for non-cycling females is to surround and control access to any local menstruating female, and to 'borrow' her signal. The signal could be amplified by use of blood-coloured substances, including pigment such as ochre, to broadcast to potential male provisioners that there is an imminently fertile female in the vicinity, but also to deter males from discriminating between cycling and non-cycling females. Through costly ritual performance, using dance and body paint, females signal to males: 'we are all menstruating females'.

This strategy succeeds as long as non-cycling females receive some of the benefits of male mating effort mobilised by the prospect of access to cycling females. It has an inbuilt reciprocity, since any fertile female alternates between cycling and not cycling. It also generates a basic sexual morality. Each time she menstruates, a female is put on the spot. Will she cheat on non-cycling females, and use her attractions for short-term gain? Or will she cooperate in using her attractions for the benefit of a wider coalition? Power (1998) argued that in cooperating, a cycling female offered a costly and reliable signal of commitment to a long-term alliance with non-cycling members of the coalition. Once she herself was pregnant and subsequently lactating, she expected to receive reciprocal benefits, derived from the signals of other cycling members of the coalition. Within such alliances of females who were sharing sexual signals and cosmetics to attract male investment, gossip would be established on a firm basis of trust.

Bantu Puberty Ceremonial: Cosmetics, Control and Secret Language

Puberty schools, for either sex, function as probationary periods, when behaviour, especially contact with the opposite sex, comes under strictest regulation. They feature centrally some trauma or ordeal which the candidate must endure to become a member of the adult community. Prior to initiation, individuals are not considered as responsible adults; their words carry no weight, they are not trustworthy (cf. Bellman 1984: 8). For girls particularly, the rites advertise onset of fertility and act as a prelude to marriage, taking place in the context of extensive female coalitions.

The key examples of female initiation discussed here are the Venda *vhusha/ domba* complex, the Bemba *chisungu* and the Kpe (or Bakweri) *liengu* schools, all Bantu speakers. The *sande* bush school of the Mande-speaking Kpelle, a classic illustration from the literature on secret societies, is drawn on for comparison. The Bantu schools maintained operative 'secret' languages even as their male counterparts had virtually become defunct (Ardener 1956: 85–86; Blacking 1969b: 69, 74). Certain common features are identifiable which offer a standard template for African girls' initiation.

First of all, the ceremonies were costly affairs. The girl's immediate kin had to pay ritual experts, providing food for her throughout as well as for visitors at coming-out feasts. The girl herself was removed from the labour force for the lengthy periods of seclusion – several months or upwards of a year in traditional circumstances. The primary impact of economic changes under colonialism was the cutting of these costs by reducing the length of seclusion (Richards 1956: 133; Bellman 1984: 9). However, the generosity of provisioning, the numbers of people drawn into celebrations and the duration of the rituals directly reflected on the status of the girl and her kin (Richards 1956: 133–134).

Secondly, older women controlled access to the girl and would be highly aggressive to male interlopers (see e.g. Stayt 1931: 107). While certain men might act as ritual officials, they often adopted a female identity, as if to stress the nonsexual, ritual relationship with the candidate (see e.g. Blacking 1969a: 10). Throughout, the subordinate status of the girl was repeatedly emphasised (Richards 1956: 67; Blacking 1969a: 6, 12; Bledsoe 1980: 68). One of several vivid metaphors for first menstruation among the Venda is 'to abuse the old ladies' (Blacking 1969a: 9). This expression, known only to women, according to van Warmelo (1932: 39–40), indicates the tension between cycling and non-cycling women.

Thirdly, there is advertisement of the girl's imminent fertility, which happens even where she has already been betrothed and is about to marry. The primary medium for this is some kind of red cosmetic – ochre in the Venda case, red camwood among the Bemba and Kpe – which connotes menstruation and which is usually passed between the girl and female associates. The rituals follow a general form of the girl first being made dirty and unkempt, then proceeding through a ritual immersion prior to an emergence ceremony which is highlighted by cosmetics.

These features of costly performance, control of access and coalitionary use of cosmetics match expectations of the 'sham menstruation' model for establishing alliances between cycling and non-cycling women. The last common aspect concerns education, though it is not always clear what girls are really learning. Richards (1956) and Bledsoe (1980) challenge the functionalist view of puberty schools as an all-purpose tribal education in norms and values, from a perspective of close involvement in Bemba and Kpelle rites, respectively. According to Richards, there was little opportunity for any formal instruction. Girl candidates would be shoved out of the way, told not to look at what was going on and usually had their heads covered in blankets (Richards 1956: 126). If any useful information was handed out, comments Richards, 'the candidates themselves would be the last people to have a chance of acquiring it' (1956: 126). Both Richards (1956: 126–127) and Bledsoe (1980: 67) explicitly deny that girls acquire any practical skills that they would not have learned anyway.

Rather than practical classes, these rites are frameworks for transmission of social knowledge that is constructed as *secret* knowledge (cf. Bellman 1984: 6). What Bemba girls learn, contends Richards, is 'a secret language'. One aspect comprises secret terms and rhymes which refer to specific actions and objects within the *chisungu* rite. Richards writes: 'What seems to the educationist to be the most mumbo-jumbo and useless aspect of the whole affair may actually constitute one of the most prized items of information to the people concerned' (1956: 127). A second aspect is a 'secret language of marriage', referring especially to the taboos that constrain the physical relationship of husband and wife. Bledsoe emphasizes that 'what young initiates do learn in the bush schools is absolute obedience to Sande leaders' (1980: 68), women who are believed to wield sanctions of infertility and death. One of the legends of *sande* is that girls are taught the art of poisoning food to keep husbands in line (Bledsoe 1980: 67). So, while a régime of total obedience is instilled in the girls, they are also being introduced to the secret arts of poisoning. Bledsoe takes this paradox to signify that the girls' ultimate loyalty is not to their husbands but to the secret society leaders 'who could command them to poison their husbands for serious transgressions against higher tribal authority' (1980: 68).

The Bemba reveal similar metaphors linking women's potential to contaminate with higher powers that may intervene between husband and wife. Because of a complex of beliefs around the magical influence of sex, blood and fire, every wife takes strenuous precautions to ensure her menstrual blood does not come into contact with the family fire (Richards 1956: 32–33). It is precisely these exigencies – an etiquette of blood and fire – that form the core of *chisungu* doctrine, which her future husband hopes and expects his bride to be taught. So, the secret 'knowledge' transmitted in these rites involves both linguistic formulae referring to the one-off event of an initiation ceremony and metaphors representing a system of taboos which regulate a woman's life persistently thereafter. When ritually enacted, these taboos invoke a moral authority superseding any mere marital authority. On occasion, this higher moral authority demands and effects physical separation of marital partners.

The Venda School of *Vhusha/Domba* as a System of Reciprocity

The traditional education among the Venda of the Transvaal offered no technological or practical training, except in 'techniques of human relationships' (Blacking 1969b: 71). In documenting Venda girls' initiation from the 1950s, Blacking writes: 'a woman who has not graduated is not "a member of the club": she has no real say in women's affairs, nor any guarantee of assistance from other women in times of crisis' (1969a: 4). The complex cycle of initiation schools, where girls would learn songs, dances and mimes, provided a framework for widespread reciprocity among Venda women.

Ideally the cycle commenced after menarche with *vhusha*, which was organised at the local village level. After being rubbed with 'dirty' red ochre on the first day, the girl spent the next four days in seclusion, where she was given over to the mercies of older girls as she attempted to learn complicated dance manoeuvres called *ndayo* (Blacking 1969a: 19). On her emergence, the girl wore special ritual dress and red ochre for a week, adopting a ritually humble posture and exaggerated form of greeting for anyone she met (Blacking 1969a: 18). Even perfect strangers could challenge the girl to respond to *milayo*, formulaic utterances in a riddlelike question-answer format (van Warmelo 1932: 49). These served as tests that she had indeed passed through the rite; if she did not know the answers, she would be ridiculed and harassed until she did. Here we can see how costly ritual signals operate as scaffolding for valid use of secret language. While the girl is still signalling her ritual graduate status, she is ruthlessly examined on her secret knowledge, so that later, when she no longer wears ritual apparel, she can prove her status using language alone.

Domba, ideally prelude to marriage, was held every three to five years in a chiefly capital. It drew together an entire age cohort of girls from surrounding districts for months or even years of practicing songs and coordinated dances, culminating in a final spectacular ceremonial dance called *domba*. Reproductive stages of menstruation, pregnancy and labour were mimed and mapped onto the landscape, renamed as parts of the female body, to effect a symbolic rebirth of the entire community (Blacking 1985: 82). Girls themselves said 'we go to *domba* because we want to learn the "laws" – *milayo*' (Blacking 1969a: 4). This body of 'esoteric knowledge', as Blacking calls it, 'refers primarily to a series of formulae in which certain familiar objects are given special names, rules of conduct and etiquette are reiterated, and the meaning of rites and symbolic objects is explained' (1969b: 69). Each ritual school had its own set of *milayo*, formulaic phrases juxtaposing apparently unconnected phenomena (Blacking 1961: 6). Van Warmelo called these 'tests of belongingness' (see Blacking 1961: 7, note 6), since the ability to recite them proves that a person has undergone the particular ritual. The girls' *milayo* mapped familiar objects onto the human body and represented relationships between the sexes. Frequently these were so sexually explicit that van Warmelo deemed them 'obscenities': penises became door hinges, arrows or the path to the council hut; pubic hair was the grass on a river bank; buttocks were gourds. Yet, according to Blacking, very few initiated women 'understand or are concerned about their symbolism' (1969b: 71). The symbolic *milayo* involve a 'special classification of the world' (Blacking 1969b:71), utilising red, white and black to divide the world into the social categories of menstruating women, men and non-menstruating women (see for example Blacking 1969b: 80, 99; van Warmelo 1932: 74). However, only a few male ritual experts, who teach *milayo* formally to the novices, showed interest in discussing this obscure symbolism (Blacking 1969b: 71).

As far as the candidates were concerned, the *milayo* functioned as shibboleths or passwords to certain privileges of association. Recitation of the proper *milayo* 'supported a woman's claim to the benefits of an inter-district, inter-tribal, pan-Venda mutual aid society' (Blacking 1969a: 5). Blacking noted one instructor warning the novices: 'If you don't listen to me carefully, you won't get any beer!' (1969b: 71). By demonstrating her knowledge of *milayo*, a woman 'will be able to go anywhere in Vendaland and establish her right to participate in any feast that is held in honour of a novice, or drink beer which is paid as part of a novice's initiation fee' (Blacking 1969b: 71).

The *milayo*, then, countered freeriding at a direct and practical level. A girl could only learn them by attending the *vhusha/domba* schools, for which she paid fees, and provided beer to the women celebrating her initiation. Once graduated, she herself had rights in the beer provided by subsequent initiates. The recurrent cycle of female initiation schools formed the backbone of Venda women's support networks. Despite predominantly patrilineal and patrilocal descent and residence rules, women maintained considerable social influence through these institutionalised alliances which excluded men. Blacking contrasted the leverage and collectivity of pagan Venda women with the sorry situation of christianised women who had dropped out of the ritual network. Forsaking tradition, they had lost power and prestige, and especially 'the prop of moral and social support from other women' (1959: 158).

Bemba *Chisungu*: Gossip, Esoteric Knowledge and Ritual Hierarchy

Audrey Richards observed the *chisungu* ceremonies of the matrilineal, largely uxorilocal Bemba people (now in Zambia) in 1931, when economic change and the onset of migrant labour had undermined traditional ritual life. Rites that once lasted at least six months now took three weeks (Richards 1956: 133). However, the mistress of ceremonies (*nacimbusa*) took pride in showing Richards exactly how things should be done (1956: 61). A midwife and ritual specialist of chiefly or royal lineage, the *nacimbusa* was crucial to the success of *chisungu* (Richards 1956: 57). For the Bemba, as the Venda, a system of reciprocity was generated via the series of initiation feasts. The view of Bemba men is revealing: 'No one', they say, 'would want to marry a girl who had not had her chisungu danced. She would not know what her fellow women knew. She would not be invited to other chisungu feasts' (Richards 1956: 120). Endurance of the trials and humiliations of *chisungu* admitted a girl to the women's community (Richards 1956: 131); without it, she had no social personality, and was unmarriageable.

As with *vhusha/domba*, red cosmetics were used recurrently to mark out ritual coalitions (Richards 1956: 124). This highlighted the key taboos of Bemba life, particularly the sexual etiquette around menstruation. The main body of esoteric lore – 'what women knew' – consisted of linguistic formulae, rhymes and songs associated with the *mbusa*, or sacred emblems (Richards 1956: 59–60, 187–212). These were either wall designs or pottery models representing animals, humans and domestic objects whose names, and meanings, were supposedly revealed only to initiated women (Richards 1956: 127). The truncated Bemba rite provided less opportunity for formal teaching than the Venda *domba*. Girls would handle the particular object and supposedly learn its 'song' from the repeated chanting of the women gathered at her *chisungu* (Richards 1956: 101–106). Actually, the learning process was cumulative. After initiation, the girl would be attached for the next year to her *nacimbusa* as a helper at subsequent *chisungu* feasts (Richards 1956: 127–128), each time learning a little more. How much she delved into the symbolism was a product of her own intellectual curiosity and ambition (Richards 1956: 131). A girl who really tried to accumulate *mbusa* lore was on the way to becoming one of the *nacimbusa*.

What *chisungu*, and the specific associations with each *mbusa*, taught was 'not the technical activities of the wife, mother and housewife, but the socially approved attitude towards them' (Richards 1956: 128). Snatches of *mbusa* songs could be used as cautionary reminders to a young wife of her duties by an older woman (Richards 1956: 163). The constant principle determining rank in Bemba society was seniority, whether of clans or individuals, expressed metaphorically by the verse 'The arm-pit can never be higher than the shoulder' – precedence was unalterable (1956: 72–73). When any food was offered or object revealed during the *chisungu*, it would first be presented to the oldest woman, and then repeatedly all the way down the age order to the candidate at the bottom of the pile (Richards 1956: 131). The charismatic figure of *nacimbusa*, one of the oldest women from a senior clan, occupied the central position in this ritual hierarchy. She also had a specific important relationship to the candidates she initiated. As midwife, 'she attends the childbed of the girls she has "danced"' (Richards 1956: 132). This placed her in a position of real power. If there was any difficulty at the birth, it was assumed that the young mother had committed adultery, and *nacimbusa* would force a confession (ibid.). It then depended on her to conceal or reveal to the in-laws 'any real or supposed bad behaviour of the girl' (ibid.). Bledsoe reports a similar situation among the Kpelle where *sande* ritual leaders exercise a jealous monopoly on knowledge of midwifery (1980: 73–74). Women are fearful and respectful of the midwives who, in case of difficult labour, may tell a woman that 'she will die unless she confesses her lovers' names or any crimes she has committed' (Bledsoe 1980: 74). The midwife is then in a position to blackmail the mother, and does so. The midwives who are most patronised because they are believed to possess the most powerful medicines belong to landowning lineages and are recognised leaders in the *sande* secret society (ibid.).

These examples illustrate that it is the speaker's status within a ritually bounded in-group that determines the likely influence and credibility of gossip, not necessarily objective truth or falsity. Clearly, competition for resources and investment may drive the extent of mafia-type extortion in these situations. The Bemba *nacimbusa* is ideally senior patrikin to the girl (Richards 1956: 57). Given preferential cross-cousin marriage (Richards 1950: 228), *nacimbusa* is probably a classificatory if not actual relative of the girl's husband, so she acts as a stern check on the girl. In the Kpelle case, *sande* leaders are strongly implicated in the vicious political jostling of landowning patrilineages (Bledsoe 1980: 78–79). Hence, the extreme pressure for 'Machiavellian' manipulation of information about adultery and paternity is easy to understand. A view of such gossip as disinterested is patently absurd.

Kpe *Liengu* Cult: Across Ethnic Boundaries

One of the best documented secret cult languages is associated with a 'kalei-doscope of beliefs' (E. Ardener 1975: 8) about *liengu* (pl. *maengu*), also called *jengu* in Duala; these are widespread among a number of tribal groups on the Cameroon coast. *Liengu* signifies a water spirit akin to a mermaid, seemingly at home in a sea-fishing environment (Ardener 1956: 93–94, 1975: 15, note 4). The Kpe (also known as Bakweri), who live on the slopes of the Cameroon Mountain, have adopted and adapted the beliefs to their own rainforest habi-tat. According to Ittmann (1972), a notable feature of the cult language was its currency across ethnic and linguistic boundaries. Ardener is cautious about Ittmann's eclectic analysis of the variety of *liengu* beliefs (1975: 15, note 4).

Nevertheless, it appears that the *liengu* language, despite phonemic differences between groups, was used and recognised by several including the Duala, Kpe, Mboko and Wovea. Ardener describes it as a code with vocabulary derived from various sources (1956: 38), while Ittmann elaborates a full grammar (1972). Despite the modern decline of the rites, scraps of the secret language remained common currency among Christian, urban, educated women until recently (E. Ardener 1975: 10).

Liengu ideology was intensively hostile to men (and to white culture) (E. Ardener 1975: 11–12). The rites were enacted 'as a response to a fit or seizure that comes mainly upon an adolescent girl but also upon older women' (E. Ardener 1975: 8). Generally, it was expected that all girls would suffer this attack by the spirits; formerly, girls might go through the rites together as a prelude to marriage, staying inside one seclusion hut (Ardener 1956: 97, 99). While Kpe men understood the process as a curing of the affliction of the spirits, women instead saw that, to solve the problem, a girl had to become one of the *liengu*. During a long seclusion when she learned to speak the spirit language, the girl was immersed in the mermaid world with its peculiar anti-male, anti-European, indeed anti-'cultural' symbolism (E. Ardener 1975: 12).

Of three different versions of the rites, the most expensive, *liengu la ndiva*, lasted over a year (E. Ardener 1975: 8–10). The classic symptom occurred when the girl fainted over a fireplace and knocked one of the stones supporting the cooking pot out of place. The *ndiva* rite (meaning 'deep water') kept the closest connection with the old water spirits. A woman would come to speak to the girl in the *liengu* language. If she showed signs of understanding, a *liengu* doctor (male or female) would be summoned who sacrificed a cock, sprinkling blood into the hole where the hearthstone had been. Clearly operative in this symbolism is opposition between blood and domestic fire, comparable to the Bemba beliefs (also echoed by the Venda). The girl in the grip of spiritual powers acts in a way directly antagonistic to domesticity and cooking.

During her months of seclusion, the girl was taught the spirit language and given a *liengu* name by a woman sponsor (E. Ardener 1975: 9). During this time, she dressed in purely natural products – bark, roots, leaves. Her hair had to grow uncontrolled and she was smeared with charcoal and oil, so that she was black, resembling the spirits (E. Ardener 1975: 11). She could only 'talk' to visitors by means of a rattle, which she used for reciting *liengu* formulae each night and morning.

At the end of seclusion in *ndiva*, the girl was carried to the river, ideally by men of her matrilineage, and pushed into the deepest part of the stream, while women sang *liengu* songs. After this, the girl was regarded as a familiar of the water spirits and as one of the *liengu* women (E. Ardener 1975: 9). In a final emergence, she was rubbed with the traditional red camwood. Following the coming-out feast, she was at last supposed by men to be immune from further attack and fit for marriage, 'rescued from the wild' as Ardener puts it (1975: 12). But 'she still continues to bear a spirit name and converses with fellow-women in the mermaid language' (E. Ardener 1975: 12).

Factors Leading to Elaboration of Mechanisms to Counter Freeriders

Examples such as the Kpe *liengu* or the Kpelle *sande* illustrate vividly that puberty schools do not exist merely to turn out docile young women who are going to be meekly amenable to their husbands. Girls are being indoctrinated in obedience, but obedience to whom? These institutions embody intra-female coalitionary strategies, generating widespread, long-term reciprocal alliances. They establish a woman's credentials as a member of a watertight 'gossiping' community. Acquisition of secret language is tied into passage through arduous ritual tests of conduct. Secret language itself comprises kernel references to named ritual actions and objects and to taboos which, once introduced at initiation, continue to govern the rest of a woman's reproductive career.

To control freeriding, it is above all important to secure reliability of in-group members, whether those are defined by clan, dialect or ethnic boundaries. This requires powerful sanctions to operate against any defector in circumstances where it is difficult for a defector to move to another group (cf. Nettle 1999). Out-group members may be assumed, as a default, to be unreliable. However, cases such as the *liengu* cults on the Cameroon coast indicate that it may be possible to forge ritual affiliations engendering goodwill across ethnic and dialect boundaries.

Factors affecting the payoffs to freeriders, noted above, are size, mobility and dispersal of population. The three groups examined here have quite different profiles. The Bemba were a sparse and widely dispersed population of shifting hoe cultivators. Richards reports a population density of 3.67 per square mile (1956: 25), with villages of between 100 and 200 inhabitants (Murdock 1967) spaced up to 20 miles apart. There would be few places for freeriders to hide. Estimates for Venda population density prior to significant urbanisation are difficult to obtain (see Stayt 1931: 1), but given their intensive forms of agriculture it is certainly considerably greater than for the Bemba. Their villages were twice as large, up to 400 inhabitants (Murdock 1967). Ardener (1956: 15) gives estimates of 122 Kpe per square mile in an overall population of 300 per square mile, indicating a degree of ethnic intermingling. Their villages were small, with less than 100 inhabitants, and so much more patchily distributed compared to the highly clumped Venda, allowing for mobility of both persons and information.

Other key factors affecting tolerance of freeriding and development of countermechanisms involve kinship and its role in labour organisation. Under the matrilineal Bemba system, a woman is unlikely to stray far from her own natal village, except in special circumstances when she is visiting or married virilocally to a headman. She would expect to be working alongside closely related women. By contrast, the Venda and Kpe women move out to marital homes where they would be in cooperation with non-kin. The Venda puberty ritual *vhusha* stresses this aspect. A mother should be last to know of her own daughter's menarche; her co-wife acts as sponsor, mobilising the community for the ritual (Blacking 1969a: 9, 10, 13). Within the puberty school, the Venda have special practices for establishing 'fictitious kinship' (Blacking 1959). Here, it is possible to see ritual elaboration arising to forge alliances in the absence of real kinship. Freeriding by close kin is more tolerable since it is mitigated by inclusive fitness (Dunbar 1999).

Risks of social defection among Bemba women would have been reduced by the factor of population dispersal, and mitigated by kinship. While the Bemba retained some ritual for admission to the women's community, they placed far less emphasis, compared to either the Venda or the Kpe, on formal instruction in linguistic mechanisms that established a woman's credentials as having paid her ritual dues. It is also unsurprising that the Bemba allowed *chisungu* to be diminished so quickly; already by the 1930s it had lost its economic purpose (that is, recruiting male labour as brideservice to the matrilineal village). By contrast, the Venda retained intact their extraordinarily complex cycle of initiation in the teeth of urbanisation and apartheid.

Special factors of economic change affected the Kpe. Formerly the staple crop had been male-cultivated plantains, but this was replaced in the early twentieth century by female-cultivated cocoyams, resulting in a labour pattern of women travelling far outside villages to collect firewood and work the farms, while men stayed at home with penned livestock (E. Ardener 1975: 7). Also appearing at this period were plantation workers, migrant labourers and strangers who contributed greatly to marital instability and divorce among the Kpe (Ardener 1956: 65; 1975: 13). Kpe women then were coming into increasing contact with strangers of both sexes, in an ethnically mixed community, as well as being particularly vulnerable to harrassment by foreign males. These factors could have promoted the coalitionary strategies exemplified by the *liengu* cult, not least its capacity for crossing ethnic boundaries. Shirley Ardener describes the dramatic direct action taken by Bakweri (Kpe) women when one of them received a particular kind of sexual insult (1975: 30). Garbing themselves with vegetation grabbed from the bush – referring to the 'wild' of *liengu* – all the women of the community converged on the offender,

demanding recompense. Surrounding him, the women sang 'songs accompanied by obscene gestures' (ibid.). While other men retreated, ashamed to watch,
he had to endure the display until the women had extracted a pig which was
divided among them all. Ardener recounts a further case occurring on one of
the ethnically mixed plantations where women combined 'regardless of tribal
origin' against the foreign offender. These are traditional African tactics against
sexual harrassment. But the particular category of insult triggering them had
connotations of 'women's secrets' revealed, with implied connection to *liengu*
(S. Ardener 1975: 33).

In the cases of the Bemba, Venda and Kpe, the degree of elaboration of secret
language associated with initiation ritual corresponds to the risks of social defection faced by women in their respective socioeconomic contexts. Conditions
where unrelated individuals must live and work together, and where people are
relatively mobile or change domicile frequently should foster freeriding. We
can predict that in those conditions countermechanisms will be elaborated.

Conclusion: Relevance, Gossip and Secret Knowledge

Reciprocity need not imply egalitarianism, particularly where asymmetric exchange takes place between elders and youth. Arguments that secret societies
function to solidarise tribal groups are simplistic. As Bledsoe warns, 'too much
emphasis on solidarity obscures important patterns of stratification in West
African secret societies' (1980: 68). The ways in which *sande* leaders, in particular, 'manipulate young women's labor and reproductive capacities dispel
the notion that the Sande society is a united egalitarian organization of women
joined in sisterhood to confront men' (1980: 77). When profits are to be made,
says Bledsoe, 'Sande leaders readily put aside women's solidarity in favor of
more lucrative coalitions' (ibid.). Their machinations intensify power differences between lineages, age groups and the sexes. But the point here is that
the threads of political and economic manipulation all run through the ritual
and secret society network. The aristocratic lineages own land, but this economic hegemony would be politically ineffective in the absence of the ritual
leadership. Ritual leaders wield a 'media tycoon' control of communications
that effectively determines who can know what.

In his study of *poro*, the male counterpart to *sande*, Bellman analyses secrecy 'according to the ways concealed information is revealed' (1984: 5). This
is what *poro* (or *sande*) teaches: how a secret can be kept, and the consequences
of inappropriate exposure. *Poro* may structure the political élite, as in Liberia,
operate illegally underground as in Guinea, or function as workers' unions, as
in Sierra Leone. In all these changeable political climates, its members discuss

and conspire 'under the security of the Poro's secrecy proscription' (Bellman 1984: 13–14). 'What must not be talked' varies according to context, but one overarching rule of secrecy, a boundary secret, secures all the subsidiary secret decisions made on a day-to-day basis. As Bellman puts it, 'the *contents* of the secrets are not as significant as the *doing* of the secrecy' (1984: 17). Boundary secrets may be illusory, fictional or even that there is no secret, but they are still a description or cipher of real social relations (cf. Murphy 1980: 203). Different cohorts of members, says Bellman, 'can be identified by their respective rights to know ... social networks can be defined according to access to types of concealed knowledge. The very identification of whether some piece of information is or is not a secret is indirectly a matter of membership identification' (Bellman 1984: 7). Display of membership through the telling or keeping of secrets 'is both a way of establishing mutual interests and a way of advancing in rank and power' (ibid.).

It is within this context of a group ritually bound to respect secrets that we should view competition for status awarded to individuals with 'relevant' information (cf. Dessalles 1998, this volume; Knight 1998). Ritual leaders such as *poro* and *sande zo* may have practical and technical know-how that is highly relevant, for instance, knowledge of the history of land rights, snake-bite medicine or midwifery. The Kpelle ethos, writes Murphy, is that 'whenever there is an important cultural skill, it is usually appropriated and controlled by a secret society' (1980: 196). Ultimately, these subsidiary societies come under authority of *poro*. Hence, the claim to relevant knowledge is based on ritual status, expressed by control of secrets whose relevance is social. As fictions, the secrets are 'irrelevant' to the external, objective world. No more or less fictional is the 'gossip' about land tenure and ownership propounded by *poro* historians, or about adultery and paternity by *sande* midwives. In the final analysis, it is ritual status that dictates relevance, not the other way round.

'Gossip' comprises manipulation of fictions in principle identical to 'secret' knowledge. As a mechanism of social bonding, gossip is by no means to be denigrated as 'small talk' (Renfrew 1998), somehow less impressive in its symbolic concomitants than full-blown symbolic language. Selection for abilities to exchange social information has tested and developed human 'Machiavellian' intelligence to the utmost. Gossip cannot be considered as some material item of trade with intrinsic value independent of context. Its value is purely social and politically determined within ritually generated communities. In this chapter, I have argued that preservation of that social value depends on a framework for concealing and revealing information. Costly signals in ritual 'flesh and blood' performance establish the framework by creating a boundary around the gossiping community. The fundamental body metaphor for such costly signals is the shedding of blood. I have drawn on examples from African ethnography to demonstrate that ritual surrounding the concealing and revealing of menstruating females forms the primary arena for establishing trust in gossip. These examples conform closely to predictions of the 'sham menstruation' model for establishing long-term reciprocity between cycling and noncycling females.

Unlike gossip, menstrual bleeding is intrinsically convincing: always and everywhere it indicates imminent fertility. Whoever can substantiate a claim to be 'menstruating' has corresponding value, hence credibility. Even men in schools of male circumcision – high-cost signals of genital bloodshed – borrow the metaphor of menstruation for other kinds of bloodshed. The secret language of the Dogon, *Sigui*, is the language of *awa*, the sacred masks (Leiris 1948: 13). Epithets of *awa* run in ritual concatenations:

'Very strong, very very very red, very strong, very red' (Leiris 1948: 60)

Taboos laid on men in respect of the masks directly parallel the menstrual taboos that structure women's lives (Leiris 1948: 6–7). The red fibres of the masks are dyed with blood, or so women and the uninitiated believe – that is the secret (Leiris 1948: 80). The day when these fibres are dyed is named 'the menstruation of men' (Leiris 1948: 78).

References

Aiello, L. C. and R. I. M. Dunbar. 1993. Neocortex size, group size, and the evolution of language. *Current Anthropology* **34**: 184–193.

Ardener, E. 1956. *Coastal Bantu of the Cameroons*. London: International African Institute.

Ardener, E. 1975. Belief and the problem of women. In S. Ardener (ed), *Perceiving Women*. London: Dent, pp. 1–17.

Ardener, S. 1975. Sexual insult and female militancy. In S. Ardener (ed), *Perceiving Women*. London: Dent, pp. 29–53.

Bellman, B. L. 1984. *The Language of Secrecy: Symbols and metaphors in Poro ritual*. New Brunswick, NJ: Rutgers University Press.

Blacking, J. 1959. Fictitious kinship amongst girls of the Venda of the Northern Transvaal. *Man* **59**: 155–158.

Blacking, J. 1961. The social value of Venda riddles. *African Studies* **20**: 1–32.

Blacking, J. 1969a. Songs, dances, mimes and symbolism of Venda girls' initiation schools, Part I: Vhusha. *African Studies* **28**: 3–29.

Blacking, J. 1969b. Songs, dances, mimes and symbolism of Venda girls' initiation schools, Part II: Milayo. *African Studies* **28**: 69–108.

Blacking, J. 1985. Movement, dance, music, and the Venda girls' initiation cycle. In P. Spencer (ed), *Society and the Dance: The social anthropology of process and performance*. Cambridge: Cambridge University Press, pp. 64–91.

Bledsoe, C. H. 1980. *Women and Marriage in Kpelle Society*. Stanford, CA: Stanford University Press.

Byrne, R. 1995. *The Thinking Ape: Evolutionary origins of intelligence*. Oxford and New York: Oxford University Press.

Byrne, R. and A. Whiten. 1988. *Machiavellian Intelligence: Social expertise and the evolution of intellect in monkeys, apes, and humans*. Oxford: Clarendon.

Deacon, T. 1997. *The Symbolic Species: The co-evolution of language and the brain*. Harmondsworth: Penguin.

Dessalles, J.-L. 1998. Altruism, status and the origin of relevance. In J. R. Hurford, M. Studdert-Kennedy and C. Knight (eds), *Approaches to the Evolution of Language: Social and cognitive bases*. Cambridge: Cambridge University Press, pp. 130–147.

Dunbar, R. I. M. 1992. Neocortex size as a constraint on group size in primates. *Journal of Human Evolution* **20**: 469–493.

Dunbar, R. I. M. 1996. *Grooming, Gossip and the Evolution of Language*. London and Boston: Faber and Faber.

Dunbar, R. I. M. 1998. Theory of mind and the evolution of language. In J. R. Hurford, M. Studdert-Kennedy and C. Knight (eds), *Approaches to the Evolution of Language: Social and cognitive bases*. Cambridge: Cambridge University Press, pp. 92–110.

Dunbar, R. I. M. 1999. Culture, honesty and the freerider problem. In R. I. M. Dunbar, C. Knight and C. Power (eds), *The Evolution of Culture*. Edinburgh: Edinburgh University Press, pp. 194–213.

Dunbar, R. I. M., N. D. C. Duncan and D. Nettle. 1995. Size and structure of freely forming conversational groups. *Human Nature* **6**: 67–78.

Enquist, M. and O. Leimar. 1993. The evolution of cooperation in mobile organisms. *Animal Behaviour* **45**: 747–757.

Hill, K. and H. Kaplan. 1988. Tradeoffs in male and female reproductive strategies among the Ache: parts I and II. In L. Betzig, M. Borgerhoff Mulder and P. Turke (eds), *Human Reproductive Behaviour: A Darwinian perspective*. Cambridge: Cambridge University Press, pp. 277–305.

Ittmann, J. 1972. *Esquisse de la Langue de l'Association Cultuelle des Nymphes au bord du Mont Cameroun*. Paris: Société d'Etudes Linguistiques et Anthropologiques de France.

Kemmerer, D. 1997. What about the increasing adaptive value of manipulative language use? *Behavioral and Brain Science* **19**: 546–548.

Key, C.A. and L. C. Aiello. 1999. The evolution of social organisation. In R. I. M. Dunbar, C. Knight and C. Power (eds), *The Evolution of Culture*. Edinburgh: Edinburgh University Press, pp. 15–33.

Knight, C. 1998. Ritual/speech coevolution: a solution to the problem of deception. In J. R. Hurford, M. Studdert-Kennedy and C. Knight (eds), *Approaches to the Evolution of Language: Social and cognitive bases*. Cambridge: Cambridge University Press, pp. 68–91.

Knight, C., C. Power and I. Watts. 1995. The human symbolic revolution: a Darwinian account. *Cambridge Archaeological Journal* **5**: 75–114.

Leiris, M. 1948. *La Langue Secrète des Dogons de Sanga*. Paris: Institut d'Ethnologie.

Murdock, G. P. 1967. *Ethnographic Atlas*. Pittsburgh, PA: Pittsburgh University Press.

Murphy, W. P. 1980. Secret knowledge as property and power in Kpelle society: elders versus youth. *Africa* **50**: 193–207.

Nettle, D. 1999. Language variation and the evolution of societies. In R. I. M. Dunbar, C. Knight and C. Power (eds), *The Evolution of Culture*. Edinburgh: Edinburgh University Press, pp. 214–227.

Power, C. 1998. Old wives' tales: the gossip hypothesis and the reliability of cheap signals. In J. R. Hurford, M. Studdert-Kennedy and C. Knight (eds), *Approaches to the Evolution of Language: Social and cognitive bases*. Cambridge: Cambridge University Press, pp. 111–129.

Power, C. and L. C. Aiello. 1997. Female proto-symbolic strategies. In L. D. Hager (ed), *Women in Human Evolution*. New York and London: Routledge, pp. 153–171.

Power, C. and I. Watts. 1996. Female strategies and collective behaviour: the archaeology of earliest *Homo sapiens sapiens*. In J. Steele and S. Shennan (eds), *The Archaeology of Human Ancestry: Power, sex and tradition*. London: Routledge, pp. 306–330.

Renfrew, C. 1998. Small talk, or why was the human revolution initially so unimpressive? Paper delivered at the Second International Conference on the Evolution of Language, University of East London.

Richards, A. I. 1950. Some types of family structure amongst the Central Bantu. In A. R. Radcliffe-Brown and D. Forde (eds), *African Systems of Kinship and Marriage*. London and New York: Kegan Paul International, pp. 207–251.

Richards, A. I. 1956. *Chisungu: A girls' initiation ceremony among the Bemba of Northern Rhodesia*. London: Faber and Faber.

Stayt, H. A. 1931. *The Bavenda*. Oxford: Oxford University Press.

van Warmelo, N. J. 1932. *Contributions towards Venda History, Religion and Tribal Ritual*. Pretoria: Government Ethnological Publications No. 3.

Whiten, A. and R. W. Byrne. (eds), 1997. *Machiavellian Intelligence II: Extensions and evaluations*. Cambridge: Cambridge University Press.

6

Play as Precursor of Phonology and Syntax

CHRIS KNIGHT

> The theme of language as play suggests inquiries into non-cognitive uses of lan-
> guage such as that found in riddles, jingles, or tongue twisters – and beyond this
> into the poetic and ritual function of language, as well as into parallels between
> language and ritual, language and music, and language and dance. It also provides
> an explanation for the obvious fact that so much in language is non-optimal for
> purposes of communicating cognitive information.
>
> Morris Halle (1975: 528)

Primate vocalisations are irrepressible, context-bound indices of emotional
states, in some cases conveying additional information about the sender's
condition, status and/or local environment. Speech has a quite different function: it permits communication of information concerning a shared, *conceptual*
environment – a world of intangibles independent of currently perceptible reality.

A suite of formal discontinuities are bound up with this fundamental functional contrast. Whereas primate vocalisations are not easily faked, human
speech signals are cognitively controlled, linked arbitrarily to their referents
and 'displaced' – hence immune from contextual corroboration (Burling 1993).
The meanings of primate gestures/calls are evaluated on an analog, 'more/less'
scale; speech signals are digitally processed (Burling 1993). When combined,
primate signals and associated meanings blend and grade into one another;
the basic elements of speech are discrete/particulate (Abler 1989; Studdert-
Kennedy 1998). Primate recipients evaluate details of signalling performance;
in speech, the focus is on underlying intentions, with listeners compensating
for deficiencies in performance (Grice 1969; Sperber and Wilson 1986). Primate vocal signals prompt reflex responses; in speech, computational processes
mediate between signal and message (Deacon 1997).

If primate calls do not reflect details of cognition, we may ask how it became possible in the human case for vocalisations to express *conceptual* processes? Insofar as a chimpanzee may be said to think in concepts, conveying these will involve facial expression, position, posture and bodily motion (Köhler 1927; Menzel 1971; Plooij 1978). Humans intuitively use the same method: when an initially functional action is replayed for purposes of communication, success is achieved through direct iconic expression of the thought (McNeill 1992). For either species, it is much simpler and more effective to involve any or all manipulable parts of the body rather than accept restriction to just hands, or just voice.

Against this background, one school of thought concludes that in the absence of a conventional code, humanity's earliest signs can only have worked as gestural replicas or icons (Hewes 1973; Kendon 1991; Armstrong, Stokoe and Wilcox 1995). During the course of human evolution – so runs the basic argument – thought-revealing gestures of the kind occasionally observed among apes (Köhler 1927; Plooij 1978) become habitually deployed. Through frequent use, these become curtailed and conventionalised, leading eventually to a system of arbitrary signs.

Recently established sign languages illustrate how iconic gestures become reduced to conventionalised shorthands, sometimes within a generation (Kegl, Senghas and Coppola 1998). Even following conventionalisation, sign languages remain more iconic than spoken ones. Yet they exhibit essentially the same hierarchical, embedded structure as spoken language, and are acquired by children just as naturally (Bellugi and Klima 1975, 1982). It appears, then, that the 'language organ' central to Chomskyan theory works as well with visuo-manual gesture as with sound. Had the evolution of syntactical competence been driven by motor control for vocal communication, as argued by Lieberman (1985), this outcome would seem difficult to explain. Even in spoken language, syntax remains to a significant extent iconic (Haiman 1985), leading Givón (1985: 214) to treat iconicity as 'the truly general case in the coding, representation and communication of experience', arbitrary convention being 'a mere extreme case on the iconic scale'. Acceptance of this principle logically excludes a vocal origin for the representational functions of language: apart from the special case of sound symbolism or onomatopoeia, it is not easy to see how iconic resemblances can be made using sound alone.

But if a language of visual signs was initially adaptive, why would it subsequently have been phased out? By comparison with manual signing, vocal communication saves time and energy, liberates the hands for other tasks and is effective around corners or in the dark. Proponents of an originally gestural modality explain the transition to a vocal one in these terms. But, asks

MacNeilage (1998: 232), if the advantages of vocalising are so decisive, how and why did visuomanual gesture take precedence in the first place? Why start with an inefficient modality and then switch to an efficient one? Why not resort to the appropriate modality from the outset? For MacNeilage, the gestural theory encounters 'an insuperable problem' at this point (1998: 232).

A further difficulty – according to MacNeilage – is that few entities in the real world allow a natural linkage between iconic gestures in both visual and vocal modalities. Admittedly, one might represent 'lion' by pouncing and roaring. Translation into a purely vocal medium is here straightforward: just omit the pounce. However, most referents are not iconically identifiable by sound. Iconic signing, moreover, exploits spatial dimensionality, an option not available in vocal-auditory signalling. This in turn implies very different principles of phonological organisation in the two modalities. Given the associated translation problems, how could the posited modality switch to vocal speech have occurred?

On the basis of such objections, MacNeilage (1998: 238) makes the strong claim that 'the vocal-auditory modality of spoken language was the first and only output mechanism for language'. This coincides with Dunbar's (1996: 141) view that gesture was never necessary – 'it can all be done by voice'.

Statements of this kind, however, pose the central question of precisely *how* it could all be done? At what point and through which mechanisms did it become technically feasible to communicate details of *conceptual thinking* by exclusively vocal means?

Precursors of Compositional Speech

Prominent recent models of the evolution of speech suggest a two-stage process beginning with the appearance of referentially functional 'words'. In Bickerton's (1996: 51) view, 'syntax could not have come into existence until there was a sizeable vocabulary whose units could be organized into complex structures'. Studdert-Kennedy (1998) likewise considers words to have emerged at an early stage. In his view, it was a steady increase in the size of the ancestral population's vocabulary which necessitated the radical restructuring of the vocal apparatus characteristic of modern *Homo sapiens* (Lieberman 1984).

Such models begin with a simple, limited lexicon, and then derive complexity from vocabulary expansion and related challenges premised upon the prior existence of words. The basic reasoning (cf. Studdert-Kennedy 1998) is as follows. Ancestral speakers increasingly needed multiple semantic distinctions, but had only limited articulatory resources to achieve this. Some primate species possess up to 30 holistically distinct vocalisations, each with its special meaning. Humans required more than this. The solution was to independently recycle the components of formerly holistic signals. This involved reduplicating each signal with variability at only certain positions – as in 'flim-flam' or 'higgledy-piggledy'. If just one component – say, the initial consonant – could be varied, while holding the remainder invariant, this would allow a vastly expanded lexicon. The argument is that during human evolution, this 'particulate' principle increasingly supplanted the 'holistic' principle of primate signalling. The development drove changes in physiology and anatomy allowing vocalisers to control lip muscles independently of tongue muscles, these independently of the soft palate and so on. The human vocal tract was in this way progressively differentiated into independently controllable parts (Studdert-Kennedy 1998: 208–209).

Note that in this scenario, 'words' are already being used *before* the evolution of the distinctively human vocal apparatus, hence prior to any correspondingly enhanced competence in differentiating syllables. Studdert-Kennedy (1998: 211) acknowledges that this evolutionary sequence bears no relationship to the stages through which children pass in acquiring speech:

If the assumption that differentiation of the hominid protosyllable evolved in response to pressure for increased vocabulary is correct, the onset of differentiation before the first words in modern children must be a relatively late evolutionary novelty, selected and inserted into the developmental sequence for whatever facilitatory effect it may have on later processes of differentiation.

Studdert-Kennedy, then, acknowledges that his model addresses one issue only to face us with an additional puzzle. If evolving humans first used words and only then began differentiating syllables, why is it that children nowadays do just the opposite, first learning to differentiate syllables and only then deploying words?

Children start babbling at an early age, when they are also displaying capacities for thinking. But at first, these two activities – babbling and thinking – remain unconnected. The infant is not thinking through its babbling. Then, at about age two, 'the curves of development' of intellect and transmission, previously separate, 'meet and join to initiate a new form of behavior' (Vygotsky 1986: 82). As the child's cognitive faculties gain control over the former babbling vocal transmission system, thought at last becomes verbal while transmission becomes intellectual. Speech is the result.

By comparison with primates, birds often display remarkable vocal ability, yet outputs lack cognitive significance (Marler 1998). As in the case of animal communication generally, cognition and vocal transmission never meet. Although this can be explained by reference to neurophysiological deficits, fundamentally the reasons are social. *Cognition* and *communication* are intrinsically divergent functions, subject to radically contrasting Darwinian selection pressures (Ulbaek 1998). Cognition is likely to enhance fitness even where social strategies are individualistically competitive; this is not true of communication. Why share valuable information with competitors who may turn out to be direct rivals? Why pass over reliable sensory evidence in favour of information received only second-hand? In resisting deception, animals respond preferentially to signals whose intrinsically hard-to-fake characteristics guarantee their reliability. This sets up selection pressures against evolution in the direction of speech.

But what if the signals simply don't matter? Suppose certain internal variations within a primate vocal sequence reflect intentional manipulation expressed only as 'idle play'. Provided no risks are entailed, conspecifics might respond with relaxed 'play' vocalisations of their own. If such call-and-response exchanges served bonding functions, sophisticated capacities for detecting and producing signal variety might evolve. We would then have the paradox that signals could be intentionally manipulated, but only on condition that little of social importance was conveyed.

This idea may have wider application than has previously been suspected. Gelada monkeys accompany their relaxed, 'friendly' social interactions with a wide range of subtly different vocalisations (Richman 1976, 1987). These include nasalised grunts, long, melodically complex inhalations, stop consonants, fricatives and glides, a range of vowel quality differences, tight voicing, muffled voicing, pitch variations and so forth. Geladas also employ a variety of rhythms and melodies. Rhythms may be fast, slow, staccato, glissando, first-beat accented or end-accented. Melodies may have evenly spaced musical intervals covering a range of two or three octaves.

Moreover, geladas in groups accurately synchronise their complex and varied vocalisations (Richman 1978). This ability is remarkable, for it involves high-speed modulation of the signal stream in response to conspecifics' *anticipated* contributions to each rhythmic sequence, with vocalisers switching between digitally contrastive alternatives. In human speech, vowels and consonants are, of course, not objective, physical units but psychologically defined entities; the fact that geladas can accurately echo and replicate one another's vocal alternations suggests that they, too, must be processing acoustic parameters of the signal stream in a digital, categorical way (cf. Harnad 1987).

Chimpanzee males often give 'long calls' together in chorus, striving to match the acoustic characteristics of each other's vocalisations (Mitani and Brandt 1994). Such chorusing and duetting leads to some local standardisation of call variants, so that neighbouring communities may even display 'dialectical' differences (Mitani et al. 1992). Each such distinctive chorus might almost amount to a 'signature' of local group identity (cf. Arcadi 1996; Mitani et al. 1992; Ujhelyi 1998). Where calls must carry over considerable distances, there is selection for salient, discrete form (Marler 1975: 16). These and comparable primate calls may be richly structured, the capacities underlying them constituting plausible precursors of the vocal competences drawn upon by humans in speech (Ujhelyi 1998).

Still more impressive are the vocalisations of those songbirds which can generate an extensive repertoire by recombining the same basic set of minimal acoustic units – avian equivalents of 'phonemes' and 'syllables'. Each species has special rules for generating songs in this way. In the case of swamp sparrows, for example, each syllable is made up of two to six different notes, themselves meaningless, arranged in a distinctive cluster. The constituent notes are all drawn from a restricted species-wide repertoire of six note types with a set of rules for assembling them into a song (Marler and Pickett 1984).

Apart from speech, the only other animal signals displaying comparable structure are the learned songs of humpback whales (Payne, Tyack and Payne 1983) and other cetaceans. 'Phonological syntax', as Marler (1998: 10–11) terms such combinatorial creativity, is not found among nonhuman primates. Admittedly, chimpanzees construct their pant-hoots and gibbons their songs by assembling novel sequences from more basic recyclable units. But in their case each individual adopts for life just one combinatorial pattern, not a variable repertoire (Marler and Tenaza 1977).

Although categorically perceived, the minimal acoustic units of birdsong do not function in the manner of speech phonemes: that is, they play no role in selecting between overall meanings. Marler (1998: 11) describes 'syntactical' birdsong as 'impoverished in referential content, but rich in idle emotional content'. The term 'idle' is well chosen here, testifying to the close relationship between such variability and the leisured creativity of animal 'play'. Like play, syntactical creativity in animal signalling reflects inner realities, not functional demands or environmental stimuli. 'The variety' writes Marler (1998: 12),

is introduced, not to enrich meaning, but to create diversity for its own sake, to alleviate boredom in singer and listener, perhaps with individual differences serving to impress the listener with the singer's virtuosity, but not to convey knowledge.

In this respect, such signalling differs not only from speech, but also from those other calls of birds, cetaceans or primates which do have meanings. Where alarms or other calls must convey reliable information, this can only be at the expense of 'syntactical' creativity or play.

'Phonological' Versus 'Lexical' Syntax

Acknowledging this dynamic, Marler (1998: 10–11) distinguishes between 'phonological syntax' on the one hand and 'lexical syntax' on the other. Phonological syntax we have just discussed. Lexical syntax in the animal world would be the rule-governed assembly and reassembly not just of phonetic representations but of semantic ones. Neither birds nor primates show evidence of syntax of this kind.

In a thought experiment, we might imagine vervet monkeys syntactically 'playing' with combinations of calls such as those warning of eagles, leopards or snakes (Cheney and Seyfarth 1990). Why is it that in real life, this never happens? In this and other cases, neurophysiological limitations have been invoked to explain observed or postulated deficits in the signalling of primates other than modern humans (e.g. Bickerton 1990, 1996, 1998). Such explanations, however, overlook a deeper problem. Combining carefree, 'playful' signalling with life-and-death functional communication is logically paradoxical. Central to the very definition of play is that no immediate function is served, no compulsion applied. If animals could freely 'play' with signals conveying life-and-death meanings, then the result would be more than 'creativity' – it would be fatal unreliability and confusion.

Against this background, the puzzle of speech is that digital alternations among low-energy signals carry weighty social consequences. Substituting a 'd' for a 't' in English, for example, will turn 'tin' into 'din' or 'mat' into 'mad'. Speakers may make such phonemic substitutions to construct utterances which, if accepted as relevant, earn corresponding social status (Dessalles 1998). Just one consonant can decide between relevance and irrelevance, or life and death – between, say, 'We will meet you tomorrow' and 'We will eat you tomorrow'. While this may be conceptualised as 'extraordinary power' (Studdert-Kennedy 1998: 202), it is important also to appreciate the social costs. How can changes in socially contestable meanings be left to the discretion of individuals who, to secure such changes, need only substitute one low-cost signal – one vowel or consonant – for another? How can listeners vest trust in a system as apparently arbitrary and open to abuse as this?

One fact is certain: in the animal world, sceptical recipients would insist on making any such substitutions costly, precluding a role for low-energy signals in deciding between socially contestable meanings (Zahavi and Zahavi 1997). This alone rules out the idea that 'lexical pressure' – in advance of ritually enforced signal reliability (cf. Power, this volume) – can have driven the evolution of syllabic differentiation or the associated restructuring of the human vocal tract. In seeking to explain early vocal preadaptations for speech, then, we appear to have no alternative but to invoke 'play', on the model of birdsong and the song sequences of cetaceans.

Language and Animal Play

It is known that children derive substantial cognitive benefits from the sense of mastery and well-being associated with imaginative play (Piaget 1962; Vygotsky 1978; Bjorklund and Green 1992; see also Bruner, Jolly and Sylva 1976). Human infants from around 18 to 24 months start playing 'pretend', a critical development prefiguring more advanced levels of mind-reading competence (Leslie 1987; Dunn and Dale 1984). Representational play with realistic toys begins at about the age when children first acquire referential words (Bates 1976). Sequences of thematically related representational play roughly coincide with first use of syntactic combinations in expressive language (Bates et al. 1979; McCune-Nicolich and Bruskin 1982). From then on, young childrens' most elaborate use of language occurs not in reality-bound, functional contexts but during make-believe play. 'In play, as in fiction', to quote one study (French et al. 1985: 24), 'one has the freedom to violate the way things really are in favour of transitory transformations of reality'. As an instrument of 'displaced reference' (Hockett 1960), speech has exactly this function.

Maternal responsiveness is strongly correlated with complexity and preplanning in childhood representational play (Spencer and Meadow-Orlans 1996). No mother could play with her infant if she were intent on 'winning'; she must know how to 'lose'. In the animal world, too, if a normally dominant individual is to play with a subordinate, it must experiment with 'losing'. Wherever inequalities exist, players must renounce physical advantages – or there will be no game. For play to flourish, safety and security must be sufficient to allow participants freedom to explore the full range of their locomotor, cognitive and social capacities, trusting in the intentions of others. In all this, suggestive parallels with language are hard to avoid.

What makes an animal's play gestures so different from the displays staged when under serious competitive pressure? Clearly, freedom from anxiety is decisive in making the difference. 'Play', as one specialist has noted (Shultz 1979: 10),

only seems to occur when the animal is essentially free of survival pressures – when it is not suffering from the heat, the cold, or the wet, when it is not being harrassed by predators, and when it is free of various physiological pressures such as hunger, thirst, drowsiness or sex.

For play to be possible, vulnerable individuals must feel able to afford the luxury of 'losing' without suffering the costs. Whereas male-male sexual contests or other fights focus repetitively on a narrow repertoire of locomotor routines, those engaged in 'play fights' may ring the changes on a varied repertoire. In play, losers and winners willingly exchange roles – a pattern reminiscent of turn-taking in conversational speech. Play participants gain cognitive benefits through identification with alternate roles in succession. Syntactical competence involves 'playing' with basic 'who-does-what-to-whom' categories such as Agent, Theme and Goal (Chomsky 1981). Social 'pretend play' draws on comparable capacities, and suggests a likely context for the evolution of such competence.

Where winning is not the intention, the play versions of actions need not be acted out in full – low-cost 'tokens' may suffice. In Kendon's (1991) model of language origins, conceptual communication begins with the partial, *tokenistic* acting out of sequences whose significance was originally functional. Worden (1998) persuasively traces syntactical competence to its roots in social intelligence. Prior to the emergence of language, it would have been in the tokens of social play that such internal intelligence became externalised most fully.

The difference between a play representation and its serious functional prototype is categorical. A puppy which mistook a play bite for its real counterpart would respond inappropriately, just as would a human listener unable to 'read behind' the literal meanings of words (Grice 1969; Sperber and Wilson 1986; Baron-Cohen 1995). A play bite resembles a real bite. But by being patently inserted in a nonfunctional context, it acquires a wholly different meaning (Bateson 1973: 150–166). When a preliminary signal is used to indicate 'What follows is play!', the effect is to systematically reverse the meanings of subsequent signals. For example, a dog may solicit play by lowering its head so as to appear nonthreatening; it wags its tail while crouched on its forelimbs, hindquarters raised (Bekoff 1977). In a pattern reminiscent of grammar, such a 'play bow' may introduce the rest of the sequence. The fact that a preliminary signal here *reverses* the 'literal' meanings of subsequent 'attacks', rather than simply augmenting or blending with them, suggests a plausible phylogenetic starting point for more complex forms of transformative, discrete/combinatorial signalling such as those involved in speech.

True imitation among apes has been most convincingly documented not in contexts of technical problem solving but during play (Visalberghi and Fragaszy 1990). Juveniles in the Arnhem Zoo, for example, have been observed amusing themselves by walking single file behind an adult group member, deliberately imitating their target's limping or otherwise distinctive gait (de Waal 1996: 72). It is in such imaginative games – in these instances suggestive of subversive humour or even 'name calling' – that young chimpanzees approximate most closely to the conceptual richness and creativity of speech.

Language and Laughter

'Mimesis' is Donald's (1991) term for putative early human emotional displays
which, in being adapted to serve intentionally communicative functions, are
brought increasingly under cognitive control. Children playing chase games
provide familiar examples, as they fill the air with partly simulated screams.
Inevitably, on hearing distant alarms, it may be difficult for others to distinguish
real from fictional danger. Among primates, selection pressures have clearly
acted to minimise such risks.

Noisy play among young primates is relatively rare, a fact which has been explained also by the danger of attracting predators (Biben 1998: 171). Where play
is accompanied by vocalising, as when squirrel monkeys 'play peep' (Biben
1998: 171) or frolicking chimpanzees 'laugh' (Goodall 1986: 371), the sounds
may assist in 'framing' other activities as 'pretend' versions of their serious
prototypes. Instances of double-deception – deceptively signalling 'play' to
trick and defeat an opponent – are not reported in the literature on primate
'Machiavellian' intelligence. Primate vocalisations, then, appear to differ from
manual or whole-body gestures in one crucial respect: being reserved for reliable communication, they resist bifurcation into 'pretend' versions on the one
hand and 'real' prototypes on the other. In the human case, this evolutionary
constraint has evidently been overcome – a fact pointing to the impact upon
social communication of distinctively human levels of safety, social security
and corresponding freedom to play.

Homo sapiens possesses radically enhanced capacities for producing vocal
signals which, like play bites, can be thought of as 'displaced' or 'fictional'.
Playful 'screams' are one example. Others are to be found in the games used by
mothers to prompt their babies to laugh. One such trick is to hide and then suddenly reappear, to the exclamation 'Boo!' (Bruner and Sherwood 1976). There is
a risk that instead of laughing, the baby may cry. This will almost certainly happen if the 'Boo!' is emitted by a stranger. But provided the context is reassuring,
the baby should overcome its initial fear response, constructing an alternative
referential frame which reverses the sound's 'literal' meaning. Laughter gives
expression to the baby's sense of mastery and relief. Involved here is a minor
revolution: the very signal most likely to cause alarm is, given sufficient trust,
the surest way to elicit laughter in the child (Sroufe and Wunsch 1972).

The same principle applies to teasing, tickling and humour more generally.
Young chimpanzees often engage in 'tickling' games, laughing all the while.
The tickle gestures are aggressive actions, but only in pretend forms (Goodall
1986: 371). In humour of the human verbal kind, a train of thought in one frame
of reference bumps up against an anomaly: an event or statement that makes

no sense in the context of what has come before. The anomaly can be resolved by shifting to a different frame of reference, in which the event at last makes sense (Koestler 1964). Recall the baby who for a split second may have been puzzled by its mother's 'Boo!' It laughs when it can place the signal in a different context, reversing its former meaning. More sophisticated jokes work in a similar way.

Pinker (1998: 552) points out that such frame shifting is not limited to the challenges of appreciating jokes. Involved here is none other than the principle of relevance (Sperber and Wilson 1986) on which the very possibility of language depends. The semantic meanings of words, taken literally, are abstract and often irrelevant. In terms of their currently perceptible contexts, they may be inappropriate – like a mother's 'Boo!' to her child. But as with babies displaying a sense of humour, human listeners do not leave matters there. On hearing such inappropriate abstractions and irrelevancies, they respond by adopting whatever frame of reference is required to make sense of them, amending or even reversing literal meanings as necessary. The aim is always to delve behind surface appearance in search of the signaller's underlying *intention*, which may be quite different (Grice 1969; Sperber and Wilson 1986).

According to Eibl-Eibesfeldt (1989: 138), the sounds characteristic of human laughter may be traced back to the rhythmic mobbing calls of group-living primates:

The loud utterance of laughter is derived from an old pattern of behavior of mobbing, in which several group members threaten a common enemy. Thus it is a special case of aggressive behavior and this component retains its original significance. If we laugh aloud at someone, this is an aggressive act, bonding those who join in the laughter. Common laughter thus becomes a bonding signal between those who are common aggressors.

Chimpanzees 'laugh' when they 'play fight'; here, the laughter indicates that the accompanying 'aggressive' behaviour is only 'pretend' (Goodall 1986: 371). We have then, as Pinker (1998: 546) points out, two candidates for precursors to human laughter: (1) a signal of collective mobbing or aggression and (2) a signal of 'pretend' aggression. These, however, are not mutually exclusive: pranks which are cruelly effective in puncturing outsiders' pretensions may amuse insiders for precisely that reason.

Laughter is contagious, irrepressible and energetically demanding. Unlike dispassionate speech, it acts as a powerful bonding mechanism. As Eibl-Eibesfeldt (1989) points out, such bonding typically reflects an in-group/out-group dynamic: collusive laughter between allies is likely to be at the expense of targets outside the group. If we assume complex structures of dominance and status to have characterised early human social life, laughter – like the antics of de Waal's chimp juveniles in the Arnhem Zoo – is likely to have signalled outbreaks of collective insubordination to those in authority. As Pinker (1998: 551) writes:

No government has the might to control an entire population, so when events happen quickly and people all lose confidence in a regime's authority at the same time, they can overthrow it. This may be the dynamic that brought laughter – that involuntary, disruptive, and contagious signal – into the service of humor. When scattered titters swell into a chorus of hilarity like a nuclear chain reaction, people are acknowledging that they have all noticed the same infirmity in an exalted target. A lone insulter would have risked the reprisals of the target, but a mob of them, unambiguously in cahoots in recognizing the target's foibles, is safe.

Laughter, then, may testify to the importance of humour as a levelling device among early human hunter-gatherers (cf. Lee 1988), helping to sustain distinctively human levels of in-group trust and mutuality on which speech in turn depends.

Can this understanding of laughter be extended to explain also the emergence of speech? Might phonology and syntax have arisen as the reverse side – the in-group 'playful' redeployment – of 'ritual' behaviour evolved originally for purposes of aggressive coalitionary display? When choral chanting and other such vocal display is used simply to demarcate in-group/out-group boundaries, form becomes everything, meaning nothing (Staal 1986: 57). Let me quote Staal (1986: 57) on how Vedic literature becomes 'meaningless' when adapted for purposes of pure ritual:

Entire passages that originally were pregnant with meaning are reduced to long 'o's'. This is precisely what distinguishes *mantras* from the original verse: to be made into a mantra, and thus fit for ritual consumption, a verse has to be subject to *formal* transformations, operations that apply to form and not to meaning. . . .

Ritual traditions have obvious social significance in that they identify groups and distinguish them from each other. They give people, in that hackneyed contemporary phrase, 'a sense of identity'. That identity, however, is often due to distinctions that rest upon meaningless phonetic variations. Thus the Jaiminīya and Kaŭthuma-Rānāyanīya schools differ from each other by such characteristics as vowel length, or because the former uses 'a' when the latter uses 'o'. Up to the present time, the Vedic schools themselves are distinguished from each other by such variations of sound that can more easily be explained in grammatical than in religious terms.

If this is accepted, then in the evolutionary past, group-on-group ritual display may plausibly have set up selection pressures for vocal imitation, syllabic differentiation and control – all in the complete absence of meaning. Along such lines, one might visualise 'war dances' to the accompaniment of assertive choral chanting, the whole display being mounted whenever a group felt threatened by local opposition. On each occasion when danger passed, however, we need not suppose complete cessation of the performance. Instead, on the model of play fighting, we might envisage elements of the formerly 'meaningless' display becoming *redeployed internally* for more complex conceptual and communicative ends. We might even follow Pinker (1998: 551) in linking successful outcomes with outbreaks of laughter. Incipiently language-like properties of both vocal and whole-body play – discussed earlier – would now characterise in-group communication, with recently evolved mimetic skills yielding a system more complex and syntactical than anything known before.

Play and the Emergence of Language

Many Darwinian attempts to explain the evolutionary emergence of language have been gradualist. By contrast, Maynard Smith and Szathmáry (1995: 279–309) view the origins of speech – together with other aspects of symbolic culture – as a 'major evolutionary transition' occurring late in human evolution. Building on this idea, I have modelled this development as one culminating in revolutionary social change (Knight 1991, 1996, 1998, 1999; Knight et al. 1995). This would locate Pinker's (1998: 551) ideas about irreverent humour within a broader context of revolutionary social upheaval. Let me now, in this new context, integrate this body of theory with the previous discussion of play.

In the scenario I favour (cf. Knight 1998, 1999), coalition members assert group identity through locally distinctive patterns of chanting and other such ritual display, coming under pressure to imitate and synchronise with 'friendly' signals (cf. Studdert-Kennedy, this volume). As in any choral ensemble, attention to internal cues is valued as an indication of commitment to the coalition, in-group status being conferred accordingly (cf. Power, this volume). Given enhanced choral diversification and frequent breaks or changes, maintenance of overall synchrony and coherence relies heavily on information conveyed internally through brief, low-energy signals. Discernible at close range, syllables differentiated by subtle vowel modulations and consonantal contrasts serve this function. Selection pressures in this context drive evolutionary differentiation of the upper vocal tract. Whereas the 'lexical pressure' model presupposes speech from the outset, this model makes no such assumptions. Citing known biological precedents and respecting Darwinian constraints, it may better explain the emergence of a high-speed, low-cost, digital encoding medium available for subsequent exaptation to serve speech functions.

Conclusion: The Emergence of Syntactical Speech

In all mammalian species, it is the young who invest most energy in play. As with human speech, there is a genetically determined 'critical period' for engaging in social play to maximum cognitive advantage. An animal deprived of play opportunities during infancy may later show a deficit in normal social skills (Biben 1998). In the human case, childhood play is not phased out but rather preserved in the elaboration of adult symbolic competence and performance (Huizinga 1970; Bruner et al. 1976: 534–704). By contrast, the playfulness of young animals is for the most part inhibited with the onset of sexual maturity. Sexual competition can provoke lethal conflict. As animals mature, their play correspondingly becomes closely involved in the determination of social rank. With increasing frequency, play fights become real fights – whereupon the play stops. Adulthood for most primates is challenging and risky, affording relatively few opportunities for that trust and abandon which is the hallmark of genuine play.

The distinctively human counterdominance strategies intrinsic to 'sham menstruation/sex strike' (Knight, Power and Watts 1995; Power and Aiello 1997; Power and Watts 1996, 1997) drive the emergence of symbolic culture by extending 'play' *into the domain of adult relationships*. Siblings and more distant relatives who might otherwise have been pitched into direct sexual rivalry are bonded in playful coalitionary opposition to the out-group. By retaining close bonds with kin-related females (cf. Power 1998, 1999, this volume), each coalition is enabled to extract increasing levels of mating effort from males. The outcome is 'bride service', an arrangement characteristic of hunter-gatherers, in which in-marrying males bring regular meat or other provisioning under supervision from their in-laws (Knight 1991, 1999). While this amounts to 'economic exploitation', Darwinian considerations clarify why minimal resistance is to be expected. In-marrying males are gaining access to the group's fertile females; moreover, they are provisioning their own probable offspring. Combative coalitions formed to secure such outcomes, meeting little organised resistance, should be highly stable. They are familiar ethnographically as unilineal lineages and clans.

What is the significance of all this for language evolution? The key point is that 'lexical syntax' (Marler 1998) presupposes digital as opposed to analog distinctions between meanings. Like distinctions between the face values of banknotes, such contrasts depend entirely on collective agreement. Take the case of kinship terms – an obvious initial focus for any human language. In hunter-gatherer kinship terminologies, 'sister' is defined in opposition to the contrastive term 'wife'. Primates could not sustain belief in such contrastive meanings, even if they had the cognitive competence. This is because their kin coalitions are neither categorically bounded nor stable. A close female relative from one standpoint will therefore be a less close relative – potentially a mate – from another. Instead of being categorically – in the eyes of a stable collectivity – 'sister' or 'wife', each female will be more or less either according to individual standpoint. Primate politics determine that other social meanings will be similarly graded and contested.

Within human systems of 'fictive' kinship, a woman is 'our sister' (or a man 'our brother') because the collectivity asserts it to be so. Children engaged in games of 'let's pretend' may likewise assert, 'this rag is mummy' or 'that stick is a horse' (Leslie 1987). In stratified societies, specified persons on a similar basis may count as 'the government' while certain small pieces of paper count as 'money'. Not necessarily dependent upon verbal language, such 'institutional facts' are expressions of *collective intentionality* (Searle 1998). To uphold them is a social, moral and – in a most fundamental sense – religious challenge (Durkheim 1965). To confuse 'sister' with 'wife', after all, would be more than mere semantic or cognitive error – it would be a violation (Lévi-Strauss 1969). Likewise if you visited my home and confused our family tablecloth with the doormat. Transgression of such categorical boundaries amounts to sacrilege. Words would lose all meaning if such boundaries could not be enforced.

The main institutional fact – the condition of all others – is that the collectivity exists. To represent this fact is to assert group self-identity, defined in opposition to the out-group. Such boundary maintenance requires serious effort, presupposing costly signals, not mere tokenistic substitutes. I have argued elsewhere (Knight 1999) that as group-living ancestral humans came under corresponding pressure to perform their war dances or sing their mantras, they shared in representing 'the sacred' as an emblem of group-level solidarity and identity (cf. Durkheim 1965). In this chapter I have suggested that during intervening periods of relaxation, however, as the performers periodically dispersed, these same representational techniques became available for redeployment in a quite different – essentially playful – atmosphere. Intentions were now once again those of distinct individuals, partitioning their shared representational resources accordingly. Processes of trust-based abbreviation and conventionalisation in this context generated a growing repertoire of low-cost tokens which, while expressive of merely personal intentions, nonetheless retained the social authority and communicable status of the whole. 'Words' were in this way 'authorised' – endowed by the ritual collective with performative force (cf. Austin 1978; Bourdieu 1991).

Finally, we may return to the 'insuperable' problem posed by MacNeilage (1998). When, how and why did the modality switch to vocal speech occur?

MacNeilage's basic argument, we may recall, is that if the vocal-auditory modality was adaptive during the later stages of human speech evolution, it must therefore have been equally adaptive from the outset. This argument would have force if it could be confirmed that the social contexts of language use remained invariant throughout the course of human evolution. But if changing social strategies are built into our models, there is no reason to suppose that a modality which is adaptive during one period must remain equally adaptive later. Where social contexts are 'Machiavellian', as is the case among primates (Byrne and Whiten 1988), constraints operate to obstruct the emergence of low-cost, conventional – in other words *fakeable* – signalling (Zahavi and Zahavi 1997). We have seen that in the primate case, the need to retain intrinsic signal credibility precludes playful cognitive expressivity in the vocal-auditory channel. Until this problem was solved, *conceptual* signalling had therefore to rely on a different modality. We may suppose that hominid use of the hands and body – whose manipulability had originally evolved in the service of noncommunicative functions – came increasingly to serve this novel purpose. Unfettered cognitive manipulability, however, was inconsistent with signal credibility (cf. Knight 1998). Mimesis (Donald 1991) may in this light have emerged in the human lineage as a compromise between these opposing pulls: hard-to-fake signals became manipulable, but only within limits. Costly, hard-to-fake and for that reason *intrinsically* convincing 'song and dance' remained central to communication wherever resistance to deception remained high.

As exogamous kin-coalitions became repeatedly successful and correspondingly stable, however (Knight 1991), the outcome was a radical intensification of in-group trust. Not only did this allow costs to be cut through adoption of conventional shorthands. A corollary was the establishment, through collective intentionality, of semantic meanings in the form of digitally contrastive collective representations. In arriving at shorthands for these, we would expect 'conspiratorial whisperers' (cf. Krebs and Dawkins 1978) to resort to the cheapest, most efficient available encoding medium. Considerations of speed and efficiency in this new context drove progressive exaptation of the phonological system, yielding syntax in the Chomskyan sense – an autonomous level of structure serving as a 'switchboard' (Newmeyer 1991) between the formerly disparate systems of vocal transmission and conceptual representation.

Acknowledgement

I would like to thank Catherine Arthur and Michael Studdert-Kennedy for their critical comments on an earlier version of this chapter.

References

Abler, W. 1989. On the particulate principle of self-diversifying systems. *Journal of Social and Biological Structures* **12**: 1–13.

Arcadi, A. C. 1996. Phrase structure of wild chimpanzee pant hoots: patterns of production and interpopulation variability. *American Journal of Primatology* **39**: 159–178.

Armstrong, D. F., W. C. Stokoe and S. E. Wilcox. 1995. *Gesture and the Nature of Language*. Cambridge: Cambridge University Press.

Austin, J. L. 1978. *How to Do Things with Words*. Oxford: Oxford University Press.

Baron-Cohen, S. 1995. *Mindblindness: An essay on autism and theory of mind*. Cambridge, MA: MIT Press.

Bates, E. 1976. *Language and Context*. New York: Academic.

Bates, E., L. Benigni, I. Bretherton, L. Camaioni and V. Volterra. 1979. *The Emergence of Symbols: Cognition and communication in infancy*. New York: Academic.

Bateson, G. 1973. A theory of play and fantasy. *American Psychiatric Association Psychiatric Research Reports* **2** (1955). Reprinted in G. Bateson, *Steps to an Ecology of Mind*. London: Paladin, pp. 150–166.

Bekoff, M. 1977. Social communication in canids: evidence for the evolution of a stereotyped mammalian display. *Science* **197**: 1097–1099.

Bellugi, U. and E. S. Klima. 1975. Aspects of sign language and its structure. In J. F. Kavanagh and J. E. Cutting (eds), *The Role of Speech in Language*. Cambridge, MA: MIT Press, pp. 171–203.

Bellugi, U. and E. S. Klima. 1982. From gesture to sign: deixis in a visual-gestural language. In R. J. Jarvella and W. Klein (eds), *Speech, Place, and Action: Studies of language in context*. New York: Wiley.

Biben, M. 1998. Squirrel monkey play fighting: making the case for a cognitive training function for play. In M. Bekoff and J. A. Byers (eds), *Animal Play*. Cambridge: Cambridge University Press, pp. 161–182.

Bickerton, D. 1990. *Language and Species*. Chicago and London: University of Chicago Press.

Bickerton, D. 1996. *Language and Human Behaviour*. London: University College London Press.

Bickerton, D. 1998. Catastrophic evolution: the case for a single step from protolanguage to full human language. In J. R. Hurford, M. Studdert-Kennedy and C. Knight (eds), *Approaches to the Evolution of Language: Social and cognitive bases*. Cambridge: Cambridge University Press, pp. 341–358.

Bjorklund, D. F. and B. Green. 1992. The adaptive nature of cognitive immaturity. *American Psychologist* **47**: 46–54.

Bourdieu, P. 1991. *Language and Symbolic Power*. Cambridge: Polity.

Bruner, J. S. and V. Sherwood. 1976. Peekaboo and the learning of rule structures. In J. S. Bruner, A. Jolly and K. Sylva (eds), *Play: Its role in development and evolution*. Harmondsworth: Penguin, pp. 277–285.

Bruner, J. S., A. Jolly and K. Sylva (eds). 1976. *Play: Its role in development and evolution*. Harmondsworth: Penguin.

Burling, R. 1993. Primate calls, human language, and nonverbal communication. *Current Anthropology* **34**: 25–53.

Byrne, R. and A. Whiten (eds). 1988. *Machiavellian Intelligence: Social expertise and the evolution of intellect in monkeys, apes, and humans*. Oxford: Clarendon.

Cheney, D. L. and R. M. Seyfarth. 1990. *How Monkeys See the World*. Chicago: University of Chicago Press.

Chomsky, N. 1981. *Lectures on Government and Binding*. Dordrecht: Foris.

de Waal, F. 1996. *Good Natured: The origin of right and wrong in humans and other animals*. Cambridge, MA: Harvard University Press.

Deacon, T. 1997. *The Symbolic Species: The co-evolution of language and the human brain*. London: Penguin.

Dessalles, J.-L. 1998. Altruism, status and the origin of relevance. In J. R. Hurford, M. Studdert-Kennedy and C. Knight (eds), *Approaches to the Evolution of Language: Social and cognitive bases*. Cambridge: Cambridge University Press, pp. 130–147.

Donald, M. 1991. *Origins of the Modern Mind: Three stages in the evolution of culture and cognition*. Cambridge, MA: Harvard University Press.

Dunbar, R. I. M. 1996. *Grooming, Gossip and the Evolution of Language*. London and Boston: Faber and Faber.

Dunn, J. and N. Dale. 1984. I a daddy: a 2-year-old's collaboration in joint pretence with sibling and with mother. In I. Bretherton (ed), *Symbolic Play: The development of social understanding*. Orlando and London: Academic, pp. 131–157.

Durkheim, E. 1965/1912. *The Elementary Forms of the Religious Life*. New York: Free Press.

Eibl-Eibesfeldt, I. 1989. *Human Ethology*. Hawthorne, NY: Aldine de Gruyter.

French, L. A., J. Lucariello, S. Seidman and K. Nelson. 1985. The influence of discourse content and context on preschoolers' use of language. In L. Galda and A. D. Pellegrini (eds), *Play, Language and Stories: The development of children's literate behavior*. Norwood, NJ: Ablex.

Givón, T. 1985. Iconicity, isomorphism and non-arbitrary coding in syntax. In J. Haiman (ed), *Iconicity in Syntax*. Amsterdam and Philadelphia: Benjamins, pp. 187–219.

Goodall, J. 1986. *The Chimpanzees of Gombe: Patterns of behavior*. Cambridge, MA and London: Belknap.

Grice, H. 1969. Utterer's meanings and intentions. *Philosophical Review* **78**: 147–177.

Haiman, J. 1985. Introduction. In J. Haiman (ed), *Iconicity in Syntax*. Amsterdam and Philadelphia: Benjamins.

Halle, M. 1975. Confessio grammatici. *Language* **51**: 525–535.

Harnad, S. 1987. *Categorical Perception: The groundwork of cognition*. Cambridge: Cambridge University Press.

Hewes, G. W. 1973. Primate communication and the gestural origin of language. *Current Anthropology* **14**: 5–24.

Hockett, C. F. 1960. The origin of speech. *Scientific American* **203**: 89–96.

Huizinga, J. 1970/1949. *Homo Ludens: A study of the play element in culture*. London: Granada.

Kegl, J., A. Senghas and M. Coppola. 1998. Creation through contact: Sign language emergence and sign language change in Nicaragua. In M. DeGraff (ed), *Language Creation and Change: Creolization, Diachrony and Development*. Cambridge, MA: MIT Press.

Kendon, A. 1991. Some considerations for a theory of language origins. *Man* (N.S.) **26**: 199–221.

Knight, C. 1991. *Blood Relations: Menstruation and the origins of culture.* New Haven, CT, and London: Yale University Press.

Knight, C. 1996. Darwinism and collective representations. In J. Steele and S. Shennan (eds), *The Archaeology of Human Ancestry: Power, sex and tradition.* London and New York: Routledge, pp. 331–346.

Knight, C. 1998. Ritual/speech coevolution: a solution to the problem of deception. In J. R. Hurford, M. Studdert-Kennedy and C. Knight (eds), *Approaches to the Evolution of Language: Social and cognitive bases.* Cambridge: Cambridge University Press, pp. 68–91.

Knight, C. 1999. Sex and language as pretend-play. In R. I. M. Dunbar, C. Knight and C. Power (eds), *The Evolution of Culture.* Edinburgh: Edinburgh University Press, pp. 228–229.

Knight, C., C. Power and I. Watts. 1995. The human symbolic revolution: a Darwinian account. *Cambridge Archaeological Journal* **5**: 75–114.

Koestler, A. 1964. *The Act of Creation.* New York: Dell.

Köhler, W. 1927. *The Mentality of Apes* (trans. Ella Winter). London: Routledge and Kegan Paul.

Krebs, J. R. and R. Dawkins. 1978. Animal signals: information or manipulation? In J. R. Krebs and N. B. Davies (eds), *Behavioural Ecology: An evolutionary approach.* Oxford: Blackwell, pp. 282–309.

Lee, R. B. 1988. Reflections on primitive communism. In T. Ingold, D. Riches and J. Woodburn (eds), *Hunters and Gatherers,* Vol. 1: *History, evolution and social change.* Chicago: Aldine, pp. 252–268.

Leslie, A. 1987. Pretence and representation: the origins of 'theory of mind'. *Psychological Review* **94**: 412–426.

Lévi-Strauss, C. 1969. *The Elementary Structures of Kinship.* London: Eyre and Spottiswoode.

Lieberman, P. 1984. *The Biology and Evolution of Language.* Cambridge, MA: Harvard University Press.

Lieberman, P. 1985. On the evolution of human syntactic ability: Its preadaptive bases– motor control and speech. *Journal of Human Evolution* **14**: 657–668.

MacNeilage, P. 1998. Evolution of the mechanism of language output: comparative neurobiology of vocal and manual communication. In J. R. Hurford, M. Studdert-Kennedy and C. Knight (eds), *Approaches to the Evolution of Language: Social and cognitive bases.* Cambridge: Cambridge University Press, pp. 222–241.

Marler, P. 1975. On the origin of speech from animal sounds. In J. F. Kavanagh and J. Cutting (eds), *The Role of Speech in Language.* Cambridge, MA: MIT Press, pp. 11–37.

Marler, P. 1998. Animal communication and human language. In G. Jablonski and L. C. Aiello (eds), *The Origin and Diversification of Language.* Wattis Symposium Series in Anthropology. Memoirs of the California Academy of Sciences, No. 24. San Francisco: California Academy of Sciences, pp. 1–19.

Marler, P. and R. Pickett. 1984. Species-universal microstructure in the learned song of the swamp sparrow (*Melospiza geogiana*). *Animal Behavior* **32**: 673–689.

Marler, P. and R. Tenaza. 1977. Signaling behavior of wild apes, with special reference to vocalization. In T. Sebeok (ed), *How Animals Communicate.* Bloomington, IN: Indiana University Press, pp. 965–1033.

Maynard Smith, J. and E. Szathmáry. 1995. *The Major Transitions in Evolution*. Oxford: Freeman.

McCune-Nicolich, L. and C. Bruskin. 1982. Combinatorial competency in play and language. In K. Rubin and D. Pebler (eds), *The Play of Children: Current theory and research*. New York: Karger, pp. 30–40.

McNeill, D. 1992. *Hand and Mind: What gestures reveal about thought*. Chicago and London: University of Chicago Press.

Menzel, E. W. 1971. Communication about the environment in a group of young chimpanzees. *Folia primatologica* **15**: 220–232.

Mitani, J. C. and K. L. Brandt. 1994. Social factors influence the acoustic variability in the long-distance calls of male chimpanzees. *Ethology* **96**: 233–252.

Mitani, J. C., T. Hasegawa, J. Gros-Louis, P. Marler and R. Byrne. 1992. Dialects in wild chimpanzees? *American Journal of Primatology* **27**: 233–244.

Newmeyer, F. J. 1991. Functional explanation in linguistics and the origins of language. *Language and Communication* **11**: 3–28.

Payne, K., P. Tyack and R. Payne. 1983. Progressive changes in the songs of humpback whales (*Megaptera novaeangliae*): a detailed analysis of two seasons in Hawaii. In R. Payne (ed), *Communication and behavior of whales*. AAAS Selected Symposia Series. Boulder, CO: Westview Press, pp. 9–57.

Piaget, J. 1962. *Play, Dreams, and Imitation in Childhood*. New York: Norton.

Pinker, S. 1998. *How the Mind Works*. London: Penguin.

Plooij, F. X. 1978. Some basic traits of language in wild chimpanzees. In A. Lock (ed), *Action, Gesture and Symbol: The emergence of language*. Lock. London and New York: Academic.

Power, C. 1998. Old wives' tales: the gossip hypothesis and the reliability of cheap signals. In J. R. Hurford, M. Studdert-Kennedy and C. Knight (eds), *Approaches to the Evolution of Language: Social and cognitive bases*. Cambridge: Cambridge University Press, pp. 111–129.

Power, C. 1999. Beauty magic: the origins of art. In R. I. M. Dunbar, C. Knight and C. Power (eds), *The Evolution of Culture*. Edinburgh: Edinburgh University Press, pp. 92–112.

Power, C. and L. C. Aiello. 1997. Female proto-symbolic strategies. In L. D. Hager (ed), *Women in Human Evolution*. New York and London: Routledge, pp. 153–171.

Power, C. and I. Watts. 1996. Female strategies and collective behaviour: the archaeology of earliest *Homo sapiens sapiens*. In J. Steele and S. Shennan (eds), *The Archaeology of Human Ancestry*. London and New York: Routledge, pp. 306–330.

Power, C. and I. Watts. 1997. The woman with the zebra's penis: gender, mutability and performance. *Journal of the Royal Anthropological Institute* (N.S.) **3**: 537–560.

Richman, B. 1976. Some vocal distinctive features used by gelada monkeys. *Journal of the Acoustic Society of America* **60**: 718–724.

Richman, B. 1978. The synchronization of voices by gelada monkeys. *Primates* **19**: 569–581.

Richman, B. 1987. Rhythm and melody in gelada vocal exchanges. *Primates* **28** : 199–223.

Searle, J. R. 1998. *The Construction of Social Reality*. London: Penguin.

Shultz, T. R. 1979. Play as arousal modulation. In B. Sutton-Smith (ed), *Play and Learning*. New York: Gardner, pp. 7–22.

Spencer, P. E. and K. P. Meadow-Orlans. 1996. Play, language, and maternal responsiveness: a longitudinal study of deaf and hearing infants. *Child Development* **67**: 3176–3191.

Sperber, D. and D. Wilson. 1986. *Relevance: Communication and cognition.* Oxford: Blackwell.

Sroufe, L. A. and J. P. Wunsch. 1972. The development of laughter in the first year of life. *Child Development* **43**: 1326–1344.

Staal, F. 1986. The sound of religion. *Numen* **33**: 33–64.

Studdert-Kennedy, M. 1998. The particulate origins of language generativity. In J. R. Hurford, M. Studdert-Kennedy and C. Knight (eds), *Approaches to the Evolution of Language: Social and cognitive bases.* Cambridge: Cambridge University Press, pp. 202–221.

Ujhelyi, M. 1998. Long-call structure in apes as a possible precursor for language. In J. R. Hurford, M. Studdert-Kennedy and C. Knight (eds), *Approaches to the Evolution of Language.* Cambridge: Cambridge University Press, pp. 177–189.

Ulbaek, I. 1998. The origin of language and cognition. In J. R. Hurford, M. Studdert-Kennedy and C. Knight (eds), *Approaches to the Evolution of Language.* Cambridge: Cambridge University Press, pp. 30–43.

Visalberghi, E. and D. M. Fragaszy. 1990. Do monkeys ape? In S. T. Parker and K. Gibson (eds), *'Language' and Intelligence in Monkeys and Apes: Comparative developmental perspectives.* Cambridge: Cambridge University Press, pp. 247–273.

Vygotsky, L. 1978. *Mind in Society.* Cambridge, MA: Harvard University Press.

Vygotsky, L. 1986. *Thought and Language.* Cambridge, MA: MIT Press.

Worden, R. 1998. The evolution of language from social intelligence. In J. R. Hurford, M. Studdert-Kenedy and C. Knight (eds), *Approaches to the Evolution of Language: Social and cognitive bases.* Cambridge: Cambridge University Press, pp. 148–166.

Zahavi, A. and A. Zahavi. 1997. *The Handicap Principle: A missing piece in Darwin's puzzle.* New York and Oxford: Oxford University Press.

PART II

THE EMERGENCE
OF PHONETIC STRUCTURE

7

Introduction: The Emergence of Phonetic Structure

MICHAEL STUDDERT-KENNEDY

> What is special to a grammatical utterance (i.e., to a linguistic event) is not that
> it has meaning, expresses feelings, or calls for a relevant response – these are all
> common to many human activities – but that it is socially transmissible.
>
> Zellig Harris (1968: 7)

In the passage above, Harris was concerned to explain why the elements of a language (phonemes, morphemes, words) are discrete, preset (that is, known to both speakers and hearers) and arbitrary. Only if the elements have these properties, he argued, can a hearer reliably transmit, or repeat, an utterance to another. If the elements were continuously variable, spontaneously invented or iconic, they would be subject to compound error in transmission, and their communicative utility would be limited.

The properties that afford reliable transmission from speaker to hearer are also those that afford reliable transmission from one generation to the next, from adult speaker to child hearer/learner. It is this aspect, transmission across generations by learning, that has enabled language to evolve, in perhaps no more than some tens of thousands of generations, from inarticulate cry to articulate speech.

All five of the following chapters deal with the transmission of words across generations. Each takes for granted a capacity for verbal symbolic reference; all but the last then address the emergence of the discrete phonetic structures on which reliable transmission of verbal symbolic reference depends. In focusing on transmission these chapters also recognise, implicitly or explicitly, the critical role of the learning child. The child's perceptual, articulatory and cognitive capacities are the filter through which words must pass from one generation to the next. That is one reason why the ontogeny of words offers our best, perhaps our only, natural model of their phylogeny. Indeed, initial steps in the emergence of language have proved recalcitrant to evolutionary theory precisely because we have lacked, until recent decades, a reliable description of how the infant progresses from gurgling to babbling to spoken words.

Adopting language development as a crucial component of our model of language evolution does not commit us to an untenable theory of ontogenetic recapitulation. The parallels between phylogeny and ontogeny on which Darwin rested much of his theory (Richards 1992) are real, but arise, at least in part, for reasons sketched over 75 years ago by Garstang (1922). First, living systems typically develop, both individually and evolutionarily, from the simple to the complex by successive steps of differentiation; second, every evolutionary step is a change in development that is inherited by later generations. In Garstang's succinct summary: 'Ontogeny does not recapitulate Phylogeny: it creates it' (1922: 82) (for a more nuanced framing, see Mayr 1982: 469ff., and for a full analysis see Gould 1977).

Thus, Garstang turned recapitulation on its head. Evolution does not drive development; development drives evolution. The phenotypes over which natural selection operates are individual ontogenies. Recognition of this fact frees us into a less rigid view of development, better suited to the diverse paths within and between languages. Language ontogeny may parallel language phylogeny not because the course is coded in the genes, as recapitulation would have it, but because it is implicit in constraints of hominid neuroanatomy and learning mechanisms, and in the logic of a developmental sequence from the simple to the complex.

Let us see how this theme plays out in the following chapters. Vihman and DePaolis open the discussion with an account of possible precursors to both verbal symbolic learning and the capacity for vocal imitation in the 'mimesis' of Donald (1998). Donald posits a preverbal mimetic stage of symbolic culture linking primate modes of episodic cognition with the purposive culture of verbal *Homo sapiens*. Mimesis is an analog mode of representing events or acts by means of bodily posture, expression and gesture, and is still a medium for much human communication. According to Donald, mimesis established 'the fundamentals of intentional expression' (1998: 60) in hominid groups. On this view, the capacity to observe the meaning of a verbal symbol arose from its precursor in comprehending mimetic action – although the leap from iconic representation in mimesis to arbitrary representation in language is still a puzzle. Similarly, mimesis is said to have put in place 'the fundamentals of articulatory gesture' (Donald 1998: 65) – although again the move from analog iconic mimesis to digital articulatory imitation still had to be made, presumably through differentiation of the vocal machinery.

In their search for parallels with mimesis in the development of the modern child, Vihman and DePaolis do not expect to 'find any simple . . . recapitulation

... of cognitive stages.' Indeed, some children reverse the probable phylogenetic sequence by producing identifiable words well before they have the cognitive capacity to use them for communication. Nonetheless, some preverbal communicative capacity must surely be in place before language can begin. Vihman and DePaolis find a functional parallel to mimetic communication in early caretaker/child interactions that set the scene for the move into language. They also find a plausible parallel to the likely lengthy process of evolving imitative capacity in what they term 'the articulatory filter' that seems to shape a child's early words. The filter is the perception-production link, rooted in proprioceptive and auditory feedback from early sound making and babbling, by which a child initially selects for imitation from the rich supply of adult words only those sound patterns that match phonetically the patterns it can already form. The child's articulatory filter parallels the evolutionary bottleneck of emerging imitative capacity through which early hominid language would have had to pass.

MacNeilage and Davis also turn to the child for a model of early phylogeny. They provide a succinct summary of their work over the past decade in which they have analysed, in persuasive detail, a sizeable corpus of data on babbling and early words. They trace a path from the unmodulated mandibular oscillation of reduplicated syllables in babble to the complex, differentiated patterns of movement by lips, tongue, and soft palate in early words. At each step the child is evidently articulating within the constraints of its limited, yet growing, capacity. The constraints clearly do not stem from perception since infants can discriminate more or less all the sounds of speech within days or weeks of birth. Rather, what MacNeilage and Davis document is the gradual opening of the articulatory filter of Vihman and DePaolis.

MacNeilage and Davis support their phylogenetic interpretation of the child's phonetic development with three main lines of argument. First, the child's progression seems to be from sounds and sound sequences that are simple and easy to those that are complex and difficult; the evolutionary sequence is hardly likely to have reversed this pattern. Second, languages themselves seem to have followed a similar course from the simple to the complex. Third, many of the child's favoured sounds and sound sequences tend to predominate in the world's languages, suggesting that they reflect biomechanical articulatory constraints within which every language has had to evolve.

The carryover of child forms into adult language reminds us again that language development, like its evolution, is social, an extended process of adaptive interchange. Not only do learners adapt to language, but language adapts to learners. Language is then an epitome of its own evolution, a summary record of its passage through successive generations of learners (cf. Deacon 1997: ch. 4). At the same time, the precise course of development varies across language communities. Thus, despite presumably universal articulatory constraints, languages differ in their phonology. Each language has come upon one of an indefinitely large number of solutions to the problem of adapting phonetic structure to the same finite vocal machinery.

If learning is the key to language evolution, then variability among languages must arise, at least in part, from variability among learners within languages. And learners do indeed vary. For example, not every English-speaking child prefers stops to fricatives in its early words, or escapes from consonant harmony by the labial-coronal gestural routine that MacNeilage and Davis describe. Yet all English-speaking children end up with much the same phonological system. The invariant terminus evidently reflects their common ambient language no less than their common vocal machinery. What we have here then is not the invariant sequence of recapitulation, but a 'canalised' run through the 'epigenetic landscape' of Waddington (1975: ch. 7), in which vagaries of individual development are buffered against extreme variation by constancies of both genome and environment.

One source of variation in phonological development, beyond the accidents of vocabulary to which a child is exposed, may lie in imitative skills. Studdert-Kennedy, also adopting an ontogenetic account of phylogeny, proposes that a critical step in the evolution of the discrete phonetic structures that support the transmission of words was the evolution of a capacity for vocal imitation, unique among primates to humans. Imitating an utterance entails analysis of a sound pattern into its underlying articulatory components (gestures, segments, syllables), storage of the components for a shorter or longer period, depending on the interval between model and copy, and reassembly of the components in correct sequence. Notice that the meaning of the utterance plays no part in the process. Here perhaps, in the act of imitation, Studdert-Kennedy argues, is where phonetic form and semantic function were first dissociated in hominid communication. The dissociation was essential for an elaborated system of learned arbitrary reference, and its consequences ramified throughout what eventually became language. From it arose independent levels of phonetic representation and memory, prerequisite for displaced reference, for the production and comprehension of syntax, and even, many thousands of years later, for writing and reading.

Arguably, then, vocal imitation was the point of breakthrough from Donald's (1998) analog mimesis into the discrete verbal symbolism that launched the entire linguistic enterprise. On such an account we would not postulate consonants, vowels and their descriptive features as axioms, but would derive them, no less than syllables, from prelinguistic perceptual and articulatory constraints on the imitative machinery.

An impressive move in this direction comes from de Boer in a remarkable paper entitled 'The emergence of sound systems through self-organisation'. De Boer explicitly rejects any notion of 'fitness' or Darwinian selection among sounds in his model. He simulates the emergence of a vowel system in a population of 'agents' who 'imitate' each other's randomly presented vowels. Axiomatic to the model are: (1) the human articulatory-acoustic space from which vowels are drawn, (2) a capacity to imitate, in the sense of an agent's being able to judge which vowel in its repertoire lies closest in acoustic space to the vowel presented, and having available an automatic 'inverse transform' from formant structure to articulatory parameters and (3) sensitivity to feedback, indicating success or failure in each imitative exchange. Note that feedback is simply a convenient way of representing within the model the effect of an agent's long-term vocal accommodation (Locke 1993: 149ff.) to the phonetic ambience. Only through vocal accommodation can an agent adjust a failed attempt to imitate a vowel, and so extend its repertoire.

Thus, each agent's vowel system emerges by local changes, one vowel at a time, from a succession of imitative exchanges with other agents. The surprising outcome, after some 2,000 exchanges, is that every agent has acquired roughly the same vowel system distributed across formant space in the familiar triangular pattern – a two-dimensional representation of the three-dimensional volume of vocal tract configurations within which every vowel must lie. No less striking is the increased tightness and stability of the system when, in an inspired stroke of verisimilitude, de Boer introduces birth, ageing and death to the simulation, and permits younger agents to change their vowel repertoires more easily than old ones.

I will not attempt to summarise further this highly original paper other than to remark that if, as he proposes, de Boer successfully extends his simulations to more complex utterances, illustrating how consonants, consonant-vowel syllables and the dynamic gestures that form them, can emerge from imitative interactions within the constraints of the human vocal tract, he will have appreciably reduced the range of phonetic properties for which a biological evolutionary explanation must be found. The focus of evolutionary study would then shift from phonetic optimisation by selection to the anatomy and physiology of the vocal tract and the capacity for imitation, from which phonetic universals would evidently emerge.

Appropriately enough, the final chapter in this part of the book models the evolution of language and its supporting physiology. All the previous chapters assume an unchanging homogeneous population equipped with a modern vocal tract and the physiological support necessary for language. Livingstone and Fyfe take the novel step of modelling the emergence of a (very simple) communication system and its genetically heritable neural substrate under various cost/benefit conditions. Their model entertains a population of agents (artificial neural networks), distributed across a sampling space, capable of sending and receiving messages, and of 'learning' to map messages received onto internal states or 'meanings'. From thousands of random learning episodes between agents, and over dozens of 'generations' marked by 'crosses' between the 'fittest' agents in groups of 'close kin', there gradually emerges a coordinated system of communication and its genetically inherited 'physiological' substrate.

Remarkably, when communication is (realistically) modeled as entailing certain costs, neither 'language' nor its 'physiology' emerges unless the communicating and interbreeding agents are 'close kin', that is, are drawn from relatively narrow neighborhoods in the sampling space. This outcome suggests that, when there are costs to communication, only individuals with a similar 'linguistic' history due to close proximity share enough 'experience' to overcome the costs, and to exploit their phenotypic variability for mutually advantageous adaptive response; and only by 'mating' among close kin can phenotypic variants in language capacity be picked up and assimilated to the genome (cf. Waddington 1975: chs. 8–10). Thus, a mathematical simulation nicely endorses a discursive argument concerning the likely role of in-groups in the emergence of language (Knight 1998; Power, this volume). Kinship evidently fosters the evolution not only of altruism, but of cooperative communication.

In conclusion, a scruple. Livingstone and Fyfe refer to their simulation as a process of 'language-physiology coevolution'. But this is somewhat misleading because coevolution properly refers to the evolutionary matching of *independent* genetic systems – clover and bumble-bee, piñon jay and pine nut, cheetah and gazelle. We do not refer to the coevolution of seeing and the eye or of hearing and the ear because, like language and its physiology, they are not independent: they are directly related as function to structure. To write of their coevolution is therefore to misrepresent the relation between two aspects of a single process, between morphology and behaviour, structure and function. Behaviour is the function that mediates between environment and animal form, engendering the selection pressures that shape morphology. In the words of Ernst Mayr: "[C]hanges in behavior generate selection forces which modify the structures involved. . . . Behavior, thus, plays an important role as the pacemaker of evolutionary change" (1982: 612).

From this vantage we see more clearly the unique self-reflexive function of language that has shaped its evolution. As I-language, language (like all behaviour) mediates between individual and environment; as E-language in the 'arena of use' (Hurford, this volume), language is itself the environment to which evolving hominid or learning child adapts. Thus, language evolved, as it still develops, under what Quine (1960: 1) aptly called 'conspicuously intersubjective circumstances'.

References

Deacon, T. 1997. *The Symbolic Species*. New York: Norton.

Donald, M. 1998. Mimesis and the Executive Suite: missing links in language evolution. In J. R. Hurford, M. Studdert-Kennedy and C. Knight (eds), *Approaches to the Evolution of Language: Social and cognitive bases*. Cambridge: Cambridge University Press, pp. 44–67.

Garstang, W. 1922. The theory of recapitulation: a critical re-statement of the biogenetic law. *Journal of the Linnaean Society (Zoology)* **35**: 81–101.

Gould, S. J. 1977. *Ontogeny and Phylogeny*. Cambridge, MA: Belknap.

Harris, Z. 1968. *Mathematical Structures of Language*. New York: Wiley.

Knight, C. 1998. Ritual/speech coevolution: a solution to the problem of deception. In J. R. Hurford, M. Studdert-Kennedy and C. Knight (eds), *Approaches to the Evolution of Language: Social and cognitive bases*. Cambridge: Cambridge University Press, pp. 68–91.

Locke, J. 1993. *The Child's Path to Spoken Language*. Cambridge, MA: Harvard University Press.

Mayr, E. 1982. *The Growth of Biological Thought*. Cambridge, MA: Belknap.

Quine, W. V. O. 1960. *Word and Object*. Cambridge, MA: MIT Press.

Richards, R. J. 1992. *The Meaning of Evolution*. Chicago: University of Chicago Press.

Waddington, C. H. 1975. *The Evolution of an Evolutionist*. Ithaca, NY: Cornell University Press.

8

The Role of Mimesis in Infant Language Development: Evidence for Phylogeny?

MARILYN M. VIHMAN AND RORY A. DEPAOLIS

Donald (1991, 1993, 1998) has proposed an imaginative evolutionary scenario involving a preverbal 'mimetic' stage of symbolic culture. Although nonverbal symbolic expression continues to play an important role in human mental life today (in art, athletics, crafts, social ritual, theater), it tends to be overlooked due to the vastly more salient role of verbal symbols. Donald characterises mimesis as the ability to reproduce or reenact an event or activity, in order to consider it, analyse it, preserve it in memory, recall it at will, compare it with other events, and refer to it at will, i.e. to communicate it to others – all without the use of language.

Such a symbolic capacity in the preverbal predecessors of *Homo sapiens* would have prepared the way for the relatively rapid development of language as a consequence of the later descent of the larynx and subsequent vocal tract changes that made the phonetic production of speech as we now know it physiologically possible. The goal of the present chapter is to think through the possible relevance, for Donald's concept of an evolutionary stage of preverbal symbolic communication or mimesis, of what is currently understood regarding the biological, social and individual origins of language in the child, bearing in mind the considerable differences in principle between the problems of phylogeny as against ontogeny.

Mimesis as Donald describes it involves a sophisticated 'modeling' of bodily posture, expression, and gesture. In contrast to the episodic memory that characterises nonhuman primates, Donald argues, *Homo erectus* showed a sufficiently complex culture – including systematic manufacture and use of tools, cooperative seasonal hunting, widespread migrations and the use of fire and cooked food – to lead us to suppose that communication based on semantic memory and its concomitant, symbolic representation, must have been in place as early as 1.5 million years ago, long before the anatomical changes that made human speech possible and that are often taken to mark the speciation of *Homo sapiens*.

Donald's characterisation of symbolic nonverbal communication derives in part from the capacities of the 'prelinguistic' but intentionally communicating child – that is, a child in the last months of the first year at the very youngest. Neither specific category-based reference nor symbolic understanding is usually attributed to children in that stage of development, however. Nonverbal symbolic representation of the kind he describes, in the absence of a productive capacity for speech or language, would typify only 'late talkers', children who have made the representational advances needed for symbolic word use (by the first half of the second year in most normally developing infants; see McCune, 1995) but whose phonetic skills and/or capacity for laying down phonological representations are slower to develop (Thal, Oroz and McCaw 1995; Rescorla and Bernstein Ratner 1996; Mirak and Rescorla 1998).

Mimesis in the Developing Infant

Precursor social behaviours in the first months of life require neither symbolic representations nor intentional or even voluntary imitation, but rather a broader, more global 'matching' response involving a seemingly instinctive sense of the essential similarity or correspondence between child and caretaker (Stern et al. 1985; Meltzoff and Moore 1993). The 'sense of self' appears to be highly precocious in the human infant, perhaps related to the representational level of self-awareness which Donald, citing Oakley (1985), sees as a relatively new element in human cognition, though it is also present to some extent in chimpanzees. It is not clear whether any nonhuman primates also have a sense of self or of the correspondence between self and mother in earliest infancy, but there is some evidence to suggest that they do not (see Plooij 1979).

What level of cognitive processing can be ascribed to the infant in the first six months of life? Maurer (1993: 119) suggests that apparent imitation in neonates is most likely the result of young infants failing to differentiate 'between changing patterns of visual and proprioceptive stimulation', i.e. between perceived other and sensed self. Her suggestion that initial sensory experiences are undifferentiated or 'synesthetic' provides one interpretation for the very young infant's 'integrative competence' (Papoušek and Papoušek 1987). Meltzoff and Moore (1993: 212) offer a related interpretation, arguing that 'there is a cross-modal equivalence between the visual pattern of the adult and the proprioceptive pattern of the self', an equivalence that lends familiarity to adult behaviours to the extent that those behaviours are present in the infant's own repertoire: 'Infants' self-produced movements provide a framework for interpreting the facial movements they see. Feeling one's own face movements infuses the seen face with special meaning' (ibid.; compare the similar function that we will posit later for the 'articulatory filter'). In short, a very basic, instinctive matching of self to other is characteristic of human infants from the start, suggesting that a deeply rooted 'premimetic' precursor of self-representation may be available to human but not to nonhuman primate infants.

Experiments with instrumental conditioning of infants aged 2, 3 and 6 months have demonstrated that what appears to be most characteristic of that period is a primitive type of episodic processing. Although the infants demonstrate recall through a motoric procedure (foot kick activates mobile), the incidental perceptual details of context and setting constitute essential elements of the memory for the infant, since changes in those details can effectively block recall (Rovee-Collier 1990). This seems to be comparable to the episodic cognition that Donald (1991: 149) ascribes to ape culture ('unreflective, concrete, and situation-bound'; Edelman (1992) uses the term 'primary consciousness' in a similar way), a predecessor of uniquely human semantic memory. Thus, higher ape–like episodic processing is combined, in the young infant, with an instinctive kind of self-representation seemingly unknown to other species. We are thus unlikely to find any simple stagelike recapitulation in ontogeny of phylogenetic cognitive stages.

By the last half of the first year, as we will show, both proprioception and the matching of self to other play a critical role in the child's move from syllabic babbling to first words (Kuhl and Meltzoff 1988; Thelen 1991; Vihman 1993b). The infant's intuitive 'body sense', on the one hand, and its powerful drive to observe and dynamically reenact the social partner's behaviours (Locke 1993), on the other, may be taken to constitute uniquely human roots for later, more sophisticated intentional and symbolic mimetic behavior (see Tomasello and Camaioni 1997). Such basic experiential motives and behavioural drives can be taken to reflect particularly deeply rooted phylogenetic characteristics of the species, innate predispositions more plausibly related to evolutionary process than any specifically linguistic preprogramming or knowledge.

The very early interactive modelling of motoric behaviors thus suggests a primitive premimetic capacity that serves as a driving force in the process of making the transition into speech, a process supported, at least in ontogeny, by the input speech stream to which normally developing infants are extensively exposed. The specific exponent of motoric modelling of speech production, the 'articulatory filter' that we will describe, could have played a similar role in phylogeny, building on the dual status of individuals as expressors (or speakers) and experiencers (listeners) to allow rapid advances in the diversity and complexity of vocal signals once speechlike production of syllables became possible for some members of the hominid community (see MacNeilage and

Davis, this volume). This is our interpretation of the role of 'self-triggered voluntary retrieval of representations' in the evolution of 'highly complex motor acts of speech', or 'articulatory gestures' (Donald 1993: 742).

In infants, a capacity for symbolic representation has been shown to constitute a prerequisite for the referential use of words which emerges in the first half of the second year (Bates et al. 1979; Goodwyn and Acredolo 1993; Vihman and McCune 1994). Infants whose phonetic and communicative skills develop early produce pre-referential, context-bound words before they begin to produce referential words, the latter occurring only in conjunction with nonverbal evidence of the child's attainment of symbolic representational capacity (McCune 1992, 1995). Other infants show gestural communication and language comprehension as well as planned play sequences that reflect symbolic understanding well before word production, which must await the maturation of phonetic abilities and/or a capacity for specifically phonological representation, or 'phonological memory' (Baddeley, Gathercole and Papagno 1998). Phylogenetically, the situation is similar to that of these 'late talkers'. Following Donald again, it seems reasonable to posit a long period of symbolic nonverbal expression in the absence of speech. Once greatly increased phonetic capacity emerged with the changed structure of the vocal tract and vocal sound-meaning associations could begin to be differentiated, dramatic changes ensued relatively quickly, since the peripheral capacity was suddenly available to express symbolic understandings in a far more efficient way (Studdert- Kennedy 1991).

Infant Entrainment into Symbolic Word Production

The Child's Empathic Identification with Caretakers

A capacity for facial and vocal matching is in place as early as the first three months of life. Whereas imitation is, according to Hauser (1996), as unique to the human species as language itself, precocious 'matching', arguably rooted in a form of emotional and vocal 'contagion' with subcortical neurological support ('the organic substrate for empathy and prosocial behavior'; see Malatesta and Izard 1984: 177; cf. also Vinter 1986), may be considered to be a prerepresentational, presymbolic basis for the later development of mimesis in Donald's sense.

Malatesta and Izard (1984) provide a helpful account of the biological and social roots of 'human social signals' in the child, tracing the development of infant facial and vocal expressions of emotion back to dyadic exchanges that begin soon after birth. By their account, a spiral of reciprocal capacities and behaviours facilitates the child's progress:

1. Infants can make discrete categorical emotion expressions (among others).
2. Mothers respond to these expressions contingently and imitate infant facial [and vocal] expressions selectively, shifting their response with infant age.
3. Infants imitate their mothers and are able to stabilise behaviours to which they experience contingent responses.

The child can be seen to advance from stimulus-bound reflexive responses (0–3 months) to a period of 'magnetic' social interaction (3–6 months), in which it is riveted to the caregiver's face in frequent face-to-face interaction (a behaviour found only late and relatively rarely in chimpanzee mother-infant dyads: Plooij 1979). In this period the child interiorises the caregiver's face and expressive style, which subsequently allows the intense dyadic interactions to 'cool off' as the child directs attention to other objects and events. The final step in this developmental trajectory is the period of more voluntary expression characteristic of the second half of the first year, when focused attention and vocal production alike first begin to assume adultlike forms (Ruff and Rothbart 1996; Vihman 1996). The transition from (1) 'biological' to (2) 'social imperative', and then to (3) individual, voluntary expression culminates in (4) the intentional (global) signalling that typifies the last months of the prelinguistic period, the immediate precursor of (5) symbolic and specifically referential behavior. Donald's mimesis seems to be an imaginative synthesis of (4) and (5), not a genuine stage of development for many or perhaps most children.

The Child's Move from Syllabic Babbling to First Words

Sometime around the middle of the first year, after an initial period of production of glottals and nasalised vowels only, followed by oral vowel production along with exploration of a range of different prosodic effects such as growling, creaking, squealing, shouting and whispering, infants quite suddenly begin to make rhythmic open-and-closed jaw movements (MacNeilage and Davis 1990), yielding what Oller (1980) has termed 'canonical babbling', the first syllabic vocalisations to show adultlike timing and to be transcribable as segmental sequences (though there is no evidence that they are so planned or produced). The emergence of rhythmic syllabic strings, which at first show little or no influence from the particular ambient language, is on a maturational schedule that suggests a biological basis (see Thelen 1981); even deaf infants may produce such syllables, with or without voicing, at around the same time (Meier et al. 1997), but in the absence of auditory feedback they fail to persevere with this vocal behaviour until many months later, if ever (Oller and Eilers

1988). The vocal tract of the infant at birth is closer to that of the nonhuman primates than to that of adult humans (Kent 1992); the change to the fully adult structure is said to take some years, yet incipient anatomical change may be supposed to underlie the dramatic shift in vocal production (Lieberman 1980).

In normally hearing infants the first slowly articulated babbles are maintained and augmented by a range of syllables which gradually increases both in paradigmatic and syntagmatic terms (diversity and complexity). (Growth in the range of consonants produced is the single most striking development in this period, and the best predictor of future phonological advance; see Stoel-Gammon 1992.) Despite earlier linguistic pronouncements as to the sharp difference between babble and words (Jakobson 1941/1968), the continuous nature of these two infant vocal systems has now been firmly established (Vihman et al. 1985).

To elaborate this important point, the first words produced by vocally expressive infants – words closely connected with routinely repeated situations ('wave bye-bye'; 'where's your shoe?') or verbal games ('what does the cow say?') – are formally indistinguishable from contemporaneous babble and are also relatively 'accurate', in that they rarely show the substitutions or transpositions of sounds that typify the first symbolic words of the next (phonological) stage of vocal development (Ferguson and Farwell 1975; Vihman 1996). Instead, these context-limited words appear to reflect holistic 'matching' of the child's own preexisting phonetic patterns to the adult input: in the child's fleeting experience of the adult speech stream (so different from the steady exposure to repeated tokens of isolated syllables provided in experimental studies of infant speech perception), those patterns familiar from the child's own often repeated productions may be presumed to stand out with particular salience, supported by advances in the neurological bases for voluntary attention in the second half-year of life. As a result of that matching process or 'articulatory filter' (Vihman 1993b) the vocally expressive child can begin to activate a capacity for phonetic memory that still depends, at first, on perceptual reminders (Rovee-Collier 1990) – hence the observed limitation of such first words to situationally embedded use.

Notice that for precociously verbal children, the production of vocalisations which holistically match adult words, supported by episodic knowledge of the 'right thing to say' in a repeatedly experienced routine or event, precedes any evidence of symbolic capacity, or the representation of either form or meaning outside of established routines. The sequence here is thus the reverse of that which Donald posits for phylogeny: given the phonetic capacity and a robust 'phonological loop', or ability to recall specific phonetic sequences which may then be deployed when the contextual basis recurs, the vocally expressive child produces identifiable words before being able to reflect on a situation, to compare and choose between competing vocal or phonetic choices (word forms) or to generalise words on the basis of semantic categorisation.

The matching process, which yields identifiable words for such a child, may play a role for children in general in the perceptual processing of speech. Whereas advances in perception in the first six months of life, before the emergence of a repertoire of adultlike syllables, is almost exclusively based on prosody, from seven to eight months on, experimental studies have shown increasingly finely tuned knowledge of or familiarity with ambient-language segmental patterns that elicit no such response in the 'precanonical' child (see Vihman 1996 and Jusczyk 1997 for reviews). The emergence of canonical syllables in the middle of the first year arms the child with a motor activity whose exercise affords increasing proprioceptive and auditory experience with segmental patterns ('articulatory filter'). We can infer that it is that experience that facilitates the infant's initial breakthrough into awareness of and eventual familiarity with particular segmental patterns in adult speech.

A spiral model of interaction between production and perception can be postulated, with the articulatory filter as the mechanism that links production and perception (see Figure 8.1; cf. Vihman 1993a; Vihman, Velleman and McCune 1994):

1. Adult words produced frequently ('repeated input patterns' in Figure 8.1), with prosodic emphasis ('infant-directed speech'), in situations of high affective value to the particular child – the first salient speech patterns for that child – leave in the child's memory some global perceptual features, such that the child's own later production of similar patterns will activate the traces of those features and thus afford the satisfaction that attends the repetition of familiar and affectively meaningful experiences.
2. Once canonical babbling is in place, each child develops its own repertoire of often produced CV syllables or 'vocal motor schemes' (VMS) (McCune and Vihman 1987), the patterns preferentially repeated reflecting the influence of salient words or phrases from the earlier period (see the arrow linking 'repeated input patterns' with 'production of stable sound patterns'; to the extent that the child's productions may in turn sometimes influence the production of adult caretakers – see e.g. Veneziano 1988; Papoušek and Papoušek 1989 – the arrow should perhaps be double-headed, but we will not explore the matter further here).
3. The first (presymbolic, pre-referential, context-limited) words produced reflect a match between child's babbling patterns (VMS) and adult patterns produced in a meaningful context ('meaning attached').

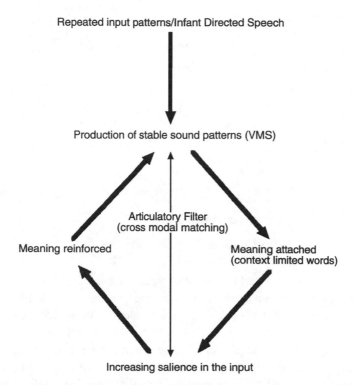

Figure 8.1. Operation of the articulatory filter in infants: Vocal Motor Scheme (VMS) production focuses child attention on similar phonetic patterns in input speech, leading to context-limited word production.

4. Repeated cycling through such a spiral of phonetic influence and lexical formation leads both to a gradual widening of the infant repertoire and a decrease in the unfamiliar patterns encountered in frequently heard verbal routines. At the same time, continuing processing of input speech will yield increasing familiarity with initially less salient words or morphemes syntagmatically associated with words already present in the child's rapidly growing production repertoire (Gerken, Landau and Remez 1990; see also Studdert-Kennedy 1991: 10, who sees in both the ontogeny and the phylogeny of language 'repeated cycles of differentiation and integration').

Steps 2 to 4 can be illustrated from Molly, one of the children whose early word production is outlined in Vihman (1996) (see also Vihman and Velleman 1989). Molly's frequently and consistently used consonants, or VMS, include the labial and velar stops and /m/ from 9 months on, with /n/ and the alveolar stop being added from 11 and 12 months, respectively. Her first words

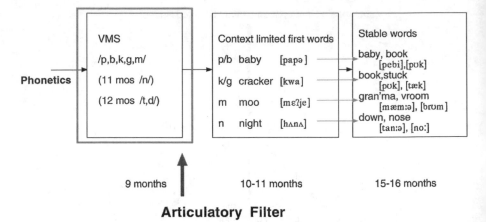

Figure 8.2. Function of the articulatory filter: Molly, 9–16 months.

(10–11 months), produced in limited contexts affording perceptual reminders of the appropriate sound pattern, were formed on the basis of these consonants and simple CV(CV) structures. By 14 months Molly had a cumulative vocabulary of over fifty words, including both nouns and relational words used referentially, yet her 'stable' words, those she produced spontaneously in the course of both of the half-hour recorded sessions sampled at 15 and 16 months, continued to be based on the consonants well established as VMSs within the first year (see Figure 8.2, which includes an exhaustive sample of stable words).

Prerequisites for the Referential Use of Words

Close analysis of the early words of 20 children acquiring English and 5 children each acquiring French, Japanese, and Swedish has made it possible to draw a number of conclusions regarding the onset of symbolic language use, typically sometime in the first half of the second year (12–18 months). Three independent strands of development appear to be necessary; the ordering of these is individual, reflecting differences in the children rather than in the input (cf. Vihman et al. 1994):

- *An understanding of the potential for communicative expression by vocal means.* This understanding, like the emergence of canonical syllables, tends to be marked by a dramatic, easily observed behavioural shift – namely, a shift from the quiet use of 'attention grunts' or other protowords, consistent vocal forms marking focal attention (typically seen in the latter part of the first year), to the louder, often insistent use of 'communicative grunts' or other protowords (Vihman and Miller 1988; McCune et al. 1996; Roug-Hellichius 1998), with the support at first of communicative gestures such as pointing; infant initiation of bouts of joint attention with the mother begins to be seen at about the same time. (Compare the account in Plooij 1979 of the faster maturing infant chimps, who selectively use biting to engage maternal attention from three to four months on.)

- *The development of sufficient representational capacity to permit comparison of word meanings across situational contexts*, resulting in the first generalised (symbolic) use of nouns and of pre-predicates known as 'relational words' (McCune-Nicolich 1981; Vihman and McCune 1994). Representational advance is identifiable also in pretend play, in which the first sequencing of play acts, or 'combinatorial pretend play', appears to constitute the critical marker (McCune 1992, 1995). (See the review of evidence of representational capacity in nonhuman primates in McCune 1999, which yields no definitive conclusions, however.)
- *The development of diversified phonetic skill (stable use of a range of different consonants, or VMS) sufficient to support identifiable word production and incipient phonological representations* in interaction with advances in representational capacity (Vihman 1996: ch. 6).

Figure 8.3 is a schematic representation of the milestones we have identified in the infant progression to symbolic word use; the time scale is individually variable, as indicated by ranges of months on the time line. We assume that the first two strands (communication and representation) constitute prerequisites to the evolution of language, which must have been in place in early hominids before the descent of the larynx began to result in changed capacity for vocal production and, eventually, in increased efficiency of vocal communication. McCune (1999) elaborates the role of protracted infant-mother interactions in the communicative development of chimpanzees as well as humans, and argues for a causative role in the evolution of language for the grunt, which occurs widely across primate species and which takes on communicative meaning in the course of infancy in nonhuman primates as well as in human infants. The scenario she develops, although different in emphasis, is entirely compatible with the present schematic model, for ontogeny as well as phylogeny.

Evidence for Phylogeny?

Donald (1991) assumes that mimetic capacity, involving symbolic representation and an elaborated system of nonverbal communication, had long been in place by the time that the modern vocal tract had evolved to the point where

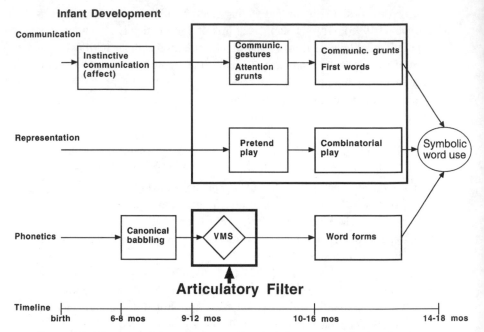

Figure 8.3. The role of the articulatory filter in infant communicative development, culminating in symbolic word use.

speech as we know it could begin to develop. That mimetic capacity would have provided the fuel for the rapid development of sound and meaning associations, accentuated by the articulatory filter, in our model, yielding the building blocks for language. Thus, unlike the developing infant, by the time early hominids had the opportunity to develop contrastive phonetic skills the cognitive function necessary for symbolic word use was already fully established. The potential similarity between ontogeny and phylogeny under our interpretation is the rapid onset of advances in language use through the implementation of an articulatory filter. Figure 8.4 constitutes a schematic proposal for the role of the articulatory filter in this development.

Assuming a long history of cohesive human mimetic culture involving close cooperative interactions, complex tool making, hunting, migrations and other group activities requiring intensive communication, the evolution of the modern vocal tract would have made rapid communicative advances possible. In this scenario, individuals exercising a nascent capacity for syllable production would serve, as do all primate communicators, as both expressors and perceivers; syllables or longer units which they produced would gain meaning from the context of production and become potential signals or, given the preexistence

Hominid Development

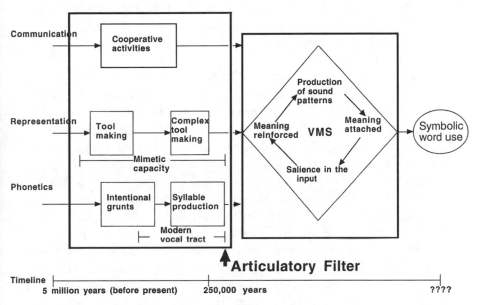

Figure 8.4. The role of the articulatory filter in hominid communicative development, culminating in symbolic word use.

of representational understanding, symbols. Repeated cycling through the chain of sound pattern production and the emergence of arbitrary lexicalisation of meanings through contextual associations, with variation in both phonetic form and semantic content, would lead to a group repertoire of meaningful symbolic forms stabilised through the action of the articulatory filter. Donald (1991: 35) proposes a similar spiral for the subsequent parallel and interactive development of distinct affective signals and first word forms: 'The existence [in phylogeny] of a primitive system of vocal communication drove a further general expansion of cognitive power [i.e. beyond the advance already represented by the mimetic stage of cognition], which in turn gradually led to complex articulate language'.

Some further speculation follows naturally from our thesis. Whatever neurological structures supported mimetic memory – gestural memory? memory for sequences? – those structures may constitute the phylogenetic precursors to those that support linguistic representation in humans today. More specifically, the phonological loop, which provides the entry point to long-term memory storage for phonetic strings and larger phonological units composed of such strings, may be more closely related phylogenetically to the processing of temporal sequences of meaningful gestures than to the processing of nonspeech auditory patterns, given the critical role of motoric production (subvocal rehearsal) in that subcomponent of working memory (Baddeley 1986; Gathercole and Baddeley 1993) and given the processing of sign language in native signers, which depends on the same brain structures as the processing of speech (Poizner, Bellugi and Klima 1991).

For phylogeny as well as ontogeny, no foreknowledge of the goal of as yet undeveloped capacities can be assumed; however, social motivations are widely believed to have played a major role in setting the stage for the origins of language in the species as in the child (e.g. Dunbar 1993). The suggestion that mimetic communication supported human cultural interactions before the evolution of phonetic capacity is compatible with the critical role of caretaker/child interactions in preparing the way for the transition to language in ontogeny. With respect to proprioception and matching, it is the development of a strong representational and intentional inventive (generative) capacity that is unique to our species. The mimetic or premimetic capacities underlying infant progress from babbling to symbolic word production may be phylogenetically older and rooted in structures which are neurologically more primitive than speech, but they cannot crystallise as language in the infant before the vocal tract is restructured to its adult-like proportions. Finally, whereas the timing of the emergence of symbolic capacity in relation to phonetic skills and communicative understanding differs across individual infants, the absence in phylogeny of both the vocal capacities and the external (environmental) modelling which infants receive in the input speech signal suggests an extended evolutionary period of mimetic development before the transition to verbal symbolic expression, or language.

References

Baddeley, A. 1986. *Working Memory*. Oxford: Clarendon.
Baddeley, A., S. Gathercole and C. Papagno. 1998. The phonological loop as a learning device. *Psychological Review* **105**: 158–173.
Bates, E., L. Benigni, I. Bretherton, L. Camaioni and V. Volterra. 1979. *The Emergence of Symbols: Cognition and communication in infancy*. New York: Academic.
Donald, M. 1991. *Origins of the Modern Mind: Three stages in the evolution of culture and cognition*. Cambridge, MA: Harvard University Press.
Donald, M. 1993. Precis of *Origins of the Modern Mind: Three stages in the evolution of culture and cognition*. *Behavioral and Brain Sciences* **16**: 737–791.
Donald, M. 1998. Mimesis and the Executive Suite: Missing links in language evolution. In J. R. Hurford, M. Studdert-Kennedy and C. Knight (eds), *Approaches to the Evolution of Language: Social and cognitive bases*. Cambridge: Cambridge University Press, pp. 44–67.
Dunbar, R. I. M. 1993. Coevolution of neocortical size, group size and language in humans. *Behavioral and Brain Sciences* **16**: 681–735.

Edelman, G. M. 1992. *Bright Air, Brilliant Fire: On the matter of mind.* New York: Basic Books.

Ferguson, C. A. and C. B. Farwell. 1975. Words and sounds in early language acquisition. *Language* **51**: 419–439.

Gathercole, S. E. and A. D. Baddeley. 1993. *Working Memory and Language.* Hillsdale, NJ: Erlbaum.

Gerken, L., B. Landau and R. E. Remez. 1990. Function morphemes in young children's speech perception and production. *Developmental Psychology* **26**: 204–216.

Goodwin, S. W. and L. P. Acredolo. 1993. Symbolic gesture versus word: is there a modality advantage for onset of symbol use? *Child Development* **64**: 688–701.

Hauser, M. 1996. *The Evolution of Communication.* Cambridge, MA: MIT Press.

Jakobson, R. 1941/1968. *Child Language, Aphasia, and Phonological Universals.* The Hague: Mouton. English translation of *Kindersprache, Aphasie und allgemeine Lautgesetze.* Uppsala: Almqvist and Wiksell.

Jusczyk, P. W. 1997. *The Discovery of Spoken Language.* Cambridge, MA: MIT Press.

Kent, R. D. 1992. The biology of phonological development. In C. A. Ferguson, L. Menn and C. Stoel-Gammon (eds), *Phonological Development: Models, research, implications.* Timonium, MD: York Press, pp. 65–90.

Kuhl, P. K. and A. N. Meltzoff. 1988. Speech as an intermodal object of perception. In A. Yonas (ed), *Perceptual Development in Infancy.* The Minnesota Symposia on Child Psychology 20. Hillsdale, NJ: Erlbaum, pp. 235–266.

Lieberman, P. 1980. On the development of vowel production in young children. In G. H. Yeni-Komshian, J. F. Kavanagh and C. A. Ferguson (eds), *Child Phonology, Vol. 1: Production.* New York: Academic, pp, 113–142.

Locke, J. 1993. *The Child's Path to Spoken Language.* Cambridge, MA: Harvard University Press.

MacNeilage, P. F. and B. L. Davis. 1990. Acquisition of speech production: frames, then content. In M. Jeannerod (ed), *Attention and Performance XIII: Motor representation and control.* Hillsdale, NJ: Erlbaum, pp. 453–475.

Malatesta, C. Z. and C. E. Izard. 1984. The ontogenesis of human social signals: from biological imperative to symbol utilization. In N. A. Fox and R. J. Davidson (eds), *The Psychobiology of Affective Development.* Hillsdale, NJ: Erlbaum, pp. 161–206.

Maurer, D. 1993. Neonatal synesthesia: implications for the processing of speech and faces. In B. de Boysson-Bardies, S. de Schonen, P. Jusczyk, P. MacNeilage and J. Morton (eds), *Developmental Neurocognition: Speech and face processing in the first year of life.* Dordrecht: Kluwer, pp. 109–124.

McCune, L. 1992. First words: a dynamic systems view. In C. A. Ferguson, L. Menn and C. Stoel-Gammon (eds), *Phonological Development: Models, research, implications.* Timonium, MD: York Press, pp. 313–336.

McCune, L. 1995. A normative study of representational play at the transition to language. *Developmental Psychology* **31**: 198–206.

McCune, L. 1999. Children's transition to language: a human model for development of the vocal repertoire in extant and ancestral primate species? In B. King (ed), *Origin of Language: What nonhuman primates can tell us.* Santa Fe, NM: SAR Press, pp. 269–306.

McCune, L. and M. M. Vihman. 1987. Vocal motor schemes. *Papers and Reports on Child Language Development* **26**: 72–79.

McCune, L., M. M. Vihman, L. Roug-Hellichius, D. B. Delery and L. Gogate. 1996. Grunt communication in human infants (*Homo sapiens*). *Journal of Comparative Psychology* **110**: 27–37.

McCune-Nicolich, L. 1981. Toward symbolic functioning: structure of early pretend games and potential parallels with language. *Child Development* **52**: 785–797.

Meier, R., L. McGarvin, R. A. E. Zakia and R. Willerman. 1997. Silent mandibular oscillations in vocal babbling. *Phonetica* **54**: 153–171.

Meltzoff, A. N. and M. K. Moore. 1993. Why faces are special to infants: on connecting the attraction of faces and infants' ability for imitation and cross-modal processing. In B. de Boysson-Bardies, S. de Schonen, P. Jusczyk, P. MacNeilage and J. Morton (eds), *Developmental Neurocognition: Speech and face processing in the first year of life*. Dordrecht: Kluwer, pp. 211–225.

Mirak, J. and L. Rescorla. 1998. Phonetic skills and vocabulary size in late talkers: concurrent and predictive relationships. *Applied Psycholinguistics* **19**: 1–18.

Oakley, D. A. 1985. Cognition and imagery in animals. In D. Oakley (ed), *Brain and Mind*. London: Methuen, pp. 99–131.

Oller, D. K. 1980. The emergence of the sounds of speech in infancy. In G. Yeni-Komshian, J. F. Kavanagh and C. A. Ferguson (eds), *Child Phonology, Vol. 1: Production*. New York: Academic, pp. 93–112.

Oller, D. K. and R. E. Eilers. 1988. The role of audition in infant babbling. *Child Development* **59**: 441–449.

Papoušek, H. and M. Papoušek. 1987. Intuitive parenting: a dialectic counterpart to the infant's integrative competence. In J. D. Osofsky (ed), *Handbook of Infant Development*. Second edition. New York: Wiley, pp. 669–720.

Papoušek, M. and H. Papoušek. 1989. Forms and functions of vocal matching in interactions between mothers and their precanonical infants. *First Language* **9**: 137–158.

Plooij, F. 1979. How wild chimpanzee babies trigger the onset of mother-infant play – and what the mother makes of it. In M. Bullowa (ed), *Before Speech: The beginning of interpersonal communication*. Cambridge: Cambridge University Press, pp. 223–243.

Poizner, H., U. Bellugi and E. S. Klima. 1991. Brain function for language: perspectives from another modality. In I. G. Mattingly and M. Studdert-Kennedy (eds), *Modularity and the Motor Theory of Speech Perception: Proceedings of a conference to honor Alvin M. Liberman*. Hillsdale, NJ: Erlbaum, pp. 145–169.

Rescorla, L. and N. Bernstein Ratner. 1996. Phonetic profiles of toddlers with Specific Expressive Language Impairment (SLI-E). *Journal of Speech and Hearing Research* **39**: 153–165.

Roug-Hellichius, L. 1998. Babble, grunts and words: a study of phonetic shape and functional use in the beginnings of language. Unpublished doctoral thesis, Stockholm University.

Rovee-Collier, C. 1990. The 'memory system' of prelinguistic infants. In A. Diamond (ed), *The Development and Neural Bases of Higher Cognitive Functions*. Annals of the New York Academy of Sciences 608. New York: New York Academy of Sciences, pp. 517–536.

Ruff, H. A. and M. K. Rothbart. 1996. *Attention in Early Development*. Oxford: Oxford University Press.

Stern, D. N., L. Hofer, W. Haft and J. Dore. 1985. Affect attunement: the sharing of feeling states between mother and infant by means of intermodal fluency. In

T. Field and N. Fox (eds), *Social Perception in Infants*. Norwood, NJ: Ablex, pp. 249–268.

Stoel-Gammon, C. 1992. Prelinguistic vocal development: measurement and predictions. In C. A. Ferguson, L. Menn and C. Stoel-Gammon (eds), *Phonological Development: Models, research, implications*. Timonium, MD: York Press, pp. 439–456.

Studdert-Kennedy, M. 1991. Language development from an evolutionary perspective. In N. A. Krasnegor, D. M. Rumbaugh, R. L. Schiefelbusch and M. Studdert-Kennedy (eds), *Biological and Behavioral Determinants of Language Development*. Hillsdale, NJ: Erlbaum, pp. 5–28.

Thal, D. J., M. Oroz and V. McCaw. 1995. Phonological and lexical development in normal and late-talking toddlers. *Applied Psycholinguistics* **16**: 407–424.

Thelen, E. 1981. Rhythmical behavior in infancy: An ethological perspective. *Developmental Psychology* **17**: 237–257.

Thelen, E. 1991. Motor aspects of emergent speech. In N. A. Krasnegor, D. M. Rumbaugh, R. L. Schiefelbusch and M. Studdert-Kennedy (eds), *Biological and Behavioral Determinants of Language Development*. Hillsdale, NJ: Erlbaum, pp. 339–362.

Tomasello, M. and L. Camaioni. 1997. A comparison of the gestural communication of apes and human infants. *Human Development* **40**: 7–24.

Veneziano, E. 1988. Vocal-verbal interaction and the construction of early lexical knowledge. In M. D. Smith and J. L. Locke (eds), *The Emergent Lexicon: The child's development of a linguistic vocabulary*. New York: Academic, pp. 110–147.

Vihman, M. M. 1993a. The construction of a phonological system. In B. de Boysson-Bardies, S. de Schonen, P. Jusczyk, P. MacNeilage and J. Morton (eds), *Developmental Neurocognition: Speech and face processing in the first year of life*. Dordrecht: Kluwer, pp. 411–419.

Vihman, M. M. 1993b. Variable paths to early word production. *Journal of Phonetics* **21**: 61–82.

Vihman, M. M. 1996. *Phonological Development: The origins of language in the child*. Oxford: Blackwell.

Vihman, M. M., E. Kay, B. de Boysson-Bardies, C. Durand and U. Sundberg. 1994. External sources of individual differences? A cross-linguistic analysis of the phonetics of mothers' speech to one-year-old children. *Developmental Psychology* **30**: 652–663.

Vihman, M. M., M. A. Macken, R. Miller, H. Simmons and J. Miller. 1985. From babbling to speech: a reassessment of the continuity issue. *Language* **61**: 395–443.

Vihman, M. M. and L. McCune. 1994. When is a word a word? *Journal of Child Language* **21**: 517–542.

Vihman, M. M. and R. Miller. 1988. Words and babble at the threshold of lexical acquisition. In M. D. Smith and J. L. Locke (eds), *The Emergent Lexicon: The child's development of a linguistic vocabulary*. New York: Academic, pp. 151–183.

Vihman, M. M. and S. L. Velleman. 1989. Phonological reorganization: A case study. *Language and Speech* **32**: 149–170.

Vihman, M. M., S. L. Velleman and L. McCune. 1994. How abstract is child phonology? Towards an integration of linguistic and psychological approaches. In M. Yavas (ed), *First and Second Language Phonology*. San Diego, CA: Singular, pp. 9–94.

Vinter, A. 1986. The role of movement in eliciting early imitations. *Child Development* **57**: 66–71.

9

Evolution of Speech: The Relation Between Ontogeny and Phylogeny

PETER F. MACNEILAGE AND BARBARA L. DAVIS

In this chapter, we present the hypothesis that the production of speech had a simple evolutionary origin, and then increased in complexity in particular ways, and that this sequence of events was similar to the one which is observed in speech acquisition. The chapter has three parts. The first is a comparison between speech and other primate call systems to identify changes which occurred in the evolution of speech. The second is a presentation of evidence from sound inventories of existing languages which suggests that speech systems have indeed increased in complexity since the advent of the first speechlike forms. Finally, we examine speech acquisition to infer in some detail what the initial patterns of speech might have been like and what forms the subsequent increases in complexity might have taken.

Basic to the present approach is the axiom that whenever a versatile movement repertoire is present in an animal, the capability for it must have been tinkered into place by evolution. In the absence of a fossil record, the ability to produce the complex movement sequences of speech appears, like the rest of language, to have evolved 'out of the blue', thus constituting a 'continuity paradox' in the words of Bickerton (1990: 7), as Darwin's theory is antithetical to *de novo* evolution. The task here is to understand how the movement versatility in speech was tinkered into place so as to give the appearance of discontinuity, in the absence of a fossil record of speech.

From Primate Calls to Speech: The Frame/Content Theory

This chapter takes as a point of departure a theory of evolution of modern human speech production based on the metaphor of 'frame and content' (MacNeilage 1998a) (see also MacNeilage 1998b, 1999). The following is a summary of the part of the theory that deals with the relation between speech and other primate call systems.

The typical call system of other primates consists of about thirty calls, each of which is a different holistic sound complex. In contrast, a typical language is made up of thousands of words, each of which tends to have the same action structure. The unique structural property of spoken words is a tendency to alternate between a relatively closed configuration of the mouth (for consonants) and a relatively open configuration (for vowels). A resultant universal unit is the syllable, defined as a vowel with a consonantal surround.

Studies of speech errors in modern adults suggest that the organisation of speech production at the cognitive level includes the placement of segmental 'content' elements (consonants and vowels) into syllable structure 'frames' (e.g. Levelt 1989). For example, a syllable frame constrains the placement of segments in spoonerisms in such a way that the displaced elements go into the same position in syllable structure that they came out of. Examples of resultant errors (Fromkin 1973) are:

Initial consonants: well made – mell wade
Vowels: add hoc – odd hack
Final consonants: top shelf – toff shelp

Perhaps most importantly, vowels and consonants never exchange with each other.

According to the frame/content (F/C) theory, this form of organisation must have evolved in the sequence 'frames, then content', rather than 'content, then frames'. The modern prohibition on serial ordering errors which mix up consonants and vowels probably evolved because the main movements associated with consonants and with vowels – mouth openings and closings produced by mandibular oscillation – are mutually exclusive. Potential motor precursors to this motor base of the cognitive frame for syllable organization (a motor frame) are types of visuofacial cyclicities widespread in other primates – lip smacks, tongue smacks, teeth chatters (Redican 1975) – which, like the syllable, involve a relatively rhythmic oscillation of the mandible between an elevated (closed mouth) and depressed (open mouth) position. This oscillation may have been borrowed from the domain of ingestive actions, where it is manifest in chewing, licking and sucking. The crucial initial step would have been the consistent pairing of mandibular oscillation with phonation (voicing) for all speech, a pairing that occasionally occurs in other primates in forms such as 'girneys' in Japanese macaques (Green 1975) and 'grunts' in baboons (Andrew 1976).

Early speech may have consisted primarily of these frame cycles either occurring alone or in a repetitive series with little or no change in detailed structure during the utterance, as is apparently typical in other primates. (We will suggest in more detail later what these frames might have been like.) Perhaps only later did the internal content of these frames move towards the complexity observed in modern speech, in which the consonants and vowels of successive syllables tend to be varied. It has been proposed that there can be frame-to-frame variety in the details of execution of communicative cyclicities of other primates (Green 1975; Andrew 1998). This is certainly an interesting claim from a phylogenetic perspective because systematic differences in internal content of frames, linked in a rule-governed way to concepts (e.g. 'lick' versus 'kill' or 'tack' versus 'cat' versus 'act') is what the action component of speech consists of.

What Is the Evidence for an Evolutionary Increase in Speech Complexity?

It is common sense that speech must have been simpler in earlier times than it is now. If the first speech output consisted primarily of single or repetitive cycles of mandibular oscillation, then the subsequent increase in complexity must have taken two forms. One of these forms must have been an increase in sound inventory. In addition, for a given inventory size there must have been an increase in the ability to vary the sequences of these sounds both within and between syllables. The evolving hominid needed to solve a variant of Lashley's classic problem of serial order in behaviour (Lashley 1951): how does an animal put together any sequence of movements?

Evidence for increase in sound inventories comes from the composition of the sound inventories of present-day languages that vary in inventory size. Lindblom and Maddieson (1988) classified consonants in the world's languages into three levels of difficulty – simple, complex and elaborated – according to the number of separate action components required in their production. They then found, in a survey of the consonant inventories of individual languages, that languages with small inventories tended to only have their 'simple' consonants. Languages with medium-sized inventories differed mainly by also including 'complex' consonants, and languages with the largest inventories tended to add 'elaborated' consonants, the most difficult category to produce. An explanation for this pattern is that languages tended to employ consonants of greater and greater difficulty as the size of their inventories increased over time.

A Possible Parallel Between Ontogeny and Phylogeny: Frames, Then Content

We have made two assertions so far. First, the first real speech production involved a combination of two motor capabilities present in all mammals – the ability to phonate and the ability to oscillate the mandible, which provided frames for speech. Second, there was a subsequent stage of increase in complexity resulting eventually in existing languages. The increase in output complexity must have been motivated by selection pressures to increase the number of possible messages while – and this is crucial for the output level – keeping the messages distinct from each other. It was this selection pressure which presumably pushed the initial language and subsequent variants into increasing motor complexity. Successive generations of hominids were faced with increasingly demanding adult models to assimilate in terms of both inventories and serial complexity, and this would have increased the time necessary to acquire speech. Speech acquisition in a modern hominid is the end state of this progression in a particular language. We will now consider the process of speech acquisition to justify and elaborate this proposal.

The Frame Stage

The first truly speechlike behavior of infants closely resembles the proposed initial frame stage of the evolution of speech. At about seven months of age a normal infant relatively suddenly begins to babble. Babbling is *defined* (Oller 1980) in terms of a relatively rhythmic alternation between an open and closed mouth accompanied by phonation, resulting in utterances such as 'bababa'. The sound repertoire in this initial stage is quite limited. Consonants are mostly labial and coronal stops ([b], [d]) and nasals ([m], [n]), and vowels are mostly in the lower left quadrant of the vowel space (vowels such as [E] in 'bed', [ae] in 'bad', [∧] in 'bud' [a] in 'father' and [ə] in 'the book'). In English this amounts to less than a quarter of the forty or so sounds of the adult language. This focus on CV syllables and repetition, with a limited sound repertoire, continues with little change through the babbling stage (7–12 months) and through the so-called fifty-word period, which lasts from about 12 to 18 months. Thus, first words are very much like babbling. Only after this does the infant begin to make major changes in the development of its repertoire of sounds and sound sequences to move towards adult levels. This first, or frame, stage will now be described in detail to support the claim that some infant output patterns resemble those of the proposed earliest phases of speech evolution.

We have called this first stage of infant speech the 'frame dominance' stage (Davis and MacNeilage 1995) because the main source of variance in output is the oscillation of the mandible with little independent contribution of the other three active speech articulators, the tongue, lips and soft palate. The most obvious sign of this frame dominance is 'reduplicative babbling'. In a single episode the infant may repeat the same open-close sequence over and over again, an action that we believe (see later) is performed solely by superimposing repeated cycles of mandibular oscillation on phonation. For example in a study of 6 infants (Davis and MacNeilage 1995), the median tendency for the second of any pair of successively produced syllables to be the same as the first was about 50%. This percentage was well above what would be expected by chance, given the overall frequencies in the corpus of the particular consonants and vowels participating in the observed CV pairs.

In addition, when the successive syllables did differ (variegation) they tended to differ in a way that could have been produced by differences in a phase of the oscillatory event, rather than as a result of a change in deployment of one of the other three articulators from syllable to syllable (Davis and MacNeilage 1995). When vowels in successive syllables differed, they tended to differ in height, perhaps resulting from an intersyllabic difference in the amplitude of the opening phase of the mandible. When consonants differed, they differed most in amount of closure, perhaps resulting from an intersyllabic difference in the amplitude of the closing phase of the mandible.

The presence of favoured patterns of co-occurrence between consonants and vowels confirmed the hypothesis that most of the variance in these early babbling patterns was the result of mandibular oscillation alone. Work done primarily in our laboratory has shown three major co-occurrence patterns between consonants and following vowels (Davis and MacNeilage 1990, 1994, 1995; Zlatic et al. 1997). Two of these patterns involve constancies in nonresting tongue position across the syllable: coronal consonants such as [d] and [n], which involve closure in the front of the mouth, tend to co-occur with front vowels such as [ɛ] and [ae]. On the rarer occasions when dorsal consonants such as [k] and [g], which involve a closure in the back of the mouth are produced, they tend to co-occur with back vowels. We have called these two patterns fronted and backed frames, respectively, and suggested that they may be achieved primarily by placing the tongue in the front or back of the mouth before the utterance even begins (MacNeilage and Davis 1990). Consequently the tongue may play only a negligible active role in the generation of these patterns.

The reason for such co-occurrences seems straightforward from a biomechanical standpoint. The tongue has a tendency to remain in a similar position in the mouth across a syllable (and between syllables too if one recalls the reduplication tendency) rather than moving from one extreme position to another. One might wish to argue that this is simply the result of immaturity. To some degree this might be true. However, if a similar tendency persists in adult languages, a different explanation is required. In a combined analysis of two studies, each of five diverse languages, by Janson (1986) and Maddieson and Precoda (1990) we found that both of these lingual CV co-occurrence patterns are also present in adult languages (MacNeilage and Davis 1993). Our contention is that if these co-occurrence patterns are sufficiently fundamental to be present in both the first speechlike attempts in acquisition and in adult languages they were probably present in the earliest hominid speech.

The third pattern found in infants is a tendency for labial consonants ([b], [m]) to co-occur with central vowels ([a], [ʌ], [ə]). In the absence of any mechanical reason for the tongue to occupy the center of the mouth when the consonantal closure is at the lips, we have called this pattern 'pure frames'. It may be produced by mandibular oscillation alone with the tongue in its rest position in the center of the mouth.

The patterns observed for labial and coronal consonants tended to be similar whether the consonants involved were oral ([b], [d]) or nasal [m], [n]) except for some nasal resonance effects on vowels in nasal contexts, which suggested that like the tongue, the soft palate tends not to change position much during these utterances (Matyear, MacNeilage and Davis 1998). These latter forms could be called nasalised frames. (Dorsal nasals such as the terminal sound in 'hang' tend to be rare at these early stages.)

In summary, babbling and early speech tend to be characterised by five types of frame – pure, fronted and backed frames, nasalised pure frames and nasalised fronted frames. For the most common of these frame types the tongue is either in a resting position (pure frames) or in what is probably the most frequent nonresting position adopted for the everyday oral activities of mammals, the fronted position. The soft palate either remains in its breathing configuration, as in the nasalised frames, or is elevated. The latter position is often said to allow more contrasts between sounds (e.g. Lieberman 1984), and there may have been a selection process that increasingly favoured it across time. We suggest that this simple picture was characteristic of the earliest stage of speech – the frame stage.

We have already alluded to the infant tendency to begin utterances with a consonant and end with a vowel, producing utterances that are strings of CV syllables. We have even found this tendency in a profoundly deaf infant prior to cochlear implantation, suggesting that it is not primarily perceptual in origin (McCaffrey et al. in press). The tendency is apparently sufficiently fundamental to be extremely common in modern languages, with the CV syllable being the only universal syllable type (Jakobson and Halle 1956). This tendency may reflect some basic constraint on deployment of the oral apparatus that transcends the demands of speech. Consequently it should be present in communicative cyclicities of other primates. Because of its fundamental status, this asymmetry in beginning and ending utterances is probably another property shared by babbling and the earliest speech.

Even the form of a departure from this CV propensity in babbling was probably present in early language. When babbled utterances end with a consonant, the consonant is relatively more often voiceless and more often a fricative than when consonants occur elsewhere in an utterance (Redford, MacNeilage and Davis 1997). This tendency is also observable in many of the world's languages (Hock 1986). Note, however, that this tendency is present even when the word does not end the utterance, but is instead embedded in continuous speech. That is, it is a word-final tendency as well as an utterance-final tendency in existing languages. When it is present word-finally the influence transcends the context (absolute final position) in which it presumably originated. These properties of babbling may be the consequence of a basic propensity to reduce the energy provided to any movement system when reaching the end of a period of use. Less respiratory or phonatory muscle contraction may tend to result in suboptimal conditions for voicing. Less articulatory force in an oral closing movement may sometimes result in a more incomplete closure. These concomitants of the cessation of movement were presumably also present in our hominid ancestors. Consequently if an early language had final consonants, it would have had this pattern.

To summarise, we have noted four properties of early infant vocal development which are sufficiently fundamental to be widely reflected in present-day languages, and consequently were probably present in the earliest speech: (1) the mandibular frame, an oral movement cycle basic to all mammals, (2) mechanically determined constraints on what consonants go with what vowels which are inherent in the biomechanics of the oral apparatus, and consequently were present before speech emerged, (3) beginning and ending movement preferences which are probably fundamental to the production of mandibular cyclicities in the oral system and (4) a necessary energy decrease when an extended movement complex is terminated. Presumably this tendency is observable in movement control systems in general.

From Frames to Frame/Content

Since the early stage of speech evolution, languages may have developed in such a way as to respond to perceptual pressures towards increase in the size of their message set. This is accomplished by the use of more sounds and sound combinations in successive generations. In what we regard as a related progression, infants acquire more sounds and sound combinations during the course of speech acquisition.

The sound repertoire of babbling consists primarily of stops, nasals, glides and vowels in the lower left quadrant of the vowel space. Sound categories that are poorly represented are fricatives, affricates and liquids, high and back vowels, and diphthongs, and a whole variety of other sounds that are uncommon in languages. This is not a subtle matter. Fricatives, affricates and liquids constitute about half of English consonants in terms of frequency of occurrence. However in an analysis of three studies of babbling in English-speaking environments involving a total of 131 infants, Locke (1983) found that no fricative, affricate or liquid occurred at a median level of more than 1% of all consonants (see also Gildersleeve, Davis and MacNeilage in press). Some people never acquire accurate production of the fricative /s/ and the liquids /l/ and /[ɹ]/. This distribution of preferences cannot be accounted for by a model according to which infants simply assimilate the pattern of relative frequencies of sounds in the ambient languages at a relatively early stage of acquisition. Most languages have the high vowels /i/ and /u/ (Maddieson 1984) presumably at least moderately frequently. The fricative /s/ occurs in most languages (Maddieson 1984), and is quite frequent in English (roughly 10% of all consonants). Liquids also occur relatively often in languages (Maddieson 1984), and are moderately frequent in English (roughly 15% of all consonants).

There is no totally objective measure of sound production difficulty. Lindblom and Maddieson (1998) classified fricatives and liquids as simple consonants. However, there is no obvious reason why the production of these sounds would be restricted by the other main source of causality of speech patterns – perception. It is generally assumed that with the possible exception of nonstrident fricatives, infants are capable of categorical perception of all consonants by the time they are a few months old (Kuhl 1985). In addition the high frequency with which infants unable to make particular sounds substitute another sound with a comparable place of articulation shows that they have a perceptual representation of the place of articulation of the sound they cannot produce.

In contrast to the situation for speech perception, factors related to speech production can be readily implicated in the low frequencies of these consonantal sound types in babbling. Fricatives, affricates and liquids each have characteristics that could contribute to an infant's inability to make them. In the case of fricatives, production requires a narrow aperture within a small range of sizes, and the establishment of an air pressure drop across the constriction sufficient to produce turbulent air flow, which is also range-limited. For affricates, it is necessary to first produce a total occlusion as in a stop and then a narrow constriction as in a fricative, both events being briefer than in simple stops and fricatives. Liquids involve a relatively unusual tongue configuration. For /l/ the tongue must simultaneously produce an occlusion in the midline and an aperture on one or both sides of the midline to produce a lateral airstream. For /ɹ/ the tongue must either be put in a retroflex configuration with the tongue tip curled backward to a degree, or it must be bunched simultaneously in regions placed one-third and two-thirds of the way along the vocal tract in order to produce the requisite acoustic effect.

In summary, fricatives require very precise articulatory positioning and air pressure control, affricates require both of these as well as an unusually brief sequence of two positions, and the liquids require complex tongue configurations. Although no objective single index of articulatory difficulty exists, in the absence of perceptual explanations for the rarity of these sounds in early speech and given that some of these sounds occur relatively often in the ambient language, the alternative explanation for their low frequencies in early speech acquisition is the presence of motor constraints. Again, we assume that if these sounds are relatively difficult for infants, they were also relatively difficult for earlier hominids, and would therefore have been added to consonant inventories only after the earliest speech.

An important way in which infants add new sounds to their inventories is by differentiation from the production of similar sounds. In perhaps the most straightforward case, mentioned earlier, before infants begin to produce fricatives reliably, they often produce stops at the same or at a closely related place of articulation. This course of development suggests that they begin to produce the fricative by modifying the degree of closure in the stop movement. Studies of the acquisition of stop consonant voicing suggest gradual changes in voice onset times towards language-specific values (Macken and Barton 1980). Both types of change illustrate a process of differentiation from available movement patterns rather than integration of existing patterns into varied lexical forms. Early hominids may have developed more movement control for more complex segments in a similar way, and languages may have added sounds in a similar way.

Infants must also increase serial complexity by placing different consonants and vowels in successive syllables. Initially, they prefer syllable reduplication, a systematic preference for repetition of the same consonant or vowel in successive syllables. If the first hominid speech was strongly reduplicative one might expect that there would be some residue of this preference in modern languages as there seems to be for lingual CV co-occurrence constraints. However, reduplication is not at all common in languages (Vihman 1978). We have recently shown that reduplication of place of articulation of consonants occurs at below chance frequencies in English and nine other languages (MacNeilage and Davis 1999). This suggests that a problem might have arisen in modern high-speed speech reception and production that was not present when speech was produced at lower speeds with smaller sound inventories. The problem may lie in the confusing effect of frequent recurrence of the same sound in working memory in both the stage of input analysis and that of output organisation. A classic finding in working memory is the confusibility of simultaneously held items with similar pronunciation (Conrad and Hull 1964). With respect to output, studies of speech errors show that they are potentiated by a 'repeated phoneme effect' (MacKay 1987): the occurrence of two examples of the same sound in close proximity tends to induce serial ordering errors.

Can anything be said in general terms about how an infant might progress from a superabundance of syllable reduplication towards some degree of prohibition of it? There are a number of reports in the literature that infants tend to make one particular relatively discrete step in departing from syllable reduplication. They begin to favor a labial-coronal (LC) consonant sequence over its opposite – 'bada' over 'daba'. In an early study, Holmes (1927) listed 14 examples of LC sequences and no examples of CL sequences in the early speech of his daughter. The infant 'Amahl' studied by Smith (1973) produced 18 LC sequences and 2 CL sequences. Ingram (1974) presented examples of the trend in one English-speaking and one French-speaking infant as part of a more general proposed strategy of 'fronting': 'That is, whatever the first consonant may be, the following one/s must be articulated either at the same point of articulation or a more posterior one' (p. 235). Ingram's analysis also included dorsal consonants, but as these tend to be a good deal rarer than labials and coronals there is less information available on them. Levelt (1994) noted a 'constraint' which 'specifically directs Labial specifications to the left edge' of words in 11 infants learning Dutch. Locke (1983) summarised individual case studies for English and Czech, in which more labial than alveolar consonants were produced in word-initial position, and more alveolar than labial consonants were produced in second position. In a study by Shibamoto and Olmstead (1978), three of four infants showed the trend in question, but one subject showed the opposite trend (4 LC sequences vs. 7 CL sequences). This is the only exception to the trend that we are aware of.

Two authors (Macken 1978; Jaeger 1997) have reported infants who produce an LC sequence even in attempting words which have the opposite sequence (e.g. 'pot' for 'top'). The consistency of this tendency and the strength of the effect in some cases led us to consider the relative frequency of this trend in the group of ten infants in the first fifty-word stage described by MacNeilage, Davis and Matyear (1997). In this study (MacNeilage et al. 1999), consonant-vowel-consonant (CVC) and consonant-vowel-consonant-vowel (CVCV) words were studied. Labial consonants were [b], [p] and [m], and coronal consonants were [d], [t] and [n]. There was a total of 252 words. Nine of the infants showed the trend towards more LC than CL sequences, and the tenth infant showed no trend. The overall ratio of LC to CL sequences was 2.55 to 1.

LC sequences are probably favoured because labial production is easier than coronal production (Jaeger 1997; MacNeilage et al. 1999). While the pure frames that contain labials are probably produced with mandibular oscillation alone, fronted frames also involve positioning the tongue in the coronal region. In addition, it has been widely reported that infants produce more labials in general in first words than in prespeech babbling regardless of whether they are reduplicated in syllables. Boysson-Bardies et al. (1992) have reported this phenomenon in infants from four different language communities, and we have observed it in eight of nine infants at the fifty-word stage (MacNeilage et al. 1997). This move towards labial preference is presumably an ease-related response to a new problem which arises when infants produce their first words – the problem of interfacing the lexicon with the motor system.

Why, in labial-coronal sequences, is the easier form placed first rather than last? We propose that an easy articulatory initiation is favored because of the high functional load involved in simultaneously *initiating* the respiratory, phonatory and articulatory components of the speech apparatus. Once the utterance is initiated, the phonatory and respiratory components presumably play a relatively uniform role in early single-word utterances, perhaps providing a window of opportunity to produce a new articulatory movement.

A dictionary count of labial-coronal preferences in ten diverse modern languages shows that the phenomenon was present in nine of them, and present at statistically significant levels in eight. (Japanese was the only exception) (MacNeilage et al. 1999). The mean ratio of labial-coronal to coronal-labial sequences was 2.18 to 1. This result suggests that the labial-coronal sequence is probably fundamental to language, and therefore was probably an important aspect of the development of frame-independent content in the history of languages.

We believe that this labial-coronal pattern is a result of self-organisation. Just as infants may more easily simulate a nonreduplicative word by beginning with a mandibular cycle not including the tongue and then adding tongue action, earlier hominids, under pressure to increase the size of the linguistic message set, could perhaps more easily have produced a new sound pattern for a new word in this manner.

The labial-coronal sequence pattern may be profitably viewed from the perspective of the 'continuity paradox' of language evolution: In a conceptual step towards the resolution of this paradox in evolutionary theory in general Gould (1977: 409) has suggested that 'external discontinuity may well be inherent in underlying continuity, provided that a system displays enough complexity'. The widespread occurrence of nonlinearities in complex systems in physics

(Prigogine and Stengers 1984) and physical aspects of biology (Kaufmann 1993) is gaining increasing attention. The events postulated here could help in the resolution of the continuity paradox for speech in the manner suggested by Gould, although at the level of *action* rather than at the genetic level suggested for Universal Grammar (Chomsky 1986) or at a strictly physical level. Starting an utterance with a simple mandibular frame and then adding tongue action allows a quantum jump in speech output complexity by providing a systematic basis for consonant variation within utterances where there may have previously been only consonant repetition. Yet the jump may have been accomplished simply by a modification of the temporal relationship between already existing movement capacities – the capacity to produce pure frames and the capacity to adopt a nonresting position of the tongue in fronted frames. While the latter capacity may have initially been restricted to frame onsets, hominids may then have become capable of implementing it after the initiation of an utterance.

To summarise our suggestions about this second expansion phase, hominids, like infants, may have added new sounds, and moved from syllable repetition to variegated syllable sequences under pressures for a larger message set, making an early quantum jump in the form of a new ability to produce labial-coronal consonant sequences.

Summary

There may be a parallel between the phylogeny of speech and its ontogeny in that both entail an initial frame stage involving very basic motor capabilities followed by a frame/content stage marked by an increase in sound inventories and serial complexity. The possibility of a parallel frame stage is suggested by evidence that some of the main features of the frame stage in infants, which are shared by modern languages, are so basic to the operation of the movement control system that they must have been influential from the very beginnings of hominid speech capacities. These features are mandibular oscillation, consonant-vowel co-occurrence constraints involving the tongue, the preference for particular beginning and end states, and phonetic preferences in final consonants. A major point of transition between the relatively simple cyclical patterns of the frame stage and the more serially complex frame/content stage may in both cases be the one between reduplicative syllabification and development of a preference for labial-coronal consonant sequences. This self-organisational step and other similar steps towards increasing serial output complexity may have made the main contribution to the present perception of a discontinuity between modern speech and the signalling systems of other primates.

Acknowledgement

This paper was prepared with support from research grant No. HD–27735 from the Public Health Service.

References

Andrew, R. J. 1976. Use of formants in the grunts of baboons and other nonhuman primates. *Annals of the New York Academy of Sciences* **280**: 673–693.

Andrew, R. J. 1998. Cyclicity in speech derived from call repetition rather than from intrinsic cyclicity of digestion. *Behavioral and Brain Sciences* **21**: 513–514.

Bickerton, D. 1990. *Language and Species*. Chicago: University of Chicago Press.

Boysson-Bardies, B., M. M. Vihman, L. Roug-Hellichius, C. Durand, I. Landberg and F. Arao 1992. Material evidence of infant selection from the target language: a cross-linguistic study. In C. Ferguson, L. Menn and C. Stoel-Gammon (eds), *Phonological Development: Models, research, implications*. Timonium, MD: York Press, pp. 369–392.

Chomsky, N. 1986. *Knowledge of Language: Its nature, origin and use*. New York: Praeger.

Conrad, R. and A. J. Hull. 1964. Information, acoustic confusion and memory span. *British Journal of Psychology* **55**: 429–432.

Davis, B. L. and P. F. MacNeilage. 1990. Acquisition of correct vowel production: a quantitative case study. *Journal of Speech and Hearing Research* **33**: 16–27.

Davis, B. L. and P. F. MacNeilage. 1994. Organization of babbling: a case study. *Language and Speech* **37**: 341–355.

Davis, B. L. and P. F. MacNeilage. 1995. The articulatory basis of babbling. *Journal of Speech and Hearing Research* **38**: 1199–1211.

Fromkin, V. A. (ed) 1973. *Speech Errors as Linguistic Evidence*. The Hague: Mouton.

Gildersleeve, C., B. L. Davis and P. F. MacNeilage. In press. Production constraints in babbling: implications for fricatives, affricates and liquids. *Applied Psycholinguistics*.

Gould, S. J. 1977. *Ontogeny and Phylogeny*. Cambridge, MA: Belknap.

Green, S. 1975. Variations of vocal pattern with social situation in the Japanese monkey (*Macaca fuscata*): a field study. In L. A. Rosenblum (ed), *Primate Behavior, Vol. 4: Developments in field and laboratory research*. New York: Academic, pp. 1–102.

Hock, H. H. 1986. *Principles of Historical Linguistics*. The Hague: Mouton de Gruyter.

Holmes, U. T. 1927. The phonology of an English speaking child. *American Speech* **11**: 219–225.

Ingram, D. 1974. Fronting in child phonology. *Journal of Child Language* **1**: 233–241.

Jaeger, J. 1997. How to say 'Grandma': the problem of developing phonological representations. *First Language* **17**: 1–29.

Jakobson, R. and M. Halle. 1956. *Fundamentals of Language*. The Hague: Mouton.

Janson, T. 1986. Cross-linguistic trends in CV sequences. *Phonology Yearbook* **3**: 179–196.

Kaufmann, S. A. 1993. *The Origins of Order: Self-organization and selection in evolution*. Oxford: Oxford University Press.

Kay, R. F., M. Cartmill and M. Balow. 1998. The hypoglossal canal and the origin of human vocal behavior. *Proceedings of the National Academy of Sciences* **95**: 5417–5419.

Kuhl, P. K. 1985. Categorization of speech by infants. In J. Mehler and R. Fox (eds), *Neonate Cognition: Beyond the blooming buzzing confusion*. Hillsdale, NJ: Erlbaum, pp. 231–262.

Lashley, K. S. 1951. The problem of serial order in behavior. In L. A. Jeffress (ed), *Cerebral Mechanisms in Behavior: The Hixon symposium*. New York: Wiley, pp. 112–145.

Levelt, C. C. 1994. *On the Acquisition of Place*. The Hague: Holland Institute of Generative Linguistics.

Levelt, W. J. M. 1989. *Speaking: From intention to articulation*. Cambridge, MA: MIT Press.

Lindblom, B. and I. Maddieson. 1988. Phonetic universals in consonant systems. In L. Hyman and C. N. Li (eds), *Language, Speech and Mind*. London: Routledge, pp. 62–78.

Locke, J. L. 1983. *Phonological Acquisition and Change*. New York: Academic.

Macken, M. 1978. Permitted complexity in phonological development: one child's acquisition of Spanish consonants. *Lingua* **44**: 219–253.

Macken, M. and D. Barton. 1980. A longitudinal study of the acquisition of the voicing contrast in American-English word-initial stops, as measured by voice onset time. *Journal of Child Language* **7**: 41–72.

MacKay, D. G. 1987. *The Organization of Perception and Action: A theory for language and other cognitive sciences*. New York: Springer.

MacNeilage, P. F. 1998a. The Frame/Content theory of evolution of speech production. *Behavioral and Brain Sciences* **21**: 499–511.

MacNeilage, P. F. 1998b. Evolution of the mechanism of language output: comparative neurology of vocal and manual communication. In J. R. Hurford, M. Studdert-Kennedy and C. Knight (eds), *Approaches to the Evolution of Language: Social and cognitive bases*. Cambridge: Cambridge University Press, pp. 222–241.

MacNeilage, P. F. 1999. Whatever happened to articulate speech? In M. C. Corballis and S. Lea (eds), *Evolution of the Hominid Mind*. Oxford: Oxford University Press, pp. 116–137.

MacNeilage, P. F. and B. L. Davis. 1990. Acquisition of speech: frames, then content. In M. Jeannerod (ed), *Attention and Performance XIII*. Hillsdale, NJ: Erlbaum, pp. 453–475.

MacNeilage, P. F. and B. L. Davis. 1993. Motor explanations of babbling and early speech patterns. In B. de Boysson-Bardies, S. de Schonen, P. Jusczyk, P. MacNeilage and J. Morton (eds), *Changes in Speech and Face Processing in Infancy: A glimpse at developmental mechanisms of cognition*. Dordrecht: Kluwer, pp. 341–352.

MacNeilage, P. F. and B. L. Davis. 1999. Consonant (vowel) consonant sequences in early words. *Proceedings of the Fourteenth International Congress of Phonetic Sciences*, San Francisco, CA: The Regents of the University of California, pp. 2489–2492.

MacNeilage, P. F., B. L. Davis, A. Kinney and C. L. Matyear. 1999. Origin of serial output complexity in speech. *Psychological Science*, **10**: 459–460.

MacNeilage P. F., B. L. Davis and C. L. Matyear. 1997. Babbling and first words: phonetic similarities and differences. *Speech Communication* **22**: 269–277.

Maddieson, I. and K. Precoda. 1990. Syllable structure and phonetic models. *Phonology* **9**: 45–60.

Matyear, C. L., P. F. MacNeilage and B. L. Davis. 1998. Nasalization of vowels in nasal environments in babbling: evidence for frame dominance. *Phonetica* **55**: 1–17.

McCaffrey, H. L, B. L. Davis, P. F. MacNeilage and D. von Hapsburg. In press. Effects of multichannel cochlear implantation on the organization of early speech. *The Volta Review*.

Oller, D. K. 1980. The emergence of the sounds of speech in infancy. In G. Yeni-Komshian, J. F. Kavanagh and C. Ferguson (eds), *Child Phonology, Vol. 1: Production*. New York: Academic, pp. 93–112.

Prigogine, I. and I. Stengers. 1984. *Order out of Chaos: Man's new dialogue with nature*. New York: Bantam.

Redford, M., P. F. MacNeilage and B. L. Davis. 1998. Production constraints on utterance-final consonant characteristics in babbling. *Phonetica* **54**: 172–184.

Redican, W. K. 1975. Facial expressions in nonhuman primates. In L. A. Rosenblum (ed), *Primate Behavior, Vol. 4: Developments in field and laboratory research*. New York: Academic, pp. 103–194.

Shibamoto, J. S. and D. L. Olmstead. 1978. Lexical and syllabic patterns in phonological acquisition. *Journal of Child Language* **5**: 417–446.

Smith, N. V. 1973. *The Acquisition of Phonology: A case study*. Cambridge: Cambridge University Press.

Vihman, M. M. 1978. Consonant harmony: its scope and function in child language. In J. H. Greenberg (ed), *Universals of Human Language, Vol. 2: Phonology*. Stanford: Stanford University Press, pp. 281–334.

Zlatic, L., P. F. MacNeilage, C. Matyear and B. L. Davis. 1997. Babbling of twins in a bilingual environment. *Applied Psycholinguistics* **18**: 455–471.

10

Evolutionary Implications of the Particulate Principle: Imitation and the Dissociation of Phonetic Form from Semantic Function

MICHAEL STUDDERT-KENNEDY

Introduction

At least three unique properties distinguish language from other systems of animal communication: unlimited semantic scope, freedom from control by identifiable external stimuli (displaced reference), and transduction into alternative perceptuomotor modalities (writing, fingerspelling). All three properties, it will be argued, depend on dissociating phonetic form from semantic function. Such a dissociation arose with the emergence of vocal imitation, a necessary condition of the protolanguage that evolved when our hominid ancestors chanced on 'the particulate principle of self-diversifying systems' (Abler 1989). This is a physical principle to which all natural systems that, in Humboldt's (1836/1972: 70) famous phrase, 'make infinite use of finite means' (physics, chemistry, genetics, language) necessarily conform. In such systems, discrete units from a finite set of meaningless elements (e.g. atoms, chemical bases, phonetic segments) are repeatedly sampled, permuted and combined to yield larger units (e.g. molecules, genes, words) that are higher in a hierarchy and both different and more diverse in structure and function than their constituents.

The particulate principle rationalises both the hierarchical structure of language and the discrete combinatorial mechanisms on which the hierarchy is raised. The principle has many implications for the evolution of language. For example, it casts doubt on the likely communicative scope of any prelinguistic symbolic system, limited to a purely analog representation of the world (e.g. Donald 1998). And the necessity for hierarchical organisation discourages the notion that syntax might have emerged before the combinatorial mechanisms of phonology were well established (Bickerton 1998: 344). My concern in what follows, however, is with implications of the particulate principle for the separation of phonetic form from semantic function, and for the emergence of an independent level of phonetic representation, preadaptive not only for displaced

161

reference and syntax, but also for the very much later cultural development of writing.

We begin by briefly considering the language hierarchy as it has generally been conceived in recent decades.

The Nature of the Language Hierarchy

Duality of Patterning

Fifty years ago André Martinet (1949) coined the phrase 'la double articulation', to describe the two-level hierarchy of phonology and syntax that characterises all human languages. Since then, 'duality of patterning', as Hockett (1958) termed the concept, has come to be generally recognised as critical to the unbounded semantic scope of language. At the lower level of the hierarchy, phonology evades the limits of a finite vocal apparatus by permuting and combining discrete articulatory actions to construct an unbounded lexicon of words. At the higher level, syntax permutes and combines words to represent a potential infinity of relations among objects, events and concepts. Despite general agreement on these functions, the questions of whether or why duality is necessary for language, why constituents are discrete and why they form a hierarchy of independent levels, were first addressed only a decade ago by William Abler (1989). The starting point for Abler's work was the relation between genetics and language.

Genes and Language

The first to see a possible parallel between the gene and language was the Austrian physicist Erwin Schrödinger (Jacob 1977; Pollack 1994). A decade before the structure of the DNA molecule was described, Schrödinger (1944) correctly predicted that the gene would prove to be a molecule with the structure of an aperiodic crystal. The molecule would offer, through rearrangements of its component atoms, a range of isomeric variants analogous to those offered by rearrangements of dots and dashes in Morse code. The vast combinatorial resources of the gene's 'code-script' (Schrödinger 1944: 62) would then suffice to specify all the diverse lines of development of every structure in the living world.

Since Schrödinger wrote, the analogy between gene and language has become a textbook commonplace (e.g. Pollack 1994), and a topic of papers by both linguists (e.g. Jakobson 1970) and biologists (e.g. Jacob 1977), although satisfactorily explained by none. Jakobson, for example, remarked: 'among all the information-carrying systems, the genetic code and the verbal code are the only ones based upon the use of discrete components which, by themselves, are devoid of inherent meaning but serve to constitute the minimal senseful unit, i.e., entities endowed with their own intrinsic meaning in the given code' (1970: 438). But how and why the parallel arose are questions he left unanswered.

Jacob went further, recognising that the principle of combining discrete units is 'not limited to language and heredity . . . [but] . . . appears to operate in nature each time there is a question of generating a large diversity of structures using a restricted number of building blocks' (1977: 188). Writing of language and heredity, Jacob also emphasised, that 'for such a system to function implies that the basic units, phonemes or chemical radicals, are by themselves devoid of meaning' (ibid.). As we shall see, this fact is crucial for understanding the early evolution of language.

Yet even Jacob stopped short of explaining why, as he wrote, 'Such a method of construction appears to be the only logical one' (1977: 188). For a particulate genetics Fisher (1930) had already supplied the logic. Fisher reasoned that, if characteristics of parents blended, they would be lost in the average of their offspring, and the characteristics of the offspring would lie between, not outside, those of their parents; variation, critical to the process of natural selection, would then diminish from generation to generation. In fact, of course, variation is conserved, or even increased, across generations, and parental characteristics may reappear unmodified in their descendants. From such facts, Fisher (like Mendel before him) inferred that biological inheritance was effected by a particulate mechanism, an inference confirmed by the description of the DNA molecule some twenty years later. Fisher's logic was the impetus for Abler's (1989) independently developed account of the gene-language parallel, which subsumes both systems under a single physical principle.

The Particulate Principle of Self-Diversifying Systems

Abler's key insights were two. First, Fisher's arguments concerning the mechanism of inheritance could be extended to the hierarchical structures of physics, chemistry and language. All four domains have an unbounded range of properties, and so 'must be based on particles rather than on blending constituents, because blending constituents would form combinations whose properties lie between rather than outside, the properties of the original constituents' (Abler 1989: 1). Here, it is to sustain variation at each level of the hierarchy that the units combined must be discrete.

Abler's second insight was that von Humboldt's (1836/1972) characterisation of language could be extended to the hierarchical structures of physics, chemistry and genetics. All four domains exploit discrete combinatorial mechanisms to 'make infinite use of finite means' (p. 70) by 'a synthetic process . . . [that] . . . creates something . . . not present *per se* in any of the associated constituents' (p. 67). It is this 'creativity', this automatic emergence of novelty, that Abler terms 'self-diversifying'. Here, then, it is for the emergence of novel structures and functions at each level of the hierarchy that the units combined must be discrete. Only because units do not blend and disappear, but combine as integral units to form new integral units, can novel structures arise whose properties are not limited by, and cannot be predicted from, the properties of their constituents.

'We cannot derive the properties of common salt from those of sodium and chlorine, nor of a protein from the genes that control its formation; in language we cannot derive the meaning of a word from the phonetic elements that compose it, nor the meaning of a proposition from the lexical meanings of its words without regard to their syntactic grouping' (Studdert-Kennedy 1998: 204). Because units cannot be derived from their constituents, each level of structure is subject to new and characteristic rules of combination, giving rise to a separate independent level of function. Hence the independence of syntax and phonology.

For a fuller account of the particulate principle than is possible here readers may turn to Abler (1989) and Studdert-Kennedy (1998). For present purposes, perhaps enough has been said to make clear that duality of patterning is not a unique cognitive property peculiar to language, but reflects rather a general physical and mathematical property of the natural world to which all self-diversifying systems necessarily conform. Under the particulate principle the axioms of earlier formulations of duality – combinatorial mechanisms and independence of successive levels in the hierarchy – receive a rational explanation.

The Dissociation of Sound and Meaning

Nonetheless, despite striking correspondences across domains, language differs from its particulate congeners in several respects. Most important are differences in the relations between form and function. For example, although we may not be able to predict the properties of a chemical compound from its component elements, or the functions of a gene from the sequence of its base pairs, these properties and functions evidently emerge from, and are in some sense intrinsic to, the physical systems of which they are parts: structure and function are inseparable, if not identical. In language, by contrast, form and function arise from distinct and incommensurate sources. The meaning of a word, or of a sentence, does not emerge from phonetic or syntactic structure as, say, water 'emerges' from the structures of hydrogen and oxygen. Rather, meaning is assigned by some arbitrary, extralinguistic process within a language community. Thus, while the particulate principle affords the hierarchical *structure* necessary to support the unlimited semantic scope of language, semantic *function* itself enters the system from outside.

The dissociation of sound and meaning has no precedent in other animal vocalisations, whose signal inventories are limited and not subject to cultural modification. The dissociation is, in fact, the critical discontinuity that separates human language from other primate systems of vocal communication – critical because, as we have seen, meaningless units at the base of a hierarchy are essential to operation of the particulate principle in all its domains. In language, it is only if they are meaningless that the same units can be repeatedly permuted and combined to form different units of meaning. And only because the basic units are meaningless can the meanings assigned to their combinations be arbitrary – as required for a lexicon of unbounded semantic scope.

The key evolutionary questions then are: What are the basic units, and how did they come to be without meaning?

Units and the Vocal Mechanism

Gestures

Several authors have proposed that the basic units of language are neither phonemes (consonants and vowels) nor their descriptive features, but gestures, such as those adopted by the theory of articulatory phonology (Browman and Goldstein 1986, 1992; cf. Bell 1911; Fowler 1996; Liberman and Mattingly 1985, 1989; Lindblom 1992, 1998; Saltzman and Munhall 1989; Studdert-Kennedy 1987, 1991, 1998; Studdert-Kennedy and Goodell 1995). Gestures are the irreducible, objectively observable units of phonetic action and perception, from which segments and syllables are formed. In the framework of articulatory phonology, a gesture is a constriction formed by lips, tongue, velum or larynx, at a certain point in the vocal tract. The function of a gesture is to shape a vocal tract configuration, controlling the flow of air so as to produce a characteristic pattern of sound. How did such gestures come to take their place at the base of the language hierarchy?

From Syllable to Gesture to Segment

Elsewhere I have sketched a possible line of phonetic evolution, modelled on the ontogeny of speech development over the first years of life (Studdert-Kennedy

1987, 1991, 1998; see also Lindblom 1992, 1998; MacNeilage and Davis, this volume). Briefly, the model takes the protosyllable, a single cycle in the repeated closed-open cycles of the mandible in a primate call, as the original unit of both articulatory action and meaning (cf. MacNeilage 1998a, 1998b). Under pressure for lexical diversity (and, as will be argued, for vocal imitation), gestures emerged from the holistic protosyllable by differentiation of the vocal apparatus into a coordinated system of more or less independent articulators; gestures were selected for acoustic distinctiveness and articulatory economy, including ease of combination and sequencing (Carré and Studdert-Kennedy 1998; cf. Lindblom 1986).

As the lexicon grew, segments (consonants and vowels) emerged to facilitate rapid, successive activation of recurrent multigestural routines within the syllabic frame. Such routines arose because certain combinations of the limited set of physiologically possible laryngeal and supralaryngeal gestures repeatedly occurred either simultaneously (as in the labial/lingual and glottal gestures for voiceless fricatives) or very closely overlapping in time (as in the labial/lingual and glottal gestures for voiced and voiceless stops, or the labial and lingual gestures for rounded vowels). Separate instructions for their simultaneous or rapidly successive and overlapping activation were then readily superseded by an integral instruction for the entire gestural constellation (i.e. segment) of which they were a part. (For fuller discussion of segments and gestural coordination, see Fowler 1996: 530ff.).

Critical to this posited evolutionary sequence and to the emergence of the gesture-segment-syllable hierarchy at the meaningless base of language was the evolution of vocal learning, or imitation. But before we come to this we must consider the vocal mechanism itself.

The Vocal Mechanism

We should not underestimate the complexity of the vocal mechanism nor the importance of its idiosyncratic properties for the evolution of language. In our preoccupation with the challenge of syntax we may be tempted to take evolution of the vocal mechanism and of its extraordinary motor facility for granted. Carstairs-McCarthy (1998: 291), for example, assumes that descent of the larynx (whether a side effect of bipedal posture or, as Lieberman (1984) has argued, directly selected for increased phonetic scope) sufficed 'to produce the full range of modern articulatory possibilities'. But 'the full range' is not merely a matter of an enlarged pharynx and the novel configurations it affords.

If we look at fluent speech as a purely motor skill, we note several salient characteristics. First is the rhythmic cycle of syllables. Cyclicity characterises all motor activities, most obviously locomotion; in speech the metrical beat of the syllables rests on finely modulated control of the respiratory apparatus, a degree of control apparently absent in other primates (Lenneberg 1967: ch. 3; MacLarnon and Hewitt 1998). Other characteristics are speed and precision: a typical rate of fluent speech (between pauses) is of the order of 6–7 syllables, or 10–15 segments, per second (Liberman et al. 1967). There would be nothing remarkable here perhaps, if the movements were repetitive – a musician's tremolo finger movements can reach 16 Hz, and hummingbirds beat their wings at over 70 Hz. Speakers, however, execute different movements of different articulators within a syllable, and different patterns of movement from syllable to syllable, all precisely phased and coordinated within a tolerance of millimetres and milliseconds.

A final characteristic of speech as a motor activity is that the form and sequence of its movements are arbitrary and internally controlled. Again, if the movements were guided by the environment, as in the swift manoeuvres of a downhill skier, or of a bird through the branches of a tree, we might find nothing extraordinary in speech. But as it is, the rapidly changing patterns of articulation, carried on the brisk beat of the syllable and on the slower rhythm of the respiratory cycle, all under endogenous control, call for a specialised premotor planning mechanism perhaps unique among motor systems. Evolution of this system, including a capacity for short- and long-term phonetic memory, must have entailed sustained selective pressure over many generations, not only for a growing lexicon, but for increasingly lengthy word strings.

We turn now to a crucial, though largely unrecognised, factor in the evolution of the speech motor system, the capacity for vocal imitation.

Imitation

The role of imitation in language acquisition has often been discounted, because, in learning to construct sentences, children clearly do more than repeat what they have heard: they extract and apply rules. They can do so, however, only because they have previously built a repertoire of words by copying their companions. The preservation of local dialects from generation to generation, not only in the words chosen for use, but in their characteristic phonetic variants, attests to the accuracy of the copies. Here I shall argue that imitation was the critical factor not only in building a lexicon, but in precipitating the dissociation of phonetic form and semantic function.

To imitate, say, a facial expression or an utterance of a conspecific is to transduce an optic or acoustic pattern into muscular actions that yield an acceptable replica of the model. No doubt the process entails empathetic recognition of a conspecific's acts as potentially one's own by means of some supramodal representation of body organs, such as Meltzoff and Moore (1997) propose in their model of facial imitation. But how, in physiological fact, do light and sound get into the muscles (Michael Turvey, in conversation)?

Studies of macaques have isolated brain cells that respond to social events, including facial displays and locomotion by a conspecific or a human (e.g. Brothers, Ring and Kling 1990). Recently, Rizzolatti and his colleagues (Rizzolatti et al. 1996) have found so-called mirror neurons in macaque cortex that fire not only when a monkey grasps or manipulates food, but also when it sees a human experimenter do the same. Moreover, these neurons lie in an area of macaque cortex arguably homologous with human Broca's area. Rizzolatti and Arbib (1998) review data from transcranial magnetic stimulation and positron emission tomography studies that demonstrate a mirror system for manual grasping in humans. They postulate 'a fundamental mechanism for action recognition' (Rizzolatti and Arbib 1998: 190) in both monkey and human, and discuss the implications of such a system for the evolution of manual gesture and speech.

Here we consider what a specialised capacity for vocal imitation implies behaviourally and cognitively for the evolution of speech and language.

Vocal Imitation

The value of imitation to a member of a social species is not hard to imagine. Yet few species imitate. The apes, and some monkeys, perhaps copy general bodily actions, but vocal learning is peculiar to a few species of songbirds, certain marine mammals, and humans (Hauser 1996).

We may never know when, or how, human vocal imitation began to evolve. We should perhaps expect it to have been a factor in, and to have coevolved with, differentiation of the vocal apparatus. Certainly, we cannot doubt that imitation was critical to the early evolution of language. Without it there could have been no shared vocabulary of learned meanings, and so no basis for the evolution of propositional utterance and syntax. As we shall see, other properties preadaptive for syntax, for displaced reference and for the cultural development of writing are also implicit in the process of imitation itself.

The Process of Vocal Imitation and the Loss of Meaning

When a child learns to say a word, it finds in the acoustic patterns of its companions' speech detailed specifications for a corresponding pattern of motor organisation. Imitating a word entails (conceptually) at least three steps: (1) analysis of the sound pattern into its underlying articulatory components,

(2) storage of the analysed structure for a shorter or longer period, depending on the delay between model and copy and (3) reassembly of the components in their correct temporal sequence.

Notice that the meaning of the word plays no part. The desire to communicate meaning may motivate vocal imitation, but meaning contributes nothing to the act itself. Imitation is a purely formal process that temporarily strips the model of whatever semantic function it may have, reducing it to its bare perceptuomotor components. Here then in the act of imitation, we may reasonably surmise, is where structure and function first came to be dissociated in hominid communication. We will return to this point.

First we should note that breaking a word into its articulatory components does not automatically set those components free for independent use in another word. In fact, early words in the speech of modern children often seem to be holistic patterns, quite unrelated to one another. For example, a young child who says *no* correctly may substitute [m] for [n] in *night*, and [b] for [m] in *moo* (Ferguson and Farwell 1975); or a child who says [nʌt] correctly in *doughnut* may say [pʌp] for *nut* in *peanut* (Studdert-Kennedy and Goodell 1995). Thus, gestures firmly executed in one context are not necessarily ready for use in another.

A striking example of motoric analysis without independent control of the analysed components comes from a deaf boy learning American Sign Language (ASL) (Akamatsu 1985). His deaf mother, lacking an ASL sign for the name of a supermarket, 'Safeway', habitually fingerspelled it as a rapid string of seven hand configurations corresponding to the English letters of the name. The boy learned to recognise the string as an integral sign, and to reproduce it; only when he was nine years old and was himself learning to fingerspell did he realize that the sign he had learned was, in fact, a string of discrete, but coarticulated handshapes (cf. Armstrong, Stokoe and Wilcox 1995: 106ff.) Despite habitual use, the handshapes had not escaped from their context.

Early acts of hominid vocal imitation may then have been holistic, or formulaic, routines. Target utterances were perhaps analysed, stored and replicated as a sequence of gestures, but they were not yet represented as a sequence of independent phonetic elements that could be marshalled for use in other contexts (cf. Wray, this volume). At this stage of evolution (as in development) phonetic structure was merely implicit in the mechanism of imitation.

The Emergence of an Independent Level of Phonetic Representation

We do not know the stages by which the vocal tract gradually differentiated into the six active articulators of modern languages (larynx, tongue root, body and blade (or tip), velum and lips). But it is evident that emergence of the gesture as a commutable unit follows naturally from the limited potential of the vocal apparatus. Each articulator has relatively few motorically and perceptually discriminable states. Moreover, none of the articulators works alone; several are active and all are at least passively engaged in every utterance (Mattingly 1991). Speakers could therefore build a sizeable repertoire of words, or formulaic utterances, only by enlisting the same articulator for the same gesture again and again in different contexts. As the number of different contexts for the same gesture increased, speed and economy of motor organisation precipitated the recurrent element as a unit of motor control, independent of its context (Lindblom 1992, 1998; Studdert-Kennedy 1987, 1991). As crystallisation of recurrent gestures (and of recurrent constellations of gestures, or segments) pervaded speakers' lexicons, there emerged a new level of representation, intermediate between signal and message.

We have been describing the elements of the newly emerged level in motor terms, on the assumption that, as argued elsewhere (Studdert-Kennedy 1998), it was through particulation of the vocal machinery that gestures first arose; but it is through their acoustic and/or optic effects that a listener recognises a speaker's gestures. The intermediate representation must therefore have been isomorphic with both act and percept and to that extent abstract; the representation must also have been specific to speech, that is, phonetic. The consequences of a new independent and abstract phonetic level, induced by the evolution of vocal imitation, ramified through much of what eventually became language.

Phonetic Memory: A Preadaptation for Displaced Reference and Syntax

In the early stages of the evolution of vocal imitation (as in the early stages of its development in the modern child) the phonetic representation of an utterance was perhaps stored little longer than necessary to execute the copy, and so little longer than the event that elicited the utterance. Lengthening the store, so that the phonetic form of a word, once learned, became a permanent entry in a speaker's vocal repertoire, had the obvious advantage of enabling a speaker to reproduce a word without a model. With the separation of a word from its model, and so from the original occasion of its use, its phonetic form became freestanding, as it were, and open to arbitrary shifts in meaning. Arguably, then, the separation of form from meaning, an incidental consequence of imitation, was the first step away from vocalisations expressing current emotional state towards vocal units ('words') of arbitrary and displaced reference. Certainly, an independent phonetic memory is necessary, though obviously not sufficient, for a sizeable vocabulary of displaced reference.

Both short- and long-term phonetic memory were also essential preadaptations for syntax. Long-term phonetic memory was necessary both to formulate and to understand the meaning of a syntactically organised utterance. Short-term, or working, phonetic memory was necessary, in speaking, to hold upcoming words in premotor store for rapid execution. Ample evidence for such a store has come from spoonerisms and other speech errors where single words, syllables, segments or gestures are exchanged or misplaced. In listening, working phonetic memory was necessary to hold words, without final commitment to meaning, while computing their syntactic relations. Without a preadapted system for storing phonetic structure, independently of its meaning, syntax could not have begun to evolve. But what exactly do we mean by phonetic structure? Where do the constraints that distinguish a word from a random string of gestures come from?

The Syllabic Origins of Phonetic Structure

Gestures and segments are not so abstract as to have entirely lost their moorings in the syllable from which they are derived: the major phonetic classes, consonants and vowels, are in fact defined by their role in controlling the flow of air over the course of a syllable. Consonants, formed by complete or narrow constrictions at the onset or offset of a syllable, impede the flow of air; vowels, the nucleus of the syllable, allow air to flow freely. Implicit therefore in the repeated opening and closing of the vocal tract over the course of an utterance is a pattern of gestural alternation that specifies the boundaries of possible words in the sequence. Thus, in evolution, the syllable or syllable string, the integrative articulatory 'frame' of which meaningless gestures and segments came to be the 'content' (MacNeilage 1998b), retained its initial status as the basic unit of meaning by virtue of the restrictions it imposed on segmental sequence.

To make this clear, consider a random number table where, by definition, we cannot predict a number, or any string of numbers, however many preceding numbers we know. Such a table is devoid of structure because all possible sequences of numbers can occur. Suppose, however, that we compose the table from an English discourse, substituting a pair of digits from 01 to roughly 40, for each phoneme. The table will now be structured because not all possible sequences of numbers can occur: the sequences will reflect restrictions on number combinations imposed by the syllable structure of English. Skilled cryptanalysts would now quickly see that the distribution of numbers was not random and, if they knew that the coded text was English, they could apply the rules of English syllable structure (and, of course, their knowledge of English words) to recover the discourse. (It was, in fact, by assuming that the language was

Greek, and the unit of transcription the syllable, that Michael Ventris deciphered Minoan Linear B (Chadwick 1958).)

My point here is that a word is defined in the first instance by its phonetic structure, secondarily by its semantic function. Definition by meaning is secondary, because meaning is unstable and varies with context. Phonetic structure, by contrast, is invariant (within the tolerance of diachronic and synchronic variation), because it arises from restrictions on the combination of gestures imposed by the biophysical structure of the syllable (MacNeilage and Davis, this volume).

Let me emphasise that I am not suggesting that all phonological constraints arise as phonetic constraints from the syllable. My point is merely that in evolution the vocal machinery itself was the only possible initial source of constraint on combinations of prephonological gestures and segments. Subsequently, of course, a diverse array of universal phonetic and language-specific phonological constraints arose, from other aspects of linguistic function, to supplement the universal rubric of the syllable.

Whatever the source of phonetic and phonological constraints, it is these constraints, not meaning, that determine whether a string of segments is, or is not, a possible word in a particular language. Recognition of this fact, many thousands of years later, was a critical step in the cultural development of writing and reading.

The Particulate Basis of Writing and Reading

Language is unique among systems of animal communication in its transduction into an alternative perceptuomotor modality. I use 'transduction' rather than 'translation' because my concern here is with writing, and writing is not an independent natural language, like a sign language, that happens to use hand and eye instead of mouth and ear. Rather, writing is parasitic on speech.

The earliest forms of writing were syllabic (Gelb 1952). Here an ambiguity may arise, in a morphosyllabic language such as Chinese, where every syllable is a unit of meaning (morpheme), as to whether a written symbol refers to the syllable as morpheme or as unit of phonetic structure. The ambiguity is reflected in the widespread, but mistaken belief that Chinese characters represent meaning directly without phonological mediation (DeFrancis 1989).

Early forms of pictographic writing did indeed represent meaning directly. But with the recognition of syllabic homonyms (syllables with the same sound, but different meanings) there became available the 'rebus principle' (DeFrancis 1989: 50), by which a syllabic symbol could be used to refer not to the syllable's meaning, but to its sound. For example, in rebus writing the symbol for the word *date* (fruit) might be used to represent the word *date* (day). By this device form and function were dissociated in writing, as they had been dissociated in speaking by the emergence of imitation.

With the invention of the rebus, therefore, true writing, capable of representing the full semantic range of language, became possible. Writing could now exploit its own form of the particulate principle with a small set of meaningless symbols, whether for syllables or for phonemes. In fact, all full writing systems (DeFrancis 1989: ch. 2) represent the phonological forms of words, with varying degrees of explicitness, depending on the language. No system represents meaning alone, or meaning without phonological mediation. From what we have argued, a purely semantic representation of any language is indeed impossible, because a phonetic structure is intrinsic to every word. Every language has phonologically permissible words that happen not to have been assigned a meaning (so-called nonsense words). No language has words that have meaning, but have not yet been assigned phonological form. Writing systems therefore differ from one another only in the phonological level (syllable or phoneme) and in the precision of their phonological representation.

Apart from the syllabaries of Chinese and Chinese-influenced languages and of a few African and Amerindian languages, alphabets derived from Phoenician consonantal orthography are the only systems in general use today (Gelb 1952: 184). The letters of an alphabet represent neither sounds nor articulations, but phonological entities (phonemes) at a higher level of abstraction than the perceptuomotor entities that we must posit to account for imitation. Each phoneme encompasses a class of phonetic variants, or allophones, that vary across phonetic contexts, dialects and even individual speakers. What is important here is that alphabetic writing represents the phonological form of a word, not its meaning. That is why we can read a text without understanding it, but cannot understand a text without reading it.

Thus, the dissociation of meaning and phonetic structure, precipitated by the evolution of vocal imitation, planted a preadaptive seed no less critical for the relatively recent cultural development of writing than for the biological evolution of displaced reference and syntax, tens of thousands of years earlier.

Summary and Conclusion

Duality of patterning, the two-level hierarchy of phonology and syntax on which the unbounded semantic scope of language rests, is a special case of the particulate principle to which all systems that 'make infinite use of finite means' (physics, chemistry, genetics, language) necessarily conform. At the base of all such systems are discrete, meaningless (intrinsically functionless) units on which, by successive combinatorial mechanisms, a hierarchy is raised.

This chapter proposes articulatory gestures as the basic units of spoken language from which phonetic segments and syllables are formed. Dissociation of phonetic form from semantic function, the critical discontinuity that separates language from all other systems of animal communication, arose as a side-effect of the evolution of vocal imitation, a capacity unique among primates to humans. To imitate a word, a speaker must analyse, store and reassemble its gestures, a purely formal process that temporarily strips the model of whatever semantic function it may have, reducing it to its perceptuomotor components.

Imitation thus gave rise to a new level of processing between signal and message, comprising a phonetic representation and a mechanism for phonetic storage. The short-term phonetic store necessary for immediate imitation proved to be a preadaptive step toward the short- and long-term phonetic memory systems necessary for displaced reference and syntax and ultimately for the cultural development of writing and reading many thousands of years later.

Acknowledgements

My thanks to William Abler, Carol Fowler, James Hurford, Alvin Liberman and Ignatius Mattingly for instructive comments on earlier versions. Preparation of the paper was supported in part by Haskins Laboratories.

References

Abler, W. 1989. On the particulate principle of self-diversifying systems. *Journal of Social and Biological Structures* **12**: 1–13.

Akamatsu, C. T. 1985. Fingerspelling formulae: a word is more or less the sum of its letters. In W. Stokoe and V. Volterra (eds), *SLR'83: Sign language research*. Silver Spring, MD: Linstok, pp. 126–132.

Armstrong, D. F., W. C. Stokoe and S. E. Wilcox. 1995. *Gesture and the Nature of Language*. Cambridge: Cambridge University Press.

Bell, A. G. 1911. *The Mechanism of Speech*. New York: Funk and Wagnalls.

Bickerton, D. 1998. Catastrophic evolution: the case for a single step from protolanguage to full human language. In J. R. Hurford, M. Studdert-Kennedy and C. Knight (eds), *Approaches to the Evolution of Language: Social and cognitive bases*. Cambridge: Cambridge University Press, pp. 341–358.

Brothers, L., B. Ring and A. Kling. 1990. Response of neurons in the macaque amygdala to complex social stimuli. *Behavioural Brain Research* **41**: 199–213.

Browman, C. P. and L. Goldstein. 1986. Towards an articulatory phonology. *Phonology Yearbook* **2**: 219–252.

Browman, C. P. and L. Goldstein. 1992. Articulatory phonology: an overview. *Phonetica* **49**: 155–180.

Carré, R. and M. Studdert-Kennedy. 1998. The origin of speech gestures. Paper read at the Second International Conference on the Evolution of Language, University of East London.

Carstairs-McCarthy, A. 1998. Synonymy avoidance, phonology and the origin of syntax. In J. R. Hurford, M. Studdert-Kennedy and C. Knight (eds), *Approaches to the Evolution of Language: Social and cognitive bases*. Cambridge: Cambridge University Press, pp. 279–296.

Chadwick, J. 1958. *The Decipherment of Linear B*. Cambridge: Cambridge University Press.

DeFrancis, J. 1989. *Visible Speech*. Honolulu, HI: University of Hawaii Press.

Donald, M. 1998. Mimesis and the Executive Suite: missing links in language evolution. In J. R. Hurford, M. Studdert-Kennedy and C. Knight (eds), *Approaches to the Evolution of Language: Social and cognitive bases*. Cambridge: Cambridge University Press, pp. 44–67.

Ferguson, C. A. and C. B. Farwell. 1975. Words and sounds in early language acquisition. *Language* **15**: 419–439.

Fisher, R. A. 1930. *The Genetical Theory of Natural Selection*. Oxford: Clarendon.

Fowler, C. A. 1996. Speaking. In H. Heuer and S. Keele (eds), *Handbook of Perception and Action, Vol. 2*. London: Academic, pp. 503–560.

Gelb, I. J. 1952. *A Study of Writing*. Chicago: Chicago University Press.

Hauser, M. 1996. *The Evolution of Communication*. Cambridge, MA: MIT Press.

Hockett, C. F. 1958. *A Course in Modern Linguistics*. New York: Macmillan.

Humboldt, W. von 1836/1972. *Linguistic Variability and Intellectual Development*. Translated by G. C. Buck and F. A. Raven. Philadelphia: University of Pennsylvania Press.

Jacob, F. 1977. The linguistic model in biology. In D. Armstrong and C. H. Van Schooneveld (eds), *Roman Jakobson: Echoes of his scholarship*. Lisse: de Ridder, pp. 185–192.

Jakobson, R. 1970. Linguistics. In *Main Trends of Research in the Social and Human Sciences* Vol.1. Paris/The Hague: UNESCO/Mouton, pp. 437–440.

Lenneberg, E. H. 1967. *Biological Foundations of Language*. New York: Wiley.

Liberman, A. M., F. S. Cooper, D. P. Shankweiler and M. Studdert-Kennedy. 1967. Perception of the speech code. *Psychological Review* **74**: 431–461.

Liberman, A. M. and I. G. Mattingly. 1985. The motor theory of speech perception revised. *Cognition* **21**: 1–36.

Liberman, A. M. and I. G. Mattingly. 1989. A specialization for speech perception. *Science* **243**: 489–494.

Lieberman, P. 1984. *The Biology and Evolution of Language*. Cambridge, MA: Harvard University Press.

Lindblom, B. 1986. Phonetic universals in vowel systems. In J. J. Ohala and J. J. Jaeger (eds), *Experimental Phonology*. London: Academic, pp. 13–44.

Lindblom, B. 1992. Phonological units as adaptive emergents of lexical development. In C. A. Ferguson, L. Menn and C. Stoel-Gammon (eds), *Phonological Development: Models, research, implications*. Timonium, MD: York Press, pp. 131–163.

Lindblom, B. 1998. Systemic constraints and adaptive change in the formation of sound structure. In J. R. Hurford, M. Studdert-Kennedy and C. Knight (eds), *Approaches to the Evolution of Language: Social and cognitive bases.* Cambridge: Cambridge University Press, pp. 242– 264.

MacLarnon, A. and G. Hewitt. 1998. Protolanguage to language: evidence from the evolution of breathing control. Paper read at the Second International Conference on the Evolution of Language, University of East London.

MacNeilage, P. F. 1998a. Evolution of the mechanisms of language output: comparative neurobiology of vocal and manual communication. In J. R. Hurford, M. Studdert-Kennedy and C. Knight (eds), *Approaches to the Evolution of Language: Social and cognitive bases.* Cambridge: Cambridge University Press, pp. 222–241.

MacNeilage, P. F. 1998b. The Frame/Content theory of evolution of speech production. *Behavioral and Brain Sciences* **21**: 499–511.

Martinet, A. 1949. La double articulation linguistique. *Travaux du Cercle Linguistique de Copenhague* **5**: 30–38.

Mattingly, I. G. 1991. The global character of phonetic gestures. *Journal of Phonetics* **18**: 445–452.

Meltzoff, A. N. and M. K. Moore. 1997. Explaining facial imitation: a theoretical model. *Early Development and Parenting* **6**: 179–192.

Pollack, R. 1994. *Signs of Life.* Boston: Houghton Mifflin.

Rizzolatti, G. and M. A. Arbib. 1998. Language within our grasp. *Trends in Neuroscience* **21**: 188–194.

Rizzolatti, G., L. Fadiga, V. Gallese and L. Fogassi. 1996. Premotor cortex and the recognition of motor actions. *Cognitive Brain Research* **3**: 131–141.

Saltzman, E. and K. Munhall. 1989. A dynamical approach to gestural patterning in speech production. *Ecological Psychology* **1**: 333–382.

Schrödinger, E. 1944. *What is Life?* Cambridge: Cambridge University Press.

Studdert-Kennedy, M. 1987. The phoneme as a perceptuomotor structure. In A. Allport, D. G. MacKay, W. Prinz and E. Scheerer (eds), *Language Perception and Production.* London: Academic, pp. 67–84.

Studdert-Kennedy, M. 1991. Language development from an evolutionary perspective. In N. A. Krasnegor, D. M. Rumbaugh, R. L. Schiefelbusch and M. Studdert-Kennedy (eds), *Biological and Behavioral Determinants of Language Development.* Hillsdale, NJ: Erlbaum, pp. 5–28.

Studdert-Kennedy, M. 1998. The particulate origins of language generativity: from sylla-ble to gesture. In J. R. Hurford, M. Studdert-Kennedy and C. Knight (eds), *Approaches to the Evolution of Language: Social and cognitive bases.* Cambridge: Cambridge University Press, pp. 202–221.

Studdert-Kennedy, M. and E. H. Goodell. 1995. Gestures, features and segments in early child speech. In B. de Gelder and J. Morais (eds), *Speech and Reading.* Hove: Erlbaum (UK), Taylor and Francis, pp. 65–88.

11

Emergence of Sound Systems Through Self-Organisation

BART DE BOER

Introduction

The research described in this chapter attempts to explain the emergence and structure of systems of speech sounds. It investigates how a coherent system of speech sounds can emerge in a population of agents and how the constraints under which the system emerges impose structure through self-organisation. If self-organisation can explain structure, then innate and biologically evolved mechanisms are not necessary. This effectively decreases the number of linguistic phenomena that have to be explained by biological evolution.

What are the phenomena to be explained by a theory of the emergence of speech sounds? The systems of speech sounds in the world's languages show remarkable regularities. First of all, certain sounds occur much more frequently than others. In the UCLA Phonological Segment Inventory Database (UPSID), a database that contains the phoneme inventories of 451 languages (the first version with 317 languages is described in Maddieson 1984), the vowels [i], [a] and [u] appear in 87%, 87% and 82% of the languages, respectively, while the vowels [y], [œ] and [ɯ] occur in only 5%, 2% and 9% of the languages. This holds even more for consonants. Some consonants, e.g. [m] (94%), [k] (89%) or [j] (84%) appear very frequently, while others, e.g. [ʀ] (1%), [ʃ] (1%) and [ʔ] (1%) appear very rarely.

The sound systems of languages also display a fair amount of symmetry. If a language has a front unrounded vowel of a given height, for example an [e] (occurring in 27% of the languages), it is quite likely that it also has the corresponding back rounded vowel [o] (which occurs in 29% of all languages, but in 85% of the languages with [e]). In the case of consonants, if a language has a voiced stop at a given place of articulation, e.g. [d] (27%) it usually also has a [t] (40% in the whole sample vs. 83% in languages with [d]).

177

Not only the inventories of speech sounds of languages show great regularities. Regularities are also found in the way speech sounds are strung together into syllables. It is said that all languages have syllables consisting of either a vowel (V) or a consonant followed by a vowel (CV). Syllables that end in a consonant are rarer, as are clusters of consonants at the onset or end of a syllable. When consonants occur in clusters, certain sequences occur much more frequently than others (Vennemann 1988). For example, a plosive followed by a nasal, e.g. [gŋ] occurs much more frequently than the inverse sequence at the *beginning* of a syllable. However, at the *end* of a syllable, the reverse is true.

Sometimes these universal characteristics are explained by innate properties of the brain (Jakobson and Halle 1956; Chomsky and Halle 1968). However, the question then becomes how these innate properties have evolved. Also, if there are innate constraints it is not clear why there is still such huge variation between different languages. It is clearly preferable to have an explanation that does not rely on innate mechanisms.

Functional explanations of the phenomena just discussed are more satisfying. A number of articulatory, perceptual and cognitive criteria have been proposed (e.g. Carré, Bordeau and Tubach 1995; Liljencrants and Lindblom 1972; Lindblom 1992; Stevens 1972). Some of these have been tested with computer simulations. These criteria can be summarised as articulatory ease, acoustic distinctiveness and minimum effort of learning.

However, these functional explanations are not the full explanation, either. They assume that the systems of speech sounds one finds are the result of an optimisation of one or more of the proposed criteria. But, it is not clear who is carrying out the optimisation. Certainly children learning a language do not optimise the system of speech sounds they learn. Rather, they try to imitate their parents (and peers) as accurately as possible. This explains the fact that people can speak the same language with different accents, from which one can identify their place of birth or their social group (Trudgill 1995).

If none of the individual speakers carries out an explicit optimisation of their sound system, but (near-)optimal sound systems are nevertheless found more frequently than nonoptimal ones, it is clear that the optimisation must be an emergent property of the interactions in the population. Therefore, if one wants to explain the sound systems that are found in the world's languages, one has to model populations of agents that imitate and learn each other's sounds under acoustic, articulatory and cognitive constraints.

A first attempt at building a computer model of a population of interacting agents for explaining the shape of vowel systems was undertaken by Glotin (1995), Glotin and Laboissière (1996) and Berrah (1998). The methods that these authors used have the drawback that the population is subject to some genetic evolution and that the agents still perform local optimisation by pushing the vowels in their vowel systems away from each other. Also the number of vowels in every agent has to be fixed beforehand in these simulations.

In this chapter a system is presented in which a population of agents that are each able to produce, perceive and learn vowels develops a coherent system of vowel sounds that conforms to the tendencies of vowel systems in human languages. The number of vowels need not be fixed beforehand, and there is no genetic evolution of the agents. Although the agents are able to change their repertoire of vowels in order to optimise success in imitation, they do so only in reaction to interactions with other agents. They also cannot change the positions of their vowels in any global way. The emerging vowel systems are therefore truly the result of the interactions between the agents. The research is mostly based on Steels's ideas on the origins of language (1997, 1998, in press), but fits in the larger recent tradition of studying the origins of language using computer simulations of populations (see also Hurford, this volume and Kirby, this volume). Steels considers language as the result of a process of mainly cultural evolution, while the universal tendencies of language can be explained as the results of self-organisation under constraints of perception and production. Steels himself has applied his ideas mainly to lexicon and meaning formation, and is now working on syntax.

In the next two sections, the agents and their interactions are described in considerable detail. The following two sections present some results of the simulations that were performed with this system and work in progress on extending the system to more complex utterances. In the final section, conclusions and a discussion of the work are presented.

The Agents

The agents are equipped with an articulatory synthesiser for production, a model of human hearing for perception and a prototype list for storage of vowels. The architecture of an agent is illustrated in Figure 11.1. All the elements of the

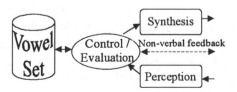

Figure 11.1. Agent architecture.

agent were constructed to be as humanlike as possible, in order to make the results of the research applicable to research in linguistics and in order to make it possible to use the agents to learn real human vowels.

An agent (illustrated in Figure 11.1) consists of three parts (S, D, V), where S is the synthesis function, D is the distance measure and V is the agent's set of vowels. The synthesiser function is a function $S : Ar \rightarrow Ac$, where Ar is the set of possible articulations and Ac is the set of possible acoustic signals. For the agents presented in this section the set of possible articulations is the set of articulatory vectors (p, h, r), where p, h, r are real numbers in the range $[0,1]$. Parameters p, h and r are the major vowel features (Ladefoged and Maddieson 1996: ch. 9) *position, height* and *rounding*. Position corresponds (roughly) to the position of the highest point of the tongue in the front to back dimension, height corresponds to the vertical distance between the highest part of the tongue and the roof of the mouth, and rounding corresponds to the rounding of the lips. Position zero means most fronted, height zero means lowest and rounding zero means that the lips are maximally spread. The parameter values for the front, high, unrounded vowel [i], as in 'leap', are $(0,1,0)$. For the back, high, rounded vowel [u], as in 'loop', they are $(1,1,1)$. For the back, low, unrounded vowel [ɑ], as in 'father', they are $(1,0,0)$.

The set Ac of possible outputs of the synthesiser function consists of vectors (F_1, F_2, F_3, F_4), where $F_1, F_2, F_3, F_4 \in \mathbf{R}$ are the first four formant frequencies of the generated vowel. These formant frequencies correspond to the peaks in the power spectrum of the vowel. When agents communicate with each other, they exchange only the formant values, not a real signal. This is done to reduce the amount of computations. A certain amount of noise is added, however. This noise consists of a random shifting of the formant frequencies, according to the following formula:

$$F_i \leftarrow \left(1 + \frac{Noise\%}{100} U(-0.5, 0.5)\right) F_i \tag{1}$$

In (1), $U(-0.5, 0.5)$ is a random number drawn from the uniform distribution between -0.5 and 0.5, *Noise%* is the noise percentage (a parameter of the system), and F_i represents the formants.

The formant frequencies are generated by a three-dimensional quadratic interpolation between 16 data points generated by Maeda's articulatory synthesiser (Maeda 1989; Vallée 1994: 162–164). The equations for calculating the synthesiser function are shown in Figure 11.2. The formant values for [i] are (252, 2202, 3242, 3938), for [u] (276, 740, 2177, 3506) and for [ɑ] (703, 1074, 2356, 3486). An important property of the synthesis function is that it is easy to calculate the formant frequencies from the articulatory description, but very hard to calculate the articulatory description from the acoustic description.

$$F_1 = \left((-392+392z)y^2 +(596-668z)y +(-146+166z)\right) x^2 +$$
$$\left((348-348z)y^2 +(-494+606z)y +(141-175z)\right) x +$$
$$\left((340-72z)y^2 +(-796+108z)y +(708-38z)\right)$$

$$F_2 = \left((-1200+1208z)y^2 +(1320-1328z)y +(118-158z)\right) x^2 +$$
$$\left((1864-1488z)y^2 +(-2644+1510z)y +(-561+221z)\right) x +$$
$$\left((-670+490z)y^2 +(1355-697z)y +(1517-117z)\right)$$

$$F_3 = \left((604-604z)y^2 +(1038-1178z)y +(246+566z)\right) x^2 +$$
$$\left((-1150+1262z)y^2 +(-1443+1313z)y +(-317-483z)\right) x +$$
$$\left((1130-836z)y^2(-315+44z)y +(2427-127z)\right)$$

$$F_4 = \left((-1120+16z)y^2 +(1696-180z)y +(500+522z)\right) x^2 +$$
$$\left((-140+240z)y^2 +(-578+214z)y +(-692-419z)\right) x +$$
$$\left((1480-602z)y^2 +(-1220+289z)y +(3678-178z)\right)$$

Figure 11.2. Synthesiser equations.

With this synthesiser all basic vowels can be generated. It is therefore *language-independent*.

A vowel v consists of elements (ar, ac, s, u), where $ar \in Ar$ is the articulatory prototype, $ac \in Ac$ is the corresponding acoustic prototype and s, u are the success and use scores (which will be explained in connection with the imitation game), respectively. The vowels are represented as prototypes as this seemed to be both a realistic and computationally effective way to represent vowels. Research in human perception of speech sounds (e.g. Cooper et al. 1952; Liberman et al. 1954) seems to indicate that humans perceive speech sounds in terms of prototypes. If human subjects are presented with acoustic signals that vary continuously from one speech sound to another (e.g. from [ga] to [ba]), they tend to perceive these signals as either the one category ([ba]) or the other ([ga]), never as something 'in between'. Perception suddenly switches somewhere in the middle. In other parts of language, such as syntax and semantics, prototypes appear to be used as well (Comrie 1981; Lakoff 1987).

An agent's vowels are stored in the set V, which we will call the vowel set. When an agent decides it has encountered a new vowel v_{new} (we will describe later how and when this is decided), it adds both the acoustic and the articulatory descriptions of v_{new} to $V : V \leftarrow V \cup v_{new}$. A sound A that the agent hears will be compared to the acoustic prototypes ac_v of the vowels v in its vowel set, and the distance between A and all ac_v ($v \in V$) is calculated using the distance function

$D : Ac^2 \rightarrow \mathbf{R}$ (to be described). It will then assume that it has recognised the vowel v_{rec} with the minimum distance to A:

$$\{v_{rec} | v_{rec} \in V \wedge \neg\exists v_2 : (v_2 \in V \cap D(A, ac_{v_2}) < D(A, ac_{v_{rec}}))\} \quad (2)$$

It should be stressed that the acoustic representations of the vowels are only stored in order to decrease the number of calculations needed for vowel recognition. Whenever an agent wants to say a vowel to another agent, it takes the *articulatory* prototype from the list and transforms it into an acoustic representation using the synthesis function S; it does not use the acoustic prototype.

The distance between two vowels is determined by using a weighted distance in the F_1-F_2' space, where F_1 is the frequency of the first formant (expressed in Bark, a logarithmic frequency scale) and F_2' is the weighted average of the second, third and fourth formants (also expressed in Barks). This distance measure is based on the distance measure described by Mantakas, Schwartz and Escudier (1986) (also described in Boë, Schwartz and Vallée 1995). The distance measure is based on weighting formant peaks differently depending on their distance relative to a critical distance c, which is taken to be 3.5 Bark.

In order to calculate F_2' two weights have to be calculated:

$$w_1 = \frac{c - (F_3 - F_2)}{c} \quad (3)$$

$$w_2 = \frac{(F_4 - F_3) - (F_3 - F_2)}{F_4 - F_2} \quad (4)$$

In these equations w_1 and w_2 are the weights and F_1 through F_4 are the formants in Bark.

The value of F_2' can now be calculated as follows:

$$F_2' = \begin{cases} F_2, & \text{if } F_3 - F_2 > c \\[2mm] \dfrac{(2 - w_1)F_2 + w_1 F_3}{2}, & \text{if } F_3 - F_2 \leq c \text{ and } F_4 - F_2 > c \\[2mm] \dfrac{w_2 F_2 + (2 - w_2)F_3}{2} - 1, & \text{if } F_4 - F_2 \leq c \text{ and } F_3 - F_2 < F_4 - F_3 \\[2mm] \dfrac{(2 - w_2)F_3 + w_2 F_4}{2} - 1, & \text{if } F_4 - F_2 \leq c \text{ and } F_3 - F_2 \geq F_4 - F_3 \end{cases}$$

$$(5)$$

The values of F_1 and F_2' for a number of vowels are shown in Figure 11.3. We can see from this figure that the distribution of the vowels through the acoustic space is quite natural. However, as it is a two-dimensional projection of an essentially four-dimensional space, not all distances between all phonemes can be represented accurately. This is especially the case with the distinction between rounded and unrounded.

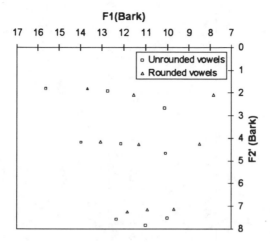

Figure 11.3. Vowels in F_1-F_2' space.

The distance between two signals, $a, b \in Ac$, can now be calculated using a weighted Euclidean distance:

$$D(a, b) = \sqrt{\left(F_1^a - F_1^b\right)^2 + \lambda \left(F_2'^a - F_2'^b\right)^2} \qquad (6)$$

The value of the parameter λ is 0.3 for all experiments that will be described.

With the synthesis function and the distance measure described in this section, the agents can produce and perceive speech sounds in a humanlike way. The results that are generated with this system can therefore be compared with the results of research into human sound systems.

The Imitation Game

The imitation game was designed to allow the agents to determine the vowels of the other agents and to develop a realistic vowel system. The imitation game is played in a population of agents (size 20 in all the experiments presented here). From this population two agents are picked at random: an *initiator* and an *imitator*. The initiator starts the imitation game by producing a sound that the imitator has to imitate. The imitator listens to the sound, and tries to analyse it in terms of the sound prototypes it already knows. It then produces the acoustic signal for the prototype it has found. The initiator then listens to this signal and analyses it in terms of its prototypes. If the prototype it finds is the same as the one it used to produce the original sound, the game is considered *successful*. Otherwise it is a *failure*. This is communicated to the imitator. The exact steps of the imitation game are illustrated in Table 11.1. Note that nonverbal feedback

Table 11.1. *Basic organisation of the imitation game*

initiator	imitator
if ($V = \varnothing$) Add random vowel to V Pick random vowel v from V $u_v := u_v + 1$ Produce signal $A_1 := ac_v$	

	Receive signal A_1.
	 if ($V = \varnothing$)
	    $v_{new} :=$ Find phoneme(A_1)
	    $V := V \cup v_{new}$
	 Calculate v_{rec}:
	 $v_{rec} \in V \wedge \neg \exists v_2 : (v_2 \in V \wedge D(A_1, ac_{v_2}) < D(A_1, ac_{v_{rec}}))$
	 Produce signal $A_2 := ac_{v_{rec}}$

Receive signal A_2.
 Calculate v_{rec}:
 $v_{rec} \in V \wedge \neg \exists v_2 : (v_2 \in V \wedge D(A_2, ac_{v_2}) < D(A_2, ac_{v_{rec}}))$
 if ($v_{rec} = v$)
    Send non-verbal feedback: *success*.
    $s_v := s_v + 1$
 else
    Send non-verbal feedback: *failure*.
 Do other updates of V.	

	Receive non-verbal feedback. Update V according to feedback signal. Do other updates of V.

is needed to indicate whether the game was a success or a failure. If one draws a parallel with human communication, nonverbal feedback can be compared to a gesture or facial expression, or to the failure to achieve a communicative goal. Making the imitation game depend on nonverbal communication might seem to introduce a very unrealistic element into the agents' learning. In the case of human children it is hardly ever directly indicated whether the sounds they produce are right or wrong. However, there are more indirect ways of discovering that the right sound was not used, such as a failure to achieve the desired goal of the communication. But our imitation game abstracts from this and assumes that a feedback signal is somehow available.

Depending on the outcome of the imitation game, the imitator can alter its vowel inventory. The way this is done is described in Table 11.2, together with a number of other routines that are used. First of all, the use and success counts u and s of the vowels that were used are updated. The use count u is increased every time a vowel is used. The success count s is only increased if the imitation game in which the vowel was used was successful.

If the imitation game was successful, the vowel that was used for imitation is shifted to sound a bit more like the signal that was heard. This is done by finding the neighbour of this vowel, whose sound is closer to the signal that was heard. The neighbours of a vowel are the six vowels that differ by a certain small value (fixed at 0.05 in all experiments described in this chapter) in only one of the three articulatory parameters. The reason for this shift is as follows: if the imitation game was successful, the vowel that was used is the same as the vowel that was used by the other agent. Shifting it to sound more like the signal that was just heard increases cohesion in the population.

If the imitation game was a failure, however, and if the vowel that was used was successful in previous imitation games (its success-to-use ratio being higher than a certain threshold, 0.8 in all games presented), then the reason the imitation game failed is probably that the vowel was confused. It is likely that the other agent distinguished two vowels where this agent distinguished only one. The confusion between the two vowels caused the imitation game to fail. It is therefore a good idea to add a new vowel, which sounds like the signal that was heard. This is done using the *find phoneme* procedure (see Table 11.2).

However, if the imitation game was a failure and the vowel that was used has a low success-to-use ratio, the vowel was probably not a good imitation of any other sound. It is therefore shifted towards the signal that was heard in the hope that it will become a better imitation.

The phoneme is not thrown away. This is done in the *other updates* routines, described in Table 11.3. This routine does three things: it throws away bad vowels that have been tried at least a minimum number of times (five times in

Table 11.2. *Actions performed by the agents*

Shift closer (v, A); return v_{best}.	**Find phoneme** (A); return v_{best}	**Update according to feedback signal**

{
 $v_{best} := v$
 for (all six neighbors v_{neigh} of v) do:
   if ($D(ac_{v_{neigh}}, A) < D(ac_{v_{rec}}, A)$)
     $v_{best} := v_{neigh}$
 }
	{
	 v_{best}
	 vowel v:
	   $ar_v = (0.5, 0.5, 0.5)$
	   $ac_v = S(ar_v)$
	   $s_v = 0$
	   $u_v = 0$
	 do
	   $v_{best} := v$
	   $v :=$ Shift closer(v_{best}, A)
	 until($v = v_{best}$)
	 }
		{
		 $u_{vrec} := u_{vrec} + 1$
		 if (feedback signal = *success*)
		   $v_{rec} :=$ Shift closer(v_{rec}, A_1)
		   $s_{vrec} := s_{vrec} + 1$
		 else
		   if($u_{vrec}/s_{vrec} > threshold$)
		     $v_{new} :=$ Find phoneme(A_1)
		     $V := V \cup v_{new}$
		   else
		     $v_{rec} :=$ Shift closer(v_{rec}, A_1)
		 }

Table 11.3. *Other updates of the agents' vowel systems*

Merge(v_1, v_2, V)	Do other updates of V
{	{
if ($s_{v1}/u_{v1} < s_{v2}/u_{v2}$)	**for** ($\forall\ v \in V$) // Remove bad vowels
$s_{v2} := s_{v2} + s_{v1}$	**if** ($s_v/u_v <$ *throwaway threshold* $\wedge u_v >$ *min. uses*)
$u_{v2} := u_{v2} + u_{v1}$	$V := V - v$
$V := V - v_1$	**for** ($\forall\ v_1 \in V$) // Merging of vowels
else	**for** ($\forall v_2$: ($v_2 \in V \wedge v_2 \neq v_1$))
$s_{v1} := s_{v1} + s_{v2}$	**if** ($D(ac_{v1}, ac_{v2}) <$ *acoustic merge threshold*)
$u_{v1} := u_{v1} + u_{v2}$	Merge(v_1, v_2, V)
$V := V - v_2$	**if** (Euclidean distance between ar_{v1} and $ar_{v2} <$
}	*articulatory merge threshold*)
	Merge(v_1, v_2, V)
	Add new vowel to V with small probability.
	}

all experiments presented). Vowels are considered bad if their success-to-use ratio is less than a threshold (0.7 in all experiments presented). Furthermore, vowels that are too close in articulatory and acoustic space can be merged. This is done in order to prevent a cluster of bad phonemes from emerging at a position where only one good vowel would be required. This has been observed in experiments without merging. The articulatory threshold for merging is the minimal distance to a neighbouring prototype (set to be 0.03 in all experiments). The acoustic threshold for merging is determined by the noise level. If two vowels are so close that they can be confused by the noise that is added to the formant frequencies, they are merged. The last change that agents can make to their vowel inventories is to add a random new vowel. This is done with a low probability (0.01 in all experiments presented). The values for the articulatory parameters of the new vowel are chosen randomly from a uniform distribution between 0 and 1.

The imitation game contains all the elements that are necessary for the emergence of vowel systems. Several different mechanisms cause variation and innovation: noise, imperfect imitations and random insertions of vowels. Other mechanisms take care of (implicit) selection of good-quality vowels: vowels are only retained if they are shared with other agents. Otherwise no successful imitations are possible, and their success score will drop. Unsuccessful vowels will eventually be removed. The merging ensures that phonemes remain distinct, so that sufficiently spaced vowel systems emerge. Note that all the actions of the agents can be performed using local information only. The agents do not need to look at each other's vowel systems directly.

Vowel Experiments

So far, only experiments with vowels have been done. These experiments have already been partly described (de Boer 1997a, 1997b). The first aim of the experiments was to show that a coherent sound system can indeed emerge in a population of agents that are in principle able to learn such a sound system, but that do not have a sound system at the beginning. The second aim was to show that the system learned has the same characteristics as human sound systems. Vowels were the signals of choice, because they are easy to represent, generate and perceive, and because the universal characteristics of human vowel systems and their functional explanations are more thoroughly described than those of other speech signals.

A typical example of the emergence of a vowel system in a population of 20 agents with maximally 10% noise is illustrated in Figure 11.4. In this figure the vowel systems of the agents in the population are shown after different numbers of imitation games. All vowels of all agents in the population are plotted on top of each other. They are plotted in the acoustic space consisting of the first formant F_1 and the weighted sum of the second, third and fourth formants

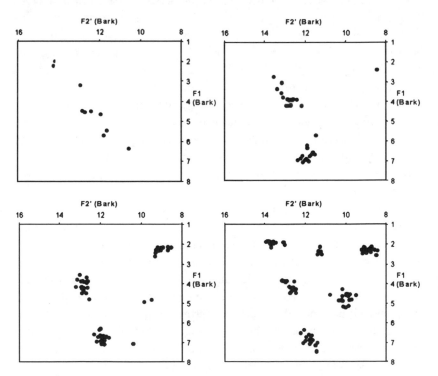

Figure 11.4.   Vowel system after 20, 200, 1,000 and 2,000 games, 10% noise.

(F_2'). The frequency of the formants is shown in the Bark frequency scale. Note that due to articulatory limitations the acoustic space that can be exploited by the agents is roughly triangular with the apex at the bottom of the graph.

The leftmost graph shows the agents' vowels after 20 imitation games. One can see hardly any structure at all; the vowels are dispersed through the acoustic space (the apparent linear correlation is an artefact). This is because initially vowels are mostly added at random. After 200 imitation games, clusters emerge. This happens because the agents try to imitate each other as closely as possible while at the same time they are under pressure to maximise the number of vowels (caused by the occasional random insertion of new vowels in the agents' repertoires). Almost every agent in the population now has two vowels: one in each cluster.

After 1,000 imitation games the available acoustic space starts to fill up, and the clusters become tighter. Every agent in the population now has at least three vowels. Some agents have more (the isolated dots in the graph), which other agents have not had the opportunity to copy yet. Finally, after 2,000 imitation games, the available acoustic space is completely covered. The system that emerges consists of tight clusters that are approximately equally spaced. The vowels that emerge are [i], [e]-[ø], [a], [o], [u] and [ɨ], which, except for the rounding of the front-mid segment, is a possible six-vowel system, such as found, for example in the Saami language of Lapland (from UPSID, based on Vallée 1994).

The noise level determines the number and size of the clusters. The higher the noise level, the lower the number of clusters, and the more widely dispersed the clusters will be. This is shown in Figure 11.5, where a system with 10% noise is compared with a system with 25% noise. Note, however, that the clusters are still spread near-optimally through the available acoustic space. Both systems are also natural. The one with 10% noise has eight vowels: [i], [e], [ɛ], [a], [ɔ], [o], [u] and [ɯ], while the one with 25% noise is the canonical three-vowel system, consisting of [i], [a] and [u]. Note that the vowel system obtained under 10% noise in this simulation run is not the same as the one obtained in Figure 11.1. This is because the population does not converge to an optimal solution, but rather to a good system, which may, apparently, consist of 6 or 8 vowels. Both systems, however, show similar characteristics of symmetry and spread of vowel clusters.

These experiments show that a coherent sound system can emerge in a population of agents, and that these sound systems show the same universal characteristics as sound systems from natural languages. However, there is as yet no transfer from one generation of speakers to the next. In real language communities speakers constantly enter (they are born) and leave (they die or

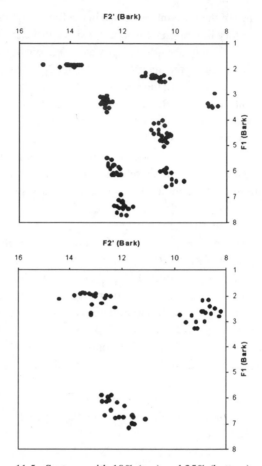

Figure 11.5. Systems with 10% (top) and 25% (bottom) noise.

move away) the community. Still, the language remains relatively stable. The simulation presented here can be used to test whether it is possible to transfer the sound system in a stable way from one generation to the next.

The succession of generations can be modelled by adding and removing agents from the population at random. These processes model the birth and death of language users. After a sufficiently long period of time, all the original agents in the population will have been replaced, and the new agents will have learned their sound system from the original population. The sound system in the population of new agents can then be compared with the original sound system. This is done in Figure 11.6. The white squares represent the positions of the original agents' vowels, and the black circles represent the positions of the vowels after 2,000 imitation games. Every 50 imitation games on average an

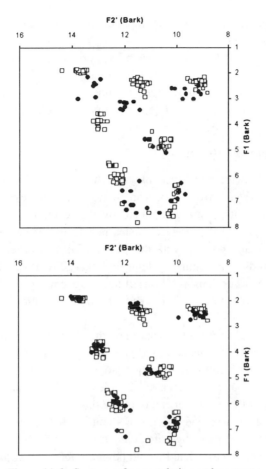

Figure 11.6. Systems after population replacement.

agent was removed from, or added to, the population. The original population consisted of 20 agents, and the final population consisted of 11 agents for the top graph and 14 agents for the bottom graph (the number of agents was not fixed, due to the independence of adding and removing agents). The noise level was a constant 10%.

In the simulation that resulted in the top graph, agents could learn equally well, independently of how long they were already present in the population. For the bottom graph, agents were used that could change their vowel repertoire more easily when they were young than when they were old. Comparing the two graphs, it can be observed that both systems preserve the approximate positions of the clusters. However, in the top graph the clusters have become more dispersed, have moved slightly, and even two clusters in the upper left corner have merged. In the bottom graph, the positions and number of clusters have hardly changed at all.

Apparently cultural transfer of sound systems is possible in both simulations. Additional stability is ensured when older agents can change their vowel systems less easily than younger agents. Apparently the older agents provide a stable target to which the younger agents can adapt their vowel systems.

Towards Complex Utterances

The experiments with vowel systems show that it is possible for coherent and realistic sound systems to emerge in a population, and that the possible structures of these sound systems are determined by the functional constraints under which they are produced, perceived and learned. However, interesting linguistic change is not really possible with this system. The vowel repertoires rapidly converge towards near-optimal systems and change relatively little after that. Some drift may occur in the positions of the vowel clusters, and clusters might even merge or split, but this is not the way in which human sound systems generally change.

Human sound change is often caused by the phonetic environment in which sounds occur. For example, nasalised vowels almost always derive from non-nasal vowels that are followed by a nasal consonant. Context is also necessary for the spread of sound changes. If an agent learns to pronounce a certain sound differently than other agents, it can only use this sound to successfully imitate other agents when the sound appears in a context that allows the other agents to disambiguate it. If there were no context, the sound could not be imitated, would become unsuccessful and would be discarded. Free variation of sounds in the population, and therefore sound change, is only possible when there is sufficient context. Therefore it is necessary to extend the system to handle longer and more complex utterances.

This is also necessary if one wants to investigate universal characteristics of consonants and syllable structure. As mentioned in the introduction to this chapter, the same general tendencies that exist for vowels also exist for consonants and syllable structure. If we want to investigate whether these can be explained with the same mechanisms of self-organisation in a population, we need to simulate an agent that is able to generate, perceive and learn complex utterances.

Work is in progress to build agents that are able to handle complex utterances. The basic imitation game will remain the same, but the architecture of the agents will be different. Their sound production system will consist of an articulatory synthesiser, based on Mermelstein's (1973) model. The degrees of freedom of this model correspond roughly to the different articulators (tongue, lips, teeth, etc.) of the human vocal tract. The movements of the articulators are simulated dynamically, taking into account their inertia. The agent's utterances are modelled as gestures (Browman and Goldstein 1995). Different articulatory gestures can be scheduled to occur in sequence, influencing each other where necessary. This system is already operational and an example output is shown in Figure 11.7.

Perception will be based on extracting features from the speech signal. These features might be the formant frequencies and their rates of change, presence of voicing, presence of noise, presence of silence, strength of the signal and so on. Associations between the different articulatory gestures and these features will have to be learned by the agents, so that they can find articulatory gestures that correspond to the acoustic signals they hear. A perception model is nearly operational. The extraction of features such as formant frequency, voicing frequency, voicing prominence and power of the signal are demonstrated in Figures 11.8 and 11.9.

The learning of the agents is the most difficult to model. The simple use of prototypes as with the vowel system is no longer sufficient. At least two levels of storage are needed: one level for the possible words (sequences of phonemes) that the agents know and another level for the articulatory gestures and their acoustic correlates (phonemes) from which these words are built up. The model will have to conform to what is known about how children learn sound systems (Vihman 1996), although much of this is controversial. Agents will first learn words as holistic patterns of gesture; they will then split these up into phoneme-like constituents under pressure of minimal storage requirements.

Once the agents have been built, it will first be tested whether a population of them is able to generate a coherent system of speech sounds. Then experiments can be run that investigate the sound changes that can take place and the extent to which the results resemble the way that human sound systems behave.

Conclusions and Discussion

The results of the simulations show clearly that coherent sound systems can emerge as the result of local interactions between the members of a population. They also show that the systems that emerge show characteristic tendencies similar to the ones found in human sound systems, such as more frequent use of certain vowels and symmetry of the system. This means that we do not need to look for evolution-based explanations for the universal tendencies of vowel systems. Apparently the characteristics emerge as the result of self-organisation

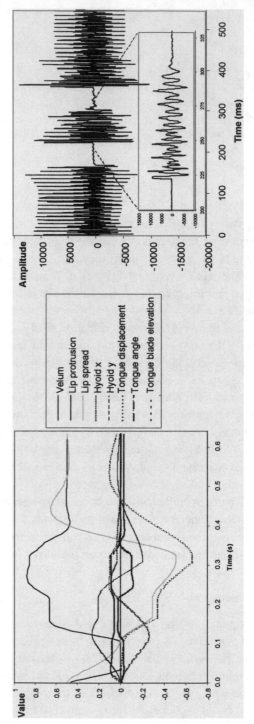

Figure 11.7. Gestural score for articulation (left) and acoustic signal: [dɐ.bu.bʰɛ] [ɔ] (right).

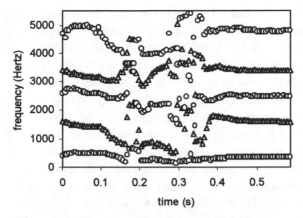

Figure 11.8. Formants extracted from artificial utterance.

under constraints of perception, production and learning. The systems that are found can be considered attractors of the dynamical system that consists of the agents and their interactions. Of course we still need an evolutionary account of the shape of the human vocal tract and of human perception, but we do not need any specific innate mechanisms for explaining the structure of the vowel systems that appear in human languages.

It has also been shown that the vowel systems can be transferred from one generation of agents to the next. For this, no change in the interactions and the behaviours of the agents have to be made, although the transfer from generation to generation is improved if older agents are made to learn less quickly than young agents. Apparently the same mechanism can be used to learn an existing vowel system as to produce a sound system in a population where no sound

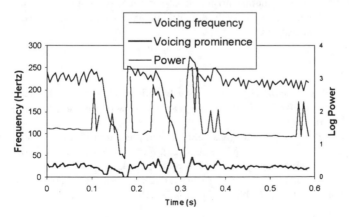

Figure 11.9. Other acoustic features.

system existed previously. This lends support to Steels's thesis that the same mechanism that is responsible for the ability to learn language is responsible for the emergence of language in the first place (Steels 1997, 1998). The use of computer simulations makes it easy for the researcher to perform experiments like these, and thus provides an extra means to test and fine-tune linguistic theories.

The ability to explain the emergence, learning and universal structural tendencies of sound systems as the result of local interactions between agents that exist in a population is a remarkable result. It indicates that not all aspects of language need to be explained by invoking biological evolution. This makes it easier to explain that language evolved in a relatively short time.

We need to test, however, whether these results also hold for utterances more complex than isolated vowels. Work is in progress to build agents that can produce and perceive complex utterances. Modelling aspects of language as the result of interactions in a population seems to be a promising way to learn more about the origins of language, especially because it provides another mechanism in addition to biological evolution for explaining the complexity and structure of language.

Acknowledgements

This research was done at the Artificial Intelligence Laboratory of the Vrije Universiteit Brussel. It is part of an ongoing research project into the origins of language and intelligence. Funding was provided by the GOA 2 project of the Vrije Universiteit Brussel. Part of the work was done at the Sony Computer Science Laboratory in Paris, France. I thank Luc Steels for valuable discussion of the ideas and the work presented here and for providing the research environment of the VUB AI Lab. I thank Edwin de Jong, Tony Belpaeme and Paul Vogt of the VUB AI Lab for their comments and suggestions, and I thank the people of the Sony Computer Science Laboratory for their hospitality. I also thank Björn Lindblom, Christine Ericsdottir and others at the Phonetics Laboratory of Stockholm University for the opportunity to present my work there and for their feedback and suggestions.

References

Berrah, A.-R. 1998. *Evolution Artificielle d'une Société d'Agents de Parole: Un modèle pour l'emergence du code phonétique*, Doctoral dissertation, Institut National Polytechnique de Grenoble.

Boë, L. J., J.-L. Schwartz and N. Vallée. 1995. The prediction of vowel systems: perceptual contrast and stability. In E. Keller (ed), *Fundamentals of Speech Synthesis and Speech Recognition*. New York: Wiley, pp. 185–213.

Browman, C. P. and L. Goldstein. 1995. Dynamics and articulatory phonology. In R. F. Port and T. van Gelder (eds), *Mind as Motion*. Cambridge, MA: MIT Press, pp. 175–194.

Carré, R., M. Bordeau and J.-P. Tubach. 1995. Vowel-vowel production: the distinctive region model (DRM) and vowel harmony. *Phonetica* **52**: 205–214.

Chomsky, N. and M. Halle. 1968. *The Sound Pattern of English*. Cambridge, MA: MIT Press.

Comrie, B. 1981. *Language Universals and Linguistic Typology*. Oxford: Blackwell.

Cooper, F. S., P. C. Delattre, A. M. Liberman, J. M. Borst and L. J. Gerstman. 1952. Some experiments on the perception of synthetic speech sounds. *Journal of the Acoustical Society of America* **24**: 597–606. Reprinted in D.B. Fry (ed), 1976. *Acoustic Phonetics*. Cambridge: Cambridge University Press, pp. 258–283.

de Boer, B. 1997a. Generating vowels in a population of agents. In P. Husbands and I. Harvey (eds), *Fourth European Conference on Artificial Life*. Cambridge, MA: MIT Press, pp. 503–510.

de Boer, B. 1997b. Self organisation in vowel systems through imitation. In J. Coleman (ed), *Computational Phonology, Third Meeting of the ACL Special Interest Group in Computational Phonology*. Somerset, NJ: Association for Computational Linguistics, pp. 19–25.

Glotin, H. 1995. *La Vie Artificielle d'une Société de Robots Parlants: Emergence et changement du code phonétique*. DEA thesis, Institut National Polytechnique de Grenoble.

Glotin, H. and R. Laboissière. 1996. Emergence du code phonétique dans une société de robots parlants. *Actes de la Conférence Modélisation des Systèmes Naturels Complexes Rochebrune 1996*. Paris: Ecole Nationale Supérieure des Télécommunications, pp. 113–125.

Jakobson, R. and M. Halle. 1956. *Fundamentals of Language*. The Hague: Mouton.

Ladefoged, P. and I. Maddieson. 1996. *The Sounds of the World's Languages*. Oxford: Blackwell.

Lakoff, G. 1987. *Women, Fire, and Dangerous Things: What categories reveal about the mind*. Chicago: Chicago University Press.

Liberman, A. M., P. C. Delattre, F. S. Cooper and L. J. Gerstman. 1954. The role of consonant-vowel transitions in the perception of the stop and nasal consonants. *Psychological Monographs* **68**. Reprinted in D. B. Fry (ed), 1976. *Acoustic Phonetics*. Cambridge University Press, pp. 315–331.

Liljencrants, L. and B. Lindblom. 1972. Numerical simulations of vowel quality systems: the role of perceptual contrast. *Language* **48**: 839–862.

Lindblom, B. 1992. Phonological units as adaptive emergents of lexical development. In C. A. Ferguson, L. Menn and C. Stoel-Gammon (eds), *Phonological Development*. Timonium, MD: York Press, pp. 131–163.

Maddieson, I. 1984. *Patterns of Sounds*. Cambridge: Cambridge University Press.

Maeda, S. 1989. Compensatrory articulation during speech: evidence from the analysis and synthesis of vocal tract shapes using an articulatory model. In W. J. Hardcastle and A. Marchal (eds), *Speech Production and Speech Modelling*. Dordrecht: Kluwer, pp. 131–149.

Mantakas, M., J. L. Schwartz and P. Escudier. 1986. Modèle de prédiction du 'deuxiéme formant effectif' F2' – application à l'étude de la labialité des voyelles avant du français. In *Proceedings of the Fifteenth Journées d'Etude sur la Parole*. Paris: Société Française d'Acoustique, pp. 157–161.

Mermelstein, P. 1973. Articulatory model for the study of speech production. *Journal of the Acoustical Society of America* **53**: 1070–1082.

Steels, L. 1997. The synthetic modelling of language origins. *Evolution of Communication* **1**: 1–34.

Steels, L. 1998. Synthesising the origins of language and meaning using coevolution, self-organisation and level formation. In J. R. Hurford, M. Studdert-Kennedy and C. Knight (eds), *Approaches to the Evolution of Language: Social and cognitive bases*. Cambridge: Cambridge University Press, pp. 384–404.

Steels, L. In press. The spontaneous self-organization of an adaptive language. In S. Muggleton (ed), *Machine Intelligence* **15**. Oxford: Oxford University Press.

Stevens, K. N. 1972. The quantal nature of speech: evidence from articulatory-acoustic data. In E. E. David, Jr., and P. B. Denes (eds), *Human Communication: A unified view*. New York: McGraw-Hill, pp. 51–66.

Trudgill, P. 1995. *Sociolinguistics: An introduction to language and society*. London: Penguin.

Vallée, N. 1994. *Systèmes Vocaliques: De la typologie aux prédictions*. Doctoral dissertation, Université Stendhal Grenoble.

Vennemann, T. 1988. *Preference Laws for Syllable Structure*. Berlin: Mouton de Gruyter.

Vihman, M. M. 1996. *Phonological Development: The origins of language in the child*. Cambridge, MA: Blackwell.

12

Modelling Language-Physiology Coevolution

DANIEL LIVINGSTONE AND COLIN FYFE

Introduction

A feature of current computational models of language evolution is that the individuals in later populations are not structurally, 'physiologically', different from those in the first. Evolution may be working on the language itself, as learned by agents which do not evolve, or on an innate communication scheme. A number of models specifically demonstrate self-organisation of communication schemes and grammars in populations that are already capable of language.

Such models do not show communities evolving from those capable of some simple protolanguage towards those capable of some fuller language. In contrast, in human evolution, vocalisations and speech provided a selective advantage that led to the exaptation and adaptation of aspects of human physiology to support improved language capacity (Deacon 1992; Lieberman 1992). This led to a process of language-physiology coevolution. From the coevolution of physiology and language, hominids developed differences from other primates, such as increased brain size and a supralaryngeal vocal tract.

The coevolution of speech and physiology in humans was also not without cost. The larger brain costs more energy to maintain, and requires a longer infancy for brain growth to be completed. The dropped epiglottis allows greater clarity and distinctiveness in speech, but increases risk of choking.

While some vocalisations are evolved responses – crying, laughter and so on – speech is learned afresh by every individual. Learning allows quicker adaptation to changes in the environment and faster solutions to environmental problems. The Baldwin effect (Baldwin 1896) explains how learning can influence evolution: individuals most capable of successfully adapting to their environment will be more likely to contribute to future generations. Thus an increase in language capabilities can occur over a population due to the higher fitness of individuals with greatest language capabilities, where the use of language provides a selective advantage.

Continuous evolution from a species capable of only a basic protolanguage to one capable of full language is then possible. Wray (this volume) describes the evolution of language from a simple protolanguage. The starting point is a learned holistic protolanguage, with capabilities similar to the verbal communication of modern primates, with a small set of words to convey general meanings. The starting point of language evolution in our model is the ability to learn and use a very limited protolanguage consisting of only a pair of signals.

We develop our model to show evolution in language agent physiology to support communication. In this model, the number of unique signals that an agent can produce defines its language ability. An agent's language ability may be greater or less than required for the agent to be able to communicate all information of interest. Where additional language capabilities may provide benefit to individuals, such evolution depends on the benefit exceeding the costs involved. We show that language negotiation can succeed in heterogeneous populations, and that it is possible to model the evolution of language ability. Finally we discuss the results with respect to the evolution of human language.

Computational Models of Language-Learning Populations

A number of recent computational models demonstrate the evolution of innate communication schemes (for example, Oliphant 1996; Cangelosi and Parisi 1996; Di Paolo 1997). Other models demonstrate the self-organisation of lexicons, grammars and sound systems in populations of language agents without evolution (see Kirby, this volume; de Boer, this volume; Steels 1996; Batali 1998).

Batali (1994) combines evolution and learning in an artificial neural network (ANN) model in which recurrent neural networks attempt to learn context-free grammars in an investigation of innate language biases and critical periods. The language agents have a fixed structure and a predetermined number of inputs and outputs. Evolution determines initial weight values for the networks, selecting appropriate values for the class of languages on which the population is trained. This model demonstrates how evolution can tune innate learning mechanisms towards certain grammars, once the mechanisms for language have developed.

In Fyfe and Livingstone (1997) a population was modelled in which the individuals learn to identify stochastic sources in an environment, and then learn a common language to communicate about the sources present in any given environment. The agents were implemented as neural networks with three layers of neurons – an environment input layer, a hidden internal-state layer and a language output layer. The language agents first learned to identify different sources in the environment before language negotiation began.

Experiments were performed with communities of agents with differing representational capabilities, i.e. different hidden-layer sizes. Communicative success was seen to improve in populations with a common representational capability, and evolution towards homogenous representation capability was observed. A weakness in this model was that the production of language was compared, but the ability to interpret signals was not tested. Thus, by producing the same word for the same environment two agents are assumed to be successfully communicating. No pressure existed to produce different signals for different environments, or to be able to decode signals.

A model using ANN agents learning to produce and interpret signals, with observational rather than reinforcement-based learning, is presented in Oliphant (1997). In Oliphant's model, ANN agents relate meanings to signals and vice-versa with winner-take-all on the produced vector, with meanings and signals represented by binary vectors with only one active value. Using a form of Hebbian learning (learning which increases the strength of a weight when the neurons connected by it both fire simultaneously), Oliphant shows successful negotiation to a common optimal language, with a different signal being used for each meaning.

Another model where a community of ANNs negotiates a shared lexicon is presented in Hutchins and Hazelhurst (1995). The agents within this model are similar to the ones presented in this chapter, although their agents are more complicated with an additional layer (used only in learning). The authors limit their investigation to the development of a shared lexicon.

Modelling Language-Physiology Coevolution

Our model comprises a population of simple language agents capable of sending and receiving messages to share information. In our model, agents learn to map messages that are sent by other agents to internal states or 'meanings'. The agents use these messages to coordinate their internal states. By learning from each other, a coordinated communication system is developed by a community of agents. An ANN architecture is used for the production of messages from each arbitrary meaning and for the reverse mapping.

We add to the model by making the expressive capability of the language dependent on hereditary genes. The genes determine the number of language nodes possessed by agents, which determines the range of signals that can be produced. This forms the basis for investigating the evolution of language ability within our model. A fitness cost according to the number of language nodes possessed by an agent is added to represent the expense of language adaptations.

Our population is composed of two-layer fully connected ANNs with N inputs and M outputs. The meaning is modelled as a bipolar (± 1) vector of length N, which is presented at the inputs of a language agent. This can be fed forward through the ANN to determine an agent's 'word' for that meaning, each output being thresholded to a bipolar value (± 1), as given in (1):

$$y_j = \sum_{i=1}^{N} x_i w_{ij} \quad \text{then } Y_j = 1 \text{ if } y_j \geq 0, \ Y_j = -1 \text{ if } y_j < 0 \tag{1}$$

where the vector $\mathbf{y}$, $y_1 \ldots y_M$, is the word generated for meaning vector $\mathbf{x}$. In all cases described, a sparse 'grandmother' coding of the meaning is used with only one value in the vector of $+1$, all others being -1. To interpret a signal vector, the signal can be fed back to generate a meaning vector. Competition can then be applied to set one bit of the vector to $+1$, and the remaining bits to -1.

One significant difference in this model from that in Fyfe and Livingstone (1997) is that the successful interpretation of the environment is taken as given. By doing away with the interpretation of a complex environment, we can concentrate on the processes of language negotiation and evolution, adding complexity when basic phenomena are better understood.

The population training algorithm for language negotiation is described in Figure 12.1. A standard training algorithm can be used for individual agent training during population training. The training signal would be presented at the pupils' outputs, the corresponding meaning at the inputs and the training algorithm used to update the weights. Language would be successfully negotiated, but with no pressure on an agent to interpret the correct meaning from a presented word, the language could use a single word for more than one meaning. It would even be possible for a language to be negotiated which used

```
1. For t training rounds
2.     pick random environment
3.     for each agent (picked in random order)
4.         pick another agent to be teacher
5.         generate training signal from teacher
6.         train pupil and teacher on signal
```

Figure 12.1. Population-training algorithm.

only one word for all meanings. To be useful a communication scheme must carry information. A negotiated communication scheme should optimise the amount of information transmittable.

A learning algorithm which ensures the emergence of an optimal communication scheme – with a different signal shared by the whole population for each meaning state – is desired. The algorithm used in Oliphant (1997) works in the case where individuals in a population are removed and replaced by new learners, but does not work in a generation-based population training algorithm. The algorithm in Figure 12.1 is used as we wish to study evolution acting on language capability over generations of the population.

Oliphant's results suggest that optimal learning is performed by an algorithm using the transmission behaviour of the population to train language reception, and the reception behaviour to train language production. In this way an agent is most likely to succeed in communicating with other members of the population. This indicates inverse learning. An inverse, top-down learning approach is presented in a number of generative models for ANN learning presented by Hinton and Ghahramani (1997). In these models there are feedback generative weights and feedforward recognition weights, and the problem of recognition is posed in terms of which hidden units could be responsible for generating the input pattern (Figure 12.2).

An additional concern is that we wish to model the evolution of language capability. Thus our population must be able to negotiate useful languages even where the users are 'physically' incapable of learning a communication scheme capable of representing all environmental states. Similarly, the earliest protolanguage users, physiologically incapable of learning a modern language, must have been able to learn useful, if restricted, languages.

In our model, language agents are represented as two-layer ANNs with a meaning layer and a language layer. Meanings are represented as sparse bipolar

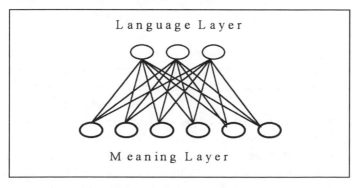

Figure 12.2. A language agent neural network. Recognition weights map language layer patterns to meanings; generative weights map meanings to patterns at the language layer.

vectors, with only one bit set to $+1$. Signals are represented at the language layer as arbitrary bipolar vectors. Thus, for N language neurons, there are 2^N possible signals or words in the language, and for M meaning neurons there are M possible meanings. Neurons in the meaning layer compete, such that any signal fed back from the language layer has only one corresponding meaning. When a signal is fed back during interpretation, it is likely that several meaning neurons will fire at different strengths, the competition allowing a single meaning to be chosen unambiguously.

The output word from one ANN is presented at the output layer of another agent ANN and fed back to produce a generated environment, defined in (2) – a 'meaning' vector – for the presented word. The error between the actual environment, x_i, and the generated environment, x_i', is used for learning by the receiver agent, as defined in (3). The error is multiplied by a learning rate, η, to determine the correction to be applied to the weights, w, connecting the layers.

$$x_i = \sum_{j=1}^{M} y_j w_{ij} \tag{2}$$

$$\Delta w_{ij} = \eta(x_i - x_i')y_j \tag{3}$$

We adapted the learning algorithm such that learning is only performed when a word is misclassified. When a word is correctly classified the receiving agent performs no learning. The learning algorithm is otherwise unchanged from (3).

More details of the model, including notes on implementation issues, can be found in Livingstone and Fyfe (1998).

Experiment 1: Language Negotiation in Populations of Homogeneous Language Capability

For our first experiment we test whether populations of networks are able to negotiate language with the learning algorithm just described. Language agents have 7 possible states, and agent populations are homogeneous, with from 0 to 7 language neurons.

We use spatially arranged populations, arranged in rings, and all communication occurs within a neighbourhood of the currently chosen agent. So, a teacher will be picked randomly according to the location of the current learner. The area of the neighbourhood is defined by a normal distribution centred on the learner. In all experiments described the standard deviation used is 0.6, placing a strong preference on immediate and very close neighbours. A ring arrangement is not necessary, but means that all agents have the same number of neighbours with the same chances of selection. With neighbourhood-limited communication the results in Figure 12.3 were produced for 300 and 1,000 training rounds

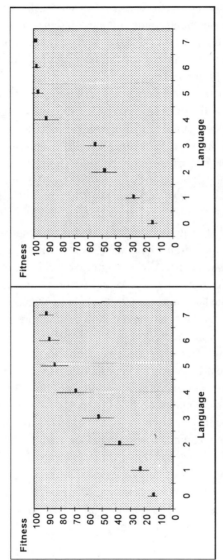

Figure 12.3. Average fitness, and standard deviation, with homogeneous populations of 0–7 language neurons measured over 10 experiment runs each case. With 300 (left) and 1,000 (right) negotiation rounds.

for populations of 40 agents, averaged over 10 runs for each language capability. Fitness is measured by computing the number of signals out of 100 received which are correctly interpreted in a separate fitness phase after completing learning. The same neighbourhoods used in language negotiation are used for communication during fitness evaluation.

With no language neurons, the performance of the agents is at chance level – on average agents guess the correct meaning 1 in 7 times. As language capability increases, so does fitness, showing that agents are successfully sharing information about their internal state. With more neurons, average success increases, and with two or more language neurons increased training time increases fitness. If training time is extended sufficiently, populations with four or more neurons will consistently negotiate a language capable of allowing all information to be shared.

The results show that using our learning algorithm, homogeneous populations are able to negotiate useful language, even where the capability for an optimal language does not exist. As the language capability increases, the success rate of communication increases. With four or more language units, the expressive power of the language exceeds the communication requirements of the environment. This has the potential for allowing multiple signals for the one meaning to be recognised correctly.

To test this, a homogeneous language population with four language units is trained for 5,000 rounds. This allows a very high degree of coordination among the agents but, due to the local communication, does not negotiate a common language over the whole population. It is observed that large neighbourhoods negotiate a common signal for a given meaning, but distant agents may have significant differences in communication schemes used. At the boundaries between neighbourhoods, agents may exist which interpret signals from different schemes correctly. This is shown in Figure 12.4. The three agents included each attained a maximal fitness score, interpreting all signals correctly. A degree of 'multilingualism' is possible in the agent communication schemes due to the redundancy in their representation capacity.

Experiment 2: Language-Physiology Coevolution

The second experiment aims to show evolution in language capability. The desired features of our model are that it should contain evolving populations of language learners whose language capability is in some way genetically determined. This adds a further constraint to the model, requiring further modification to allow agents of differing language capability to communicate. For this, we assume in these experiments that all agents have full language interpretation

```
Meaning 0                               Meaning 4
   Agent   4  -1   1  -1  -1               Agent   4   1  -1  -1  -1
   Agent   5  -1   1  -1   1               Agent   5   1   1  -1  -1
   Agent   6  -1   1  -1  -1               Agent   6   1  -1  -1  -1
Meaning 1                               Meaning 5
   Agent   4   1   1   1   1               Agent   4   1  -1  -1   1
   Agent   5   1  -1   1   1               Agent   5   1  -1  -1   1
   Agent   6   1  -1   1   1               Agent   6   1  -1  -1   1
Meaning 2                               Meaning 6
   Agent   4   1   1   1  -1               Agent   4  -1  -1   1   1
   Agent   5   1   1   1  -1               Agent   5  -1  -1   1   1
   Agent   6   1   1   1  -1               Agent   6  -1  -1   1   1
Meaning 3
   Agent   4  -1  -1   1  -1
   Agent   5  -1  -1   1  -1
   Agent   6  -1  -1   1  -1
```

Figure 12.4. The signals used by three adjacent agents for seven environmental states. Each meaning is represented by a bipolar (+ and –1 values) signal vector; e.g. to indicate meaning 0, agent 5 would send the signal (−1,1,−1,1). All three scored maximum fitness, interpreting all signals correctly, despite differing communication schemes.

capability, but genetically determined, variable language production capability. This is simply implemented by setting any language bits above an agent's capability to 0 when it produces a signal. A genetic binary string, representing 0 to 7 active production neurons in the language layer, determines the language ability of an agent.

When a signal with a number of zeroes is interpreted, only the bipolar signal bits affect the meaning found by feeding the signal back, the zeroes providing no information. Given the learning algorithm in (3), a zero signal bit also ensures that no learning is performed where no signal input is received. In this way, agents with greater language production ability than others can produce signals that can be learned by others.

Explicitly, if the three agents represented in Figure 12.4 had 2, 3 and 4 active production neurons in the language layer, they would produce the following signals to indicate meaning 0: (−1, 1, 0, 0), (−1, 1, −1, 0) and (−1, 1, −1, −1). When an agent receives a signal at its language layer, it receives and tries to interpret the complete signal, even if it is unable to produce such a signal.

As a heterogeneous population negotiates language, agents are able to learn to interpret signals from more language-capable neighbours. Agents in the neighbourhood of a language-capable agent have higher fitness than those further away. As fitness is demined by the ability to interpret the signals of others, the language-capable agent itself receives no benefit from its ability to produce clear signals (Figure 12.5). Since greater language production ability provides no direct benefit to an agent, it will not be favoured by

No. of language neurons	1	1	1	5	1	1	1
Fitness	29	26	42	26	35	33	24

Figure 12.5. Number of language neurons and fitness scores for a small population sample in a heterogeneous population of language agents. The central agent has a greater language production ability than that of the other agents, and its immediate neighbours benefit from the good signals it provides.

natural selection. The language-capable agent is behaving altruistically, helping agents in its neighbourhood with no benefit for itself. Another selection mechanism is required. Oliphant (1994) shows that spatially organising a population can enable the evolution of altruistic behaviour through the 'selfish gene' effect.

The same neighbourhood functions used for communication between agents are also used when selecting parents for successive generations. After fitness has been evaluated, the new generation is formed. A parent is picked randomly according to the relative fitnesses of all agents. A mate is picked for this parent according to the neighbourhood distribution. Two agents are then placed into the next generation, their language ability determined by applying crossover and mutation operators to the parent genes. A mutation rate of 0.005 per bit is used. Offspring are placed in the next generation in positions similar to those occupied by their parents in the previous generation.

This approximates kin selection, by placing close kin in similar neighbourhoods and enabling kin selection. Additionally, good signallers receive a more direct benefit. By increasing fitness of a neighbour, a good signaller increases the likelihood that it will be selected as the second partner for mating. The issue of spatial constraints on the evolution of communication is also discussed in Di Paolo (1998), based on a model in which agents can increase their chance of reward from social partner selection by occupying space in a dense cluster of agents.

A number of runs were performed, all starting with homogeneous populations with a single language production neuron. Two typical results can be seen in Figure 12.6. In these experiments there is a relatively rapid increase in the language capability of the population. In all runs the language capability evolves to an extent that the language is able to express all meanings. The populations do not evolve homogeneously.

In addition to the spatial selection providing a secondary benefit to a good signaller, the kinship rules make survival harder for defectors – agents which provide poor signals. Individual defectors can enjoy a free ride from good signallers, but groups of defectors form, providing each other with poor signals, limiting their survival and reproduction.

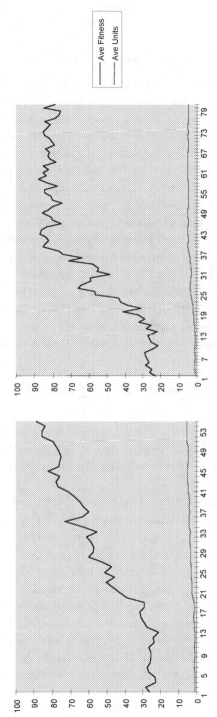

Figure 12.6. Average fitness and language neurons against generation. Two runs showing coevolution of language with language production capability. 300 training rounds per generation.

Experiment 3: Costly Language-Physiology Coevolution

With our model we aim to show how language may be adopted by a population despite the cost associated with possessing such an ability. For this purpose a fitness penalty is added to the model. By applying a penalty according to the number of language units, language-capable agents are penalised and less capable agents get a free ride. For the results that follow, each agent is penalised by an arbitrary four fitness points per active language node it possesses. Other penalties have been used without qualitatively altering results.

With spatial selection, as previously described, the population still evolves to a more language-capable one. Results of two experiments are shown in Figure 12.7. In both experiments, several generations pass before increased language ability evolves. The language ability may then evolve slowly, in gradual increments, or rapidly, in a smaller number of larger increments.

As seen in the results of Experiment 1 (Figure 12.3), at least four language neurons are required to achieve maximum fitness. This would incur a 16-point fitness penalty in the present experiments, resulting in a maximum possible fitness of 84 points. In both runs, near-maximum fitness is achieved.

Experiment 4: Negotiation and Evolution Without Spatial Organisation

We have stated the importance of spatial organisation for the previous sets of results. In this experiment we demonstrate this importance by reducing the strength of spatial selection and observing the results, which are in accord with Oliphant (1994).

The radius of neighbourhoods can be changed, larger neighbourhoods weakening the effects of spatial organisation, and the effects on language negotiation and evolution observed. Larger neighbourhoods weaken the effect of kin selection, as agents will usually not be communicating with their 'kin', and reduce the likelihood that a good signaller agent will be selected as the partner of another agent to which good signals have been provided.

This is less serious where there is no cost of communicating – a very wide neighbourhood is reached before evolution of language fails. Where there is a cost, even small increases in neighbourhood size prevent the evolution of language. This is demonstrated in Figure 12.8. These graphs show that some form of spatial organisation is necessary for the evolution of an altruistic language ability.

Spatial organisation also has an effect on language negotiation in this model. With small neighbourhoods, language forms in tight clusters. Close neighbours

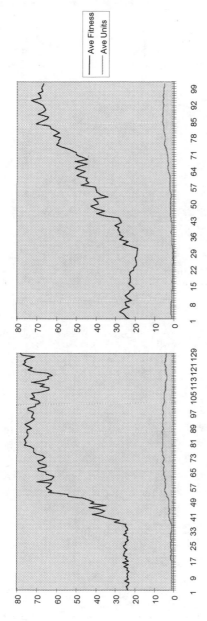

Figure 12.7. Average fitness and language neurons against generation. Two runs showing costly coevolution of language with language production capability. 300 language training rounds per generation:

211

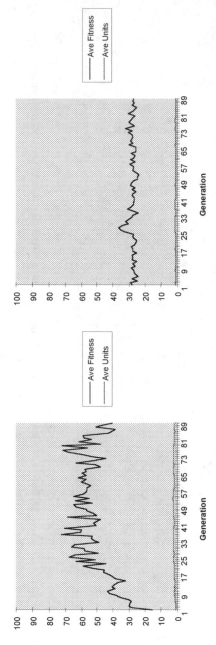

Figure 12.8. Evolution of language with reduced pressure from kin selection. *Left*, standard deviation 12, noncostly language. *Right*, standard deviation 3, costly language.

share negotiated languages, while two agents selected from distant points may be unable to communicate with each other. With larger neighbourhoods, the clusters are larger and ultimately global coordination of language can occur.

Discussion

The experiments discussed so far show evolution in the language ability of populations of simple language agents. We now consider the relevance of this to the evolution of language in hominids.

Our artificial language lacks almost all of the properties of a real language – in particular there is no grammar – no word morphology or sentence syntax. All communication consists of single words for single meanings. At the same time our artificial language also differs from human involuntary nonverbal vocalisations, such as laughter, crying or screaming, in that the communication scheme is learned rather than inherited.

Our model can be considered an abstract representation of the evolution of language – language provides an unspecified selective benefit to groups of kin who are able to share information. A number of different ideas concerning the 'original' selective benefits of language exist, it being widely agreed, however, that language does indeed confer a selective benefit. But language is clearly used to serve a great many functions (Dunbar 1997). Embodied experiments on the evolution of language focus on very specific uses of language, and some work has been carried out on evaluating the adaptive value of specific features or uses of language (for example, Cangelosi and Harnard 1998). 'Disembodied' experiments, such as those presented in this chapter, simply accept that language provides a benefit, and directly reward agents for successful communication.

Although not grounded in an environment, the language ability of the agents in our model can be considered as their ability to learn useful languages – with inevitable cost and potential benefit. Our model clearly shows that despite physiological costs, such abilities can evolve. This process takes a number of generations before succeeding in a population. Individuals of different abilities frequently coexist within populations. To allow language agents of differing abilities to communicate we have given all agents a full capability to receive and learn signals, even those above their own production ability. This detail is also important for the evolution of language. For the evolution of language to occur over a period of time, it is necessary that language be learnable and useful at every stage of phylogenetic evolution.

Burling (this volume) argues that for the evolution of language to occur, the ability to comprehend language must exceed that necessary to produce it. He further argues that it is the act of interpreting an action that turns it into a signal. Lyn and Savage-Rumbaugh (1998) provide evidence for the language-learning abilities of pygmy chimpanzees, which by far exceed their ability to produce language. Similarly in our model the ability to learn to interpret signals exceeds the ability to produce them. Within our model the ability to comprehend language is fixed throughout although it is clear that the ability to understand, as well as to produce, language has evolved.

To conclude, some models have highlighted selection mechanisms required for evolution of altruistic language users or for the self-organisation of lexicons and grammars. Further models supporting evolutionary theories of language are required that demonstrate evolving populations in which agents are able to negotiate and learn useful languages at all stages of their evolution. This has been achieved, at a high level of abstraction, in the model presented here. We have shown communities of varying abilities negotiating and using language successfully. Language ability has been seen to evolve gradually in communities of agents, and agents of differing abilities have been able to coexist within those communities with kin selection favouring individuals which are more language-capable. Prospects for further work include the evolution of agents capable of rudimentary grammars from grammar-incapable agents and information-theoretic studies of evolving communication schemes.

Acknowledgements

Thanks are due to Mike Oliphant for his helpful comments on an earlier draft of this chapter.

References

Baldwin, J. M. 1896. A new factor in evolution. *American Naturalist* **30**: 441–451.

Batali, J. 1994. Innate biases and critical periods: combining evolution and learning in the acquisition of syntax. In R. Brooks and P. Maes (eds), *Proceedings of the Fourth Artificial Life Workshop*. Cambridge, MA: MIT Press, pp. 160–171.

Batali, J. 1998. Computational simulations of the emergence of grammar. In J. R. Hurford, M. Studdert-Kennedy and C. Knight (eds), *Approaches to the Evolution of Language: Social and cognitive bases*. Cambridge: Cambridge University Press, pp. 405–426.

Cangelosi, A. and D. Parisi. 1996. The emergence of a 'language' in an evolving population of neural networks. Paper read at the 18th Conference of the Cognitive Science Society, San Diego, CA.

Cangelosi, A. and S. Harnard. 1998. Adaptive advantages of 'hearsay' over direct sensorimotor experience. Paper read at the Second International Conference on the Evolution of Language, University of East London.

Deacon, T. W. 1992. Brain-language coevolution. In J. A. Hawkins and M. Gell-Mann (eds), *The Evolution of Human Languages*. Redwood City, CA: Addison-Wesley, pp. 273–303.

Di Paolo, E. A. 1997. An investigation into the evolution of communication. *Adaptive Behavior* **6**: 285–324.

Di Paolo, E. A. 1998. Spatio-temporal and structural constraints in the evolution of communication. Paper read at the Second International Conference on the Evolution of Language, University of East London.

Dunbar, R. 1997. *Grooming, Gossip and the Evolution of Language*. London: Faber and Faber.

Fyfe, C. and D. Livingstone. 1997. Developing a community language. Poster presented at the Fourth European Conference on Artificial Life, Brighton.

Hinton, G. E. and Z. Ghahramani. 1997. Generative models for discovering sparse distributed representations. *Philosophical Transactions of the Royal Society B*. **352**: 1177–1190.

Hutchins, E. and B. Hazelhurst. 1995. How to invent a lexicon: the development of shared symbols in interaction. In N. Gilbert and R. Conte (eds), *Artificial Societies: The computer simulation of social life*. London University College, London Press, pp. 157–189.

Lieberman, P. 1992. On the evolution of human language. In J. A. Hawkins and M. Gell-Mann (eds), *The Evolution of Human Languages*. Redwood City, CA: Addison-Wesley, pp. 21–47.

Livingstone, D. and C. Fyfe. 1998. A computational model of language-physiology coevolution. *Computing and Information Systems Departmental Journal* **5**: 55–62, University of Paisley.

Lyn, H. and E. S. Savage-Rumbaugh. 1998. Observational word learning in bonobos. Paper read at the Second International Conference on the Evolution of Language, University of East London.

Oliphant, M. 1994. Evolving cooperation in the non-iterated prisoner's dilemma: the importance of spatial organization. In R. Brooks and P. Maes (eds), *Proceedings of the Fourth Artificial Life Workshop*. Cambridge, MA: MIT Press, pp. 349–352.

Oliphant, M. 1996. The dilemma of Saussurean communication. *BioSystems* **37**: 31–38.

Oliphant, M. 1997. *Formal Approaches to Innate and Learned Communication: Laying the foundation for language*. Doctoral dissertation, University of California, San Diego.

Steels, L. 1996. Emergent adaptive lexicons. In P. Maes, M. Mataric, J.-A. Meyer, J. Pollack and S.W. Wilson (eds), *From Animals to Animats 4: Proceedings of the Fourth International Conference on Simulation of Adaptive Behavior*. Cambridge, MA: MIT Press, pp. 562–567.

PART III

THE EMERGENCE OF SYNTAX

13

Introduction: The Emergence of Syntax

JAMES R. HURFORD

The chapters in this part of the volume reflect a movement in the late 1990s away from a focus on the genetic evolution of the innate Language Acquisition Device towards accounts invoking cultural and linguistic evolution as well. This is not to deny that the human linguistic capacity evolved biologically, but to acknowledge that such evolution was slow and complicatedly entangled with other aspects of human evolution. The whole part is neatly sandwiched by its first and last chapters, contributed by generative linguists. The first of these argues against narrowly biological adaptationist accounts of language evolution, and the last (complementarily but quite independently, as it happens) casts its contribution to language evolution research in the form of a clearly historical exercise in linguistic reconstruction. The chapters in the middle of this sandwich are no less meaty, many of them setting out on a complementary quest for accounts of how languages could have evolved relatively rapidly into their particular complex modern shapes by nonbiological mechanisms, within a relatively static biological frame of reference.

Several themes connect the chapters in this part, reflecting the general movement just described. These themes are:

- Complex innate principles of the language faculty, such as subjacency, cannot be accounted for by mechanisms of adaptive biological evolution (Lightfoot, Newmeyer).
- More generally, certain features of grammar were or are nonadaptive (Carstairs-McCarthy, Wray).
- Central features of syntactic structure are exaptations of preexisting nonsyntactic structure (Carstairs-McCarthy, Bickerton).
- Syntactic structures evolve (at least in part) on the basis of preexisting semantic representations (Bickerton, Kirby, Hurford).

- Protolanguage evolves into language via stages of holistic/formulaic expression (Kirby, Hurford, Wray).
- Syntactic rules emerge from unstructured data via a new breed of learners, capable of segmentation and generalisation (Wray, Kirby).
- Items of linguistic structure are selected and perpetuated in the historical cycle of language transmission by mechanisms favouring generality (Kirby, Hurford, Worden).
- The processes of language evolution through a historical cycle of learning and exemplification are modelled computationally (Kirby, Hurford, Worden).

One might have expected syntactic theorists to have been prominent in the literature on human evolution, given that what is most remarkable about humans is their capacity for syntactically complex language. But until very recently, syntactic theorists have kept away from evolutionary theorising. This avoidance has tended to apply to linguists in general; paradoxically, mainstream scholarly linguists have typically been outnumbered in speculation on the evolution of language by anthropologists, psychologists and palaeontologists (witness the list of contributors to Lock and Peters's massive handbook (Lock and Peters 1996)).

Why have linguists traditionally been so reticent in contributing to evolutionary debates? The very complexity of human languages, especially their syntactic components, of which linguists above all (and one might even say only linguists) have been fully aware, is a severe obstacle to theorising. Although evolutionary biology is a well-established field, one notices a similar reticence among many biologists to engage in evolutionary speculation, because biologists, above all, know how complex the explananda are. Just characterising the intricacies of human syntax has been work enough for linguists, let alone worrying about how it all might fit into an evolutionary scenario. But the time for turning to the evolution of such complexity had to come.

As the chapters in this part of the volume illustrate, the time has come, and linguists are now getting involved in evolutionary theorising. Less than a decade ago, it would have been impossible to assemble such a coherent set of contributions by scholars who have made their reputations in nonevolutionary aspects of linguistics. Here, now, we have such an assembly of linguists from markedly different backgrounds, some willing to outline actual mechanisms by which syntactic complexity may have emerged, and others (well, just one, actually) clearly sceptical of such attempts, but taking them seriously enough to mount a closely reasoned counterargument.

It remains the case that the linguists most concerned with the complexity of the explananda are those with least sympathy for proposed evolutionary explanations. In this part, David Lightfoot's chapter acts as a salutary counterweight to any tendency to assume, without detailed argument, that any universal aspect of the syntax of human languages must be adaptive. Although Lightfoot is the only contributor in this part who voices what might be taken as a negative note on theories of language evolution, in fact his arguments in no way clash with the tenor of the other chapters. This is an indication of how far and how quickly theorising about the evolution of syntax has shifted in the decade since Pinker and Bloom's influential paper (Pinker and Bloom 1990).

Popular science books can give an impression of simple intellectual battle-lines drawn up with Dawkins, Pinker and Dennett on one side (the 'adaptation-ists') and Chomsky, Gould and Lewontin on the other. As Andrew Carstairs-McCarthy's chapter notes, 'What both sides in this debate have generally had in common, so far, is an all-or-nothing attitude: either grammar is adaptive or it is not. But from the point of view of evolutionary biology, that attitude seems oversimple.' Pinker and Bloom's conspicuously drawn parallel between the structure of the eye and the structure of human languages certainly tended to start people thinking along straightforwardly adaptationist lines about the complexity of language. Yet, for all its virtues in reviving discussion of the evolution of language, it is clear that Pinker and Bloom's analogy is in many ways misplaced. The eye evolved separately many times, whereas human lan-guage has only evolved once; the evolution of the eye took tens of millions of years, at least, whereas it seems that the evolution of human language was faster by several orders of magnitude; and there is clearly a social, communicative dimension to the evolution of language that is lacking in the case of the eye. Pinker and Bloom argued that the innate human capacity to acquire language was likely to have been selected by orthodox Darwinian processes. Thus it seemed, at the beginning of the 1990s, that work on the evolution of syntax was set to take a decidely adaptationist (and biological) course. Lightfoot's chapter in this volume can be seen in this context. It echoes his position in a commentary on another broadly adaptationist proposal from the early 1990s (see Newmeyer 1991; Lightfoot 1991). Lightfoot here discusses some quite complex and ab-stract constraints on grammatical structures, underdetermined by any evidence that learners are likely to observe, and hence attributable to a definite bias in the learning mechanism. He shows how these constraints have a dysfunctional effect, actually preventing speakers from expressing certain messages in what would seem to be the most straightforward way. It should be no surprise that any complex system has advantages and disadvantages; efficiency is always a matter of compromise between costs and benefits.

None of the chapters in this part argue for biological adaptation of brain structures as the central mechanism behind the emergence of complex syntax. None of them deny the existence of selective pressures, either, but adaptation is not their prime focus. Thus, Carstairs-McCarthy's central argument is that a particular feature of language, for a long part of its prehistory, was not well adapted. Derek Bickerton advances an explicitly exaptationist position: (much of) syntactic complexity is built on nonlinguistic structure that existed before. Alison Wray also argues explicitly that much of grammar is dysfunctional for day-to-day communicative activities. The computational models of Simon Kirby and Jim Hurford are consonant with Bickerton's view, as they assume mental representational structures which preexist communication, and which give rise to linguistic structures. The title of Kirby's paper is 'Syntax without natural selection', emphasising its nonadaptationist stance. Kirby, Hurford and Worden all assume a constant biological endowment, in the shape of specific learning mechanisms, which enables cultural evolution of languages. Finally, Newmeyer's chapter does not continue his earlier (1991) broadly adaptationist arguments, but deals with the evolution of languages within the context of an unchanging biological endowment, and includes an argument specifically against a particular form of adaptive evolution (genetic assimilation, or the Baldwin Effect) as an account of properties of the innate human capacity for syntax.

Lightfoot's chapter, and the second part of Newmeyer's, bear testimony to the great complexity of syntactic structure. Nonlinguists are apt to dismiss arguments by linguists on the grounds that they are too complicated. This is like concluding that general relativity can't be true because you can't understand it. And just as it would be wrong to disbelieve in electrons and quarks because you can't experience them directly, it is wrong to discount linguists' arguments involving invisible (and inaudible) elements of linguistic structure, such as the brackets, indices and traces which are at the centre of Lightfoot's, and to some extent Newmeyer's, arguments. In the hope that it will help nonlinguists to get the drift of such arguments, some points of background from syntactic theory are given at the end of this introduction, in a brief appendix.

The first and last chapters in this part, Lightfoot's and Newmeyer's, are by linguists who have made their names within the Chomskyan tradition of generative grammar. The level of technical syntactic detail in their arguments exceeds that of the intervening chapters, which tend toward programmatic, 'big-picture' statements. There remains a significant gap to be bridged between such programmatic proposals and the degree of detailed knowledge that has now been accumulated about the syntax of languages. I will give three examples.

Carstairs-McCarthy makes a broad structural proposal for the origin of the category 'grammatical subject': it arose, he suggests, from a structural parallel with the syllable-structure category 'onset'. But in many languages, specific constraints apply to grammatical subjects, as opposed to (direct or indirect) objects. Lightfoot's examples (11)–(14) illustrate this: wh-items cannot be extracted from the subjects of tensed clauses, whereas such extractions from other functional positions are normally grammatical. Carstairs-McCarthy's account of the origin of the category 'subject' does not address the specific properties that generative grammarians have identified as peculiar to subjects.

Bickerton claims 'In fact, it has proved possible to derive most if not all of the basic principles of universal grammar from a small set of primitives which includes only the obligatory representation of thematic roles, a general economy measure ("all constituents without independent reference must choose the nearest available referent") and a pragmatic assumption ("no two arguments of a clause can refer to the same referent unless one of them is lexically marked to this effect")'. It is not clear that this broad claim extends to many of the examples given by Lightfoot.

A third example of the large gap between those concerned with syntactic detail and the 'big-picture' (or 'broad-brush') theorists of the evolution of syntax is seen in the simple syntaxes of the emergent languages in Kirby's and Hurford's computer models. Their simulated populations converge on languages whose grammars can be completely described on one sheet of paper, obviously falling far short of the complexity of real languages.

So what is the value of such big-picture proposals as are included in this collection? A clue lies in the very course of syntactic theorising over the last forty years. Undoubtedly, generative grammar has expanded, with the result that vastly more detailed knowledge has now been accumulated about the syntax of languages than ever before. And some of this detailed knowledge is expressible in generalisable form, as in the case of the subjacency constraints mentioned by Lightfoot and Newmeyer. The field has also moved very fast, so that today's theoretical arguments are typically quite different from those of even a decade ago. This is often not because the old arguments have been settled, but rather because the very speed at which the field has changed has resulted in the implications for large areas of language being left unresolved. Furthermore, syntactic theory has fragmented into a host of rival theories. See, for example, the large number, at least a dozen, of alternative generative theories surveyed and summarised in Brown and Miller (1996).

In brief, narrow syntactic theorising, despite undeniable gains, is in a state of considerable turmoil, and needs to start looking beyond its traditional horizons for explanatory principles of kinds that it has not previously considered. No contributor to this volume denies the central part played by the specific dispositions of human language learners in the structuring of language. But the chapters here place language acquisition in the wider context of the arena of use, history and evolution. In this wider context, types of explanation for universals in syntactic structure become available which are either alternative or complementary to those appealing to the special nature of the language acquisition device.

Carstairs-McCarthy draws attention to significant structural parallels between syllable structure and simple clause structure. It is suggested that the human capacity for mental representation of signals was constrained, at both the syllabic and the clausal level, and for many millennia, by the same structural straitjacket. For Carstairs-McCarthy, the step to modern syntactic structures came later, with a capacity to represent recursively embedded structures. It seems reasonable to suppose that a capacity to represent non-self-embedding hierarchical structures preceded a capacity to handle recursion. Although Bickerton, Kirby and Hurford take as given a capacity for representing recursively self-embedded (semantic) structures, there is in fact no necessary conflict between Carstairs-McCarthy's proposal and theirs. Carstairs-McCarthy does not suggest that *Homo erectus*'s representations of meanings were constrained in the same way as his representations of possible signals. It is possible, and would be an instructive exercise, to put Carstairs-McCarthy's and Bickerton's (and Wray's) proposals together into a finer-grained and more detailed story.

For Bickerton, recursively hierarchical syntactic structure is an exaptation from preexisting semantic structure. The major shift between protolanguage and modern language came with a steep rise in signal-processing capacity. Although Bickerton does not single out recursive self-embedding as a special problem, it is clear that self-embedding does pose special processing problems (for example in a system where the online store of the structure currently being processed cannot reliably record and distinguish more than one structure of the same category). Carstairs-McCarthy's move to recursion and Bickerton's 'catastrophic' shift in signal-processing capacity perhaps coincided. If they did, both authors concur in locating this shift at around three hundred thousand years ago, coinciding with the appearance of late archaic to modern *Homo sapiens*.

Wray argues cogently that protolanguage is still with us. There has been a tendency to talk of Bickertonian protolanguage 'giving way to', or being wholly supplanted by, modern language. Bickerton concurs with Wray that such was not the case: 'there is no need to suppose that in catastrophic changes of state, one state supersedes or abolishes the other. . . . We need not imagine parents who spoke only protolanguage with children who spoke like us'. Wray's and Bickerton's views coincide on the implications of the high cost of processing grammatically articulated language.

Bickerton's implicit assumptions about the nature of the semantic structure preexisting modern language are quite different from Wray's explicit view of the semantics of protolanguage. Bickerton envisages discrete and distinct mental categories corresponding to predicates and their arguments; in protolanguage there could have been 'words' corresponding to argument concepts and others corresponding to predicate concepts. The step from protolanguage to language involved externalising the syntax of semantic representations (more or less like predicate logic, without quantifiers, for Bickerton), so that, roughly, the forms corresponding to predicates became verbs, the forms corresponding to arguments became nouns, and the larger forms expressing embedded propositions became subordinate clauses. Thus, for Bickerton, the seeds of reference and predication are already present in the semantics of the protolanguage. The meanings of protolanguage utterances were essentially truth-conditional. (In fact, natural languages do not fit the syntax of predicate logic as neatly as Bickerton implies, as common nouns, adjectives, prepositions and verbs are all semantically predicates, and only proper nouns correspond to the atomic arguments of predicate logic.)

Wray's view of the semantics of protolanguage is quite different, with messages being essentially holistic speech acts, centrally pragmatic in function, and without inbuilt reference and predication. For Wray, reference and predication emerge with the segmentation of protolanguage utterances into smaller meaningful parts. This illustrates another difference between Bickerton and Wray. One can identify two views of the move from protolanguage to language, which one can label 'synthetic' and 'analytic'. Bickerton takes the synthetic view. The original words of protolanguage had meanings which became the atomic constituents of the meanings of the larger utterances of full language. The original words of protolanguage were strung together to make the phrases and sentences of full language. Wray takes an analytic view. The original words of protolanguage had meanings which became the meanings of high-level constituents in full language. The original words of protolanguage were dissected into parts which came to express the atomic meanings of full language.

Thus Bickerton and Wray diverge along two separate dimensions. For Bickerton, protolanguage meanings were truth-conditional, and the step to language was synthetic; for Wray, protolanguage meanings were pragmatic ('interpersonal'), and the step to language was analytic. The two dimensions are independent, as Kirby's chapter in this part in fact assumes a kind of truth-conditional semantics for presyntactic stages of language, but combines this with a model of an analytic move from syntaxless early language to later syntactic language. Kirby and Hurford differ along the same analytic/synthetic dimension as Wray and Bickerton. One can summarise the positions as in Table 13.1.

These various background assumptions about the move from presyntactic protolanguage to language are not argued for in any great detail by these authors (and especially not by Kirby or Hurford). The present analysis is intended to point out directions for future debate. It is notable that the 'Pragmatic/Synthetic'

Table 13.1. *Perspectives on protolanguage*

		Move from Protolanguage to Language was:	
		Analytic	Synthetic
Protolanguage meanings were:	Truth-conditional	Kirby	Bickerton Hurford
	Pragmatic	Wray	

cell in Table 13.1 is empty. It is more difficult, though not actually impossible, to conceive of a Pragmatic/Synthetic scenario. In such a scenario, there would presumably have been protolanguage referential 'words' for I and you, two of the central atomic components of any speech act meaning (illocution).

Kirby's chapter is one of the first in a current spate of research reports which describe fully implemented computational models of the evolution of languages with (simple) syntax in a population of learners. The chapter builds on, and significantly extends, the work of Batali (1998) (in the predecessor volume to this one). This new trend, the computational modelling of evolving populations, with individuals endowed with quite complex behaviours, is made possible by the spectacular advances in computing power of the last decade. A collection of such work appears in a companion volume to this (Briscoe in press), which contains a survey article on these works (Hurford in press).

As mentioned earlier, Kirby models the emergence of syntex 'analytically'; the essential capacity in his learners which gives rise to syntax is a capacity to segment utterances and generalise over chance coincidences in the meanings of identical segments of different utterances. This is just the same process as envisaged by Wray in her chapter.

Hurford's chapter in this part follows Kirby's lead, modelling the evolution of a syntactic language from an initial languageless state in a population of learners. Hurford adds recursive power to the model (but see now Kirby in press) and focuses on the way in which the mechanism of social transmission of language tends to select general (i.e. syntactic) mappings between meanings and forms. Hurford models the evolution of syntax 'synthetically', via learners with a capacity to invent constructions in which previously learned atomic forms are included.

Kirby's and Hurford's computational models highlight a kind of language evolution which is not driven by clearly functional pressures, such as a pressure toward easily parsable structures, or toward socially useful meanings. The very fact that the history of a language passes through stages of data compression (language learning) and exemplification (language use) is sufficient to guide a language over time toward general, regular structures. Kirby and Hurford emphasise different kinds of generalisation and regularisation, with Kirby arguing persuasively that this historical process favours the evolution of one of the most basic features of language, namely compositionality of meaning. The compositionality principle states that the meaning of a whole is a function of the meanings of its parts and of the way the parts are put together. Compositionality is so basic to language that it is usually simply taken for granted, and the idea of explaining why languages should be organised in this way is seldom contemplated. But Kirby's chapter shows how the historical compression-exemplification cycle leads to the evolution of compositional languages.

Worden's chapter shares with Kirby's and Hurford's a degree of formal explicitness, and similarly reports on a computationally implemented model. It begins to bridge the gap between the level of syntactic detail typical of generative treatments of syntax and the kinds of big-picture theorising more typical in work on the evolution of language. With a quite specific model of syntactic structure, derived in part from various extant generative theories, Worden, like Kirby and Hurford, explores the implications of the historical passage of a language through the cycle of learning and exemplification, and offers specific explanations for several widespread characteristics of language. Worden differs from Kirby and Hurford in introducing functional pressures into the historical picture, including ease of learning and usefulness of meaning. Kirby and Hurford do not deny the relevance of such functional pressures, but leave them out of consideration in their 'purer' models, as a way of disentangling the contributions made by function on the one hand and the basic fact of historical transmission by exemplification on the other. Several of the features of language which Worden's model explains are examples of the kind of generality and regularity which Kirby's and Hurford's models also explain. The details of implementation in the three models are all rather different, but they converge on strikingly similar conclusions, with respect to the emergence of syntactic regularities in languages.

Finally, Newmeyer's chapter is a strikingly bold attempt, the first of its kind, to argue for a particular ordering of the major sentence constituents in the earliest human language, SOV. Like all such bold speculations (including Bickerton's concept of protolanguage), it will raise many questions. The fact that Newmeyer has thrown this suggestion into the ring, with arguments that can be taken seriously, is of great value. He has shown that it is possible to advance sensible arguments relating to what might previously have been thought to have been an unanswerable question.

Appendix on Syntactic Notation

Speakers of a language have mental representations of the grammatical structure of sentences in that language. While ordinary native speakers clearly do not, consciously or otherwise, store such scholarly grammatical labels as 'Noun', 'Verb' and 'CP' in their heads (any more than electrons carry little labels on them saying 'electron'), the organisation of speakers' knowledge of their language in the brain is in terms of such differentiated categories. Speakers mentally represent sentences in their language as partitioned into nonarbitrary chunks, each with its own characteristic contribution to the meaning and over-all well-formedness of the sentence. In the notation of Lightfoot's examples, such chunks ('constituents') are marked off by matching left and right square brackets, sometimes labelled with a subscript indicating the structural type of the chunk, e.g. [$_{CP}$that Kim hit Tim]. The structural type of a constituent is crucial to the meaning and well-formedness of the sentence in which it oc-curs. The wrong type of constituent in the wrong place can be a reason for ungrammaticality.

Speakers' knowledge of their language includes both positive and negative knowledge – knowledge of what is a well-formed expression in the language, and also knowledge of what couldn't be a well-formed expression in the lan-guage. Linguists argue on the grounds of both well-formed and hypothetical ill-formed examples. Ill-formed examples are examples that a native speaker, on due reflection, judges to be so. A star, or asterisk, prefixed to an exam-ple indicates that the string of words so prefixed is ill-formed in the language in question. In linguistic argumentation, sets of asterisked and non-asterisked examples are typically juxtaposed and the difference in well-formedness thus indicated is attributed to the effect of some general principle of grammatical structure applying to a minimal structural difference between the examples. When reading syntactic arguments, you need to slow down a bit, but it's not as bad as maths. Hint to nonlinguists: for each set of juxtaposed examples, identify the minimal difference between asterisked and non-asterisked examples, and relate this to the surrounding discussion.

Speakers' knowledge of their language is abstract enough to include elements which have no phonetic realisation. Linguists postulate these in order to give the most general account of the whole (infinite) set of judgments that a speaker can make about strings of words. In Lightfoot's chapter, such invisible elements are variously indicated by: GAP, 0 (zero), and e (mnemonic for 'empty'). To be reminded of the justification for such invisible elements, a simple exercise is to take a short substring containing them out of the whole example, and consider whether, on its own, such a substring would be well-formed. For instance, one of Lightfoot's examples is: *Who_i do you think [e_i Ray saw e_i]?* Reading this whole sentence aloud (without the brackets and subscripted e's, as they are inaudible elements of structure), it can be heard that this is a perfectly commonplace English question. What then is the point of the e_i? Consider just the last e_i in the example. Try saying just the last two words on their own, i.e. **Ray saw*. This could be expected to be well-formed, since it forms a proper constituent of the larger sentence (marked as such by the square brackets around it), but, on its own **Ray saw* is, at best, elliptical. *Ray saw what?* we are inclined to ask. In the larger sentence *Who do you think Ray saw?* this elliptical feeling does not arise, because as native English speakers, we know that the 'gap' after the verb *saw* is legitimated by the sentence-initial *who*.

Newmeyer's arguments also include examples with such empty categories. His Japanese examples (17) and (19) are probably particularly hard for a non-Japanese-speaking nonlinguist to disentangle. The first thing to note is that in Japanese, as in most SOV languages, relative clauses precede their head nouns. So, for example, the noun phrase *the man who owns a dog* would in Japanese look more like a quasi-English string **dog-own man*. Furthermore, such preposed relative clauses, as Newmeyer's example shows, can be used to express meanings that in English cannot be expressed with parallel postposed relative clause constructions. Newmeyer's example is parallel to something like *the man who owns the dog that barked*, but which comes out in Japanese like the quasi-English **e_i owns dog barked man*, where the 'gap' shown by e_i is coreferential with man.

Finally, the relationship between the invisible element and its legitimating word elsewhere in the sentence is often referred to by linguists, as by Lightfoot here, as 'movement', as if the legitimating element had once been in the place of the invisible marker, and migrated, leaving a 'trace' behind it. The relationship between the 'moved' element and its 'original' location is indicated by giving them common subscripts.

References

Batali, J. 1998. Computational simulations of the emergence of grammar. In J. R. Hurford, M. Studdert-Kennedy and C. Knight (eds), *Approaches to the Evolution of Language: Social and cognitive bases*. Cambridge: Cambridge University Press, pp. 405–426.

Briscoe, E. J. (ed) In press. *Linguistic Evolution through Language Acquisition: Formal and computational models*. Cambridge: Cambridge University Press.

Brown, E. K. and J. Miller (eds). 1996. *Concise Encyclopedia of Syntactic Theories*. Oxford: Pergamon.

Hurford, J. R. In press. Expression/induction models of language evolution: dimensions and issues. In E. J. Briscoe (ed), *Linguistic Evolution through Language Acquisition: Formal and computational models*. Cambridge: Cambridge University Press.

Kirby, S. In press. Learning, bottlenecks and the evolution of recursive syntax. In E. J. Briscoe (ed), *Linguistic Evolution through Language Acquisition: Formal and computational models*. Cambridge: Cambridge University Press.

Lightfoot, D. 1991. Subjacency and sex. *Language and Communication* **11**: 67–69.

Lock, A. and C. Peters. 1996. *Handbook of Human Symbolic Evolution*. Oxford: Clarendon.

Newmeyer, F. 1991. Functional explanation in linguistics and the origin of language. *Language and Communication* **11**: 3–28.

Pinker, S. and P. Bloom. 1990. Natural language and natural selection. *Behavioral and Brain Sciences* **13**: 707–784.

14

The Spandrels of the Linguistic Genotype

DAVID LIGHTFOOT

Universal Grammar

Under one view, a grammar is a mental entity, represented in the mind/brain of an individual and characterising that individual's linguistic capacity.[1] It emerges on exposure to some linguistic environment, which triggers the development of a grammar from some structured initial state, common to the species. That initial state is 'Universal Grammar', the part of the genotype which is relevant for the emergence of a grammar. Linguists say that a child is exposed to some primary linguistic data, and that UG develops into some particular grammar (1a); more generally, one could characterise the phenomenon as in (1b): a child is exposed to a trigger experience, and the linguistic genotype develops its phenotypical properties.

(1) a. primary linguistic data (UG → grammar)
b. trigger experience (linguistic genotype → phenotype)

Under this perspective, what has evolved in the species is not a set of languages, nor grammars, but the language faculty itself – the linguistic genotype, UG. If we are to investigate 'the evolution of language' in the species, we shall ask about the evolution of UG.

UG is plastic (consistent with knowing Hopi or Ewe), modular, algebraic, and (unlike anything found in animal communication) computational. It has principles and parameters, and dictates that grammars consist of a lexicon and computational operations. To illustrate the computational operations and to get a sense of how linguists reason about UG, let us consider one property.

A UG Condition on Movement Traces

English grammars have an operation whereby the complementiser *that* may be deleted (2). So we have structures like (3), where *that* may be present or not

('0' for zero, an absent complementiser).

(2)   Delete *that*.
(3) a. It was apparent [that/0 Kay left].
    b. The book [that/0 Kay wrote] arrived.
    c. It was obvious [that/0 Kay left].

This operation does not apply in languages like Dutch and French, where the counterparts of *that*, *dat* and *que*, are invariably present. Nonetheless, this English-specific operation is learnable, because children are likely to hear sentences in both forms, sometimes with the complementiser present, sometimes not. Therefore the operation in (2) meets the basic requirements for inclusion in English grammars.

However, as with virtually every grammatical operation, we find that many aspects are not determined by normal childhood experience. Certain instances of *that* may not be deleted. Consider (4), where only the structures with *that* actually occur in speech.

(4) a. It was apparent yesterday [that/*0 Kay left].
    b. The book arrived yesterday [that/*0 Kay wrote].
    c. [That/*0 Kay left] was obvious to all of us.
    d. Fay believes, but Kay doesn't, [that/*0 Ray is smart].

This is a standard poverty-of-stimulus problem. Since children are not told that the ungrammatical variant in, say, (4c) does not occur, principles of UG must be implicated. Linguists have argued that complementisers can be deleted only where they head the complement of some adjacent overt word (see Hornstein and Lightfoot 1991 for one account). In (4a–d), each instance of *that* heads something which is not the complement of the preceding word; consequently it may not be deleted.

It was discovered that the same condition applies to the traces of movement. In a sentence like *Who did Jay see?*, *who* leaves a trace when it moves from the complement of *see* (5a). In more complex movement, where *who* is understood in an embedded clause, *who* moves first to the front of its clause (CP) and only then to its final position, leaving a coindexed trace with each movement (5b). In (5), all traces head the complement of the adjacent overt word, and therefore they are licit.

(5) a. Who_i did Jay see e_i?
    b. Who_i did Jay say [$_{CP}e_i$ that Fay saw e_i]?

This entails that alongside *Who was it apparent that Kay saw?*, we do not find **Who was it apparent yesterday that Kay saw?* The structure would be (6a): the clause is not a complement of the adjacent word *yesterday*, and the trace at the front of the embedded CP (bold) is illicit. If *yesterday* is not present, then the clause is the complement of and adjacent to *apparent* and the trace is licit (6b).

(6) a. *Who$_i$ was it apparent yesterday [$_{CP}$e$_i$ that [Kay saw e$_i$]]?
    b. Who$_i$ was it apparent [$_{CP}$**e$_i$** that [Kay saw e$_i$]]?

Consider some other contexts where this condition has been invoked. (7a) illustrates a conjunction, in which the second verb may be unpronounced (7b). In cases like (7b), we say that there is a 'gapped' verb, which is understood to be present in the position indicated, but not pronounced. This means that the trace of a wh- word to the right of the gap in (7c,d) is not the complement of an overt word, rendering these structures ungrammatical.

(7) a. Jay introduced Kay to Ray, and Jim introduced Kim to Tim.
    b. Jay introduced Kay to Ray, and Jim GAP Kim to Tim.
    c. *Which man$_i$ did Jay introduce e$_i$ to Ray, and which woman$_j$ (did) Jim GAP e$_j$ to Tim?
    d. *Jay wondered what$_i$ Kay gave e$_i$ to Ray, and what$_j$ Jim (did) GAP e$_j$ to Tim.

The same point holds for a deleted *that* to the right of a gapped verb (8b) and a trace at the front of an embedded clause (8c). The deleted *that* and the trace at the front of the CP do not head the complement of an adjacent, overt word; consequently the structures are ungrammatical.

(8) a. Jay thought Kay hit Ray, and Jim GAP [$_{CP}$that Kim hit Tim].
    b. *Jay thought Kay hit Ray, and Jim GAP [$_{CP}$0 Kim hit Tim].
    c. *Who$_i$ did Jay think Kay hit e$_i$, and who$_j$ (did) Jim GAP [$_{CP}$e$_j$ (that) [Kim hit e$_j$]]?

There are more subtleties which follow from this particular condition of UG, governing the distribution of movement traces and holding of the speech of every mature speaker of English. A simple possessive noun phrase like *Jay's picture* is three-ways ambiguous. Jay might be the owner of the picture, its painter or the person portrayed, i.e. the object. The structure for the reading in which Jay is the object, the person portrayed, is (9): *Jay* moves from the complement position to the possessive position, leaving a trace in the usual fashion. The trace is the complement of the noun *picture*.

(9) [$_{DP}$Jay$_i$'s [$_{NP}$picture e$_i$]]

But now consider an expression like *the picture of Jay's*. Here Jay is the owner or the painter of the picture, but not the object – the expression can not refer to a picture in which Jay is portrayed. Again, this is something that most non-linguists are not aware of and something which is not imparted explicitly to children. Again, a condition of UG must be involved, and it is our condition on the traces of movement. The intended structure is (10a), and the trace (indexed) is the complement of another empty element, understood as 'picture', but no overt lexical element governs it (cf. (9)). The case is similar for *the picture is Jay's* (10b) and *the picture which is Jay's* (10c), which also lack the object reading for *Jay* and whose structures have an illicit trace.

(10) a. *the picture of [$_{DP}$Jay$_i$'s [$_{NP}$e **e**$_i$]]
      b. *the picture is [$_{DP}$Jay$_i$'s [$_{NP}$e **e**$_i$]]
      c. *the picture which is [$_{DP}$Jay$_i$'s [$_{NP}$e **e**$_i$]]

UG includes principles of this type and linguists postulate them on the basis of arguments from the poverty of the stimulus.

Explaining Evolution

In asking how the human language faculty may have evolved, we are faced with some immediate problems. First, there is no useful comparative data from other species with some form of 'primitive language'. Second, we have no real substantive data on the neural architecture which subserves the operation of our grammars, at least not beyond very gross notions (and unenlightening so far, for our purposes) about brain localisation; in fact, this point is true of all cognition, except for some aspects of low-level vision. Furthermore, we have no idea whether there was one big, homogeneous mutation yielding UG in all its present glory, with all the individual principles and parameters emerging at the same time.

There is a novel approach to the evolution of functions: the approach of palaeoneurology. If a human mental organ evolved, investigators might be able to identify a physical correlate of the mind that is manifested in the fossil records. Jerison (1976) tried to trace the 'index of encephalisation', a measure of actual brain size relative to the size of the brain that can be expected for a certain species, given a certain body weight and size. It is known that the human being's most distinctive anatomical feature is the central nervous system, and that human evolution has been marked above all by progressive increase in cranial capacity. Jerison aimed to establish the brain and body sizes of fossil vertebrates and identified periods where there was a four- and fivefold increase in relative brain size for the average mammal.

Jerison's work suggests that the human brain may have evolved in a series of explosions and qualitative changes, and not gradually. Presumably something like this happened for most physical features, since evolution typically is a discontinuous process, prizing only those innovations which are big enough and effective enough to be adaptive. Even if relevant facts are in short supply, one may speculate that perhaps something similar happened in the evolution of the mental genotype in humans. As with the emergence of the heart or upright posture, so with language. Nobody has any idea of how this happened with physical or mental organs; there are no principles which allow us to predict that from some organism some particular property must evolve. That is not to say that these developments are inexplicable, but only that they are unexplained at the present state of knowledge. From that perspective the evolution of the human heart and mental organs are on a par.

We know nothing of the circumstances under which this evolutionary development took place. Nonetheless, there have been many papers and books in recent years on the evolution of language. It is worth revisiting the matter in the context of the perspective I have sketched and in the context of recent discussions about natural selection. At the risk of oversimplifying, it is useful to distinguish two positions (Gould 1997).

Singularists and Pluralists

The singularists invoke just one factor to explain evolutionary development: natural selection. The result of natural selection is adaptation, the shaping of an organism's form, function and behaviour to achieve enhanced reproductive success, the Darwinian *summum bonum*. In the context of the evolution of UG, the singularists say that selective forces shaped individual components of UG. For the singularists, these items are adaptive. The idea is that various principles of UG evolved by selective demands in a kind of 'mosaic evolution'. The term is Newmeyer's (1991), and the view is shared by Dennett (1995), Maynard Smith and Szathmáry (1995), Pinker (1997) and Pinker and Bloom (1990).

The pluralists, on the other hand, appeal to more than natural selection in explaining evolution. In particular, they try to understand the limits to the variation on which natural selection works. Natural selection may explain the development of some central characteristics of language, but other factors narrow the range of options. For example, Brandon and Hornstein (1986) argued that the general algebraic character of the language faculty was selected for. A species able to convey and understand an unbounded number of stimulus-free messages would presumably have had a reproductive advantage in a fluctuating and variable environment. It would have been able to give and receive warnings about a wide range of dangers and predators, and engage in abstractions, for example abstractions about predators which *might* be present, although not currently

visible or audible. This might have been a more effective way of responding
to predators than by genetic tracking. So the fact that an organism has a language faculty allowing unbounded, stimulus-free messages may be explained
by selection. But this does not entail that all aspects of UG were adaptive: there
is no discernible selective advantage for an organism whose grammars permit
elements to move only locally (Lightfoot 1991).

The linguistic singularists have flourished at a time when Richard Dawkins,
Daniel Dennett and others have articulated a conviction that every evolutionary
change of any importance is due to the shaping effects of natural selection, and
that adaptation emerges as a universal result and proof of the selective forces
(e.g. Dawkins 1995; Dennett 1995). They have been joined in recent years by
proponents of 'evolutionary psychology' (Barkow, Cosmides and Tooby 1992;
Wright 1994).

Robert Wright has a deep faith in the power of natural selection:

The thousands and thousands of genes that influence human behavior – genes that
build the brain and govern neurotransmitters and other hormones, thus defining our
"mental organs" – are here for a reason. And the reason is that they goaded our
ancestors into getting their genes into the next generation. If the theory of natural
selection is correct, then essentially everything about the human mind should be
intelligible in these terms. The basic ways we feel about each other, the basic kinds
of things we think about each other and say to each other, are with us today by
virtue of their past contribution to genetic fitness. (Wright 1994: 28)

Natural selection has now been shown to plausibly account for so much about
life in general and the human mind in particular that I have little doubt that it can
account for the rest. (Wright 1994: 383)

The pluralists allow that forces in addition to natural selection may be at work
in guiding evolutionary developments. Despite the attempts of the singularists
to cloak themselves with the mantle of true Darwinism, Darwin (1859/1968:
69) closed the introduction to his *Origin of Species* by saying 'I am convinced
that natural selection has been the main but not the exclusive means of modification'. There *are* alternatives. The fundamental properties of all physical systems surely play some role in determining the kinds of mutations that organisms
and specific organs might undergo, for example the fact that organisms cannot
transfer themselves instantaneously from Maryland to Cornwall, or become invisible on demand (surely a property which would convey selective advantage,
if it were possible). Similarly, complex biological systems may be subject to
particular principles. One thinks for example of the nature and behaviour of
cells, of the properties of exons and introns and of other fundamental aspects of
the biological world which were not specifically selected for. In 1917 D'Arcy

Thompson discussed constraints on the shape and functioning of biological forms, finding certain geometric forms recurring in many unrelated organisms: hexagons, spirals following the Fibonacci series, and so on (Thompson 1961). It is reasonable to believe that constraints yielding these repeated forms hold independently of the effects of natural selection. Recently the biomathematician Ian Stewart has written the book that D'Arcy Thompson might have written if he were alive today (Stewart 1998).

It is, in principle, an empirical matter whether any particular property of an organism evolved because it was selected for. It might have arisen as a by-product of something else that was selected for, perhaps induced by physical or biological principles, or perhaps as an accidental consequence of some other change. For example, hemoglobin was adaptive, because natural selection would have favoured the acquisition of a molecule which would carry oxygen from our lungs to the rest of our body and carbon dioxide on the reverse route. However, the redness of our blood is an epiphenomenon of the structure of hemoglobin, and lobsters and other animals have green blood. It is, therefore, a mistake to seek an adaptive account for why our blood is red (Lewontin 1978). After all, a gene might not be selected but might be dragged along on the same chromosome as some quite unrelated gene which *is* selected.

Since organisms are often complex and highly integrated, any adaptive change must automatically spin off structural by-products. Those by-products may later be coopted for useful purposes, but they didn't arise as adaptations. The human brain is a good example of a complex organ, and may have evolved to its large size for adaptive reasons – for some set of activities that our ancestors could only perform with bigger brains. But this doesn't entail that all attributes of universal human nature must be adaptations. We can read and write, and these capacities are now highly advantageous for humans, but the mental machinery for them must have originated as a spandrel that was coopted later (Gould and Lewontin 1979).

Some properties of organisms are not selected for and are not accidental by-products, but emerge because of deep, physical principles which affect much of life. For example, organisms as diverse as robins, redwoods and rhinos obey exactly the same mathematical laws governing the way size affects structure, physiology and life history. Those laws, the 'scaling relations', are a near-universal feature of life. They reflect fundamental limits on the kinds of things that evolution can make, and they arise from the interaction of a few simple physical principles.

Living things, from microbes to whales, vary in size by a factor of a billion trillion, 21 orders of magnitude; they come in a profusion of body designs, and inhabit quite different environments – earth, air and water. Despite this stupefying complexity, organisms obey remarkably simple scaling laws. Across thousands of species, the rules mandate that the larger the animal, the slower its metabolism. Similar relationships have been found for variables such as respiration rate, heart rate, life span, proportion of body weight devoted to skeleton, length of pregnancy and more. Make a mouse the size of an elephant, and it wouldn't last the day, because it wouldn't have enough surface area to dissipate the heat generated by the superactive mouse metabolism, and it would cook itself to death in short order.

Scaling follows precise mathematical relationships. Three 'power laws' have turned out to have widespread effects. The *three-quarter power law* describes, for example, metabolic rate (a body's total energy consumption per unit of time): this varies as the three-quarter power of an animal's mass. So a creature that is 10,000 (10^4) times more massive than another – say, the difference between a mouse and a large hog – will have a metabolic rate only 1,000 (10^3) times as large: the mouse uses energy at about .2 watts, the hog at around 200 watts. The *one-quarter power law* applies to life span, which generally varies as the one-quarter power of weight. So an animal that is 10^4 more massive than another typically lives only ten (10^1) times longer. Elapsed times for blood circulation and gestation scale by the same factor. So does the cross-sectional area of mammalian aortas and of tree trunks: a tree with a mass 1,000 times that of a sapling will have a trunk cross-section only 5.6 times larger. Heart rate scales as a negative one-quarter power under the *minus one-quarter power law*: the larger the animal, the slower its heart beat. A 110-pound human has a pulse of about 70 beats per minute, and creatures 10,000 times smaller (around 5 grams, like a shrew or a hummingbird) have heartbeats 10 times faster.

What has been mystifying about these three laws is the appearance of one-fourth as the common factor in all these relationships. Now West, Brown and Enquist (1997) have proposed a model which generates accurate scaling equations from three principles. First, the organism's energy supply network has to be a branching 'fractal' system (like blood vessels in animals or vascular conduits in plants), in which the sum of the area of all daughter branches is equal to the area of the parent. Second, the smallest branch (such as a capillary in animals) is the same dimension, no matter how large the organism. And third, the organism is assumed to employ the minimum energy necessary to distribute resources around its volume. Their model – a unique combination of the dynamics of energy transport and the mathematics of fractal geometry – has produced results that conform well with observations of living systems, including the enigmatic one-quarter-power scaling, and they derive the three-quarters power law for metabolism, along with many other relations. It may seem remarkable that equations apply to organisms at all, but now there is a theoretical basis for understanding the central role of body size in all aspects of biology.

Physical laws of the type just discussed describe the limits to evolutionary change, in the same way that the principles of UG describe the limits to grammatical change at the phenotypical level. They define the terrain on which natural selection works, and they illustrate the pluralists' multifactored approach to evolution, which goes beyond the working of natural selection. The physical laws shape the limits of the way that evolutionary changes take place, and they are quite independent of the workings of natural selection.

If evolutionary change takes place in explosive, catastrophic developments within the channels defined by physical and biological laws, then one expects complex changes which are, in certain respects, nonadaptive. In the next section, I shall offer a new kind of argument that UG is not shaped entirely by the workings of natural selection. I shall claim that certain features of UG are to some extent dysfunctional, hence nonadaptive, hence spandrels in the sense of Gould and Lewontin (1979), a by-product of something else.

We saw that the UG condition on the distribution of movement traces does a lot of work: it enables us to distinguish many well-formed and deviant structures of English, and to do so in such a way that we can accurately distinguish what is learned and what is not learned by children acquiring English. Now I want to show that this condition, despite the work it does, is actually maladaptive in well-defined ways. This demonstration concerns a subcase of the condition, according to which subjects of tensed clauses are unmoveable (what Bresnan 1972 called the Fixed Subject Constraint – henceforth the FSC); they are unmoveable because in general their traces, not heading the complement of an adjacent overt lexical item, would violate our condition.

The Condition Is Partially Dysfunctional

We noted earlier that English embedded clauses are introduced by a complementiser which may or may not be pronounced; the unpronounced (or 'deleted') complementiser occurs only where it heads the complement of an adjacent overt word. This is also true if a wh- item moves from the embedded object position (11a).

(11) a. Who$_i$ did you think [e$_i$ that/0 Ray saw e$_i$]?
b. *Who$_i$ did you think [e$_i$ that **e$_i$** saw Fay]?

However, a *who* may not move from an embedded subject position if *that* is present (11b), and the reason is that the subject trace (bold) would not be licit. The same is true of indirect questions introduced by a word like *how*: subjects cannot move (12a) but objects can (12b).

(12) a. *Who$_i$ do you wonder [e$_i$ how [e$_i$ solved the problem]]
        b. Which problem$_i$ do you wonder [e$_i$ how [John solved e$_i$]]

A wh- word also may not move from a subject position if the indirect question is part of a relative clause. In (13a), the wh- word has been moved from an underlying object position (where the trace is the complement of *bought*). By contrast (13b) is totally impossible, where the trace is in subject position and not a complement; [e$_i$ bought e$_j$] is not the complement of *what*.

(13) a. This is the sweater which$_i$ I wonder [who bought e$_i$]
        b. *This is the student who$_i$ I wonder [what$_j$ **e$_i$** bought e$_j$]

English has an operation whereby a 'large' phrase may occur in a displaced position at the far right of its clause, leaving a trace as usual. In (14a) the trace of the moved element, *all the students from L.A.*, is the complement of the verb *introduced*. In (14b) the trace is in a subject position, but the subject of a nontensed or 'infinitival' clause, and it heads the complement of the verb *expect*. Finally, in the ungrammatical (14c) the subject trace does not head a complement.

(14) a. I introduced e$_i$ to Mary [all the students from L.A.]$_i$
        b. I expect [e$_i$ to be at the party] [all the students from L.A.]$_i$
        c. *[**e$_i$** are unhappy] [all the students from L.A.]$_i$

So the UG condition on traces has a negative effect, blocking the movement of wh- items from the subject of tensed clauses. To this extent, the UG condition is dysfunctional. It apparently conflicts with the desire/need to ask questions about subjects of tensed clauses, just as one may ask questions about entities in other structural positions. The evidence for this claim is that individuals adopt strategies to circumvent the effects of the UG principle in certain contexts, and these strategies are manifested quite differently in individual languages. Because they vary so much, the individual strategies cannot directly reflect genetic principles. There are three classes of strategies used in different languages, each of which permits an ad-hoc learned device which licenses extraction from a subject position:

(15) Three strategies to license an extracted subject
        a. Adjust the complementiser to license the extraction.
        b. Use a resumptive pronoun in the extraction site.
        c. Move the subject to a nonsubject position and then extract.

English exploits strategy (15a) and permits extraction of a subject if the complementiser *that* is not present, as in (16). Here the lowest (rightmost) trace (the subject) heads the complement of the higher trace at the front of the CP (through coindexing), and that trace heads the complement of the verb *think*. In the comparable (11b) and (12a) the subject trace was illicit. In other words, subjects of tensed clauses in English are moveable only if the complementiser is unpronounced; that permits the subject trace to be licit. (I avoid technical issues concerning the role of indices.)

(16) Who$_i$ did you think [$_{CP}$e$_i$ [e$_i$ saw Fay]?

Consider now French, where the complementiser *que* is never deleted. Again we see that objects may be extracted freely (17b), but that a subject is not extractable in a comparable way (17c). French speakers can adjust the complementiser to the 'agreeing' form *qui* if it is followed by a trace. This effectively legitimates the trace (17d).

(17) a. Je crois [$_{CP}$que Marie a   vu   Jean].
        'I think   that Mary has seen John.'
     b. Qui$_i$ crois-tu [$_{CP}$e$_i$ que Marie a   vu e$_i$]?
        who think you   that Marie has seen
        'Who do you think Marie has seen?'
     c.*Qui$_i$ crois-tu$_{CP}$[e$_i$ que e$_i$ a vu Jean]?
     d. Qui$_i$ crois-tu$_{CP}$[e$_i$ qui e$_i$ a vu Jean]?

Again we see a very specific, ad-hoc device, in this case an operation changing *que* to *qui*, whose sole motivation is to permit extraction of a subject.

Rizzi (1990) found similar devices in a variety of languages, which permit extraction of subjects. West Flemish behaves similarly to French: the usual form of the complementiser is *da* (18a) but a special 'agreeing' form *die* occurs where a subject is extracted (18b).

(18) a. den vent da$_i$ Pol peinst [e$_i$ da Marie e$_i$ getrokken   heet]
        the man that Pol thinks   that Marie photographed has
        'the man that Pol thinks that Marie has photographed'
     b. den vent da$_i$ Pol peinst [e$_i$ die e$_i$ gekommen ist]
        the man that Pol thinks   that come   is
        'the man that Pol thinks has come'

Hebrew also does not allow extraction of a subject (19a), in accordance with our condition on movement traces. Objects extract freely (19b). But subjects are extractable if a special device applies adjusting the complementiser, in this case cliticising the complementiser *še* onto an adjacent head (19c). In (19c) the complementiser cliticises onto the negation *lo*, vacating the complementiser position and permitting the subject trace to head the complement clause.

(19) a. *Mi_i ein- ex joda'at ['im **e**_i mešaret ba-milu'im]?

who not you know whether serves in reserves?

'who do you not know whether (he) serves in the reserves?'

b. Et mi_i ein- ex joda'at ['im ha- milu'im me'aifim e_i]?

Acc+who not you know whether the reserves tire?

'who do you not know whether the reserves tire (him)?'

c. Mi at ma'mina [še- lo ohev salat xacilim]?

who you believe that not likes salad eggplants

'who do you believe does not like salad with eggplants?'

Norwegian shows a special complementiser *som* only in embedded questions with an extracted subject (20a); its function seems to be to license a trace which otherwise would violate our UG condition. It never occurs with an extracted object (20b).

(20) a. Vi vet [hvem_i som/*0 e_i snakker med Marit]

we know who that talks with Mary

'We know who talks with Mary.'

b. Vi vet [hvem_i *som/0 Marit snakker med e_i]

we know who that Mary talks with

'We know who Mary talks with.'

The second general strategy (15b) is to replace the illicit trace with a 'resumptive' pronoun. Swedish exploits this strategy: (21a) shows that if a wh- word moves from an embedded subject position to the right of a complementiser, the resumptive pronoun *det* is required. On the other hand, if no complementiser is present, no resumptive pronoun is allowed (21b) (Engdahl 1985).

(21) a. Vilket ord_i visste ingen [hur det/*e_i stavas]?

which word knew no one how it/e is-spelled?

'Which word did no one know how it is spelled?'

b. Kalle_i kan jag sla vad om e_i/* han kommer att klara sig.

Kalle can I bet about e/he is going to succeed

'Kalle, I can bet (*he) is going to succeed.'

The West African language Vata adopts the same strategy, but even for movement in a simple, unembedded clause. Again we see the familiar subject-object asymmetry: an extracted subject has a resumptive pronoun in its underlying position, never a trace (22a), but vice versa for an extracted object (22b).

(22) a. Alo_i *(o_i) le saka la?

who he eat rice WH?

'who eats rice?'

b. Yi$_i$ Kofi le (*mi$_i$) la?

what Kofi eat it   WH

'what does Kofi eat?'

Italian manifests a third strategy (15c): moving the subject first to a nonsubject position and then moving it to the front of the CP. Subjects may occur to the right of the verb phrase (23a), and that is the position from which they are extracted, as shown in (23b), where the trace occupies a complement-like position.

(23) a. Credo [che abbia telefonato Gianni]

I-think that has   telephoned Gianni

'I think that Gianni has telephoned'.

b. Chi$_i$ credi [che abbia telefonato e$_i$]?

who you-think that has   telephoned?

'Who do you think has telephoned?'

The Arabic dialect Banni-Hassan employs a similar device. This language exhibits a morphological distinction between a postverbal subject *miin* and its preverbal counterpart *min*. If the complementiser *innu* occurs (24a), then the postverbal subject form is required. In other words, if the complementiser is present, a trace in the preverbal subject position would not head a complement, and consequently the element must move from the postverbal position, showing the appropriate morphology. On the other hand, if the complementiser is absent, then the subject position heads the complement, as illustrated for English in (16). The preverbal subject is then a possible extraction site, and the pronoun shows the appropriate preverbal morphology (24b).

(24) a. Miin/*min$_i$ Fariid gaal [innu *pro* kisar e$_i$ al- beeda]?

who   Fariid said that   broke the egg?

'Who did Fariid say broke the egg?'

b. Min/*miin$_i$ Fariid gaal [0 e$_i$ kisar al-beeda]?

We have discussed a superficially bewildering range of data, but they have become quite comprehensible. UG blocks extraction of subjects. However, for reasons of expressibility, speakers need to extract subjects; that is what the evidence from specific languages shows. Because of the constraints of UG, speakers are forced to adopt ad-hoc strategies which either eliminate illicit traces (Swedish, Vata), provide a postverbal alternative to them (Italian, Banni-Hassan) or adjust the complementiser so as to license them in some special fashion (English, French, West Flemish, Hebrew, Norwegian). Each of the devices we have examined is learnable, if children are prohibited genetically from extracting embedded subjects in the normal case. That is, children are exposed

to positive, accessible data which demonstrate the language-specific operation
that adults use: the deletability of *that* in English, the operation changing *que* to
qui in French or the need for a resumptive pronoun only in subject positions in
Swedish and Vata. We therefore have accounts for the specific languages which
meet our basic requirements. We can also see that a condition of the linguistic
genotype may be countermanded by the needs of expressivity; to that extent,
the condition is dysfunctional.

The restriction on subject movement is nonadaptive, and part of our evidence
is that it does not hold transparently at the level of individuals; individuals do
extract subjects, in apparent violation of the condition on movement traces.
But we have seen that these individual phenomena only make sense against
the backdrop of a condition at the genetic level, which therefore evolved in
the species. It evolved in the species despite the fact that it is dysfunctional.
If nonadaptive elements evolve, then we need something other than natural
selection to drive evolutionary developments. The particular subcase we have
discussed, the restriction on the movement of subjects, is a by-product of the
more general condition on movement traces, a spandrel.

The spandrels of San Marco are by-products of a particular architectural
design, and the restriction on the movement of subjects is a by-product of the
general condition on movement traces. That general condition may well be
functionally motivated, possibly by parsing considerations. In parsing utterances, one needs to analyse the positions from which displaced elements have
moved. Our UG condition restricts traces to certain well-defined positions, and
that presumably facilitates parsing. The FSC, however, and the phenomena
that it subsumes constitute a spandrel, a dysfunctional by-product of that more
general condition.

Conclusion

There can be no doubt that UG principles are implicated in the phenomena
discussed. If future work provides a more general UG account, which does not
use the technicalities invoked here, it must in any case prohibit the movement
of embedded subjects, and capture the effects of the FSC. To that extent, any
account will be nonadaptive.

A condition which blocks the extraction of subjects is dysfunctional, blocking expressions which are needed; in that case, the FSC is a spandrel and could
not have been selected for. The whole package of UG may have been adaptive as a whole, but the singularists cannot be right: it is not necessary to look
for adaptive accounts of the subparts of UG. Specific elements of UG like the
condition on the extraction of subjects are spandrels in the sense of Gould

and Lewontin (1979), nonadaptive by-products of something else. But then, of course, precisely the same argument could be true of UG as a whole: UG may have evolved as an accidental side effect of some other adaptive mutation. This means that one may not take as certain even the scenario that the general algebraic character of the language faculty was selected for. Natural selection may have played no direct role in the evolution of UG specifically. We do not know, but natural selection is not the only possibility.

This conclusion will come as no surprise to Stephen Jay Gould, who has speculated that the language faculty as a whole is a spandrel (Gould 1991). Similarly Massimo Piattelli-Palmarini (1989). Nor will it surprise molecular biologists who have emphasised the internal forces motivating genetic change. They adapt Francis Galton's image of organisms as perfectly round billiard balls, which are struck at some angle and with some force by a cue, roll over a perfectly flat surface and come to rest at one of an infinite number of points which can be predicted by calculating the angle and force of the cue and the dimensions of the plane on which they roll. Adapting this image, they suggest that organisms may instead be thought of as polyhedrons, which will move only if subjected to a significant force; there will be rapid movement, and they will come to rest at one of only a finite number of endpoints, because of the intrinsic properties of their shape. This view builds on the early insights of D'Arcy Thompson, who identified forms which recur pervasively in unrelated species, suggesting that there are physical laws – like the scaling laws discussed earlier – which drive species to adopt familiar forms (Thompson 1961). Our conclusions will also not surprise complexity theorists like Waldrop (1992), Kauffman (1991) and Stewart (1998), who have argued that complex, dynamical systems can sometimes go spontaneously from randomness to order, and that this may be a plausible driving force for evolutionary change.

The complexity theorists have argued that the forms which are subject to selection are generated by laws of complexity. Dynamical systems follow trajectories that inevitably flow into attractors, which 'trap' the system and create order. Kauffman notes that 'selection has always had a handmaiden. It is not, after all, the sole source of order, and organisms are not just tinkered-together contraptions, but expressions of deeper natural laws. . . . the patterns of life's bursts and burials are caused by internal processes, endogenous and natural' (1995: 8, 15). The task, then, is to find how much work selection does, and how effective the underlying physical laws are.

There are alternatives which go beyond natural selection, and it is worth the time of linguists to consider some of them. Current understanding suggests that some effects of UG are dysfunctional, hence spandrels evolving as a by-product of something else and not the result of adaptive change favouring survival to reproductive age. Therefore, no extreme form of adaptationism is necessary or plausible.

One possibility is that a mental organ evolved with a capacity for 'discrete infinity', which manifests itself in grammars, the number system and music, all of which would have therefore evolved together. And it is possible that due to physical laws a mental organ of that type could only have the properties that the human brain now has. We do not know enough to deny this possibility. In principle, it is an empirical matter to decide to what extent evolutionary development is due to selection by external forces, and how much is due to the demands of internal laws. In practice, of course, the empirical work is hampered by a dearth of relevant facts.

Evolutionary change at the genetic level is similar to phenotypical change in grammars in that both take place in fits and starts, when environmental factors tweak existing systems in some fashion. However, in neither case do environmental factors suffice to shape the resulting changes. The principles of UG provide the channels along which grammatical change may proceed, and physical laws define the terrain on which evolutionary change takes place.

Note

1.   This chapter adapts material from Lightfoot (1999, ch. 9).

References

Barkow, J., L. Cosmides and J. Tooby (eds). 1992. *The Adapted Mind: Evolutionary psychology and the generation of culture*. Oxford: Oxford University Press.

Brandon, R. and N. Hornstein. 1986. From icons to symbols: some speculations on the origins of language. *Biology and Philosophy* **1**: 169–189.

Bresnan, J. W. 1972. *Theory of Complementation in English Syntax*. Doctoral dissertation, M.I.T.

Darwin, C. 1859/1968. *The Origin of Species by Means of Natural Selection*. Harmondsworth: Penguin.

Dawkins, R. 1995. *River Out of Eden: A Darwinian view of life*. New York: Basic Books.

Dennett, D. 1995. *Darwin's Dangerous Idea: Evolution and the meaning of life*. New York: Simon and Schuster.

Engdahl, E. 1985. Parasitic gaps, resumptive pronouns, and subject extractions. *Linguistics* **23**: 3–44.

Gould, S. J. 1991. Exaptation: a crucial tool for an evolutionary psychology. *Journal of Social Issues* **47**: 43–65.

Gould, S. J. 1997. Evolution: the pleasures of pluralism. *New York Review of Books*, June 26.

Gould, S. J. and R. Lewontin. 1979. The spandrels of San Marco and the Panglossian paradigm: a critique of the adaptationist programme. *Proceedings of the Royal Society of London B* **205**: 581–598.

Hornstein, N. and D. Lightfoot. 1991. On the nature of lexical government. In R. Freidin (ed), *Principles and parameters in comparative syntax*. Cambridge, MA: MIT Press.

Jerison, H. 1976. Paleoneurology and the evolution of mind. *Scientific American* **234**: 90–101.

Kauffman, S. 1991. Antichaos and adaptation. *Scientific American*, August: 78–84.

Kauffman, S. 1995. *At Home in the Universe: The search for laws of self-organization and complexity*. Oxford: Oxford University Press.

Lewontin, R. 1978. Adaptation. *Scientific American* **239**: 156–69.

Lightfoot, D. 1991. Subjacency and sex. *Language and Communication* **11**: 67–69.

Lightfoot, D. 1999. *The Development of Language: Acquisition, change, and evolution*. Oxford: Blackwell.

Maynard Smith, J. and E. Szathmáry. 1995. *The Major Transitions in Evolution*. Oxford: Freeman.

Newmeyer, F. 1991. Functional explanation in linguistics and the origin of language. *Language and Communication* **11**: 3–28.

Piattelli-Palmarini, M. 1989. Evolution, selection, and cognition: from 'learning' to parameter setting in biology and the study of language. *Cognition* **31**: 1–44.

Pinker, S. 1997. *How the Mind Works*. New York: Norton.

Pinker, S. and P. Bloom. 1990. Natural language and natural selection. *Behavioral and Brain Sciences* **13**: 707–784.

Rizzi, L. 1990. *Relativized Minimality*. Cambridge, MA: MIT Press.

Stewart, I. 1998. *Life's Other Secret*. New York: Wiley.

Thompson, D. 1961. *On Growth and Form*. Abridged edition, edited by J. T. Bonner. Cambridge: Cambridge University Press.

Waldrop, M. M. 1992. *Complexity: The emerging science at the edge of order and chaos*. New York: Simon and Schuster.

West, G. B., J. H. Brown and B. J. Enquist. 1997. A general model for the origin of allometric scaling laws in biology. *Science* **276**: 122–126.

Wright, R. 1994. *The Moral Animal: Why we are the way we are – the new science of evolutionary psychology*. New York: Random House.

15

The Distinction Between Sentences and Noun Phrases: An Impediment to Language Evolution?

ANDREW CARSTAIRS-MCCARTHY

1. Introduction: Grammar as Historical Accident

Consider the details of how grammar (particularly syntax) operates in contemporary human languages: how phrases and clauses are structured, how they can be combined and subordinated, and how some elements can control or govern others. For many of these details, no off-the-cuff functional explanation suggests itself. For example, why can *Algernon* be interpreted as coreferential with *he* or *him* easily in (1)–(3) but not easily in (4) (Langacker 1969)?

(1) While Algernon wasn't looking, Penelope bit him in the leg.
(2) While he wasn't looking, Penelope bit Algernon in the leg.
(3) Penelope bit Algernon in the leg while he wasn't looking.
(4) Penelope bit him in the leg while Algernon wasn't looking.

The complexity of such details, and the lack of immediately obvious explanations for them, is the main reason why all versions of grammatical theory have become such elaborate and often intimidating edifices in recent years.

A linguist interested in grammatical evolution must confront the issue of adaptation. Has grammar reached its present elaborated state because people who use this sort of grammar have been more efficient at reproducing themselves than have other people? Directly contrary answers have been given. 'No', says Chomsky, as cited by Newmeyer (1998): adaptation has little if anything to contribute to expaining why grammar is the way it is. This view is echoed by Lightfoot (1999, this volume) and in part by Bickerton (1990, 1995, 1998, this volume). On the other hand, Pinker and Bloom (1990) and Newmeyer (1991) say 'yes' (cf. Pinker 1994, 1997). Pinker and Bloom argue that a structure which serves a complex function may be exploited to fulfil a simpler one (for example, a television set can serve as a paperweight), but not vice versa; therefore, given the complexity of the functions which language fulfils, it must have evolved primarily to fulfil those functions, rather than as a by-product or 'spandrel' of structures or organs which evolved for other reasons.

What both sides in this debate have generally had in common, so far, is an all-or-nothing attitude: either grammar is adaptive or it is not. But from the point of view of evolutionary biology, that attitude seems oversimple. Consider for comparison the question whether the human hand is adapted for its present functions. The biologist George C. Williams (1992, 1996) points out that, in many respects, the answer is a resounding 'yes'. But these respects do not include the fact that we have two hands rather than four. That is simply an accident, due to the fact that the first fish to come on land and evolve into amphibians happened to have two pairs of lateral fins rather than three or more. Other examples of historical accident are the structure of the vertebrate eye and the configuration of the sperm ducts, which connect the testes with the penis in male mammals. From the point of view of good design, one would expect that no unnecessary tissue should intervene in the eye between the lens and the light-sensitive cells of the retina, and that the sperm ducts should be short, since the scrotum and penis are close together. In fact, neither expectation is correct. In the eye of vertebrates (unlike cephalopods), nerve fibres intervene between the lens and the retina, while in male mammals each sperm duct loops back over the ureter, and is thus several centimetres longer than necessary. Both facts illustrate how evolution, even when it seems most clearly to be guided by functional pressures (such as a pressure to see better, or to keep the testes cool), operates without any of the planning and foresight which we associate with the term 'function' when applied to human activity. Having set out down a particular road, it cannot turn back and begin again, so to speak, even though, from the point of view of a designer with foresight, a short-term loss of fitness might be compensated amply by greater efficiency in the long run. And it is instances of poor design such as this which are particularly enlightening about evolutionary history, because they are much more likely to be residues of historical accidents than to have been selected for as aids to reproductive success.

Are there similar residues in contemporary grammar? If so, they too should be particularly enlightening about how language got to be the way it is. Elsewhere (Carstairs-McCarthy 1999) I have argued that even so basic a feature of grammar as the distinction between sentences and noun phrases (NPs) is just such a residue. In Sections 2 and 3 I will summarise those arguments before suggesting in Sections 4 and 5 that this particular instance of mediocre grammatical design may help to account for a puzzle about the pace of human evolution in a nonlinguistic area, namely the apparently very slow technical and cultural development, amounting to virtual stagnation, of the varieties of human traditionally grouped under the label *Homo erectus*.

I say 'may help to account for', not 'accounts for'; I do not present my suggestion as the whole story about *erectus*'s stagnation. But, even if further research should show that I overestimate the linguistic factor in it, I hope to have persuaded readers that there is no need to choose between a strictly adaptive and a strictly nonadaptive view of grammatical structure. It is worth investigating how much of grammar, even of those aspects of grammar most tightly controlled by biology, is as it is through historical accident; and both linguistic and nonlinguistic evidence may shed light on this.

2. The Sentence-NP Distinction as an Evolutionary Problem

Every human language distinguishes syntactically between sentences, as in (5), and noun phrases, as in (6):[1]

(5)   John arrived yesterday.
(6) a. John
   b. John's arrival yesterday
   c. the present King of France

It may seem strange to suggest that this syntactic distinction presents any sort of evolutionary problem. Whatever course language evolution took, one may think, it was bound to provide for a distinction between, on the one hand, what is referred to and, on the other hand, assertions made (or questions asked) about what is referred to. Is not the sentence-NP distinction just the syntactic counterpart of that essential fundamental distinction? Against this objection I will offer here just two brief counters, referring the reader elsewhere for details (Carstairs-McCarthy 1998, 1999).

Firstly, one can perfectly well envisage a kind of syntax where the distinction between asserting and referring is not encoded grammatically, so that one expression would do duty for both *John's arrival yesterday* and *John arrived yesterday*. An example is the syntax of the hypothetical language which I have called 'Uniformitarian' (1998) or 'Monocategoric' (1999). In this language there is a distinction between 'expressions' (such as *snake, you, John* and *Mary*) and 'operators' (such as *yesterday, disappear, seem* and *tell*). Complex expressions are formed by combining an operator with an appropriate number of preceding expressions, simple or complex, which constitute its arguments, as in (7) (where brackets are supplied as aids to parsing):

(7) a. you snake see
   b. [you snake see] yesterday
   c. [[[you snake see] yesterday] disappear] seem
   d. John Mary [[you snake see] yesterday] tell

At first sight, this may look much like an actual human language with verb-final word order, such as Japanese. There is a crucial difference, however. In Monocategoric, unlike Japanese, there is no grammatical coding of a distinction between 'nominal' and 'sentential' interpretations. For example, (7b) could be rendered in English as 'You saw a snake yesterday' or 'your seeing a snake yesterday' or 'the snake you saw yesterday'. Before readers rush to protest that such ambiguity would be intolerable, they should reflect that there is plenty of ambiguity in actual syntax that we take in our stride because contexts steer us towards one interpretation or another, and just the same would apply in Mono-categoric. For example, (7b) is contained within both (7c) and (7d), which steer us firmly towards interpretations for it which in English would be classified as respectively nominal (*'The snake you saw yesterday* seems to have disap-peared') and sentential ('John has told Mary that *you saw a snake yesterday*'). So Monocategoric, even though it lacks a syntactic sentence-NP distinction, cannot be dismissed as representing a direction in which syntax could not con-ceivably have evolved.

Secondly, one might expect logicians and philosophers of language to pro-vide clear-cut reasons why linguistic expressions exhibit not one but two ways of fitting the world, namely by being true and by successfully referring. Yet when one searches for such reasons one returns empty-handed. Philosophers generally take the distinction between truth and reference for granted, however much they may disagree about the analysis of the two notions; and such motiva-tion as they offer always seems to circle back to that very syntactic distinction between sentences and NPs which we are interested here in explaining.

The origin of this distinction ought therefore to be a serious issue for re-searchers on language evolution. In Section 3 I will sketch an answer. But the focus of this chapter is not on the answer itself but on certain expectations about human evolution which arise from it. A reader may well be persuaded that these expectations are fulfilled, while still remaining sceptical about the hypothesis which gives rise to them – though I hope that, if readers are so persuaded, they will look on the hypothesis more kindly.

3. A Scenario for the Origin of the Sentence-NP Distinction

A few decades ago, humans were thought to differ from other primates in a wide variety of ways: not just in having language and being bipedal but also in using tools, obeying social norms and taboos, engaging in warfare, communicating about external states of affairs as well as internal wants and feelings, and being able to deceive. Today most of these latter Rubicons have dried up, in the sense that all these capacities have been found to be present to at least a rudimentary degree in some nonhuman primates. This poses a difficulty, at least prima facie, for any claim that all aspects of language (its grammatical structure as well as its ranges of use) are derivable ultimately from (for example) social functions such as grooming or the detection of freeloaders. It is now clear that those social functions need to be fulfilled in primate societies other than human ones; so why should it be humans in particular who developed language?

A more parsimonious and to that extent more plausible evolutionary story will be one which attributes a crucial role to characteristics which are still generally agreed to distinguish humans from all other primates. One of these is bipedalism. Another is the configuration of the oral and nasal cavities and the arrangements for breathing and swallowing: in adult humans, alone of all mammals, these involve a chamber (the pharynx) through which both air and food pass, en route to the lungs and stomach respectively. I have argued elsewhere that these peculiarly human characteristics do indeed play a crucial role in language evolution (Carstairs-McCarthy 1998, 1999). In summary, the argument runs like this.

For whatever reason, our ancestors became first predominantly and then exclusively bipedal (exclusively bipedal, that is, in their normal locomotion; they could still use their hands in climbing when necessary, just as modern humans can). Since the head was now balanced on top of the spinal column rather than projecting in front of it, anatomical changes were favoured whereby the spinal column entered the skull further forward than formerly, so that the skull base was shortened and the larynx, formerly high in the neck (as in other mammals and in new-born humans) was squeezed downwards. This reconfiguration created the peculiarly human pharynx, just mentioned. An adverse consequence of this reconfiguration, which might have been expected to inhibit it, was an increased risk of choking. But one positive consequence was a greater diversity of vocalisation possibilities, with the pharynx as a new resonating chamber distinct from the mouth, and with the back of the tongue (lying opposite the soft palate) supplying a new locus for constriction of the airflow in addition to the front of the tongue and the lips.[2] This facilitated a larger vocabulary of 'calls'. But there was a limit to the extent to which the new vocalisation possibilities could be exploited through vocabulary expansion alone. A different mode of exploitation would have been by stringing calls together. The more this happened, however, the greater the advantage that would accrue from reliable interpretation of such call strings. (Does 'seek termite nest Koko find' mean 'Look for the termite nest which Koko found' or 'Koko was looking for a termite nest and found one' or even 'I've found the termite nest which Koko was looking for'?) In other words, the greater would be the advantage accruing from having a regular pattern of syntax.

Where was syntax to come from, however? A handy source would be any already existing neural mechanism for imposing a regular pattern on speech. Such a pattern could indeed be found, namely in the syllabic 'frames' associated with mandibular oscillations (MacNeilage 1998). After larynx lowering, these frames were combinable with a greater variety of segmental 'content', that is vowel-like sounds produced at the open phase of the oscillation (syllable nuclei) and consonant-like sounds produced at the closed phase (syllable margins). The syllabic frame was thus available to provide a model for a sentential frame, into which individual calls (we can now perhaps call them 'words') could be fitted as 'content', just as consonants and vowels supply the 'content' of the syllable.

Syllable nuclei and margins are not on a par, however, in terms of syllable structure. In particular, we find in contemporary languages the following contrasts or asymmetries:

(a) Syllable margins are distinct from syllables.
(b) Consonants occur only within syllables (as margins to a nucleus), not on their own.
(c) All syllables must have a nucleus but (in nearly all languages) some syllables may lack marginal consonants. As a consequence, vowels may occur on their own, constituting minimal syllables.
(d) The onset margin (preceding the nucleus) is privileged over the coda (following it), inasmuch as, given a choice, consonants are assigned to onsets rather than to codas, and some languages disallow codas entirely whereas none disallows onsets.

The suggestion that the neural control of syllable structure is what was coopted for syntax will therefore gain credibility if syntax displays contrasts which may conceivably be derived from (a)–(d). Here are some candidates:

(a′) Noun phrases are syntactically distinct from sentences (as discussed in the previous section).
(b′) Noun phrases generally occur within sentences (e.g. as arguments to verbs) rather than on their own. (When a noun phrase occurs on its own, it usually constitutes an elliptical sentence; that is, discourse or pragmatic cues permit reliable reconstruction of a sentential context for it.)
(c′) A sentence typically has a verbal or 'stative' element as its syntactic 'head'.
(d′) Some nonverbal material typically has a privileged status within the sentence, e.g. as 'subject', as 'topic', or by preverbal position.

In order to put this syllabic scenario for the origin of syntax on a firm footing, much more certainly needs to be said. A crucial question, clearly, is how close the parallels between (a)–(d) and (a′)–(d′) really are. I argue elsewhere

(Carstairs-McCarthy 1999) that they are too close to be plausibly regarded as accidental. But in one respect the parallel between sentence and syllables expressed in (a) and (a') is not close at all, at least in modern languages. One of the differences between syllables and syllable margins is that a syllable cannot appear in a marginal position in a larger syllable; that is, syllables cannot be nested in larger syllables. But there is no parallel difference between sentences and noun phrases. Sentences can and do appear in positions where noun phrases also occur, so that sentences can indeed be nested in larger sentences. This sort of recursion is a fundamental feature of syntax as it operates today, and, although other kinds of nesting occur too, the nesting of sentences inside sentences is the prime illustration of it. So, if syllable structure is not recursive, the syllabic scenario for the origin of syntax must be wrong (one may think).

That would be an overly hasty conclusion, however, because the syllabic scenario does not purport to explain everything about how the grammar of contemporary languages works (that is, everything about contemporary Universal Grammar, in Chomskyan terms). Rather, it purports to explain how syntax got started, and in particular why it still incorporates a distinction, namely between sentences and NPs, which is more mysterious than it at first seems. The fact that the syllabic scenario predicts that the earliest form of syntax would not have permitted sentential recursion need not count against it automatically. Which way it should count, for or against, is a factual issue, to which we will return in Section 5. First, however, we need to look in more detail at precisely what the syllabic scenario leads us to expect as the syntactic counterpart of characteristic (a). This will permit a more precise characterisation of the kinds of thing that could and could not be said with a syntax that conforms rigidly to a syllabic model.

4.   Precise Implications of the Syllabic Model for Syntax

Syllables such as /kæt/ and /ki:/ (phonological representations of the monosyllabic English words *cat* and *key*) are not just strings of speech sounds. Rather, as stated in Section 3, there is evidence from a variety of sources (including comparative phonology and developmental psycholinguistics) in favour of distinguishing between the vocalic nucleus and the consonantal margins, and also between the onset margin and the coda margin. Most, though not all, phonologists see the second distinction as reflecting a closer bond between the nucleus and coda than between the nucleus and onset, and hence posit a 'rhyme' constituent, consisting of the nucleus and any accompanying coda, intermediate between the syllable and the individual speech sound (Blevins 1995). These considerations point to an internal structure for /kæt/ and /ki:/ as follows:

(8) $[_k{}_{onset}[æ_{nucleus} t_{coda}]_{rhyme}]_{syllable}$
(9) $[_k{}_{onset}[i:_{nucleus}]_{rhyme}]_{syllable}$

One way to arrive at a syntax which mimics this structure directly is to relabel 'syllable' as 'sentence', 'onset' as 'NP-subject', 'coda' as 'NP', 'nucleus' as 'verb' or 'stative', and 'rhyme' as 'VP' (standing for 'verb phrase'). These relabellings reflect the parallels cited at (a)–(d) and (a')–(d') in the previous section. The shared element 'NP' in the labels for the counterparts of onset and coda reflects the shared status of onsets and codas as syllable margins. Substituting lexical material for consonants and vowels, we can get syllable-style sentences as follows:

(10) a. $[Mary_{NP\text{-}subject} [hit_{verb} John_{NP}]_{VP}]_{sentence}$
      b. $[John_{NP\text{-}subject} [see_{verb} Mary_{NP}]_{VP}]_{sentence}$
(11) $[Mary_{NP\text{-}subject}[angry_{stative}]_{VP}]_{sentence}$

Admittedly, just inserting lexical material into relabelled syllabic frames tells us nothing directly about how these lexical strings should be interpreted. But, if syntax originated in humans who possessed at least the social intelligence of contemporary great apes, then a natural use to which such frames could be put would be to encode predicate-argument structure (who does what to whom) more reliably than was possible through word strings of the 'seek termite nest Koko find' variety.

For any predicate with one argument, such as *angry*, that argument will naturally occupy the NP-subject position in the frame. For any predicate with two arguments, such as *hit*, a convention would need to be established as to which would occupy the NP-subject position, but once established the convention would ensure reliable interpretation. The filled frame in (10a) therefore provides a natural syllabic-syntax rendering for either of the English sentences *Mary hit John* or *John hit Mary*, depending on which of the two arguments of *hit*, the agent or the goal, is required to occupy the NP-subject position. Likewise, (10b) provides a natural rendering for either *John saw Mary* or *Mary saw John*, depending on which of the two arguments of *see*, the experiencer or the theme, is required to occupy the NP-subject position.

Sheer familiarity with the sort of structures illustrated in (10) and (11) may make it seem obvious that predicate-argument structure should be encoded linguistically in this way. But in fact it is far from obvious. Firstly, the Monocategoric syntax sketched in Section 2, which lacks a sentence-NP distinction, illustrates just one alternative method of encoding predicate-argument structure, namely by means of 'operators' and 'expressions'. In actual languages, too, predicate-argument structure can be encoded otherwise than by sentences; for example the noun phrases *Mary's attack on John* and *John's glimpse of Mary* have just the same predicate-argument structure as *Mary hit John* and *John saw Mary*. Secondly, the privileging of one piece of nonverbal material by assigning to it a status such as 'subject' (another respect in which English syntax differs from Monocategoric) does not link up with predicate-argument structure in any consistent way. This is shown by the diversity of semantic roles which the subject may express, according to the possible glosses of (10). Why then are 'subjects' so widespread, being invoked in the description of so many languages? This has been a long-standing puzzle for syntactic theorists (Li 1976). But it ceases to be a puzzle if subjects are merely one kind of syntactic homologue for syllable onsets, so as to constitute a historical accident or piece of evolutionary residue in the sense of Section 1.

Examples (10) and (11) illustrate syntactic counterparts of the well-formed syllables in (8) and (9). Consider now the following ill-formed syllable:

(12) $[k_{onset}[æ_{nucleus}[k_{onset}[i{:}_{nucleus}]_{rhyme}]_{syllable}]_{rhyme}]_{syllable}$

What is wrong with (12) is that it incorporates the whole syllable /ki:/ in the coda position occupied in (8) by /t/. It is not that the phonetic sequence [kæki:] cannot exist; it is simply that, in any language in which it occurs, it must be analysed as a sequence of two syllables rather than as one syllable with another embedded inside it. It follows that, in any syntax modelled closely on syllable structure, the following sentence would be ill-formed too:

(13) $[John_{NP\text{-}subject}[see_{verb}[Mary_{NP\text{-}subject}[angry_{stative}]_{VP}]_{sentence}]_{VP}]_{sentence}$

A vital point to observe is that this ill-formedness is not due to any semantic anomaly or difficulty of interpretation. If a natural interpretation can be found for (10b) in terms of predicate-argument structure, one can be found for (13) too: it can be glossed in English as 'John saw that Mary was angry'. For us, as speakers of contemporary human languages, it is hard to visualise a linguistic world in which precise syntactic tools are available to say something which means 'John saw Mary' but not something which means 'John saw that Mary was angry'. Yet that restriction will indeed obtain in a world where permissible sentence structures conform rigidly to syllabic models.

The ill-formed syllable (12) illustrated an attempt to embed a syllable in coda position. Equally ill-formed will be a syllable with another syllable in onset position:

(14) $[[k_{onset}[i{:}_{nucleus}]_{rhyme}]_{syllable}[æ_{nucleus}\ t_{coda}]_{rhyme}]_{syllable}$

Again, it is not that the phonetic sequence [ki:æt] cannot exist; it is simply that, in any language in which it occurs, it must be analysed as a sequence of two syllables (or perhaps a single syllable with a diphthongal nucleus). It follows likewise that, in any syntax modelled closely on syllable structure, the following sentence would be ill-formed too:

(15) [[Mary$_{\text{NP-subject}}$[angry$_{\text{stative}}$]$_{\text{VP}}$]$_{\text{sentence}}$[hit$_{\text{verb}}$John$_{\text{NP}}$]$_{\text{VP}}$]$_{\text{sentence}}$

Again, this ill-formedness is not for want of a plausible interpretation of (15) in predicate-argument terms. It could perfectly well mean 'Mary, being angry, hit John', with the constituent '[Mary angry]' functioning much like a 'head-internal' relative clause in some contemporary languages. Yet here too we have an illustration of a kind of sentential content which, though perfectly expressible with the syntactic tools of contemporary languages, is not expressible by means of a syntax which conforms strictly to a syllabic model.

Dunbar (1996) paints a picture of early hominid language users for whom the principal functions of language are grooming (to establish and maintain interpersonal relationships) and gossip (to keep track of potential freeloaders). Bickerton (this volume) similarly emphasises the role in early language of a 'cheater detection mechanism'. For such language users, it will be advantageous to be able to convey unambiguously such messages as (16) and (17):

(16) John was the one who who helped Mary to stop Alice from stealing fruit from Bill.

(17) Fred has had a grudge against Geoff ever since Geoff failed to support him in his quarrel with Boris over Natasha.

But in a syntax strictly modelled on syllable structure in the fashion I have outlined, the best achievable equivalents will be circumlocutions on the following lines:

(18) Bill had fruit. Alice stole fruit. Mary stopped Alice. John helped Mary.

(19) Fred wanted Natasha. Boris got Natasha. Fred quarrelled with Boris. Geoff abandoned Fred. Fred dislikes Geoff.

Not only will sentential recursion be impossible, but even a predicate with more than two arguments, such as *steal* (as in 'A stole B from C'), will be hard to accommodate. So, if Dunbar and Bickerton are broadly correct about what language was first used for, the syllabic scenario for syntactic evolution implies a serious mismatch between what our earliest language-endowed ancestors were cognitively equipped to say on the basis of their social intelligence and what they were syntactically equipped to say. If such a mismatch really existed, we might expect to find some evidence for it both in the archaeological record and in the way in which cognitive and syntactic endowments were eventually brought more closely into line, as they have been in contemporary human language. I will argue in the next section that there is indeed evidence of both kinds which is consistent with such a mismatch, and which the syllabic scenario may therefore help to explain.

5. Archaeological and Later Linguistic Evidence

Archaeologists have often commented on the cultural and technical inertia displayed by the various human types traditionally included under the label *Homo erectus*, between about 1.5 and 0.3 million years ago (e.g. Mithen 1996). Some have argued that this period of stagnation corresponds to a period when human brain size remained fairly constant, sandwiched between earlier and later bursts of increase: the earlier transition from australopithecines through *Homo habilis* to *Homo erectus*, and the later transition to *Homo sapiens neanderthalensis* and *Homo sapiens sapiens* (Aiello 1996). Admittedly, absence of evidence is not evidence of absence, and there is no telling what variety of artefacts *erectus* may have made out of perishable materials. Some *erectus* were certainly expert makers of wooden spears (Thieme 1997). Nevertheless, it remains true that *erectus*'s most elaborate stone tool, the Acheulean handaxe, remained substantially unchanged for thousands of years. Why such conservatism?

One factor, I suggest, may have been linguistic. The preadaptation for syntax supplied by the neural control of syllabically organized speech, consequent on the lowering of the larynx and the development of the two-tube vocal tract, was a less than ideal preadaptation. Predicate-argument structure is naturally recursive, as Bickerton (1998) points out: that is, a predicate and its argument(s), such as *Mary was angry*, can together constitute an argument of a higher predicate, as in *John saw that Mary was angry*. Yet the syllabic preadaptation for syntax steered linguistic development in *erectus* away from any grammatical mode of expression for this semantic nesting. Moreover, syllable-derived syntax could not easily encode predicate-argument structures with more than two arguments. Instead, it steered *erectus* towards the familiar but nevertheless otiose sentence-NP distinction, yielding sentences with a kind of binary structure which reflects the privileged status of onsets in syllables, but which lacked (and still lacks) any clear-cut cognitive or communicative function. If evolution operated with foresight rather than blindly, it might have foreseen the shackles that this sort of syntax would impose on *erectus*'s communicative and perhaps also cognitive development (insofar as language influences cognition), and would have backpedalled in order to try again. But evolution could not sacrifice short-term fitness for long-term gain in this case, any more than it could in the development of the mammalian sperm duct or the vertebrate eye.

The principal recent champion of the hypothesis that *erectus*'s cultural inertia had a linguistic cause, at least in part, is Bickerton. According to him, *erectus* possessed not language but protolanguage: an ability to produce strings of individually meaningful 'words', but no syntax to enable such strings to be decoded reliably. In particular, protolanguage was not hooked up to predicate-argument structure, and so could not be used for the sort of precise gossip illustrated in (16) and (17). Full language emerged only with the transition to modern humans, involving new neural linkages between phonetic structure and predicate-argument structure (Bickerton 1990, 1995, 1998, this volume). An obvious question, then, is whether my scenario has any advantages over Bickerton's.

Bickerton's scenario certainly seems broadly consistent with what is known about human evolution. The difficulty is that it is also consistent with other radically different evolutionary paths which the great apes (including humans) might have taken. For Bickerton (as for most researchers) the lowering of the larynx is primarily a consequence of selection pressures for improved speech once the evolution of other features of language (vocabulary expansion and grammar) had got under way; it is not (as I have suggested) an independently motivated precursor of those other features. So Bickerton's scenario provides no ready explanation for why it should have been us, the bipedal apes, who developed language, rather than quadrupedal apes such as chimpanzees or gorillas. As is now generally agreed, these other great apes have a social intelligence which ought to have been just as adequate to trigger the development of language as that of prelinguistic hominids – if social intelligence really played the triggering role that Bickerton claims for it.

This is not a fatal objection to Bickerton's scenario. There may indeed have been special factors other than bipedalism and larynx lowering which favoured language development in humans rather than in other apes. For example perhaps foraging on the savannah could be assisted by more elaborate oral communication in ways that foraging in the forest could not. But for the time being such special factors remain largely speculative, and are in any case grafted onto Bickerton's scenario rather than an integral part of it. In my scenario, by contrast, no such special factors need to be invoked. Rather, language could scarcely have arisen in any other ape because no other ape produces vocalisations analysable as sequences of syllables. So, at least, for the time being, my scenario has the advantage of parsimony.

Admittedly, the linguistic shackles which I have described were thrown off, or at least loosened, eventually: the syntax of modern languages allows for recursion, for predicates with more than two arguments, and for much else which is not obviously foreshadowed in syllable structure. An archaeological transition which suggests itself as the counterpart of this linguistic development is the transition to *Homo sapiens*, beginning around three hundred thousand years ago. But even if the two changes were indeed simultaneous, what enabled grammar to break out of its syllabic straitjacket precisely at that time, after failing to do so for a million years? I have no answer to that question. That is a shortcoming of my scenario. However, it is a shortcoming shared with every other account of language evolution, so far as I can see, including Bickerton's. Besides, even if my scenario does not explain the timing of post-*erectus* grammatical changes, it goes a considerable way towards explaining the form which these changes took.

It is not surprising that embedded sentences should have the same syllable-derived structure as simple ones, exhibiting the same contrasts (a')–(d'). But in modern syntax it is not just sentences which exhibit internal structure; phrases of all kinds, such as noun phrases and prepositional phrases, do so too. What form should we expect this internal structure to take? In view of the obvious differences in meaning and syntactic function between a typical noun and a typical preposition, for example, there is little reason to expect that the internal structures of their respective phrases should be parallel, either with each other or with that of the sentence. Nevertheless, they are indeed parallel. This claim, first mooted by Chomsky (1970) and developed by Jackendoff (1977), has proved to be one of the most robust and long-lasting features of generative grammatical theory. Each phrase is said to have a 'head' which determines its syntactic status, and which is typically accompanied by a 'complement'; this head-complement unit, in turn, can be accompanied by a 'specifier' in order to constitute a complete phrase of the relevant kind (in syntactic terminology, to constitute a 'maximal projection' of the head). The subject-verb-object structure of a simple English sentence is merely one manifestation of a more general specifier-head-complement structure.

From the point of view of the questions which concern us here, this parallelism suggests that sentential recursion arose not as an independent innovation but as simply one effect of the development of a syntax for all phrases, not just for simple sentences. This development in turn involved not some radically new syntactic mechanism but rather the generalisation of a syllable-derived structure to new syntactic units. Paradoxically, the syntactic liberalisation which now permits sentences such as (16) and (17) arose not through an abandonment of the syllabic model but rather through a wider application of it.

The syllabic scenario, as formulated in Section 3, was not devised to account for the internal structure of units other than sentences. But that structure, as it has been described by syntactic theorists with no axe to grind on grammatical evolution, turns out to be just what we expect if we assume both (1) that the syllabic scenario for the origin of sentence structure is correct and (2) that, as we are often reminded by evolutionary biologists, evolution works by conservative tinkering, not by radical innovation. To succeed in evolutionary terms, a solution to a problem does not have to be good; it merely has to be better (from the point of view of reproductive success) than no solution at all. When circumstances arose where syntax would confer a reproductive advantage, evolution provided *erectus* with just such a mediocre solution. Later, when for some reason it began to be feasible for humans to gain reproductive advantage through replacing some of *erectus*'s 'words' with internally structured phrases, precisely the same mediocre solution was recycled.

6. Conclusion: Grammar as a Mixed Blessing

It is easy to see the development of language as an unmixed blessing. How can it not be an advantage for a species to have at its disposal a means of producing and understanding complex messages rapidly and easily? Recently, researchers such as Knight (1998) and Power (1998) have questioned that assumption. The very ease and versatility of speech make it cheap to use for deception, or, more broadly, for gaining advantages over one's fellows. By contrast, signals which are expensive to produce, like elaborate plumage as part of a mating display, are hard to fake and therefore reliable. Why, then, would voluntary vocal messages have ever come to be regarded as sufficiently trustworthy for language use to become general? Subtle questions such as these have led to imaginative proposals about the circumstances of earliest language use, invoking links with ritual in hunter-gatherer communities and with the use of pigments for body decoration – links which are far from obvious but which will therefore be all the more persuasive if they can be firmly established.

Research on the structure, rather than the use, of the earliest forms of language has not so far benefited from similarly subtle questioning. As I mentioned in Section 1, grammatical evolution has generally been seen in black-and-white terms: either grammar is not adaptive at all so evolution cannot explain it, or else grammar must have evolved (because it has a biological basis) so it must be adaptive. In this chapter I have suggested that a more nuanced approach may be illuminating. Grammar could in some respects have been radically different while still fulfilling (perhaps even fulfilling better) the communicative or cognitive functions which are usually posited for it; therefore grammar as it is may in these respects reflect historical accidents which will shed important light on how language evolved.

As for links with domains outside grammar proper, the main foci of research on grammatical evolution hitherto have been semantics (particularly predicate-argument structure and its association with social intelligence), discourse structure (the role of the topic-comment distinction), and parsing efficiency. While not denying the importance of such links, I would like to suggest that domains less obviously connected with what syntax is for, such as syllable structure, will be potentially more enlightening if they can be established. Whether or not my argument in favour of precisely that link is accepted, I hope to have persuaded readers of the value of looking in grammar for historical accidents of the kind whose evolutionary relevance is emphasised by George C. Williams.

Acknowledgements

What I say about human evolution in general draws heavily on what I learned as a result of a month's visit to Professor Leslie Aiello and her colleagues at University College London in 1996. She and they are of course not responsible for my interpretations or misinterpretations, however. The work was supported by a grant from the Marsden Fund in New Zealand.

Notes

1.   Although nearly all linguists would agree with this claim, Gil (1994) argues that Riau Indonesian is a counterexample to it. Whether or not Gil is correct about Riau Indonesian (which I will not discuss here), his position supports the view that a distinction between sentences and noun phrases is not syntactically inevitable.
2.   Another positive consequence, pointed out to me by Jeffrey Laitman, was the possibility through mouth breathing of moving greater volumes of air in and out of the lungs. This may have promoted stamina in bipedal running – a significant advantage in a new savannah habitat.

References

Aiello, L. C. 1996. Hominine preadaptations for language and cognition. In P. Mellars and K. Gibson (eds), *Modelling the Early Human Mind.* Cambridge: McDonald Institute for Archaeological Research, pp. 89–99.
Bickerton, D. 1990. *Language and Species.* Chicago: University of Chicago Press.
Bickerton, D. 1995. *Language and Human Behavior.* Seattle: University of Washington Press.
Bickerton, D. 1998. Catastrophic evolution: the case for a single step from protolanguage to full human language. In J. R. Hurford, M. Studdert-Kennedy and C. Knight (eds), *Approaches to the Evolution of Language: Social and cognitive bases.* Cambridge: Cambridge University Press, pp. 341–358.
Blevins, J. 1995. The syllable in phonological theory. In J. A. Goldsmith (ed), *Handbook of Phonological Theory.* Oxford: Blackwell, pp. 206–244.
Carstairs-McCarthy, A. 1998. Synonymy avoidance, phonology and the origin of syntax. In J. R. Hurford, M. Studdert-Kennedy and C. Knight (eds), *Approaches to the Evolution of Language: Social and cognitive bases.* Cambridge: Cambridge University Press, pp. 279–296.
Carstairs-McCarthy, A. 1999. *The Origins of Complex Language: An inquiry into the evolutionary beginnings of sentences, syllables and truth.* Oxford: Oxford University Press.

Chomsky, N. 1970. Remarks on nominalization. In R. A. Jacobs and P. S. Rosenbaum (eds), *Readings in English Transformational Grammar*. Waltham, MA: Ginn, pp. 184–221.

Dunbar, R. 1996. *Grooming, Gossip and the Evolution of Language*. London: Faber and Faber.

Gil, D. 1994. The structure of Riau Indonesian. *Nordic Journal of Linguistics* **17**: 179–200.

Jackendoff, R. 1977. *X̄ Syntax: A study of phrase structure*. Cambridge, MA: MIT Press.

Knight, C. 1998. Ritual/speech coevolution: a solution to the problem of deception. In J. R. Hurford, M. Studdert-Kennedy and C. Knight (eds), *Approaches to the Evolution of Language: Social and cognitive bases*. Cambridge: Cambridge University Press, pp. 68–91.

Langacker, R. W. 1969. On pronominalization and the chain of command. In D. A. Reibel and S. A. Schane (eds), *Modern Studies in English: Readings in transformational grammar*. Englewood Cliffs, NJ: Prentice-Hall, pp. 160–186.

Li, C. N. (ed). 1976. *Subject and Topic*. New York: Academic.

Lightfoot, D. 1999. *The Development of Language: Acquisition, change and evolution*. Oxford: Blackwell.

MacNeilage, P. F. 1998. The frame/content theory of evolution of speech production. *Behavioral and Brain Sciences* **21**: 499–546.

Mithen, S. 1996. *The Prehistory of the Mind*. London: Thames and Hudson.

Newmeyer, F. J. 1991. Functional explanations in linguistics and the origins of language. *Language and Communication* **11**: 3–28.

Newmeyer, F. J. 1998. On the supposed 'counterfunctionality' of universal grammar: some evolutionary implications. In J. R. Hurford, M. Studdert-Kennedy and C. Knight (eds), *Approaches to the Evolution of Language: Social and cognitive bases*. Cambridge: Cambridge University Press, pp. 305–319.

Pinker, S. 1994. *The Language Instinct*. New York: Morrow.

Pinker, S. 1997. Evolutionary biology and the evolution of language. In M. Gopnik (ed), *The Inheritance and Innateness of Grammars*. New York: Oxford University Press, pp. 181–208.

Pinker, S. and P. Bloom 1990. Natural language and natural selection. *Behavioral and Brain Sciences* **13**: 707–784.

Power, C. 1998. Old wives' tales: the gossip hypothesis and the reliability of cheap signals. In J. R. Hurford, M. Studdert-Kennedy and C. Knight (eds), *Approaches to the Evolution of Language: Social and cognitive bases*. Cambridge: Cambridge University Press, pp. 111–129.

Thieme, H. 1997. Lower Palaeolithic hunting spears from Germany. *Nature* **385**: 807–810.

Williams, G. C. 1992. *Natural Selection: Domains, levels and challenges*. New York: Oxford University Press.

Williams, G. C. 1996. *Plan and Purpose in Nature*. London: Weidenfeld and Nicholson.

16

How Protolanguage Became Language

DEREK BICKERTON

1. Introduction

The present chapter presents the evolution of language as a sequence of three stages. The first stage is the derivation of the basic structure of syntax from a social calculus set up to handle reciprocal altruism (Section 2). The second stage consists of the long delay hypothesised between the birth of protolanguage and the emergence of true language, the cause of this delay being the limited coherence of neural signals in prelinguistic brains (Section 3). The third is a stage of Baldwinian evolution commencing after the emergence of basic syntactic structure and possibly continuing at least until the human diaspora that began approximately ninety thousand years ago (Section 4). In Section 5, some possible objections to these proposals are considered.

Nothing will be said here about protolanguage, its emergence or the selective pressures that drove that emergence. It will simply be assumed along the lines of previous work (Bickerton 1990, 1995) that between two and three million years ago there developed a structureless protolanguage. Whether this protolanguage originally consisted of signs, (proto)words or a mixture of these is immaterial to the present discussion; it is not unreasonable to suppose, along with Burling (this volume), that at its inception, protolanguage was indeed mixed. For expository convenience it will be assumed in what follows that protolanguage was spoken, but nothing of significance turns on this. The protolanguage vocabulary doubtless increased over time, but its users, for reasons to be discussed, are presumed to have been unable to produce or comprehend utterances of more than four or five units, a limit that might not have been significantly exceeded even in the period immediately prior to the first appearance of true syntax.

2. Reciprocal Altruism, the Social Calculus and the Roots of Syntax

How could syntax, an evolutionary novelty, ever have emerged? Some would argue it is not unique, that it merely constitutes a particulate (Studdert-Kennedy 1998), hierarchical (Simon 1967) structure such as may be found in many other natural phenomena. However, while it is true that syntax, in common with many other phenomena, is indeed hierarchical, that by itself does not tell us very much. Each hierarchy has its own units and subunits and its own modes of organising these. Properties that syntax seems not to share with other particulate, hierarchical structures include (but are not necessarily limited to) the following:

1. Units that constitute descriptions (of real or imagined entities) that are indeterminate in length (phrases).
2. Units that consist of clusters of lower-level units (as in (1)) together with one (and not more than one) unit (a verb) to which all members of the cluster relate in some manner (clauses).
3. Restrictions on the function (thematic role) and number of first-level units that can combine to form second-level units.
4. Absence of restrictions on the number of second-level units that can combine to form third-level units (sentences).

Granted, hierarchical, particulate structuring probably characterises many if not all the complex systems known to us. However, that is just a beginning. Within the class of such structured systems there exist significant differences (Newmeyer 1983: 103). To ignore such differences is to place crippling restrictions on our understanding of the phenomena concerned.

This point can hardly be overemphasised, given remarks such as the following (Dunbar 1998: 107): 'No doubt non-linguists ought to hesitate before commenting on matters relating to the grammatical structure of languages, but these structures of language are not, in themselves, relevant to questions about the function of language *or its evolution*' (emphasis added). However, there can be no question that grammar, in common with all other components of language, evolved. It is therefore crucial that any account of the evolution of language should explain, not merely how grammar (in particular, syntax) evolved, but why it has the precise set of properties that it has, rather than a different set that (other things being equal) evolution might have provided it with.

In principle there are five, and probably no more than five, ways in which syntax could have emerged:

1. Through macromutation.
2. Through the operation of 'laws of form'.
3. As a 'spandrel'.
4. Through gradual accumulation of rules.
5. Through exaptation.

The first (although previously assumed by the present author, see Bickerton 1990) is unacceptable to a large majority of biologists. The second (see for example Piatelli-Palmerini 1989) usually contains references to the structural properties of crystals, fractal studies and so forth, but to the best of my knowledge no one has yet put the suggestion in a form concrete enough to be discussed. The same applies to the third (for the architectural and biological definitions of 'spandrel', see Gould and Lewontin 1984). We know the kind of superimposition of two arches that produces architectural spandrels, but no one has suggested what might be the equivalent of arches in the case of syntax.

The fourth, with its automatic appeal to neo-Darwinian gradualism, is perhaps currently the most popular approach (Pinker 1994; Pinker and Bloom 1990; Newmeyer 1991). However it faces severe problems yet to be dealt with by its proponents. One concerns the nature of syntax itself. According to Pinker, grammars intermediate between protolanguage and full human language could have had 'modules with fewer rules' (1994: 366). Such a picture mirrors what we know of *physical* evolution. To propose that the giraffe's neck or the peacock's tail could not have evolved gradually would merely invite derision. Unfortunately, more abstract aspects of evolution prove less tractable. One need only consider the proposal that syntax progressed from a grammar with n rules to a grammar with $n + 1$ rules in the context of what is nowadays accepted without question by most syntacticians: that syntax, contrary to what was supposed by generative grammarians of the 1960s and 1970s, does not consist of a simple aggregate of rules. Indeed, according to what is probably the deepest and most thorough school of thought in the field (Chomsky 1981, 1995), syntax consists of a small handful of principles which interact systematically with one another. It is highly implausible that such interdependent principles could have been arrived at by any merely incremental process.

Another and perhaps even more severe problem arises from the nature of the initial step. Natural selection (which all proponents of this approach accept) works on variation: it selectively increases the distribution of variations that are adaptive. But how could there be a variation in syntactic ability before there was any syntax?

For all who study the evolution of language, syntax must somehow be grounded in conceptual structure. But no one has yet even attempted to spell out how any individual variation in the complexity of conceptual structure or in the degree of skill with which conceptual structure was utilised could have had implications for an initial step into syntax. Thus gradualism in the evolution of syntax remains an article of faith rather than a logically based hypothesis.

Thus of the five possibilities listed earlier, the likeliest, at least at present, is some form of exaptation. The question therefore becomes one of determining which if any among preexisting primate traits or capacities could have yielded the properties required by syntax. Given the emphasis placed nowadays on social intelligence as a factor in language evolution, it should come as no great surprise that a particular aspect of social intelligence supplies just the required properties.

That aspect is a consequence of reciprocal altruism (Trivers 1971, 1985). The concept of reciprocal altruism has proved extremely fertile in behavioural studies, receiving both theoretical (Axelrod and Hamilton 1981; Axelrod 1984) and observational (Strum 1987; de Waal 1996) support. Reciprocal altruism is widespread among apes and not uncommon in monkey species. It may well have evolved to counterbalance the tyranny exercised in many animal species by alpha males and thus give members of reciprocal-altruism alliances a greater chance of reproductive success. Such alliances are cemented by means of mutual grooming, food sharing (among chimpanzees for instance fruit, which is plentiful, is seldom if ever shared but meat, which is rare, is very frequently shared), support in disputes in which either animal was involved and so on.

Some of the ways in which reciprocal altruism works are well described by Strum (1987: 134–135) for baboons (genetically further from humans than chimpanzees but, as terrestrial primates, behaviourally closer in several respects):

Friendships were almost formal systems of social reciprocity. The underlying understanding seemed to be, 'If I do something good for you now, you'll do something good for me later'. The balance sheet would be set up in an individual's favor by a combination of good deeds and hard-won trust. *This was quite a sophisticated process when one took into account the time that might pass between credits and debits.* A new male coming into [the troop] acted as if he had thought to himself, 'To be successful in this troop, I'll need a few female friends, several infant friends ... and some male allies.' He would then set out to acquire them. Weeks, even months later, he would call in his dues. (Strum 1987: 135, emphasis added)

The 'balance sheet' is perhaps even more sophisticated than Strum suggests. To create it, an animal cannot merely tag other individuals as 'owing'. Since it is in the interests of either animal to obtain as much as possible from the alliance while giving as little as possible, all alliances are subject to cheating. And as Pinker points out, 'A subtle cheater reciprocates enough to make it worth the altruist's while, but returns less than he is capable of giving, or less than the altruist would give if the situation were reversed. That puts the altruist in an awkward position . . . [The altruist] does have one type of leverage, though. If there are *other* trading partners in the group who don't cheat at all, or who cheat subtly but less stingily, she can give them her business instead' (Pinker 1997: 403, original emphasis).

Accordingly, there would have been a strong selective pressure for the development of a social calculus that would keep track of the behaviours not just of one other animal in the group, but of all those with which a given animal interacted closely (for a suspect ally would need to be replaced, and it would then be necessary to evaluate candidates for its replacement). Such a social calculus would have to automatically determine the current status of any dyad: had member A done more favours for B, or vice versa? An animal that could not tell whether it was being cheated would not prosper if there were animals in its vicinity reliably able to detect cheaters and freeloaders.

But how exactly could a social calculus of this kind work? While a global summation of all interactions remains a possibility, it is at least questionable whether monkey or even ape minds could have achieved a category with such a high level of abstraction. In light of what is known about linkages between specific actions and the firing of specific sets of neurons in macaques (Perrett et al. 1985), it would seem rather more plausible to suppose that different types of action (grooming, food sharing etc.) would have been tabulated separately. However, ego and alter were at different times performers of these actions (Agents), the acted-upon, where the action was something like grooming (Themes) or the recipients of the acted-upon, where the acted-upon was food in a context of sharing (Goals). Note that these categories could not, like status categories or kinship categories, be tied to given individuals or sets of individuals; they had to be categories abstract enough to be instantiated by different individuals at different times.

One of the components of human memory is what is known as 'episodic memory' (Tulving 1984a). Episodic memory is what enables us to recall particular events and sequences of events. Note that in such recall we are invariably able to state, with respect to any remembered action, who or what was acted upon, and (where appropriate) who or what performed the action and who or what it was directed towards. The evolution of episodic memory (like the evolution of so many human cognitive capacities) remains, almost a century and a half after Darwin, a total mystery. But there is no reason to tie it to the possession of language: although its presence is impossible to demonstrate in species without narrative capacity, some researchers (Olton 1984; Tulving 1984b) are prepared to accept that other species possess it in some degree. Certainly, at some period in human ancestry episodic memory must have evolved, and the crucial thematic roles must have been mapped onto it, enabling us to recreate the thematic structure of any given event. While, for the reason stated, we cannot confirm the presence of episodic memory in any other primate species, the need for maintaining the social calculus over extended periods of time suggests that such a memory may have been well-established among our remote ancestors.

Note that the three thematic roles discussed (Agent, Theme, Goal) are precisely those that are obligatorily mapped onto sentence structure. All verbs specify and obligatorily require some kind of Theme, a subset of verbs in addition have an obligatory Agent, and a subset of that subset also requires a Goal. Thus all verbs fall into one of the three categories determined by the number of obligatory thematic roles (one-place, two-place and three-place predicates). Furthermore, the existence of thematic roles and their obligatory nature potentially yield the basic building blocks of syntax: the phrase and the clause. A phrase is simply an argument of a verb (that is, a referent that takes part in the action of a given verb on a given occasion) with its appropriate thematic role, and a clause is simply a verb plus a series of phrases (its obligatory arguments plus any optional ones). Moreover, since syntax gives no limiting definition as to what an argument can consist of, arguments can be clauses as well as phrases, thereby building in the possibility of infinite recursivity.

In contemporary studies of syntax, thematic roles are not usually regarded as its cornerstones. This is because thematic roles have semantic content as well as syntactic implications; the doctrine of the autonomy of syntax, which since Chomsky (1957) has been crucial to syntactic theory, automatically disqualifies any such Janus-faced entities from a central role. However, synchronic description is one thing and evolutionary explanation quite another. Once we turn from the goal of synchronic description to that of evolutionary explanation, it becomes apparent that it is precisely the Janus-faced nature of thematic roles – one foot in semantics, the other in syntax – that makes them the most plausible mechanism for the introduction of syntax into a hitherto asyntactic protolanguage. Moreover, the precise nature or number of thematic roles (long controversial in syntactic theory, see e.g. Carlson 1984) matters less than the fact that verbs obligatorily assign arguments (one to three), the number of which is predictable from the verb itself. What this means is that if you know the semantics of a verb, you know how many arguments will be obligatorily represented (for 'sleep' one, for 'break' two, for 'give' three and so on). This is true for whatever language you choose: there is no language in which the verb that means 'sleep' takes two obligatory arguments, the verb that means 'break' takes three, but the verb that means 'give' takes only one.

Knowing the requirements of a given verb and recognising the existence and nature of units intermediate between the single word and the complete utterance (that is, phrases and clauses) at one and the same time enables hearers to rapidly parse and comprehend sentences, and provides speakers with a fixed template around which words can be assembled. In fact, it has proved possible to derive most if not all of the basic principles of universal grammar from a small set of primitives which includes only the obligatory representation of thematic roles (as just described), a general economy measure ('all constituents without independent reference must choose the nearest available referent as antecedent') and a pragmatic assumption ('no two arguments of a clause can refer to the same referent unless one of them is lexically marked to this effect'). A full account of this derivation can be found in the appendix to Calvin and Bickerton (2000).

Once again, it should be emphasised that the fact that such a derivation proves possible is in itself a strong argument in favour of the theory of syntactic origins presented here. As stated earlier, a viable theory of language evolution should explain why the properties of syntax are what they are, and not otherwise.

However, it should also be pointed out that the social calculus was not the only, but merely the most crucial, factor encouraging abstract representations of thematic roles. The capacity to represent agency may have much longer roots, given that agency implies causation, understanding causation permits prediction, and the ability to predict is highly adaptive. However, it is doubtful whether any aspect of animals' lives would have encouraged abstract role representations to the same extent as a social calculus would.

Since reciprocal altruism appears in a number of primate groups, the existence of such a calculus probably long predates the emergence of protolanguage. It is therefore reasonable to ask why, when protolanguage first emerged, the social-calculus analysis of thematic roles was not immediately mapped onto it. To understand that, we need to understand the status of the human brain at the time when protolanguage emerged.

3. Signal Coherence and Syntax

If the present account is correct, protolanguage emerged when the hominid brain was in the region of 600cc. Since then it has more than doubled in size. This increase in size has often been regarded as the force that drove language and indeed all typically human attributes (including consciousness). Chomsky for instance has pointed out that 'We have no idea, at present, how physical laws apply when 10 to the tenth neurons are placed in an object the size of a basketball, under the special conditions that arose during human evolution' (1982: 321).

However, as pointed out in Bickerton (1990, 1995) there is a marked discrepancy between brain expansion and human mental powers which is amply revealed in the fossil record. When the brain doubled in size, hominids didn't get twice as smart. Artefactual production and behavioural changes from *Homo habilis* to Neanderthals are insignificant compared to those found once our own species emerged, and unless there is no relationship whatsoever between intelligence and the products of intelligence (including tools and behaviour), an enlarged brain did not, in and of itself, significantly enhance the former.

That it appears to have finally done so in our case suggests the presence of some kind of threshold effect. In Bickerton (1998) I tried to account for this effect by the proposal that the social calculus (there referred to as a cheater detection mechanism) resided in one portion of the brain, protolanguage in another, and that there was no significant linkage between these regions.

There are several problems with this solution. First, if thematic roles are stored in episodic memory, as implied here, it is hard to see why the protolanguage, which was surely used for (among many other things) telling tales of past events, could not access them. Second, in any case, all brain regions are linked to one another; indeed, as regards the neocortex, some researchers (Braitenberg and Schuz 1992) estimate that no two neurons are separated by more than three synaptic relays.

Moreover, what is sometimes referred to as Hebb's rule (Hebb 1949) states that neurons that are frequently active together will strengthen their connections. Now, given that there are obvious social benefits from enhanced communication, it would have been in the interests of hominids to attempt to map their role-assigning representations of events onto their protolanguage. If they had had any success at all in doing so, by Hebb's rule the connections involved would have strengthened. If they failed, then it was because something was preventing them from mapping these social calculus–derived representations onto their speech. Thirdly, the way the brain now seems to be organised, into nonlocalised but dedicated circuits (in ways that do not exclude the possible plurifunctionality of particular circuit components) rather than into strictly localised Fodorian modules, renders unlikely any radical separation scenario lasting millions of years.

The work of Calvin (1996a, 1996b; Calvin and Bickerton 2000) suggests an interesting alternative. The task of constructing sentences (or, if it comes to that, trains of thought) places demands on the brain that probably no nonhominid brain had been called upon to satisfy. It is worth considering in some details what those demands were, and why they differed.

First consider what brains of other species have to do. Note to begin with that the things which only humans can do are not limited to complex activities such as mathematics or philosophy, nor even to those for which language is a prerequisite. They include tap-dancing, rhythmic drumming, representational drawing, doing jigsaw puzzles and playing simple games the rules of which can be ostensively, rather than verbally taught. What do such tasks require? Common to all of them, simple and complex alike, is the maintenance, over what in terms of brain activity are long periods, of coherent patterns of neural signalling that are neither necessarily stimulated nor necessarily supported by stimuli from the external world.

Moreover, none of the many behaviours we share with other species seems to require long-term maintenance of neural firing patterns. Most if not all of these behaviours are triggered and maintained by external stimuli. In addition, we must take into account the fact that most if not all of the messages that nonhuman brains transmit (as well as many that human brains transmit) do not require a high level of coherence. They serve to focus increased vigilance in particular directions, they process messages from sensory organs, they transmit instructions to motor organs to perform responses to stimuli. Such messages do not have to be maintained without external stimulation for long periods, they do not normally have to merge with other messages to form complex wholes, and if they are distorted in transmission, errors that result can often be corrected through proprioceptive feedback.

The case is very different when we utter sentences. A high degree of signal coherence is required here. To take a concrete example, compare the following two sentences:

> Do you know how to make a rabbit stew?
> Do you know how to make a rabbit spew?

An anonymous referee of this chapter supposed that only a phonological error was involved here but was wrong. Granted, the difference between the two sentences lies only in one feature (point of articulation) of one phoneme; if one means the former, but carelessly produces the latter, it is because the motor organs have been accidentally instructed to produce a voiceless stop consonant with bilabial rather than the appropriate alveolar closure. However, the implications of this seemingly trivial slip are far-reaching and involve semantics and syntax as well as phonology. As regards semantics, 'Make a rabbit stew' means 'cook a dish in which rabbit is the principal ingredient'; 'make a rabbit spew' means 'cause a rabbit to vomit'. As regards syntax, in the first sentence 'a rabbit stew' is a complex noun phrase; in the second 'spew' is a verb, 'a rabbit' is its subject and 'a rabbit spew' is a clause, not a noun phrase. In other words, a single transmission error affecting a single distinctive feature of a single phoneme can completely change the syntax and semantics of a sentence.

It might be objected that the need for signal coherence is overestimated here. Pinker and Bloom (1990) note that many examples of clipped, telescoped or otherwise incoherent speech are perfectly comprehensible. But such an objection is misguided. While a sequence such as 'skid crash hospital' may be perfectly comprehensible, it is only so because any speaker of English can quickly access the extended (and of course fully grammatical) equivalent, 'Her car got into a skid, it crashed and she was taken to hospital'. What a speaker without such resources (for example, a hominid limited to protolanguage) could do with such sequences is problematic; it seems likeliest that the small percentage of truncated and distorted utterances that our highly developed language faculty still produces can be processed only in light of a vast percentage of fully grammatical utterances, to one or more of which they can be related.

Now consider what the brain has to do in order to utter a commonplace sentence like 'Do you know how to make a rabbit stew?' As a first approximation, let us assume the existence of an 'executive brain' (Donald 1998) that knows what it is doing, and determines in advance what it will say. That brain must first assemble nine words of appropriate meanings and category membership in just one out of hundreds of thousands of possible combinations. Exactly how it does this we do not know, but patterns of neural activity that somehow represent the words concerned must somehow join, merge or blend into a single structure. What happens when two word representations meet – whether the activity patterns representing each are merely added to one another, or whether a third pattern is formed that somehow retains the identities of the merged units – remains a topic of research for the twenty-first century. However, in addition to this process (repeated eight times for the nine-word sentence 'Do you know how to make a rabbit stew?'), several distinctive features for each of the twenty-three phonemes that make up the nine-word sentence also have to be selected (with the possibility of a single wrong choice causing disastrous results), associated with the appropriate lexical units and arranged in their correct order. As Donald (1998: 57) points out, 'Language is really a gigantic meta-task, requiring the co-ordination of an entire hierarchy of subtasks and sub-subtasks, regulated from working memory'.

Such a metatask would impose massive and unprecedented demands even on an executive brain. But suppose there is no executive brain, and the brain as a whole is just as Dennett (1991) has described it: a place that has nowhere where 'everything comes together', but in which a Darwinian struggle among potential thoughts and utterances is constantly taking place.

Of course, in a sense the same is true of our experience of the external world, the Jamesian 'blooming, buzzing confusion' from which our senses have to extract those features directly relevant to our homeostasis. But here we have gatekeepers, the three attention systems described by Posner and Rothbart (1992). However, those attention systems are focused on the external world, and have had hundreds of millions of years in which to learn to distinguish the kinds of phenomena that have direct relevance to their users' lives from the far more numerous phenomena that can safely be disregarded. What gatekeepers exist to monitor internally generated, mental phenomena? Apparently none. Far from being conducted in the calm, well-lit surroundings of the 'executive suite' (Donald 1998: 53), the metatask of language is performed in what is more like an eastern bazaar, with everyone shouting their wares at the tops of their voices.

Such a procedure, carried out in such surroundings, places demands on the coherence of signals that far exceed any procedures that animals of other species are required to carry out. Accordingly Calvin (1996a, 1996b), building on suggestions contained in studies of neural transmission (Enright 1980; Somers and Koppel 1993; Lund, Yoshioka and Levitt 1993), has proposed that a significant increase in signal coherence was required for language to be launched.

Calvin's proposal allows us to make sense of the fossil record, particularly as it relates to brain growth. The size of the human brain, or to be more precise, our species' degree of encephalisation (Jerison 1977), is perhaps the most distinctive physical characteristic of *Homo sapiens sapiens*. But how, exactly, would brain size affect language and thought? According to Calvin, the increase in number of available neurons corresponds to the difference between a quartet and a choir. In a quartet, it becomes immediately apparent when one or more of the singers is off key or out of tune; in a choir, a number of singers may be off key or out of tune, but their errors are lost in the chorus of dozens of voices. In a similar fashion, small numbers of neurons attempting to relay the same message will not achieve the degree of coherence obtained if very large numbers perform the same task. Assume that neurons tend to make neighbouring neurons synchronise their firing patterns by a process of entrainment similar to that by which two grandfather clocks, placed in close proximity, tend to synchronise the swings of their pendulums. Under such circumstances, competing messages will spread or contract as more and more neurons are recruited by one firing pattern or lost by another. Provided that the number recruited is sufficient to pass some kind of coherence threshold, the pattern that recruits the most neurons will win the struggle and (if the pattern represents a sentence) achieve utterance at the expense of competing patterns.

The foregoing hypothesis can be related to the overall development of language as follows. Initially (perhaps two to three million years ago, the precise time does not appear to be significant) our ancestors had a well-developed social calculus capable of assigning roles to the participants in any action, and an extremely primitive and structureless protolanguage. Obviously they would, if they could, have mapped the former onto the latter forthwith. Alas, selective pressures are relatively powerless in the face of infrastructural deficits. To assemble a full thematic structure prior to utterance, as modern humans do, would have required the maintenance of fully coherent signals through several merges. With brains little larger and more efficient than those of contemporary apes, the best those remote ancestors could do would have been to send individual words singly to the motor organs of speech (which is what, apparently, contemporary pidgin speakers do, see Bickerton 1995). This would have resulted in extremely slow speech (speech delivery by contemporary pidgin speakers is also very slow), placing a heavy burden on working memory. Because of this burden and because of the parsing problems presented by protolanguage's lack of structure, protolanguage utterances (like those of contemporary pidgins, see Bickerton 1983) would have consisted of short bursts of, at most, four or five words.

Among modern humans, four- or five-word utterances are normally produced not by sending successive words individually to the organs of speech, but rather by combining those words prior to sending them. But to create even a sentence of only five words in this way would require at least a three-level hierarchy of combinatory processes, or merges (assuming that the brain can assemble units in parallel – if it cannot, more levels are required): level one, join A to B and C to D; level two, join AB to CD; level three, join E to ABCD.

In other words, in order even to execute short sentences the way modern humans do it, the brain would have had to maintain a high level of signal coherence through at least three and perhaps four signal merges. Suppose that to send a coherent message through one merge requires n neurons. Then to sustain that message through two merges would require $2n$ neurons – a doubling of available capacity. But to sustain a message through three merges would require only an additional increment of 50%, and to sustain it through four merges, only a 33% increase. The increase in combinatory capacity, however, grows as the increment required for it diminishes: one merge yields two-word sentences, 2 merges yield sentences of 3 or 4 words, 3 merges yield sentences of 4 to 8 words, 4 merges yield sentences of 5 to 16 words, 5 merges yield sentences of 6 to 32 words.

What results from this is not an all-or-nothing switch, but rather an extremely steep gradient. Until the brain achieves a capacity of at least three merges, it is more efficient to operate in protolanguage mode (no merging, one-word-at-a-time production) and pay the cost in low-speed utterance to gain relatively reliable transmission. However, once the three-merge threshold has been crossed, the combinatory, true-language mode permits the production of ever longer and more complex sentences in exchange for relatively small increments in numbers of available neurons.

Is the foregoing a gradualist or a catastrophic scenario? In terms of the shift from a protolanguage strategy to a true-language strategy – combining words before despatching them to the organs of speech, rather than (as in protolanguage) despatching them individually – it is clearly catastrophic. You either use one mode or the other. While it is true that modern humans can switch from one mode (when using their native language) to the other (when speaking a pidgin or a foreign language they are only beginning to master), there was clearly a stage in hominid development when this was impossible, because the number of merges through which contemporary brains could sustain coherent neural signals was insufficient to support the true-language mode. When brains did achieve this level of development, syntax (at least the core of syntax – subsequent refinements are discussed in Section 4) was immediately accessible; that is to say, the social-calculus template of actions and the thematic roles they assign could be mapped directly onto linguistic output, and could be interpreted and comprehended via the same calculus.

In this sense, then, the emergence of syntax was catastrophic. It is no less catastrophic because it was preceded by a long period of gradual change. But all catastrophic events share this nature. The paradigm case is the glass placed under a dripping tap; the glass gradually gets fuller, but nothing else happens until the water reaches the rim of the glass and immediately starts to pour over it. One state – water contained – yields catastrophically to another – water spilling – without any change whatsoever in the gradualness of the agency involved.

However, there is no need to suppose that in catastrophic changes of state, one state supersedes or abolishes the other. The glass under the tap continues to contain water, and speakers can (to this day, as noted) switch back and forth between linguistic and protolinguistic modes. Nor were the initial manifestations of the change in capacity necessarily abrupt. We need not imagine parents who spoke only protolanguage with children who spoke like us. Doubtless, especially towards the end of the *erectus* period, there were sporadic individuals who pushed at the boundaries of protolanguage, just as conversely there are individuals today who, as a result of autism or other language-affecting syndromes, cannot escape beyond those boundaries. However, it may be hypothesised that a larger number of the first type appeared in southern Africa, probably within the last two hundred thousand years, and that it was this chance agglomeration that launched our species.

4. Baldwin Effects, Parsing and Speaker-Hearer Conflicts

But even when the thematic grid of the social calculus had been exapted, much remained to be done. While protolanguage was still the only form of linguistic communication, there were no selective pressures to refine and speed up motor control of speech, to strengthen the links between the many cortical and even subcortical (Crosson 1992; Courchesne and Allen 1997) areas implicated in language, or to improve parsing capabilities – as regards the latter, in the absence of syntax there was nothing to parse! However, once the thematic grid could be mapped onto output, a cascade of consequences was unleashed. Since all the developments listed in this paragraph made for faster, yet at the same time more comprehensible, speech, and since (in a species at this stage of development) facility of speech would surely have improved an individual's fitness with respect to mate access, leadership and so on, the social pressures for improvement would have been extremely strong.

Space limitations make it impossible to deal here with all of these consequences, so what follows will be limited to a consideration of parsing problems. Although, as shown in Section 2 (see also Calvin and Bickerton 2000), parsing would have been greatly improved, it would not have been optimal in real time because processing the argument structure of each clause was the only way to establish phrasal and clausal boundaries. In modern language, those boundaries are additionally marked in a variety of ways: by prepositions and postpositions, by determiners, by complementisers and by affixes of many kinds. 'Sister says can't come Thursday' is fine as a telegram – written messages don't need fast processing – but isn't a grammatical sentence of English, unlike the synonymous 'Your sister says that she can't come on Thursday'. Speech does have some shortcuts, but they are limited, and in turn depend on the existence of a boundary-marking grammatical morphology.

There would, therefore, have been a strong selective pressure on early language speakers to innovate measures by which phrasal and clausal boundaries would be (fairly) unambiguously marked, and this pressure would have generated what are known as Baldwin effects. Baldwin (1896) – see Richards (1987) for an extended account of Baldwin's theories and their place in the development of the theory of evolution, and Hinton and Nolan (1987) for an updated version of those theories – proposed that behavioural change in a species could bring about subsequent biological changes by selectively favoring among random developments just those traits that were adaptive in terms of the new behaviour. The processing of complex sentences certainly constituted such a behavioural change, and would have favoured those individuals whose nervous systems developed in ways that improved such processing.

It is therefore hypothesised that there was a period of competition between varying solutions to the problem of boundary marking. For instance one way of marking the boundaries of phrases is by preceding and/or following them with some otherwise meaningless unit. Thus, for example, Palauan precedes all arguments of a verb (and even the verb itself) with the morpheme i. However, the redundancy of such a measure is high; the boundaries of many phrases are already adequately marked by items such as prepositions, some of which (particularly directional items such as equivalents of 'to' or 'from') probably preceded true language.

Here it is necessary to consider the conflict of interest between the speaker and the hearer; those interests differ from one another almost as much as do the reproductive interests of men and women (Buss 1989; Ripley 1993), except that individuals of both sexes switch between the roles of speaker and hearer several hundred times a day. The conflict of interest is in essence the following: hearers want all the information they can get, redundant or not, to ensure comprehension, whereas speakers want to reduce the amount of information they provide, for ease of articulation and economy of effort.

A compromise between speaker and hearer could have led to something like the proviso, 'Each argument must be accompanied by a non-argument'. Such a compromise could, by Baldwinian evolution, have come about initially in behaviour (speakers consciously and deliberately pairing arguments and non-arguments), and the efficiency of this technique would then have given an evolutionary advantage to individuals whose nervous systems began, with increasing accuracy, to attach arguments to non-arguments automatically. Certain facts about language and the brain – for instance, that all arguments have noun heads and that verbs (which are non-arguments), prepositions and other items are not stored in the same brain areas as nouns (Ojeman 1983; Damasio 1994) – should make it possible for the brain to distinguish arguments from non-arguments ('Don't directly merge stuff from the temporal lobe with stuff from elsewhere').

A further speaker-hearer tradeoff that would have been operative once syntax developed concerns completeness of representation. For the hearer, things need to be explicit; hearers don't want to have to puzzle over, say, which of two possible masculine referents is intended by the pronoun 'he'. Speakers, on the other hand, seek to minimise effort, for example by referring with reduced forms (such as pronouns) or, better still, omitting items altogether if their reference is clear. Again a compromise had to be reached; items could be omitted if their reference could be recovered by systematic means (that is, automatically, rather than by paying attention to context, pragmatics, etc.). Presumably (since the effects of the compromise seem to be the same in all languages), Baldwinian evolution has similarly instantiated in the nervous system algorithms for ensuring that the reference of omitted items is automatically recoverable. For a full account of these algorithms, see the appendix to Calvin and Bickerton (2000).

We may assume that the resolutions of these speaker-hearer conflicts and the absorption of those resolutions into the human genome (in the form of automatic pairing of arguments with non-arguments, and automatic assignment of reference to omitted constituents) were far from instantaneous. They may have taken tens of thousands of years, although they must presumably have reached completion by the time the Australian population was separated from other human populations – that is, fifty or sixty thousand years ago.

5. Some Possible Objections

The foregoing account of language evolution inevitably contains much that is speculative, as well as novel, and is thus subject to a number of possible objections. In this section I shall attempt to deal with some of these objections.

With regard to the increment in signal coherence that is here claimed to have made mapping from the social calculus to linguistic utterances possible for the first time, it might reasonably be objected that most mammals, all primates and a fortiori the species immediately ancestral to ours were and are capable of executing complex and flexible sequences of sensory-motor activities that would seem to entail an already high level of signal coherence, more than enough to sustain a signal through the three or four merges necessary to transcend protolanguage. However, such a supposition ignores the radical differences between such activities and those necessary for the production of sentences. These differences include, but are not limited to, the following:

a. General sensory-motor activities are normally reactions to (and sustained by) external stimuli, while production of sentences is not normally a reaction to external stimuli or sustained by these.
b. General sensory-motor activities involve minor variations on stereotyped routines that have been honed by evolutionary forces for many millions of years, while production of sentences represents an evolutionary novelty, and sentences differ from one another in unpredictable ways.
c. General sensory-motor activities enjoy the benefit of attention mechanisms that monitor, sort and prioritise external stimuli, whereas no such mechanisms regulate the internal stimuli that most often initiate sentence production.

In other words, it is much more difficult to sustain the coherence of an internally generated signal in the face of inevitable competition from internal sources than it is to sustain the coherence of an externally generated signal where dedicated attention mechanisms reduce the interference from other stimuli.

A more radical objection might question the very nature of the mechanism itself. How do we know that human brains can maintain coherence of more complex neural signals over longer periods than nonhuman brains? In the absence of direct experimental evidence, this question is indeed a challenging one. But the significant fact here is that, while no such evidence supports such a mechanism, there is none that explicitly contradicts it, either (Terence Deacon, personal communication). The plain fact of the matter is that, since no one prior to Calvin (1996a, 1996b) had placed the issues in these terms, no one has looked for the relevant evidence. Now, perhaps, they will.

It is well worth searching for evidence, because the proposal has immense explanatory power. It would account, not merely for the appearance of structured language, but for all of the significant differences between humans and other species. For the power to sustain signal coherence over time in the absence of external stimuli is what underlies not only language, but the human capacity to plan ahead, to model solutions in the brain before attempting them in real life, to create and execute novel strategies – in short, the whole suite of behaviours that together yield the unique flexibility and creativity of our species. In addition to this, it explains the paradoxical nature of human brain evolution – that the brain in growing to its present size yielded only minor changes in primate behaviour, while the modern brain, quite stable in size, supports a range of novel and constantly changing behaviours.

Mention of brain size raises another possible objection to these proposals. If hominisation had a neural threshold, and if brains of a critical size are crucial elements in the crossing of this threshold, then Neanderthals, with brains as large or larger than those of modern humans, should have had similar capacities to those of modern humans and, as the more adapted of the two (sub?) species to conditions in Ice-Age Europe, should not in so short a time have been driven to extinction.

There are a number of possibilities here. First, although Neanderthals may have been at least our equals in brain size, it is not clear that they were our equals in encephalisation. It seems likely that their stockier, less gracile bodies required a larger proportion of their brains for housekeeping tasks, leaving a correspondingly smaller area for the type of development envisaged here. Second, we must take into account the fact that in certain areas such as the Near East, Neanderthals and modern humans coexisted for tens of thousands of years without any decisive advantage for one over the other, and indeed

without significant differences in the quality, range or originality of their artefacts. Third, there is no reason to suppose that a difference as radical as true
language versus protolanguage is required to explain why modern humans replaced Neanderthals so quickly. In much shorter spaces of time, groups of
modern humans have replaced other groups with identical biological capacities; it took only decades, not millennia, for Europeans to replace Tasmanians,
for instance.

The precise nature of Neanderthal capacities and of human-Neanderthal
interactions remains tantalisingly obscure, and is still controversial (see Mellars
1998 for a recent summary). One of several possible scenarios would go as
follows. A hundred thousand years ago, modern humans and Neanderthals had
both crossed the signal-coherence threshold, but both then had to undergo the
cascade of consequences that followed this event. A relatively minor delay in
say the development of sophisticated phonology among Neanderthals, which
could have been due to differences in cranial structure, could have given a
decisive edge to modern humans. Alternatively, some kind of critical population
mass, necessary for rapid cultural development, might have been reached by
modern humans somewhat in advance of Neanderthals. In our present state of
knowledge, little is served by debating such possibilities, since there is nothing
here concrete enough to require rethinking of the proposals in this chapter, given
their explanatory power.

6. Conclusion

The evolution of syntax, then, was not a simple matter, and it may be useful to
recapitulate here the stages that have been hypothesised:

1. At a period long prior to the pongid-hominid split, there developed among
   primates a social calculus that included abstract representations of actions
   and their participants (thematic roles); these were preserved in episodic
   memory.
2. Over two million years ago, there developed in the hominid line a structureless protolanguage.
3. For the next two million years, protolanguage continued but could not develop into true language because the level of signal coherence that the human
   brain could achieve was too low to map the thematic structure of the social
   calculus onto utterances.
4. At some time within the last two hundred thousand years, an adequate coherence level was achieved in a group that became the ancestors of modern
   humans, causing the emergence of basic phrasal-clausal structure.

5. Crossing the coherence threshold unleashed a cascade of consequences including the development of grammatical morphology and parsing algorithms that were incorporated into the human genome by Baldwinian evolution.

References

Axelrod, R. 1984. *The evolution of co-operation*. New York: Basic Books.
Axelrod, R. and W. D. Hamilton. 1981. The evolution of co-operation. *Science* **211**: 1390–1396.
Baldwin, J. M. 1896. A new factor in evolution. *American Naturalist* **30**: 441–451.
Bickerton, D. 1983. Creole languages. *Scientific American* **249**: 116–122.
Bickerton, D. 1990. *Language and Species*. Chicago: Chicago University Press.
Bickerton, D. 1995. *Language and Human Behavior*. Seattle, WA: University of Washington Press.
Bickerton, D. 1998. Catastrophic evolution: the case for a single step from protolanguage to full human language. In J. R. Hurford, M. Studdert-Kennedy and C. Knight (eds), *Approaches to the Evolution of Language: Social and cognitive bases*. Cambridge: Cambridge University Press, pp. 341–358.
Braitenberg, V. and A. Schuz. 1992. Basic features of cortical connectivity and some considerations on language. In J. Wind, B. Chiarelli, B. H. Bichakjian, A. Nocentini and A. Jonker (eds), *Language Origin: A multidisciplinary approach*. Amsterdam: Kluwer.
Buss, D. 1989. Sex differences in human mate preference: evolutionary hypotheses tested in 37 cultures. *Behavioral and Brain Sciences* **12**: 1–49.
Calvin, W. H. 1996a. *How Brains Think*. New York: Basic Books.
Calvin, W. H. 1996b. *The Cerebral Code*. Cambridge, MA: MIT Press.
Calvin, W. H. and D. Bickerton. 2000. *Lingua ex Machina: Darwin and Chomsky reconciled*. Cambridge, MA: MIT Press.
Carlson, G. 1984. On the role of thematic roles in linguistic theory. *Linguistics* **22**: 259–279.
Chomsky, N. 1957. *Syntactic Structures*. The Hague: Mouton.
Chomsky, N. 1981. *Lectures on Government and Binding*. Dordrecht: Foris.
Chomsky, N. 1982. Discussion of Putnam's comments. In M. Piatelli-Palmerini (ed), *Language and Learning: The debate between Jean Piaget and Noam Chomsky*. Cambridge, MA: Harvard University Press, pp. 310–324.
Chomsky, N. 1995. *The Minimalist Program*. Cambridge, MA: MIT Press.
Crosson, B. 1992. *Subcortical Functions in Language and Memory*. New York: Guildford.
Courchesne, E. and G. Allen. 1997. Prediction and preparation: fundamental functions of the cerebellum. *Learning and Memory* **4**: 1–35.
Damasio, A. R. 1994. *Descartes' Error: Emotion, reason and the human brain*. New York: Putnam.
Dennett, D. C. 1991. *Consciousness Explained*. Boston: Little, Brown.
de Waal, F. 1996. *Good Natured: The origins of right and wrong in humans and other animals*. Cambridge, MA: Harvard University Press.

Donald, M. 1998. Mimesis and the Executive Suite: missing links in language evolution. In J. R. Hurford, M. Studdert-Kennedy and C. Knight (eds), *Approaches to the Evolution of Language: Social and cognitive bases*. Cambridge: Cambridge University Press, pp. 43–67.

Dunbar, R. 1998. Theory of mind and the evolution of language. In J. R. Hurford, M. Studdert-Kennedy and C. Knight (eds), *Approaches to the Evolution of Language: Social and cognitive bases*. Cambridge: Cambridge University Press, pp. 92–110.

Enright, J. T. 1980. Temporal precision in circadian systems: a reliable neuronal clock from unreliable components? Science **209**: 1542–1544.

Gould, S. J. and R. C. Lewontin. 1984. The spandrels of San Marco and the Panglossian paradigm. In E. Sober (ed), *Conceptual Issues in Evolutionary Biology*. Cambridge, MA: Bantam Books.

Hebb, D. O. 1949. *The Organization of Behavior: A neuropsychological theory*. New York: Wiley.

Hinton, G. and S. Nowlan. 1987. How learning can guide evolution. *Complex Systems* **1**: 495–502.

Jerison, H. J. 1977. The theory of encephalization. In S. J. Diamond and P. A. Blizard (eds), *Evolution and Lateralization of the Brain*. Annals of The New York Academy of Science, Vol. 299. New York: New York Academy of Science, pp. 601–606.

Lund, J. S., T. Yoshioka and J. B. Levitt. 1993. Comparison of intrinsic connectivity in different areas of macaque monkey cortex. *Cerebral Cortex* **3**: 148–162.

Mellars, P. 1998. The fate of the Neanderthals. *Nature* **395**: 539–362.

Newmeyer, F. J. 1983. *Grammatical Theory: Its limits and possibilities*. Chicago: University of Chicago Press.

Newmeyer, F. J. 1991. Functional explanation in linguistics and the origins of language. *Language and Communication* **11**: 3–28.

Ojeman, G. A. 1983. Brain organization for language from the perspective of electrical stimulation mapping. *Behavioral and Brain Sciences* **6**: 189–230.

Olton, D. S. 1984. Comparative analysis of episodic memory. *Behavioral and Brain Sciences* **7**: 250–251.

Perrett, D., P. A. J. Smith, A. J. Mistlin, A. J. Chitty, A. S. Head, D. D. Potter, R. Broenniman, A. P. Milner and M. A. Jeeves. 1985. Visual analysis of body movements by neurones in the temporal cortex of the macaque monkey. *Behavior and Brain Research* **16**: 153–170.

Piatelli-Palmerini, M. 1989. Evolution, selection and cognition: from learning to parameter setting in biology and the study of language. *Cognition* **31**: 1–44.

Pinker, S. 1994. *The Language Instinct*. New York: Morrow.

Pinker, S. 1997. *How the Mind Works*. New York: Norton.

Pinker, S. and P. Bloom. 1990. Natural language and natural selection, *Behavioral and Brain Sciences* **13**: 707–784.

Posner, M. I. and M. K. Rothbart. 1992. Attentional mechanisms and conscious experience. In A. D. Milner and M. D. Rugg (eds), *The Neuropsychology of Consciousness*. New York: Academic, pp. 91–111.

Richards, R. J. 1987. *Darwin and the Emergence of Evolutionary Theories of Mind and Behavior*. Chicago: University of Chicago Press.

Ripley, M. 1993. *The Red Queen*. New York: Macmillan.

Simon, H. A. 1967. *The Sciences of the Artificial*. Cambridge, MA: MIT Press.

Somers, D. and N. Koppel. 1993. Rapid synchronization through fast threshold modulation. *Biological Cybernetics* **68**: 393–407.

Strum, S. C. 1987. *Almost Human: A journey into the world of baboons*. New York: Random House.

Studdert-Kennedy, M. 1998. The origins of generativity. In J. R. Hurford, M. Studdert-Kennedy and C. Knight (eds), *Approaches to the Evolution of Language: Social and cognitive bases*. Cambridge: Cambridge University Press, pp. 202–221.

Trivers, R. L. 1971. The evolution of reciprocal altruism. *Quarterly Review of Biology* **46**: 35–57.

Trivers, R. L. 1985. *Social Evolution*. Menlo Park, CA: Benjamin/Cummings.

Tulving, E. 1984a. Elements of episodic memory. *Behavioral and Brain Sciences* **7**: 223–238.

Tulving, E. 1984b. Relation among components and processes of memory. *Behavioral and Brain Sciences* **7**: 257–263.

17

Holistic Utterances in Protolanguage: The Link from Primates to Humans

ALISON WRAY

Introduction

No account of how human language originated should ignore two fundamental contextualising questions: how was communication achieved before? and what, precisely, is 'human language' anyway? Both of these apply, irrespective of one's views on whether full human language was qualitatively the same as or different from its precursors, and/or whether it appeared suddenly or evolved gradually into its current state. While much of what has been written recently takes some account of what human language might have evolved out of, I think that many problems arise from a general misconception about what full human language consists of today. The position that seems to be taken is the one represented in Figure 17.1. It is generally accepted that primates communicate using highly effective, though limited, holistic noise/gesture systems in which any given 'utterance' with a meaning takes its identity from the whole, not the sum of meaning-laden parts. Full human language, on the other hand, is standardly portrayed as an analytic, grammar-based system. This leaves protolanguage as the forum for the entire transition, one which entails the appearance of arbitrary phonetic representation, lexical reference, phrase structure and morphology. Consequently, there is an uneasy relationship between, on the one hand, the dynamism that needs to be invoked in order to bridge the gap within what is, for some, a very narrow time window, and, on the other, the level of stability that we might prefer to associate with the success of day-to-day interaction over a lengthy period of, relatively speaking, cultural and intellectual stagnation (Gowlett 1992: 353; Mithen 1996: 116).

The Nature of Human Language

Viewing full human language in this way, however, overlooks an important feature of our everyday linguistic communication: much of what we say is

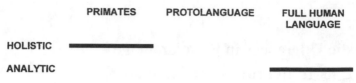

Figure 17.1. The common view of primate and human communication.

formulaic – prestored in multiword units for quick retrieval, with no need to apply grammar rules (e.g. Becker 1975; Bolinger 1976; Sinclair 1991; Nattinger and DeCarrico 1992; Ellis 1996; Wray 1998, 1999; Wray and Perkins 2000). In other words, we operate, in part, holistically when we produce and decode language, using a range of types of prefabricated word string, including ones which:

- are undisputably holistic in nature, because they can't be generated by the grammar, e.g. *by and large; to go the whole hog,*
- are grammatically sound but semantically holistic, e.g. *to pull someone's leg; the oldest profession,*
- appear both grammatically and semantically ordinary but have transformational restrictions, e.g. *I didn't sleep a wink, *I slept a wink; He was fed up, *The encounter had fed him up* (Irujo 1986; Flavell and Flavell 1992),
- consist of a specific form of words with an agreed social or interactional function, e.g. *happy birthday; I now pronounce you man and wife; if you'd like to . . . ,*
- are the frame for a paradigm of strings made 'novel' by the insertion of open-class items into slots, e.g. *NP be-TENSE sorry to keep-TENSE you waiting* (Pawley and Syder 1983),
- are indistinguishable from novel utterances, except that, within a certain speech community or individual's idiolect, they are preferred over other equally possible formulations, e.g. *put the kettle on, will you?* versus *please would you make me a hot drink?*

I term these collectively *formulaic sequences,* which is intended to be an inclusive epithet devoid of too much of the connotational baggage associated with many of over forty words that I have found so far in the literature (Wray and Perkins 2000). The forms and functions of formulaic sequences in our everyday language, as well as their role in first and second language acquisition and in aphasic speech, are reviewed in Wray (1999).

   It seems, then, that human language has a holistic as well as an analytic component. Our starting point, therefore, should be the one depicted in Figure 17.2.

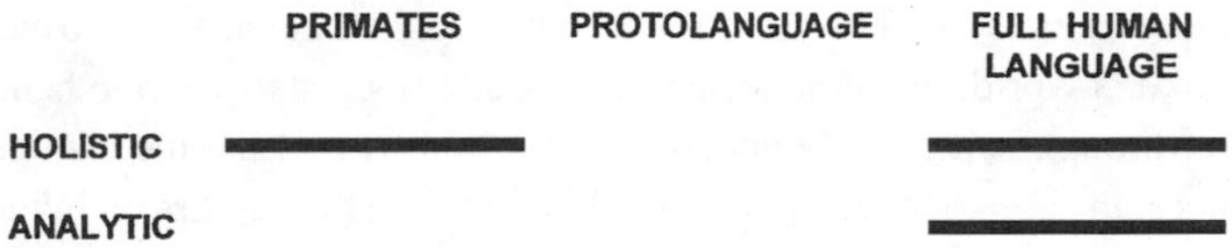

	PRIMATES	PROTOLANGUAGE	FULL HUMAN LANGUAGE
HOLISTIC	▬▬▬▬▬		▬▬▬▬▬
ANALYTIC			▬▬▬▬▬

Figure 17.2. A revised view of primate and human communication.

Was Protolanguage Holistic?

Given the existence of holistic language before and after protolanguage, can a case be made for continuity? Certainly continuity should not simply be assumed. The holistic processing strategy manifests itself often and independently in humans, as in memory for faces and the proceduralisation of movement sequences like car driving (Givón 1989: 256ff.). Even within language there appears to be no single *linguistic* motivation for the adoption of holistic processing (Wray 1998; Wray and Perkins 2000). It is, then, not impossible by any means that the holistic language we use today has nothing in common with the holistic communication used by primates other than that it is holistic. However, Occam's razor gives us a compelling reason for believing that they are the same thing. As we shall see, when we compare the functions of formulaic sequences today with those for which holistic noise/gesture utterances appear to be used in primates, we find a strikingly close correspondence (Reiss 1989; Goodwin 1996).

The functions of holistic language in human communication. Formulaic sequences are rarely the *only* way of expressing a given idea, but they are undoubtedly very often the *preferred* or *normal* way. Although *Do not step on the lawn* and *Please perform an act of kindness for me* are comprehensible, we are much more likely to encounter *Keep off the grass* and *Would you do me a favour*? It seems as if utterances with certain kinds of functions, such as requesting, commanding, bargaining and so on, have a tendency to take on a preferred form. What they have in common is that they are used to effect a response in the hearer. We use them to get others to change our world for us, whether physically (*pass me the salt; present arms!*), mentally/intellectually (*tell me what happened; could you repeat that?*) or emotionally (*say you love me; leave me alone*). As such, it seems plausible that the advantage in their being formulaic is that it makes them easier for the hearer to recognise and decode, something that is clearly entirely in the speaker's interests in this kind of directive utterance. If the speakers do match their output to what they believe the hearer will most successfully decode, then there are some important corollaries for understanding how languages come to be the way they are.

Besides utterances whose function is to manipulate the hearer into changing the speaker's world, two other categories of utterance also seem to benefit the speaker through being easily understood by the hearer. Like the manipulative sequences, these also require a reaction, but this time they centre on influencing the hearer's perception of the speaker's identity. Identity entails a balance between (1) being an individual and (2) being part of, and having a status within, significant groups. Both are important for our mental health and, arguably, for our survival. We signal our group membership to those around us by adopting the 'in' phrases of the speech community, joining in with communal chants, and using institutionalised forms of words, including ritual performatives (see also Dunbar 1996). We assert, express and alter our place in the group hierarchy by using threats, put-downs, agreed forms of address and so on (all characteristically, though not obligatorily, formulaic), and even by quoting (formulaicity in another guise) those whom we admire. We ensure that we are also viewed as individuals by having personal turns of phrase and by using a range of formulaic devices to attract attention and keep it, such as story openers, turn claimers, turn holders, fillers and discourse pointers.

All of the above relate to social interaction, and their formulaicity seems to reflect the anticipated easiest processing route for the hearer. However, if formulaic sequences are indeed stored whole, demanding no more decoding effort than 'big words' (Ellis 1996: 111) (or a little more if the sequence is a frame containing some open-class items), then formulaicity also ought to offer direct benefits in production; and this has, indeed, been proposed. By being prefabricated, formulaic sequences seem to relieve pressure on our language production mechanisms by offering a processing option whereby 'we do not have to go through the labor of generating an utterance all the way out from S every time we want to say anything' (Becker 1975: 17; see also Bolinger 1976; Sinclair 1991; Ellis 1996). Three types of sequence can be identified as particularly benefiting the speaker in this way. First, there are the formulaic sequences that are simply the *customary* way of expressing an idea. For example, although we say *quarter past* and *half past* the hour, we do not say *third past* but rather *twenty past* (Pawley and Syder 1983). For no apparent reason other than common practice, some of the utterances that are possible in a language seem to become the idiomatic ones (for an individual or a speech community). Such strings are, if Becker, Sinclair and the others are right, either memorised whole in the form received from others, or else begin as novel utterances and become 'fused' (Peters 1983) into a single unit in response to the frequency with which they are needed. Either way, they aid production by being the default choice for expressing common ideas.

Also offering relief to processing are pause fillers and memory enhancers. Pause fillers (e.g. *That's a very good question* and *Another thing that I want to say, and I think this is very important, is . . .*) are sequences that are relatively low in semantic content, and which can be uttered more or less automatically when utterance planning might otherwise cause a hiatus in production. Finally, memory enhancers are formulaic sequences which provide access to information otherwise difficult to recall. The mnemonic is one example. *Every Good Boy Deserves Fun*, for instance, provides, in its initial letters, the names of the notes on the treble stave in music. Memorising lengthy texts is another way of using our facility with prefabricated language to ensure that material we need later is easily to hand without the need to reconstruct it using the lexicon and grammar.

The function of holistic noise/gesture signals in chimpanzees. Reiss (1989: 295–296) categorises chimpanzee cries into four of Searle's (1979, 1983) five speech act classes: *commissives*, including threats and offers, *directives*, including food begging, requests for grooming and dominance displays and challenges, *expressives*, such as social greetings, and *assertives*, such as the food call. With the exception of the last, it is clear that these map closely onto the socio-interactional functions identified in human language. Chimps use their noise/gesture system to effect changes in their world, maintain social structure and express the place of the individual within it. But they do not harness it as an entity in its own right, either as a means of accessing other information (e.g. mnemonics) or as a processing shortcut. The *assertives* class, however, seems somewhat anomalous. Reiss defines the assertive as 'express[ing] belief about some state of affairs' (1989: 286) with the intended perlocutionary effect being that the hearer believes (1989: 289). This looks very like a referential function, yet I shall argue that reference did not appear until after the protolanguage period. In actual fact, drawing on evidence from Terrace's work with Nim, Reiss goes on to demonstrate that what seems at first to be reference in chimp utterances actually has a manipulative subtext (that is, *thirsty* means *give me a drink*) (1989: 297f.).

Similarities and differences. It seems, then, that the functions of holistic utterances in chimp communication are a subset of those in human language. In both species they are used for social interaction, where their purpose is the manipulation of the hearer, either to act in the interests of, or to recognise the identity and status of, the speaker. Given this cross-species correspondence, it does indeed seem reasonable to suppose that in protolanguage too, day-to-day social interaction was achieved by means of holistic utterances. This continuity

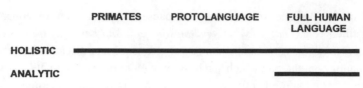

Figure 17.3. The continuity view of holistic processing.

is represented in Figure 17.3. I shall argue later that the other functions of holistic language in humans relate to the development of grammar and of reference at the *end* of the protolanguage stage, so I shall assume for the present that protolanguage users did not have the metalinguistic skills required for performatives and mnemonics, nor any need for pure information exchange, devoid of hearer action implications.

Explanatory Advantages of Continuity

The emergence of grammar. Accounts in which communicational success, and hence survival, are determined by what the lexicon and grammar could do alone, are hard-pressed to explain the following:

- the survival advantage of referential words (in isolation or simple formations) over the noise/gesture communication system that we must assume preceded it,
- how a simple grammar (half a grammar – cf. Pinker and Bloom 1990) could be adequate either communicationally or intellectually,
- why a simple word-juxtaposition system should develop into a complex grammatical and morphological system at all,
- why we should have ended up with precisely the kind of grammar we have, particularly as it misaligns with our communicational needs, giving us:
  - grammatical sentences that are incomprehensible (e.g. centre-embedded ones),
  - ungrammatical sentences that are perfectly comprehensible (e.g. many of those violating PRO-drop, subjacency, etc.),
  - countless grammatical sentences that never get round to being uttered, while others are uttered many times (Bolinger 1976; Coulmas 1979),
  - problems with fluency as soon as we have something intellectually difficult to say.

If, on the other hand, holistic utterances provided a continuity in basic day-to-day social interaction during the transition from protolanguage to full human language, this separates out the appearance of the grammar faculty from the demands of everyday routine communication, something which it neither sits easily with nor which seems to reflect its real shape and capabilities. Specifically, rather than looking for reasons why principles and parameters might have made communication more successful, or else why they should be a natural by-product of some other aspect of the grammar faculty which did so, communication can be taken right out of the picture.[1] This leaves the way clear for some more appealing and plausible explanations for the origin of grammar, such as that:

- word-sized concepts and referentiality emerged as a means of organising creative thought and planning,
- the hierarchically structured grammar evolved as a way of better marshalling thought, by creating a stacking and embedding system for juxtaposing ideas in different ways (Pinker and Bloom 1990: 771; Gibson 1996).
- grammatical language was first used not for interpersonal communication but for 'talking to oneself', that is, so that the speech-brokered phonological loop (Baddeley 1992) could be used as add-on memory capacity – an extra place to deposit information during complex thought.

As survival and reproductive success depend on getting what you need and being integrated socially, grammar would not be greatly beneficial to an individual unless it coexisted with, and reinforced, the existing communicational system. To have an internal grammar *instead* of the ability to produce the holistic utterances might mean you were *smarter* than those around you, but it wouldn't get you a share of the food, ensure you were looked after in sickness, or, as a nonparticipant in the group, do much for your chances of attracting a mate and passing on your grammar-enhancing genes. Even a Nobel prize–winner needs to know how to order a pizza, and success in procreating depends a great deal more on having a good chat-up line and a facility with pillow talk than it does on an impressive publications list.

The kernel of the continuity account, then, is that the selectional advantage of grammatical ability depended upon the continued existence of the holistic socio-interactional communication system. A crucial corollary is that the state of the grammar at any given point would not have been the major determiner of the survival chances of the individual within the group (compare Lightfoot, this volume). This is because however long it took to develop the grammar – one day, one generation or a thousand generations – basic interaction and social cohesion would have been protected by the continued availability of the holistic system. This means that the account to be presented of how protolanguage became transformed, can accommodate equally well a 'catastrophic' appearance of grammar (e.g. Bickerton 1998) (implicit in Figure 17.3) or a gradual one, and, if the latter, either developing *before* it came into communicational use (Figure 17.4a) or with some supplementary communicational role of its own (Figure 17.4b).

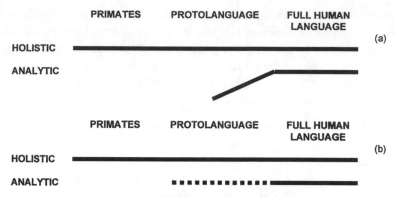

Figure 17.4. Possible onsets of protolanguage.

The transition to arbitrary phonetic representation. The continuity approach also offers some explanatory advantages regarding the much earlier transition from a mimetic and/or iconic noise/gesture system to one based on arbitrary phonetic representations. This is, of course, actually two transitions, which need not be linked in time. Arbitrary representation could be nonphonetic (as in the vervet's warning cries and the latent ability of gorillas, chimps and bonobos to handle arbitrary symbols, demonstrated in their use of human language) – this might lead us to suggest that abstract representation came first. On the other hand, phonetic sounds could be an integral part of an iconic/mimetic system, as Richman (1976) seems to have found in gelada monkeys. What most clouds the picture, however, is the assumption, in so many accounts, that the first language-like utterances were single words. Such accounts need to explain:

- whether words had a mimetic/iconic realisation *before* they got an arbitrary phonetic realisation, and if not, how they came to be coined in their specific phonetic form (whatever that was),
- the relative timing of the development of fine articulatory movement and the origin of word use.

Not only are these questions immensely difficult to answer, but because of the time frames imposed by such approaches, the various transitions tend to get forced into narrow periods associated with other events, such as the second African migration (e.g. Tomasello 1990), one or another 'cultural explosion' (e.g. Mithen 1998) or even the spread of agriculture (Renfrew 1998). The more sudden the transitions, the more it is necessary to place the burden of explanation onto single genetic mutations and onto a selectional advantage strong enough to annihilate the descent lines of all but those with the trait. While there is nothing wrong per se with looking to chance advantageous mutations as the explanation for substantive changes in the nature of language, there is a real danger that such explanations amount to no more than a dressed-up version of 'and then a miracle occurs'.

However, if, as proposed here, arbitrary phonetic representation developed not in the service of individual words but of complete, holistic utterances (possibly combined with gestures), long before words or grammar appeared, the whole process can be envisaged to have occurred gradually, fully exploiting the potential for minor latent abstracting abilities with or without selectional advantages (as found in the great apes – Savage-Rumbaugh, Shanker and Taylor 1998) to instigate small steps in the development of arbitrary representation, without the burden of proving their worth in survival terms at every stage. The speed of change could be determined by the developing ability of the species to achieve more general intellectual aspects of abstraction, such as pattern identification, the anticipation of events and simple set theory (which I shall suggest is central to the operation of a holistic protolanguage).

Furthermore, in the service of even such limited abstractional representation, the vocal tract, perhaps already in command of some phonetic articulations (as in geladas) would soon come under selectional pressure, by giving the most cleanly articulating individuals a greater capacity to create discrete meaningful utterances. Coupled with this would be a pressure for fine auditory discrimination, without which one would be unable to tell utterances apart and would consequently miss out on aspects of the group's communication. Certainly, the pressures for finesse in both production and discrimination would be greater in the context of holistic communication than in a language with a small set of combinable morphemes. These would, as in today's languages, require only a fraction of the total inventory of phonetic distinctions we have ended up being able to make.

A Holistic Protolanguage

Simply to suppose that human protolanguage was holistic does not in itself get us very far. We need to envisage what it would have been like, what it would have been able to do and *not* do, and how a changeover might occur from a holistic protolanguage to full human language (Wray 1998).

Utterances in Protolanguage

Here are some examples of the sort of utterance that might be found in a hypothetical phonetically arbitrary holistic protolanguage used for interpersonal manipulation and for the expression of group and personal identity. (Kirby, this volume, begins his simulation of language evolution with something very

similar to this, though in his case, the meanings are referential rather than
interactional in function.)

tebima	*give that to her*
mupati	*give that to me*
kumapi	*share this with her*
pubatu	*help her*

There is no phonological similarity between sequences with similar meanings,
because they are holistic. There is no part of *tebima* that means *give* or *to her*.
Simply the whole thing means the whole thing. There is no significance to
the CV structure used here, nor to the use of three syllable strings. Within the
bounds of memorisability and minimal differentiation, strings of any length and
any phonological structure might be used.

Levels of Abstraction and Generalisability

The translations into English above contain pronouns, which implies that one
utterance could be used in a set of generic situations. To have a separate utterance
for *give the stone to Mary, give the stone to Edith, give the stick to Mary* and so
on, would require an enormous inventory: too many to remember and too many
to differentiate even with a large set of phonetic distinctions. In proposing this
particular level of abstraction I am attributing to protolanguage users a capability
in set theory, but I don't think that this is too unreasonable a claim. Of course,
there is no reason to assume that classifications would necessarily be by sex or
proximity. I simply use these for our convenience. It must be emphasised that
having an utterance which can be applied to any female, and which is translated
into English using the word *her*, does not mean that such a protolanguage has a
word for *her*. Rather, it has, amongst its inventory of discrete phonetic strings
with specific whole-utterance meanings (such as those just given), a subset that
are used only when (in this case) the beneficiary is a female.

Absence of Reference and Description

It follows from the previous sections that there is no place in such a protolanguage for individual words with a referential or descriptive function. However,
more than this, the discussion in the first section suggests that there is no need
for *utterances* with these functions either, only for ones that effect a change or
which either express compliance with or attempt to alter the social status quo.
This does not mean, of course, that reference (at least) is not *entailed* in utterances that have another function, but only that there is no specific utterance set

that refers or describes for the sake of it. Vervet monkeys can 'refer' to different predators (Seyfarth, Cheney and Marler 1980) but only within the context of a warning (Deacon 1992: 129). The leopard aspect of *beware of the leopard* does not have its own separate representation, nor do the cries used for the three predator warnings stand in any paradigmatic relationship by virtue of some common *beware of the* . . . element in their form.

Plausibility

It may seem that even using set classifications to generalise the use of a given sequence, the inventory of individual phonetic sequences required to say everything would be too large to remember. However, you do not need all that many utterances to keep a society ticking over: you have formulaic commands and requests to get others to do what you want, you have formulaic threats, declarations of superiority, admissions of inferiority and so on, to maintain and alter the group hierarchy, and you have formulaic comforters and sweet nothings to oil the wheels of the relationships (cf. Dunbar 1996). A protolanguage without reference or description for their own sake needs far fewer potential sentences than we need today. In such a language, it would not be possible to say *it's a lovely day* or *this stone is heavy*, nor would it be possible to be creative or say something novel, beyond the occasional coining of a new arbitrary sequence with its own interactional function, something that is no more problematic to envisage than the invention of a new monomorphemic word today. Yet there is no reason why such a protolanguage, with agreed holistic sequences for the narrow range of everyday interactions, should not be perfectly stable over a long period. There would be lots of things that couldn't be said, but then a protolanguage of this kind would not be there for saying things, but rather for getting things done and for preserving social stability.

The Appearance of Grammar

Why Did Grammar Appear?

Stability in the protolanguage enables us to envisage it as more than a transitory stage. The flipside is why, if protolanguage was so effective, grammar should ever have appeared at all. There are two ways of answering this. One is to point to the weaknesses and limitations of such a protolanguage – its unwieldiness, its heavy demands on memory, its restrictions on creative expression. The other, explored earlier, is to view grammar as an intruding influence, spawned not by the protolanguage but independently, as a result of other operations. These two combine to provide a scenario in which the capacity for grammar and individual words was not *needed*, but once it was there, was pretty useful – not for doing protolanguage better, but for other things, such as sharing with another person the complex thought that the internal grammatical mechanisms made it possible to have.

A Scenario

For the sake of convenience, I will assume here that the capacity for grammar appeared in the way suggested by Bickerton (1998), but this doesn't have to be the case for the account to work. In particular, Bickerton's view is that the transition was sudden but, as already stated, the continuity account works equally well with a sudden or a gradual appearance of grammar. The sudden/gradual distinction is not a helpful one in any case. Pinker and Bloom, who favour a gradual appearance of grammar through natural selection, nevertheless incorporate a key transition point in their account, whereby 'a parent with no grammatical rules at all and just rote associations . . . [has] an offspring with a single rule' (1990: 722). This (in itself) is sudden and significant, even if its buildup and followup are gradual. For an exploration of whether our full complement of grammatical skills and constraints appeared all at once, the reader is referred to dedicated discussions, such as those of Berwick (1998) and Lightfoot (this volume).

Bickerton describes the key development as the connection of two preexisting modules: the one that provided phonetic representations for, in his case, words, but in this account, entire sentences, and a theta-role module, which kept track of relationships and participants in events. Bickerton suggests that an individual with such a connection would expect to have phonetic representations of theta roles (that is, of the agent, theme and so on). In his account, this leads to the assignment of theta roles to preexisting referential vocabulary items and, automatically, the beginnings of grammar, as two such words in a sequence have an order relationship relative to the action word they are combined with (Bickerton 1998: 352).

Segmentation

However, if the protolanguage upon which this innovation works had not referential words but arbitrary sequences that conveyed within their meaning *implicit* theta roles, then the connection of the two modules would lead the individual to look for a part of that arbitrary sequence that specifically referred to the theta role. The result would be the first stages of segmentation: the dividing up of previously unanalysed material into meaningful subunits, something which has been observed in both first- and second-language acquisition (e.g. Peters 1983; Wong Fillmore 1976). Going back to our examples, in a protolanguage where *tebima* meant *give that to her*, the individual might ask which part of it meant *to her*. The answer, of course, is none of it, because the sequence is arbitrary. But if in two or more sequences there were chance matches between phonetic segments and aspects of meaning, then it would seem as if there was a constituent with that meaning. So if, besides *tebima* meaning *give that to her,* *kumapi* meant *share this with her*, then it might be concluded that *ma* had the meaning *female person + beneficiary*.

Of course, one would want to set the threshold somewhat higher than one confirmatory example. In a large inventory of arbitrary strings, there would, naturally, be lots of counterexamples (see next subsection), but if we envisage these first segmenters dealing with input as it happened to come at them, then from time to time, by chance alone, two, three, or even more utterances that supported a hypothesis would occur in close succession. Just how often this happened, and how quickly a hypothesis might start to look robust, would depend on how many different utterances the speakers regularly used, how long the utterances were and what size the phonetic inventory was.

The Effect of Counterexamples

Once random attempts at segmentation provided a hypothesis (e.g. that *ma* meant *female person + beneficiary*), then various things might happen when counterexamples were encountered. In some cases, the hypothesis would be discarded because the counterexamples discredited it. In other cases, however, some form of hypercorrection of the counterexamples might occur. Three types of hypercorrection are possible: (1) changing a form to match the hypothesised pattern, (2) the dividing up of the semantic space, and (3) the introduction of arbitrary post-hoc morphogrammatical distinctions. The second and third of these could be particularly powerful tools of language formation. In the case of (1), the phonetic string in the counterexample is altered to fit the pattern: as *ma* 'means' *female person + beneficiary*, there should be a *ma* in *pubatu* (*help her*), so one is either added (e.g. *mapubatu*) or one segment already present and phonetically similar is altered (e.g. *pumatu*). In (2), it is the meaning part of the counterexample that is altered. Specifically, the meaning of the utterance is assumed to have been misunderstood. The reasoning goes: if *pubatu* really meant *help her* (as I thought it did), then it would have *ma* in it. As it doesn't, it must mean something else, such as *help your mother, help the older woman, help Jemima*. To reinterpret *help her* as *help your mother* is to divide up the semantic space. It imposes a post-hoc justification for breakdowns in the apparent pattern, by shifting the focus to different semantic levels. In this way, the natural semantic hierarchies that come with the ability to perceive sets, but which would have featured in protolanguage only as a way of generalising the application of formulaic sequences, could suddenly spawn the labelling of referents at every level. For the first time, individual referential nouns would appear, including proper names, their phonetic form determined by the arbitrary segment they seem to be associated with. In (3), the introduction of arbitrary post-hoc morphogrammatical distinctions, a different type of rationalisation is imposed: as *ma* means *female person + beneficiary*, and there is no *ma* in *pubatu* (help her), it must be the case that when you refer to *female person + beneficiary* in the context of *help*, you use a different word from the one you use when you refer to *female person + beneficiary* in the context of *give*. This could provide the beginnings of case morphology and maybe even verb classes.

What Happened Next?

The progress of the segmented language. Because of the continuity of holistic utterances alongside these developments, the possession of even a small vocabulary and very simple grammar could never disadvantage an individual, for it would only ever supplement the socio-interactional system. This also means that there would be no onus on any individual fully to 'crack' the code, that is, to segment everything and come up with a complete lexicon, morphological system and grammar. Rather, these could emerge gradually over many years, through the passing down of the accumulated body of knowledge, augmented by each generation of segmenters, who would further rationalise and hypercorrect both that and the residue of unprincipled source material, until, in the end, some sort of form, meaning, function and distribution had been assigned to every segment (compare Kirby, this volume). The 'segment' would be of variable phonetic length, depending on what happened to be picked out in the segmentation process, or what happened to be left over when everything around it had a 'meaning'. Stray sounds left without a meaning might be dropped, given some status as a particle, explained away as the expression of some phonologically determined variant of an adjacent word, or attached to a more distant morpheme to form a infix-tolerant root.

The progress of a segmenting people. It is difficult for most accounts to separate out the need for all modern humans to have descended from a single line of ancestors who had the language 'blueprint' from the need for there to have been only one original language. But in this account more scenarios are possible. Whether already speaking their own segmented language or just carrying the potential to segment, migrating 'segmenters' could appropriate the holistic protolanguages of groups with whom they lived and interbred, making a facility with the emerging grammar such a culturally desirable and selectionally advantageous asset that the ultimate demise of the original stock was assured. Thus, full human language could arise out of any holistic utterance set, without there having been any single 'original' language.

A Continuing Role for Holistic Sequences

The superiority in novel information exchange of a rule-based hierarchical system over a holistic one is unequivocal. Its structural characteristics mean that 'even totally novel combinations of morphemes can . . . be assigned unambiguous new meanings as soon as they are heard . . . [which] gives almost unlimited possibilities for language to adapt to new contexts' (Deacon 1992: 128). So why, now we have our full human language grammar, should we still be using holistic utterances? In the light of the preceding discussion, the answer is clear. If grammar did not evolve directly for communicative purposes, why should it be particularly good at achieving them? Social communication, for manipulating your world and establishing and maintaining your place within it, is repetitive and fast-moving. It demands quick reactions if you want to get yourself heard, requires decoding and encoding at the same time, and, while entailing the extraction of only relatively small amounts of novel meaning, needs them to be swiftly squared with the pragmatics of the situation. The analytic language function characterised by a wide vocabulary, hierarchical structure and subtle grammatical interactions is qualitatively much more powerful but is cumbersome and expensive in its processing demands, particularly on-line memory (e.g. Bolinger 1976; Peters 1983; Pawley 1985). To use it for mundane exchanges many of which need to be in a predictable form to achieve their communicative function, would waste its creative capability, and would divert it from the preparation of utterances which do require novelty. Why use a highly trained engineer to operate a simple factory machine, when an untrained operator could do it, freeing up the engineer for other things (Wray 1992: 10)?

Once we fully engage with the possibility that our grammatical abilities came about as a means for better internal concept management, and not for linguistic expression, it is easy to envisage how their subsequent harnessing for the exchange of ideas with other people might be a matter of fitting a quart into a pint pot. Our support systems, especially short-term memory capacity, seem to be insufficient for our powerful analytic faculties to operate at full stretch, hardly surprising if they were never previously under pressure from a grammar and they did not evolve in tandem with one. It was demonstrated earlier that, of the two major functions of formulaic language today, only one, the socio-interactional, corresponds with the communicational behaviour of chimpanzees. We can now account for this. It is only once the grammar appeared that the second function for formulaic sequences became necessary. Where before they helped the speaker to ensure the successful reception of the message, they now were enlisted to help ensure the successful production as well. They offered shortcuts in the production of commonly needed referential utterances, so that the rather overstretched processing hardware would not crash in its attempt to support the powerful new grammar.

Our use of formulaic language today, then, may be crucial to the successful application of the grammar faculty in unplanned speech, funnelling off the delivery of common socio-interactional exchanges, and making it possible to produce what are relatively small amounts of novel information within a fluent and comprehensible frame. We have taken the best of two systems and use them side by side: the more ancient holistic one to achieve our communicative needs efficiently, and the newer analytic one to explore and talk about new ideas and to achieve the unexpected.

Note

1. Such a separation makes some sense of Chomsky's (1980: 230) assertion that 'we must reject the view that the purpose of language is communication'. Chomsky deals, of course, exclusively with the analytic grammar.

References

Baddeley, A. 1992. Working memory: the interface between memory and cognition. *Journal of Cognitive Neuroscience* **4**: 281–288.

Becker, J. 1975. The phrasal lexicon. *Bolt Beranek and Newman Report No. 3081, AI Report No. 28*: 1–35.

Berwick, R. 1998. Language evolution and the Minimalist Program. In J. R. Hurford, M. Studdert-Kennedy and C. Knight (eds), *Approaches to the Evolution of Language: Social and cognitive bases*. Cambridge: Cambridge University Press, pp. 320–340.

Bickerton, D. 1998. Catastrophic evolution: the case for a single step from protolanguage to full human language. In J. R. Hurford, M. Studdert-Kennedy and C. Knight (eds), *Approaches to the Evolution of Language: Social and cognitive bases*. Cambridge: Cambridge University Press, pp. 341–358.

Bolinger, D. 1976. Meaning and memory. *Forum Linguisticum* **1**: 1–14.

Chomsky, N. 1980. *Rules and Representations*. Oxford: Blackwell.

Coulmas, F. 1979. On the sociolinguistic relevance of routine formulae. *Journal of Pragmatics* **3**: 239–266.

Deacon, T. 1992. Biological aspects of language. In S. Jones, R. Martin and D. Pilbeam (eds), *The Cambridge Encyclopedia of Human Evolution*. Cambridge: Cambridge University Press, pp. 128–133.

Dunbar, R. 1996. *Grooming, Gossip and the Evolution of Language*. London: Faber.

Ellis, N. C. 1996. Sequencing in SLA: phonological memory, chunking and points of order. *Studies in Second Language Acquisition* **18**: 91–126.

Flavell, L. and R. Flavell. 1992. *Dictionary of Idioms*. London: Kyle Cathie.

Gibson, K. R. 1996. The biocultural brain, mental hierarchies, and continuity approaches. Paper presented at the International Conference on the Evolution of Language, Edinburgh.

Givón, T. 1989. *Mind, Code and Context*. Hillsdale, NJ: Erlbaum.

Goodwin, R. Q. 1996. A functional perspective on the communicative abilities of apes and children. Paper presented at the International Conference on the Evolution of Language, Edinburgh.

Gowlett, J. A. J. 1992. Tools: the palaeolithic record. In S. Jones, R. Martin and D. Pilbeam (eds), *The Cambridge Encyclopedia of Human Evolution*. Cambridge: Cambridge University Press, pp. 350–360.

Irujo, S. 1986. A piece of cake: learning and teaching idioms. *ELT Journal* **40**: 236–242.

Mithen, S. 1996. *The Prehistory of the Mind*. London: Thames and Hudson.

Mithen, S. 1998. Thought, language and the manufacture of handaxes. Paper presented at the Second International Conference on the Evolution of Language, University of East London.

Nattinger, J. R. and J. S. DeCarrico. 1992. *Lexical Phrases and Language Teaching*. Oxford: Oxford University Press.

Pawley, A. 1985. On speech formulas and linguistic competence. *Lenguas Modernas* **12**: 84–104.

Pawley, A and F. H. Syder. 1983. Two puzzles for linguistic theory: nativelike selection and nativelike fluency. In J. C. Richards and R. W. Schmidt (eds), *Language and Communication*. New York: Longman, pp. 191–226.

Peters, A. 1983. *Units of Language Acquisition*. Cambridge: Cambridge University Press.

Pinker, S. and P. Bloom. 1990. Natural language and natural selection. *Behavioral and Brain Sciences* **13**: 707–784.

Reiss, N. 1989. Speech act taxonomy, chimpanzee communication, and the evolutionary basis of language. In J. Wind, E. G. Pulleybank, E. De Grolier and B. H. Bichakjian (eds), *Studies in Language Origins, Vol 1*. Amsterdam: Benjamins, pp. 283–304.

Renfrew, C. 1998. Small talk, or why was the 'Human Revolution' initially so unimpressive? Paper presented at the Second International Conference on the Evolution of Language, University of East London.

Richman, B. 1976. Some vocal distinctive features used by gelada monkeys. *Journal of the Acoustical Society of America* **60**: 718–724.

Savage-Rumbaugh, S., S. G. Shanker and T. J. Taylor. 1998. *Apes, Language, and the Human Mind*. New York: Oxford University Press.

Searle, J. 1979. *Expression and Meaning*. Cambridge: Cambridge University Press.

Searle, J. 1983. *Intentionality: An essay in the philosophy of mind*. Cambridge: Cambridge University Press.

Seyfarth, R. M., D. L. Cheney and P. Marler. 1980. Monkey responses to three different alarm calls: evidence for predator classification and semantic communication. *Science* **210**: 801–803.

Sinclair, J. 1991. *Corpus, Concordance, Collocation*. Oxford: Oxford University Press.

Tomasello, M. 1990. Grammar yes, generative grammar no. Commentary on Pinker and Bloom. *Behavioral and Brain Sciences* **13**: 759–760.

Wong Fillmore, L. 1976. *The Second Time Around: Cognitive and social strategies in second language acquisition*. Doctoral dissertation, Stanford University.

Wray, A. 1992. *The Focusing Hypothesis: The theory of left hemisphere language re-examined*. Amsterdam: Benjamins.

Wray, A. 1998. Protolanguage as a holistic system for social interaction. *Language and Communication* **18**: 47–67.

Wray, A. 1999. Formulaic language in learners and native speakers. *Language Teaching* **32**: 213–231.

Wray, A. and M. R. Perkins. 2000. The functions of formulaic language: an integrated model. *Language and Communication* **20**: 1–28.

18

Syntax Without Natural Selection: How Compositionality Emerges from Vocabulary in a Population of Learners

SIMON KIRBY

Introduction

How can we explain the origins of our uniquely human compositional system of communication?[1] Much of the recent work tackling this problem (e.g. Bickerton 1990; Pinker and Bloom 1990; Newmeyer 1991; Hurford, Knight and Studdert-Kennedy 1998) explicitly attempts to relate models of our innate linguistic endowment to neo-Darwinian evolutionary theory. These are essentially functional stories, arguing that the central features of human language are genetically encoded and have emerged over evolutionary time in response to natural selection pressures.

In this chapter I put forward a new approach to understanding the origins of some of the key ingredients in a syntactic system. I show, using a computational model, that compositional syntax is an inevitable outcome of the dynamics of observationally learned communication systems. In a simulated population of individuals, language develops from a simple idiosyncratic vocabulary with little expressive power, to a compositional system with high expressivity, nouns and verbs, and word order expressing meaning distinctions.[2] This happens without natural selection of learners – indeed, without any biological change at all or any notion of function being built into the system.

This approach does not deny the possibility that much of our linguistic ability may be explained in terms of natural selection, but it does highlight the fact that biological evolution is by no means the only powerful adaptive system at work in the origins of human language.

The Origins of Syntax

Pinker and Bloom (1990) argue that an analysis of the design features of human language, and of syntax in particular, leads to the conclusion that the best way of understanding their origins is as biological adaptations. The central questions that should be asked in their view are:

Do the cognitive mechanisms underlying language show signs of design for some function in the same way the anatomical structures of the eye show signs of design for the purpose of vision? What are the engineering demands on a system that must carry out such a function? And are the mechanisms of language tailored to meet those demands? (Pinker and Bloom 1990: 712)

Pinker and Bloom claim that the features of grammar which they are interested in form part of the innate endowment of humans and work together to make 'communication of propositional structures' possible. For example, the existence of linear order, phrase structure and major lexical categories together will allow a language user to 'distinguish among the argument positions that an entity assumes with respect to a predicate' (Pinker and Bloom 1990: 713), suggesting that their presence in human languages requires a biological/adaptationist explanation.

There have been many authors (see e.g. Hurford 1998 for a recent review) who have argued that it is useful to look at syntax as a product of natural selection – Newmeyer (1991, 1992) for example looks in detail at the features of the 'Principles and Parameters' model of syntax and gives them an evolutionary explanation. The reasons for this are clear, as Pinker and Bloom (1990: 707) point out: 'Evolutionary theory offers clear criteria for when a trait should be attributed to natural selection: complex design for some function, and the absence of alternative processes capable of explaining such complexity. Human language meets these criteria.'

I will show in this chapter that, for at least some features of syntax, there are in fact 'alternative processes capable of explaining such complexity', and that some of the qualitative evolution of human language proceeded without natural selection. The kind of evolution we will be looking at is not biological, but relies on a notion that languages themselves act as complex adaptive systems (Hurford, this volume; Worden, this volume; Kirby 1999, 1998a; Christiansen 1994; Deacon 1997; Kirby 1997; Briscoe 1997; Gell-Mann 1992).

The particular feature of syntax that will be explored in this light – and one which subsumes many of Pinker and Bloom's list – is compositionality. Cann (1993: 4) gives the following definition of the principle of compositionality, a universal of human language:

The meaning of an expression is a monotonic function of the meaning of its parts and the way they are put together.

This definition makes it clear that, although compositionality is often taken to be a property of semantics, it is actually a property of the system that links forms and meanings.

A Computational Approach

If we are to fully understand the ways in which a learned, culturally transmitted system such as language can evolve we need some sophisticated population models of learners. Simple theorising about the likely behaviour of complex adaptive systems is not good enough. As Niyogi and Berwick (1997) point out, our intuitions about the evolution of even simple dynamical systems are often wrong. Recently, many researchers have responded to this problem by taking a computational perspective (for example, Hurford 1989, 1991; MacLennan 1991; Batali 1994; Oliphant 1996; Cangelosi and Parisi 1996; Steels 1996; Kirby and Hurford 1997; Briscoe 1997; Hurford this volume).

This chapter follows on from this line of work, and also borrows from language learning algorithms developed in computational linguistics (namely, Stolcke 1994) in order to see if a significant portion of the evolution of syntax can be modelled without assuming biological change. In many ways, this work is a logical extension of the work of Batali (1998), who simulates a population of recurrent neural networks.

Features of a Desirable Model

In order to be a successful model of the cultural adaptation of language, the computational simulation has to have a set of key features. These set out our minimum requirements. In general, we wish to make the model as simple as possible initially, and see if the complex behaviour that we are looking for emerges without extra assumptions. The basic requirements are:

1. Individuals that *learn observationally*. In other words, all the knowledge in the population is learned by individuals observing others' behaviour. Following Oliphant (1997), I use this term to contrast the model with ones which assume that learning proceeds through explicit reinforcement.
2. A gradual turnover of members of the population over time. By ensuring that members of the population are not 'immortal' we can see that there is true historical/cultural transmission of knowledge through the system.
3. No selection of individuals. In order to show that biological evolution is not a factor in the results of the simulation, the 'death' of members of the population should be completely random and not related in any way to their success at communication.
4. Initial nonlinguistic population. Those individuals that make up the initial population should have no communication system at all. This means that any biases that emerge in later states of the simulation are purely a product of the learners and the population model.

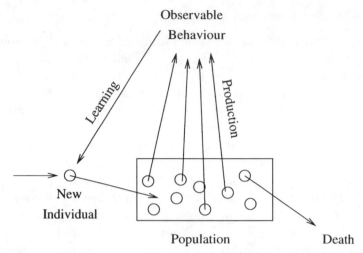

Figure 18.1. A framework for modelling populations of observational learners (from Oliphant 1997).

The basic structure of the model is similar to that used by Oliphant (1997). Figure 18.1 shows Oliphant's diagram of how we can model populations of observational learners. The simulation maintains a population of individual learners which produce observable behaviour. Occasionally, individuals will die and be removed from the population. These individuals will be replaced with new individuals which learn from the body of observable behaviour that the population has produced. There is actually not much more than this to the computational model. All that remains is to define what is meant by 'observable behaviour', and to expand on how we model individuals that can produce and learn this behaviour.

Utterances

For a model of a population of communicating individuals, we clearly need something for our individuals to talk about – in other words, we must provide the simulation with a set of possible meanings. For the purposes of demonstrating emergent compositionality, it is important that this set of meanings be structured in some way. If meanings were not decomposable then it would be impossible for there to be a compositional system for communicating those meanings.

Each meaning in the simulation is a triple of attribute-value pairs. The three attributes can be glossed as *Agent*, *Patient* and *Predicate*. The set of possible values is divided into two classes, which can be glossed as *Objects* and *Actions*.

The *Agent* and *Patient* attributes can be paired only with *Objects*, whilst the *Predicate* attribute can be paired only with *Actions*. The *Object* class contains the values *Mike, John, Mary, Tünde* and *Zoltan*. The *Action* class contains the values *Loves, Knows, Hates, Likes* and *Finds*. An example meaning in this scheme could be: *<Agent = Zoltan, Patient = Mary, Predicate = Knows>*, which we can think of as being equivalent to the English sentence 'Zoltan knows Mary'. Essentially, the individuals' meanings are all about who did what to whom.[3] For purely implementational reasons, meanings with the same value for *Agent* as *Patient* are disallowed. This leads to a complete semantic space made up of 100 possible meanings.

The individuals in the simulation communicate through a serial channel with discrete symbols concatenated into a string. They have five of these basic symbols: a, b, c, d and e, which can be thought of as phonetic gestures. In principle, there is no limit on the length of an utterance, and the shortest possible utterance is one symbol long.

The observable behaviour in the model (which corresponds to the top part of Oliphant's diagram) is made up of pairs of meanings and symbol strings. This builds in an assumption that the intended meanings of utterances are, at least some of the time, accessible to learners.

Individuals

In order to be able to produce utterances, the individuals in the model must have some way of representing a communication system internally, and a way of inducing such a representation from experience. There are many ways in which we might implement this. In Batali (1998) for example the communication system is represented as a set of connection weights in an artificial neural network, and these weights are learned using a standard algorithm. The techniques used in the simulations described in this chapter are described in detail in Kirby (1998b), but a flavour of them will be given here.

Internal representation. Each individual represents its communication system as a context-free grammar.[4] Importantly, the space of possible grammars is huge, and almost all of them are not language-like at all. In other words, by choosing a grammatical framework like this, we are not building in any unwanted inherent biases towards a compositionally structured system. Context-free grammars allow us to express a range of systems from completely noncompositional to highly compositional.

Although in this chapter I do not intend to go into much of the purely technical detail behind the simulations, it is worth illustrating what a context-free grammar looks like, and how it can be compositional or noncompositional. Two examples should make this clearer. The first is a (very simple!) noncompositional grammar[5] that produces the string *zoltanknowsmary* meaning *<Agent = Zoltan, Patient = Mary, Predicate = Knows>* :

S/ *<Agent = Zoltan, Patient = Mary, Predicate = Knows>* →
zoltanknowsmary

This grammar has only one rewrite rule for the category S (i.e. sentence). The grammar can be interpreted as stating: 'A sentence that means *<Agent = Zoltan, Patient = Mary, Predicate = Knows>* can be expressed as the string of symbols *zoltanknowsmary*'. This grammar is obviously noncompositional since the meaning of the sentence is not built up from the meaning of parts of that sentence.

The second example grammar also produces the same string/meaning pairing:

S/ *<Agent = x, Patient = y, Predicate = p>* → $N/x\ V/p\ N/y$
V/ *<Knows>* → knows
N/ *<Zoltan>* → zoltan
N/ *<Mary>* → mary

This grammar can be interpreted as stating: 'A sentence can be made up of something of category *N* followed by something of category *V* followed by something of category *N*, if the meaning of that sentence is constructed by assigning the meaning of the first *N* to *Agent*, the second *N* to *Patient* and the *V* to *Predicate*. In turn something of category *V* that means *<Knows>* can be expressed as a string of symbols *knows*, something of category *N* that means *<Zoltan>* can be expressed as *zoltan*, and something of category *N* that means *<Mary>* can be expressed as *mary*'. This grammar contrasts with the previous one in being compositional, in that the meaning of the whole is built up from the meanings of its parts.

Invention. The initial individuals in the population have no linguistic knowledge – at the start of the simulation runs no one is able to say anything. For anything to get off the ground there must be a way for novel forms to be produced. It is assumed that occasionally individuals, even though they have no normal way in which to express a certain meaning, will nonetheless produce some invented string of symbols.

There are different ways in which this might be done. The simplest approach is to produce a completely random string of symbols. Another possibility, used by Hurford (this volume), is to break down the meaning that is to be expressed into its atomic components, and then try to 'synthesise' a symbolic representation of the sum of those components, perhaps by checking a lexicon for any matches to these atomic meanings. So, for example, if an individual was trying to express <*Agent = Zoltan, Patient = Mike, Predicate = Knows*>, then Hurford's technique would check to see if there was a way to say 'Zoltan', 'Mike' and 'Knows' in isolation, and put together an utterance by combining these parts.

However, Hurford's (this volume) goal is not to model the emergence of compositionality, so his approach may not be the best one to use in this simulation. Indeed, a synthetic approach to some extent is bound to build in the central feature of compositionality – that the meaning of the whole is composed of the meanings of its parts. Moreover, Wray (1998, this volume) suggests that language evolution did not proceed through the synthesis of small components into larger syntactic units, but rather that protolanguage consisted of holistic (i.e. noncompositional) utterances for complex meanings.

Given this, it would seem sensible to opt for a random invention technique. However, this is rather unrealistic for some cases. For example, imagine that you, as an English speaker, do not know the word for a new object that you have never seen before. It seems implausible that, if you needed to express a meaning that mentioned this object somewhere in it, you would utter a completely random string of phonetic gestures for the whole sentence.

Instead, whenever individuals invent a new form for a particular meaning, they do not introduce new structure, but equally, they do not throw away structure that is already part of the language they have acquired. The computational implementation of this invention strategy is described in detail in Kirby (1998b). Briefly, the invention algorithm used by the simulation generates random strings where the speaker has no grammatical structure, but for meanings that can be partially expressed with a particular grammar will only randomise those parts of the string that are known by the speaker not to correspond to expressible meaning.[6]

Induction. Each individual in the simulation acquires a grammar based on experience of meaning-form pairs produced by the rest of the population. The simulation uses a simplified version of an algorithm developed by Stolcke (1994) for induction of context-free grammars with semantics. Full details of the methodology are given in Kirby (1998b). Essentially, the learning process involves two steps:

1. *Incorporation.* On receiving a meaning-form pair, the algorithm immediately builds a grammatical model for that pair which makes no generalising assumptions about it. In other words, the inducer will simply add a

(completely noncompositional) rule to the grammar that states directly that a legal sentence in the language has the given form and corresponds to the given meaning. (For example an incorporated rule for the English sentence 'Zoltan knows Mary' would look very like the first simple grammar rule given in the section on internal representation.)

2. *Merging*. Having built a grammatical model of a single utterance, the algorithm seeks to merge this model with the existing model for any previous utterances. Merging involves making changes to the rules in the grammar in such a way that two or more rules in the grammar become more similar to each other. The rationale behind this is that learning can be viewed as compression of training into a compact hypothesis (Osborne and Briscoe 1997). If two rules in the grammar become identical, then one is redundant and is deleted. The merging algorithm thus tends to produce 'minimal length' grammars for the observed utterances.

In practical terms, the way in which the induction algorithm seeks to merge the grammar will introduce constraints on the space of possible grammars that the learners can acquire. For example, the learners described in this chapter cannot acquire recursive grammars (see Kirby in press for a simulation in which recursion is possible). This is not a serious concern, however, since the simple 'who did what to whom' meanings that they have to convey are not recursive anyway.

The Population Dynamic

Given a computational model of an individual we need to set out the ways in which a population of individuals interacts. The population in the simulations reported here is made up of ten individuals at any one point in time, organised in a ring. In other words, each member of the population has two neighbours. Figure 18.2 shows how this population is updated over time. On each cycle through the inner loop of Figure 18.2, the speaker is 'instructed' to produce a randomly chosen meaning. Especially at the start of the simulation, the speaker may well not be able to produce a string that corresponds to that meaning with the grammar that it has internalised. At this point, one of two things may happen: either the speaker says nothing, or the speaker may try and invent a new string (as described earlier). The rate at which inventions are introduced can be easily controlled in the simulation. For the results reported here, speakers produce inventions on average one time out of every fifty. If, on the other hand, the speaker can produce a string which corresponds to the meaning, then it does so,

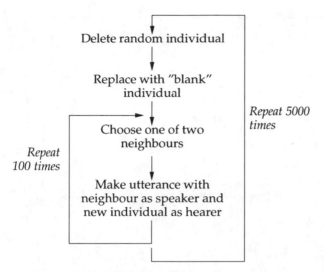

Figure 18.2. The main loop used in the simulations.

although noise is simulated in the model by replacing this string with a random one one time out of a thousand. The key points here are:

- Each individual learns only from utterances (form-meaning pairs) produced by its neighbours.
- The makeup of the population changes over time.
- Individuals are replaced entirely at random.
- The probability that one individual will hear all forms for all the possible meanings is vanishingly small.[7]

Results

This section looks in some detail at one particular run of the simulation. The behaviour of the simulation is consistent from run to run, so a careful analysis of one case is worthwhile.

The initial population is made up of ten individuals, none of which have any knowledge of language – that is, they have empty grammars. The simulation loop described in Figure 18.2 is then initialised and left to run until the behaviour of the population stabilises (after several thousand generations). Periodically, various measures of the population's behaviour and knowledge are taken:

1. *Meanings*. The number of meanings that an individual can express (without invention).
2. *Size*. The number of rules in an individual's grammar.[8]

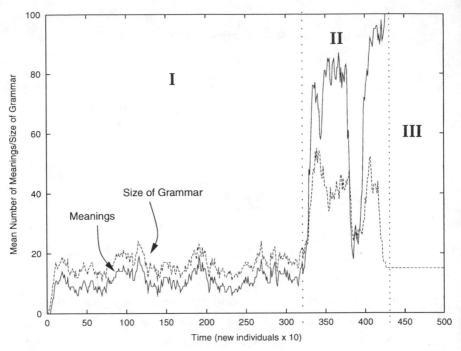

Figure 18.3. The population average of size, meanings and coverage over 500,000 sentences, where a 'sentence' is an instruction to a speaker to produce a random meaning. The graph is divided into three stages signifying major 'phase changes' in the grammars of the population.

3. *Grammars*. The actual grammars of the individuals in the simulation can be directly inspected, so that we can analyse any internal structure to the language that evolves in the community.

A graph of the population average of meanings and size over a run of 5,000 cycles through the simulation is given in Figure 18.3. The graph has been partitioned into three stages between which the population appears to make 'phase transitions' into radically different types of behaviour. In particular, the relationships between the two measures graphed and also the structure of the grammars changes radically at these points. These stages are present in every run of the simulation, although the timing of the transitions is variable.

Stage I

In the first few cycles of the simulation run nothing much happens. No individuals in the population have any grammar, so they have no way of producing utterances. Each time an individual is asked to produce a string for a particular

Table 18.1. *Vocabulary list for a random individual (Stage I)*

Meaning (glossed in English)	String
John finds Mary	aceabbceeeabeea
John finds Zoltan	ceadaeeabbe
John hates Zoltan	ecdceaabdda
Mary finds Zoltan	adabeeb
Mary hates John	ddadbbbbabeedaeee
Mary hates Tünde	adababcccecadcbce
Mary hates Zoltan	ceeaebeebcecabdee
Mary loves Tünde	abacdddbe
Mike hates Mary	adddbdcceaa
Zoltan hates John	d
Zoltan hates Mike	e

randomly chosen meaning, it consults its grammar and discovers it has no way of producing a string so it says nothing. Consequently the new individuals have no exemplars for acquisition, and also end up with empty grammars. Recall, however, that there are occasional random *invention* and *noise* events. Whenever one of these occurs, the new individual has something to internalise: a pairing of a randomly constructed string of symbols with a randomly chosen meaning. Then, if this individual is later called upon to produce an utterance with that meaning, that same string of symbols will again appear in the input of a new learner.

This process of random invention and reuse leads to the situation that is stable throughout the first emergent stage in the simulation. The population can express only a small percentage of the meanings, using a small grammar. In fact, the grammars in this stage are basically vocabulary lists, with each complex meaning being expressed as an arbitrary unanalysed string of symbols. One such vocabulary list for a random individual picked out of the population at this stage is shown in Table 18.1. Notice that only 11 out of the full 100 meanings can be expressed by this individual, and there is no consistent way in which the meanings are related to the strings. For example, *John hates Zoltan* is expressed as *ecdceaabdda* while *Zoltan hates John* is expressed as the completely unrelated string *d*. This complete lack of structure is confirmed when we look at a tree diagram produced by using the grammar of this individual to parse the string *aceabbceeeabeea* (Figure 18.4).

Stage II

The second stage in the simulation results is marked by a sudden change in the population measures. The number of meanings covered increases dramatically,

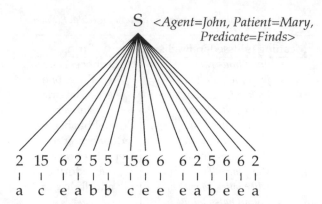

Figure 18.4. A stage I phrase structure tree showing the utterance *aceabbceeeabeea* meaning *John finds Mary*. Note the complete flatness of the structure. The numbers attached to the nodes are the actual arbitrary category labels assigned by the learning algorithm. Notice (as discussed previously) that each terminal symbol has an associated preterminal category. So the symbol *a* has been arbitrarily assigned the category label 2 by the learner.

as does the size of the grammar. More importantly, the number of meanings becomes greater than the number of rules in the grammar. It is clear from this that the language is no longer simply behaving as a list of unanalysed vocabulary items for complex meanings as it was in Stage I.

In fact, the grammars at this stage are far more complex and byzantine than the earlier ones. The details of what is going on in the language of the population at this stage are hard to figure out. There are, however, a few points that should be noted. Firstly, there are now syntactic categories that are intermediate between the sentence level and the level of individual symbols. Importantly, some of these intermediate categories, or *words*, have a semantics of their own. We can see this from the example tree in Figure 18.5. Here, as we can see from this parse tree, the substring *ce* means *John* in the context of the string *dceddd*. This utterance is therefore partly compositional.

Stage III

After a second abrupt change, the population switches into a third and final stage. This stage appears to be completely stable, and in no runs do significant changes occur after this point. The transition is marked by a sudden increase of the number of meanings that can be produced to the maximum value and by a drop in the size of the grammars.

A look at the behaviour of an individual in this stage reveals a marked contrast with the typical behaviour earlier in the simulation. Some of the utterances

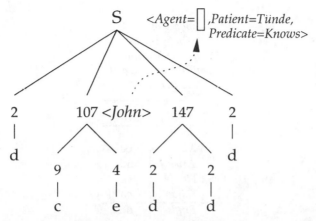

Figure 18.5. A stage II tree showing *dceddd* meaning *John knows Tünde*. The arrow shows how the meaning of the whole is partially composed from the meaning of one of its lower constituents. Notice, again, that arbitrary numerical category labels have been assigned by the inducer. There are two types of label here, however. We have preterminal labels as before such as 2, 4 and 9, which stand in for the terminal symbols, but there are also intermediate categories such as 107 and 147, which begin to look more like the standard lexical categories we find in real language, which rewrite to strings of preterminals.

of a typical individual are shown in Table 18.2. This individual is able to express all 100 possible meanings because there is a regular correspondence between meanings and forms. Each string is composed of three substrings, which correspond to the predicate, the patient, and the agent, in that order. Table 18.3 and the example tree in Figure 18.6 make this clearer. Not only is this language completely compositional but, by directly inspecting the grammars of

Table 18.2. *Utterances of a typical individual (Stage III)*

Meaning (glossed in English)	String
John finds Mary	daecde
John finds Mike	daadde
John finds Tünde	daccde
· · ·	· · ·
John hates Mary	cdecde
John hates Mike	cdadde
· · ·	· · ·
Mary finds John	dadeec
· · ·	· · ·
Zoltan loves Tünde	ceccca

Table 18.3. *Strings composed of substrings correspond to the predicate, the patient and the agent (Stage III)*

Meaning	String
John	de
Mary	ec
Mike	ad
Tünde	cc
Zoltan	ca
Finds	da
Hates	cd
Knows	ee
Likes	ae
Loves	ce

the individuals, it can be shown that the language also groups all the objects (*Mary, Zoltan, Mike, Tünde* and *John*) under one syntactic category (62) and all the actions (*Likes, Loves, Knows, Finds* and *Hates*) under a second category (66). In other words, this language encodes the classic noun/verb distinction syntactically.

The language is a VOS language in that the verb is the first word in the sentence, and the semantic roles of the two following nouns are determined by word order such that the first noun is the patient and the second the agent. The

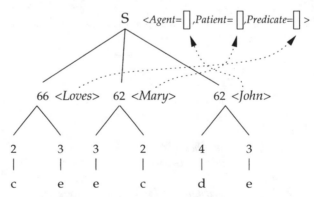

Figure 18.6. A stage III tree showing ceecde meaning *John loves Mary*. Here, the arbitrarily assigned category label 66 could be glossed as 'verb' and the label 62 as 'noun'.

emergent ordering differs from run to run, but the general pattern is the same: a noun/verb distinction encoded in the lexicon with the agent/patient distinction encoded by word order.[9] The eventual grammar size in this run is 15 rules. This works out as 1 top-level sentence rule, 10 lexical rules (one for each noun and verb), and 4 preterminal rules (one each for the symbols a, c, d and e as the symbol b happens not to be used in this language).

Summary of the Results

What we have seen in this run, and in every run of the simulation that has been attempted, is the emergence from randomness of simple yet language-like syntax in a population that is not constrained to learn only a compositional language.

The communication system of the population that quickly emerges from nothing is an impoverished, idiosyncratic vocabulary of one-word utterances – in fact, nothing more than an inventory of calls expressing unanalysed meanings. This system is passed on only 'culturally' through observational learning by new individuals, and there is nothing else inherited by later generations from earlier ones.

After many generations, the system that is used to express meanings balloons in complexity. Utterances are no longer unanalysed strings of symbols. They are made up of common chunks of several symbols. Some of these chunks even have meanings of their own, although they are not regularly used to signify these meanings in a larger context. The language of the population now goes through radical and unpredictable changes over time as the range of meanings that are readily expressible changes wildly. The language appears to be brittle in some way and liable to break and lose its expressive power suddenly.

At some point, all this changes, and the population converges on a simple system, a syntactic system. Now, every sentence is made up of nouns and verbs (drawn from a concise lexicon lacking synonymy and homonymy) in a fixed order which encodes meaning distinctions compositionally, and every possible meaning can be expressed.

Why Does This Model Work?

The individuals in the simulation simply observe each others' behaviour and learn from it, occasionally inventing, at random, new behaviours of their own. From this apparent randomness, organisation emerges. Given that so little is built into the simulation, why is a compositional syntax inevitable?

To answer this question, we need to look at how languages persist over time in the population. Language exists in two forms, both in reality and in the

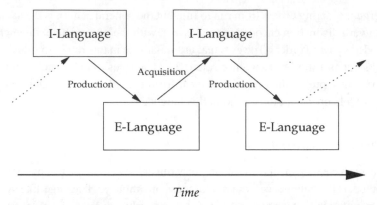

Time

Figure 18.7. The cycle of language acquisition and use, which maps I-language objects to E-language objects and vice versa. These transformations act as bottlenecks for the information flowing through the system. For a particular feature of language to survive over time, it must be faithfully preserved through these mappings.

simulation (Chomsky 1986; Hurford 1987; Kirby 1999):

> *I-language*. This is (internal) language as represented in the brains of the population. It is the language user's knowledge of language. In the simulation, the I-language of an individual is completely described by its grammar.
>
> *E-language*. This is the (external) language that exists as utterances in the arena of use (Hurford 1987). In the simulation, we can describe E-language by listing the form-meaning pairs of an individual.

These two types of language influence each other in profound ways. E-language is a product of the I-language of speakers. However, the I-language of language learners is a product of the E-language that they have access to (see Figure 18.7). A particular I-language or E-language can fail to persist over time because the processes that map from one to the other and back again are not necessarily preservative.

We can divide up I-language into units – *replicators* – that may or may not persist through time. The persistence of an I-language over time is related to the success of the replicators that make up that language. In other words, the languages which are more easily transmitted from generation to generation will persist.

Within a population, certain replicators actually compete for survival. That is, the success of one must be measured relative to the success of others in the population at that time. These competing replicators are those rules which potentially express the same meaning. If there are two ways of saying *John loves Mary*, then on a particular exposure to this meaning, the learner can obviously only hear one of them. Therefore, on one exposure, only one of the rules (or, more properly, set of rules) that can be used to express *John loves Mary* has a chance of being induced by the learner.

At face value, it would seem that the two competing rules (or rule sets) will have an equal chance of being chosen for producing the meaning, so the replicative success of all rules in a language should be equal. This would be true *if each rule only ever expressed one meaning*. However, if one rule can be used to express more meanings than another, then, all other things being equal, that rule will have a greater chance of being expressed in the E-language input to the learner. In this case, the more general rule is the better replicator.

For a more concrete example, consider a situation where, in the population of I-languages, there are two competing rules. One is a rule that expresses *John loves Mary* as an unanalysed string of symbols – essentially as one word. The other rule expresses *John loves Mary* as a string of symbols, but can also be used to express any meaning where someone loves Mary. So, the latter rule can also be used to express *Zoltan loves Mary* and so on. Further imagine that both rules have an equal chance of being used to express *John loves Mary*. The more general rule is still a better replicator, because for any randomly chosen set of meanings, we can expect it to be used more often than the idiosyncratic rule. Its chances of survival to the next generation are far more secure than those of the idiosyncratic rule.

Of course, the more general rule will not be learned as easily as the idiosyncratic rule. In the simulations described, an idiosyncratic pairing of one meaning to one form takes only one exposure to learn, but the most general rule takes several. However, the idiosyncratic rule only covers one meaning, whereas the most general rule covers 100. It is clear, therefore, that the probability of acquiring a particular rule given a random sample of meanings increases with the generality of that rule. The success of I-languages which contain general rules seems secure.

The picture that emerges, then, is of the language of the population acting as an adaptive system in its own right. Initially, the rules are minimally general, each pairing one string with one meaning. At some point, a chance invention or random noise will lead a learner to 'go beyond the data' in making a generalisation that the previous generation had not made. This generalisation will then compete with the idiosyncratic rule(s) for the same meaning(s). Given that generalisations are better replicators, the idiosyncratic rules will be pushed out over time. The competition will then be replayed amongst generalisations, always with the more general rules surviving.

The inevitable end state of this process is a language with a syntax that supports compositionally derived semantics in a highly regular fashion. The grammar for such a language appears to be the shortest (in terms of number of rules) that can express the entire meaning space. The shorter the grammar, the higher the generality of each of the rules – the shortest grammar that can still do the job of expressing meanings is therefore the one made up of optimal replicators.

There is an interesting way in which this replicator-based theory can be tested using the simulation. If the emergence of compositionality is due to the differential success of competing replicators, then there should be effects introduced by changing the frequency of particular meanings. For example, if one meaning is expressed particularly frequently by speakers, any rule that contributes to the production of a string for that meaning will be a good replicator. In the simulation results presented so far, idiosyncratic rules have died out because they contribute to a relatively small portion of E-language. However, if one meaning is particularly frequent, then we should find that an idiosyncratic form for that meaning will survive longer.

To test this, the simulation was run again, but the maximum number of utterances was doubled to 200. The meaning *John loves Mary* was made far more frequent so that it made up approximately half of the utterances. The results of such runs are consistent with the idea that replicator dynamics are driving the evolution of language in the simulation. The pattern of change in the simulation is similar to the one described earlier, with three stages showing evolution towards compositional syntax. Even in the final stage, however, an idiosyncratic, noncompositional way of saying *John loves Mary* survived.

This mechanism – whereby frequent meanings can withstand the pressure to become compositionally expressed – may explain some features of human languages. For example, in morphology, suppletive forms tend to correlate with highly frequent meanings. The past tense form of the frequent verb *go* is the noncompositional *went*, not *goed*. The ordinal versions of the English numbers after *three* are compositional – *third, fourth, fifth* etc. – but the more frequent *first* and *second* are not.

Conclusion

In this chapter I have argued the case for an appreciation of the role of truly linguistic evolution (as opposed to biological evolution) in the emergence of syntax. Human language is unique amongst communication systems in being compositional. It is also unique in the natural world in being a phenomenon that persists over time through observational learning. These two facts are clearly connected. Once an observationally learned communication system is off the ground, the dynamics introduced make the emergence of compositionality inevitable without further biological change.

Notes

1. This research was carried out at the Collegium Budapest Institute for Advanced Study and at the Language Evolution and Computation Research Unit in the Department of Linguistics at Edinburgh, funded by ESRC grant R000236551. Much of the work described was carried out in collaboration with Mike Oliphant and Jim Hurford. Some sections of this chapter are available in an earlier technical report (Kirby 1998b), which also has an appendix dealing with the model more formally.
2. For parallel, and in certain ways contrasting, work, see Hurford (this volume).
3. I hope it will be clear that in choosing these particular attributes and values I am not making any claims about what sort of things real individuals want to talk about. The terms 'Agent', 'Patient' and 'Predicate' are purely devices to help us think about these triples as meanings. They could equally well have been given numbers (as indeed they are in the computational implementation of the model). The important feature of this semantics is that it has inherent structure, albeit a very simple one.
4. Actually, the grammars are *probabilistic attribute grammars* (Stolcke 1994). These are context-free grammars which are enriched with statistical information and a simple semantics.
5. The illustrative formalism used here is essentially identical to the one used internally in the simulation. It is just like a traditional phrase structure grammar, with semantics attached to category labels (after a slash) and variables indicated in bold. In the simulation, these rules also have frequency counts attached to them. Furthermore, the category labels (such as N and V in our example) are assigned arbitrary numerals in the simulation. This means that the learner does not have a limit on the number of categories that might be postulated.
6. In the simulation results reported here, the completely novel utterances invented by the speakers were set to vary randomly in length between 6 and 10 symbols. In addition, during partial invention of utterances, the lengths of the invented strings could increase or decrease by one symbol with a small probability. The purpose of these arbitrary variables was to allow the string length to be potentially infinite, but likely to remain within a workable range. In fact, as the results to be described show, the languages that emerge seem to favour shorter utterances that can still express the meaning space.
7. There are 100 different possible meanings, and a maximum of 100 utterances heard by each individual. Even if an individual is lucky enough to hear 100 utterances in its lifetime, the chances that these will cover the entire meaning space are $\frac{100!}{100^{100}}$.
8. The size is calculated by inspecting each individual's context-free grammar, and counting the number of rewrite rules. Notice that there are more rules than meanings initially in the graph. This is because for purely technical reasons (discussed more fully in Kirby 1998b) each letter in an individual's language has an associated rewrite rule. In other words, the grammar contains an intermediate 'preterminal' layer between sentences/vocabulary and strings of symbols. This does not affect the results of the simulation in any interesting way, but it does mean that the measure of

grammar size is slightly higher than might otherwise be predicted. In fact, usually each language will use all five terminal symbols *a*, *b*, *c*, *d* and *e*, so there will be five extra rewrite rules in the grammar.

9.   Although the result of this run is full compositionality, in that the sentence rule does not add any atomic semantic content, this is not always the case. Occasionally, one of the atomic meanings does not become lexicalised as a noun or a verb, and an idiosyncratic sentence rule is used to express meanings that include the missing word.

References

Batali, J. 1994. Innate biases and critical periods: combining evolution and learning in the acquisition of syntax. In R. Brooks and P. Maes (eds), *Artificial Life IV*. Cambridge, MA: MIT Press, pp. 160–171.

Batali, J. 1998. Computational simulations of the emergence of grammar. In J. R. Hurford, M. Studdert-Kennedy and C. Knight (eds), *Approaches to the Evolution of Language: Social and cognitive bases*. Cambridge: Cambridge University Press, pp. 405–426.

Bickerton, D. 1990. *Language and Species*. Chicago: University of Chicago Press.

Briscoe, E. J. 1997. Language acquisition: the bioprogram hypothesis and the Baldwin Effect. Manuscript, Computer Laboratory, University of Cambridge.

Cangelosi, A. and D. Parisi. 1996. The emergence of a language in an evolving population of neural networks. Technical Report NSAL-96004, National Research Council, Rome.

Cann, R. 1993. *Formal Semantics: An introduction*. Cambridge: Cambridge University Press.

Chomsky, N. 1986. *Knowledge of Language*. New York: Praeger.

Christiansen, M. 1994. *Infinite Languages, Finite Minds: Connectionism, learning and linguistic structure*. Doctoral dissertation, University of Edinburgh.

Deacon, T. W. 1997. *The Symbolic Species: The co-evolution of language and the brain*. New York: Norton.

Gell-Mann, M. 1992. Complexity and complex adaptive systems. In J. A. Hawkins and M. Gell-Mann (eds), *The Evolution of Human Languages*. Reading, MA: Addison-Wesley

Hurford, J. R. 1987. *Language and Number: The emergence of a cognitive system*. Cambridge, MA: Blackwell.

Hurford, J. R. 1989. Biological evolution of the Saussurean sign as a component of the language acquisition device. *Lingua* **77**: 187–222.

Hurford, J. R. 1991. The evolution of the critical period for language acquisition. *Cognition* **40**: 159–201.

Hurford, J. R. 1998. The evolution of language and languages. In C. Knight, R. I. M. Dunbar and C. Power (eds), *The Evolution of Culture*. Edinburgh: Edinburgh University Press, pp. 173–193.

Hurford, J. R., C. Knight and M. Studdert-Kennedy. (eds). 1998. *Approaches to the Evolution of Language: Social and cognitive bases*. Cambridge: Cambridge University Press.

Kirby, S. 1997. Competing motivations and emergence: explaining implicational hierarchies. *Language Typology* **1**: 5–32.

Kirby, S. 1998a. Fitness and the selective adaptation of language. In J. R. Hurford, M. Studdert-Kennedy and C. Knight (eds), *Approaches to the Evolution of Language: Social and cognitive bases*. Cambridge: Cambridge University Press, pp. 359–383.

Kirby, S. 1998b. Language evolution without natural selection: from vocabulary to syntax in a population of learners. Technical Report EOPL-98-1, Department of Linguistics, University of Edinburgh.

Kirby, S. 1999. *Function, Selection and Innateness: The emergence of language universals*. Oxford: Oxford University Press.

Kirby, S. In press. Learning, bottlenecks, and the evolution of recursive syntax. In E. J. Briscoe (ed), *Linguistic Evolution Through Language Acquisition: Formal and computational models*. Cambridge: Cambridge University Press.

Kirby, S. and J. R. Hurford. 1997. Learning, culture and evolution in the origin of linguistic constraints. In P. Husbands and I. Harvey (eds), *Fourth European Conference on Artificial Life*. Cambridge, MA: MIT Press, pp. 493–502.

MacLennan, B. 1991. Synthetic ethology: an approach to the study of communication. In C. G. Langton, C. Taylor, J. D. Farmer and S. Ramussen (eds), *Artificial Life II*. Reading, MA: Addison-Wesley, pp. 631–657.

Newmeyer, F. J. 1991. Functional explanation in linguistics and the origins of language. *Language and Communication* **11**: 3–28.

Newmeyer, F. J. 1992. Iconicity and generative grammar. *Language* **68**: 756–796.

Niyogi, P. and R. Berwick. 1997. Populations of learners: the case of Portuguese. Unpublished manuscript, M.I.T.

Oliphant, M. 1996. The dilemma of Saussurean communication. *BioSystems* **37**: 31–38.

Oliphant, M. 1997. *Formal Approaches to Innate and Learned Communication: Laying the foundation for language*. Doctoral dissertation, University of California, San Diego.

Osborne, M. and T. Briscoe. 1997. Learning stochastic categorial grammars. Technical report, Computer Laboratory, Cambridge University.

Pinker, S. and P. Bloom. 1990. Natural language and natural selection. *Behavioral and Brain Sciences* **13**: 707–784.

Steels, L. 1996. Emergent adaptive lexicons. In P. Maes, M. Mataric, J.-A Meyer, J. Pollack and S. W. Wilson (eds), *From Animals to Animats 4: Proceedings of the Fourth International Conference or Simulation of Adaptive Behavior*. Cambridge MA: MIT Press, pp. 562–567.

Stolcke, A. 1994. *Bayesian Learning of Probabilistic Language Models*. Doctoral dissertation, University of California at Berkeley.

Wray, A. 1998. Protolanguage as a holistic system for social interaction. *Language and Communication* **18**: 47–67.

19

Social Transmission Favours Linguistic Generalisation

JAMES R. HURFORD

Introduction

This study[1] focuses on the emergence and preservation of linguistic general-isations in a community. Generalisations originate in the innate capacities of individuals for language acquisition and invention. The cycle of language trans-mission through individual competences (I-languages) and public performance (E-language) selects differentially among innately available types of generali-sation. Thus, certain types of general pattern tend to survive in the community's language system as a consequence of social transmission.

Computational simulations are described in which a population that initially shares no common signalling system converges over time on a coordinated system. For the emergence of shared vocabularies, the dynamics of such systems are now well understood (see for example Oliphant 1997 and Steels 1996a, 1996b, 1997, in press).

This chapter demonstrates how systems with syntax can emerge from the same fundamental population dynamics. The essential ingredients of the com-putational model are:

1. Individuals are capable of cognitively representing complex meanings.
2. Individuals who have no rules for signalling meanings have a repertoire of sounds which they may randomly emit when attempting to 'express a meaning'.
3. Individuals are capable of inferring, or postulating, general correlations in observed pairings of complex meanings and strings of sounds.
4. Once inferred by an individual, a connection between a complex meaning and a sound sequence becomes the default basis for the expression of complex meanings by that individual.

This model incorporates no Darwinian selection of individuals by fitness, and no selection of meaning-form pairings by utility or psycholinguistic complexity. Although these classical evolutionary factors are relevant to the evolution of language(s), this chapter abstracts away from them in an attempt to discover what contribution may be expected from the purely mathematical workings of any system of social transmission with the four properties listed.

In such models, the language acquirer is also, in the early stages of the process, a language creator. In the later stages of the process, when the population has converged to a common system, the language acquirer is a language maintainer.

The work described here draws from, and builds upon, work by Batali (1998) and Kirby (this volume).

Assumptions

The take-home conclusion of this chapter is that general rules emerge and survive in the Arena of Use. This conclusion is argued on the assumption that a language has a two-stage life cycle. In its history, a language exists in, and passes through, individual brains as grammars, or 'I-language' (internalised language), and through communities as utterances and their interpretations, or 'E-language' (externalised language). The Arena of Use is where E-language exists.[2]

Rules are acquired by speakers of a language, on the basis of exposure to utterances of the preceding generation. Learners have dispositions to make certain generalisations, and not to make other logically conceivable generalisations, over the data they observe. Naturally, the common generalising tendencies of language acquirers affect the shape of the language as it is transmitted from one generation to the next. But factors outside individuals' heads also influence the differential conservation of general patterns in the continuing language. A learner might have no innate preference between rival generalisations that are equally possible from the observed evidence, and might choose at random between alternative rules expressing these different generalisations. But such generalisations, although equally available to an acquirer, can have disproportionate consequences in the acquirer's eventual adult performance.

There are degrees of generalisation. 'Any odd number above 2 can be expressed by the morpheme X' and 'Any prime number above 2 can be expressed by the morpheme X' are both generalisations about numbers, but the former is more general in that it covers more numbers than the latter. A child given limited data compatible with either generalisation might choose either. A learner who internalised the 'odd' generalization would, as an adult, be likely to produce some meaning-form pairs not covered by the 'prime' generalisation, so that the 'odd' generalisation would be more likely to be the one made by successive generations. A learner who happened to make the 'prime' generalisation would use X for prime numbers, and would use (or invent) a morpheme (or morphemes) other than X for nonprime odd numbers. If all numbers are equally likely to be expressed, there will necessarily be more exemplars in the Arena of Use of the 'odd' generalisation than of the 'prime' generalisation.

The generalisations that a learner acquires (i.e. the individual's grammar rules) determine the output performance data which will be the basis of the next generation's acquisition. Generalisations which give rise to larger proportions of the linguistic data in the Arena of Use will be better represented in the next generation's input. Thus the basic mechanism of language transmission itself will tend to favour patterns conforming to generalisations which embrace greater numbers of examples.

The examples just given depend on a subset relation between sets of potential meanings. All other things being equal, generalisations over supersets will be more likely to be perpetuated in the historically transmitted language than generalisations over subsets. (Prime numbers (over 2) are a subset of odd numbers (over 2).) In addition to such formal factors, external factors (for example, sheer usefulness or conventions associated with common social interactions) can also influence the relative frequencies of linguistic data items. A generalisation which happens to cover examples which are more frequent has a boosted likelihood of being propagated into the next generation.

The method for exploring the coherence and scope of these ideas is computer modelling of the evolution of simple languages in a community. The framework of these computer models is described in what follows.

Speaking/Invention and Hearing/Acquisition

The simulated communities start with no language at all. What permits a shared communication system to 'get off the ground' is the inventive capacity of individuals. Each individual is simultaneously a potential speaker/inventor and hearer/acquirer. The process of invention is computationally modelled by allowing speakers, when they are 'prompted' to express some meaning for which they have not learnt any corresponding signal, to select a signal at random[3] from a predefined, potentially infinite set of forms. The process of invention cannot go beyond the bounds of the innately specified set of possible meaning-form mappings. For any given simulation experiment, there is a limited set of innately permitted types of mapping between meanings and forms. In this work, the innately specified possibilities for meaning-form pairings were experimentally manipulated in order to explore the contribution that innate dispositions and constraints impose on the structure of the language that eventually emerges in the community.

It is also assumed that speaking/invention and hearing/acquisition are parallel applications of the same principles of language use. The central assumption about language use is that the processes of speaking and hearing both call upon the same internalised declarative mappings between meanings and forms, i.e. competence grammars. These mappings can take the simple form of lexicons, in which atomic meanings are paired with atomic forms, in a list. Or, more complexly and realistically, the meaning-form relations can also be partly specified by compositional rules, stating that particular configurations of forms have complex meanings which are a function of the meanings of the constituent forms and the particular shape of the construction containing them. The meaning-form pairings that can be specified by such compositional rules are defined and constrained in various experimental ways in this study.

More specifically, a speaker who has already learned a pairing between a particular atomic meaning and a particular form (i.e. internalised a lexical entry) would, if prompted to express this meaning, simply look up the meaning and 'speak' the corresponding form. If the speaker is prompted with an atomic meaning for which it has no lexical entry, it speaks a form randomly selected from a large predefined set of possible syllables. This invention process is genuinely random, and in no way guided by the grammars or behaviour of other individuals in the community. Inventors make no effort to invent forms consistent with existing usage.

If a speaker is prompted to express a complex (i.e. nonatomic) meaning, there are again two possibilities. If the speaker has already learned a rule mapping this general type of meaning onto either a specific form or a general type of form, the rule would be applied, and the appropriate form would be spoken. But if the speaker has learned no such rule, then again invention is invoked, and the speaker either (1) speaks a random atomic syllable or (2) selects at random from a specified set of general rules mapping complex meaning-types compositionally onto corresponding form configurations, and follows that rule to speak a particular form, a string of syllables. In the latter case, following the rule involves, recursively, a prompt to express the meanings which are subparts of the original complex meaning. The probabilities with which options (1) and (2) are followed are varied experimentally.

Rule learning is only associated with the act of hearing. Inventors do not learn from their own inventions. That is, after inventively selecting a random syllable, or string of syllables, to express some meaning, inventors do not 'learn from themselves' and internalise a corresponding rule. Thus a speaker/inventor would, if prompted with the same meaning on several occasions, almost certainly invent different forms for it. The diversity thus created is something for hearers/learners to cope with.

Turning now to the behaviour of hearer/acquirers, learners acquire their grammars on the basis of positive information only. An individual who has already learned a pairing between a particular atomic meaning and a particular form would, on observing this same meaning-form pairing used by another speaker, simply do nothing. If, however, the hearer, while in the learning phase of its life, observes a novel atomic meaning-form pair, this new pair is added to the hearer's lexicon. If a hearer/learner observes the use by another speaker of a particular complex meaning paired with a particular form, then either (1) a 'brute force' rule is acquired relating this meaning to this form, or (2) the hearer structures the parts of the meaning in some permitted way, consistent with the given meaning-form pair, and acquires a general rule relating this meaning-type to this form-type, and applies the hearing/learning procedures, recursively, to the parts. Again, the probabilities with which options (1) and (2) are followed are varied experimentally. There is no sense in which a learner's growing knowledge is evaluated against any 'target grammar'.

Several more technical assumptions are made about the ways in which speakers and hearers make use of their internalised gramars or rule sets. Firstly, it is assumed that acquired rules take precedence over 'innate' dispositions. This has been implicit in the discussion so far, in that invention on the part of a speaker, or learning on the part of a hearer, is only called upon where the individual does not already possess a rule specifying the relevant meaning-form pair. A second assumption is that earlier-acquired rules take precedence over later-acquired rules. This embodies in a very simple way the principle that speakers' uses are roughly influenced by the frequency with which they observe meaning-form pairings. If a particular meaning-form pairing is more widespread in the community than some other, the likelihood is that the more frequent pairing will be observed earlier by a learner.

The World of Meanings

The simulated agents can talk to each other about a little universe, borrowed from Cann's (1993) semantics textbook. This universe includes some people (Fiona, Bertie, Ethel, Jo), a cat (Prudence), and a dog (Chester). These individuals can have properties such as being happy, running or singing; they can be in dyadic relationships with each other, such as liking or loathing; and they can participate in the triadic relationship of giving (the humans can give the animals to each other). So far, this is within the bounds of first-order predicate logic, but the simulation also allows embedding of a proposition as second argument of the two-place predicate *SAY* (whose first argument must be human). This embedding is recursive, up to an arbitrary limit. The simulation does not deal with logical quantification.

Here is a list of some possible messages, expressed in a simple predicate-argument format.

> *HAPPY(FIONA)*
> *LIKE(FIONA,BERTIE)*
> *LOATHE(BERTIE,FIONA)*
> *GIVE(ETHEL,BERTIE,CHESTER)*
> *SAY(JO,(HAPPY(FIONA)))*
> *SAY(ETHEL,(GIVE(JO,BERTIE,PRUDENCE)))*
> *SAY(BERTIE,(SAY(FIONA,(RUN(ETHEL)))))*

The simulated speakers and hearers are not themselves members of the little universe about which they exchange messages. Thus Fiona, Chester et al. are like the community's gods, ever present and ever talked about.

The meanings which simulated individuals could be prompted to express ranged from atomic 'concepts', such as *FIONA, LOATHE* or *GIVE,* to complex propositions, such as *SAY(FIONA,(GIVE(BERTIE,JO,CHESTER)))*.

About Rules

The simplest kind of rule that a learner can acquire is a lexical entry specifying a pairing of an atomic meaning with a single syllable, represented as a number. For example:

> *WEALTHY :* vom
> *JO :* tot
> *SAY :* bit

It is also possible for a learner to acquire a rule linking a whole proposition with a single syllable. For example:

> *WEALTHY(BERTIE) :* gaq
> *SAY(FIONA,(HAPPY(CHESTER))) :* lih
> *LOATHE(CHESTER,PRUDENCE) :* mis

For the first three experiments to be described, there was also a single type of rule for expressing whole propositions in a compositional way, by specifying a particular ordering of subexpressions corresponding to the meanings of the parts of the whole proposition.[4] An example of such a rule, for a one-place predication, is:

$PRED(ARG1) \rightarrow$ <F-ARG1, F-PRED>

This translates as 'To express a proposition consisting of a one-place predicate and a single argument, use a string consisting of the form for the argument, followed by the form for the predicate'. Another example is:

$PRED(ARG1,ARG2,ARG3) \rightarrow$ <F-ARG3, F-PRED, F-ARG1, F-ARG2>

This translates as 'To express a proposition consisting of a three-place predicate and three arguments, use a string consisting of (1) the form for the third argument, (2) the form for the predicate, (3) the form for the first argument, and (4) the form for the second argument.'

Such rules are essentially constituent-ordering rules, i.e. rules for ordering the forms which express predicates and their arguments. There are two different ways of ordering a predicate form and a single argument form, six different ways of ordering a predicate form and two argument forms and so on. Note that such rules contain no autonomous syntactic categories, being simply 'translation rules' from semantic representations to 'phonetic' representations. I do not believe that natural languages in fact manage without such autonomous syntactic categories in (at least some of) their rules; the present treatment is clearly a simplification.

Note that there are two ways of expressing a whole proposition, either compositionally as a string of expressions for the constituent meanings, or noncompositionally (holistically) as a single syllable. The compositional method is in a clear sense more general than the holistic method.[5] Rules of the compositional sort use variables over the meaning constituents and the corresponding elements in the output syllable string. Such a rule will apply to any proposition with the appropriate number of arguments. A holistic rule, on the other hand, is completely specific, applying to just one particular proposition, e.g. *LIKE(FIONA,BERTIE)*. We will see that the cyclic process of production and acquisition over many generations favours the perpetuation of the more general type of rule, at the expense of the more specific type of rule.

Rule invention. An inventor who produces a syllable string corresponding to some given propositional meaning, for which there was previously no rule, chooses at random an arbitrary ordering of the constituents of the given meaning, and then expresses the meaning constituents in the order chosen. In some cases, this second round of meaning expression may be straightforward, simply involving lexical lookup of the expressions to be used for the constituent meanings. In more complex cases, the speaker/inventor may have no existing rule for expressing some of the constituent meanings, and in such cases further calls to the invention procedure are made. In sum, an inventor, prompted to express a proposition (and not taking the simple single-syllable option), goes through the following operations:

1. Randomly order the immediate constituent terms (predicate and argument(s)) of the proposition.
2. Utter a string of expressions for the constituent terms, in the order selected. For each constituent term, the speaker is prompted in the same way as for the higher-level meaning, so that there may be recursive calls to this procedure.

In an extreme case, a speaker/inventor prompted to express some complex proposition, could utter a long string of syllables, each one invented, in an invented order.

As an example of speaking involving some rule invention, suppose that a speaker has only the following rules:

WEALTHY : vom
JO : tot
SAY : bit
PRED(ARG1) → <F-ARG1, F-PRED>

Now this speaker is prompted to express the meaning:

SAY(FIONA,(WEALTHY(JO)))

The top-level proposition here is a two-place predication, with the predicate *SAY*, first argument *FIONA*, and second argument the proposition *WEALTHY (JO)*. The speaker has no rule for expressing a two-place predication, and so must invent one. The speaker picks a random ordering of the three constituents, let us say the 'SOV' order *(FIONA,(WEALTHY(JO)),SAY)*. Now the speaker is prompted to express each of these constituent meanings in the order chosen. The first is *FIONA*; the speaker has no expression for *FIONA*, and must therefore invent one. Let's say this speaker picks the random syllable *kuf*. Moving on now to the second meaning constituent, the proposition *(WEALTHY(JO))*, the speaker already has a rule for expressing such one-place predications; this rule calls for the expression of the single argument to precede the expression of the predicate. Accordingly, the speaker is prompted to express *JO*. The speaker has a rule for *JO*, which is expressed as the syllable *tot*. The speaker also has a rule for the predicate *WEALTHY*, specifying the syllable *vom*. All that remains is to express the predicate *SAY*, for which there happens also to be an existing rule, specifying the syllable *bit*. In sum, the outcome of this process is that the speaker utters the string of syllables:

<kuf, <tot, vom>, bit>

The output syllable strings in these simulations retain any bracketing inherited from the nesting of propositions inside each other in the meaning representations. Thus, in these simulations, the embedding structure, but not the linear order, of an expression for a complex meaning is derived from the embedding structure of the complex meaning itself. This bracketing is available to the simulated hearer/acquirers. Undoubtedly, there are both realistic and unrealistic aspects to this treatment. In natural languages, syntactic clause embedding tends to reflect the embedding of propositions at the semantic level. On the other hand, clearly, hearers do not receive completely explicit signals of bracketing. In further work, it will be interesting to remove these brackets and implement a full string-parsing mechanism in hearers, which could conceivably give rise to bracketings other than those present in the original meaning representation. In the fourth experiment to be described, the bracketing of the output string did not correspond exactly to that of the input meaning representation.

Rule acquisition. When speaker/inventors use some new forms in an utterance, they do not remember them. But a hearer/acquirer who observes the meaning-form pair generated by a speaker/inventor can acquire the rules which were used in generating it. A simple case of acquisition would involve a single lexical item. Say, for example, a hearer observes a speaker uttering the syllable *jam* for the atomic meaning *BERTIE*. If a hearer did not already have a lexical entry linking this syllable to this meaning, he would acquire it. Likewise, if a hearer for the first time hears a single syllable used to express a complex meaning, say *LOATHE(BERTIE,CHESTER)*, he would acquire a rule linking this complex meaning to the observed syllable. The case of acquiring an ordering rule is somewhat more complex, but follows the same principles as were explained earlier for the case of rule invention. An example follows.

Suppose the hearer has only the following lexical entries:

WEALTHY : vom
JO : tot

This hearer does not yet have any general rules for expressing propositions. The hearer observes a speaker producing the meaning-form pair:

WEALTHY(JO) : <vom, tot>

In this example, as it happens, the expression for the predicate precedes the expression for its argument. The hearer/acquirer notes that this is the order of elements which has been used, and accordingly internalises the general rule:

$$PRED(ARG1) \rightarrow \text{<F-PRED, F-ARG1>}$$

The hearer/acquirer generalises a constituent ordering rule on the basis of a single examplar.

Whereas in the speaking/invention process it is possible for a particular production to involve more than one invention, in the hearing/acquisition process, a limit of one rule acquisition per observation is applied. Thus, it is not possible to learn a general rule for a construction and a number of the lexical entries involved all at the same time. This has the effect of imposing a typical bottom-up ordering on the language acquisition process. A learner learns atomic lexical correspondences before learning constructions, as in the example just given. It is, however, possible for a learner to acquire a new atomic lexical entry after the acquisition of a construction in which it is used. For example, the hearer/learner in the above example might next observe the meaning-form pair:

$$WEALTHY(FIONA) : \text{<vom, but>}$$

Having already acquired both a lexical entry for *WEALTHY* and a rule stating how one-place predications are expressed, the hearer can acquire the next lexical entry:

$$FIONA : \text{but}$$

The Simulation Cycle

The simulation program ran repeatedly through the following steps, starting with a 'blank' population consisting of some adults and some children.
   Repeat

1. Do steps (a)–(f) a few hundred times:
    (a) select a random adult, A.
    (b) select a random child, C.
    (c) select a random meaning, M.
    (d) A expresses meaning M to C using utterance U.
    (e) C observes meaning-form pair M-U.
    (f) C, if possible, acquires new rule(s) on basis of M-U and any previously acquired rules.
2. N children become adults.
3. N oldest adults are removed.

This model of population turnover, with speaking and learning, is essentially similar to both Kirby's (this volume) and Batali's (in press).

In all the experiments to be reported, there were, at any given time, four adult speaker/inventors and one child hearer/learner.[6] These numbers are unrealistically small, of course, but they made for fast runs. Some experiments with larger populations were carried out, and these converged more slowly on results essentially similar to those to be reported, so there is no reason to believe that the general conclusions would be different given larger populations.

The Experiments

Within the framework just sketched, four experiments were carried out, progressing from the illustration of quite simple principles to the exploration of slightly more complex cases.

Experiment 1: Syntactic Rules Supersede Idiosyncratic Lexical Items

As noted, the community started with no language at all. The speakers in the first generation had not themselves gone through a language-learning experience, and therefore, when prompted to express any particular meaning, always had to resort to invention. The hearer/acquirer was thus presented with an uncoordinated jumble of randomly invented meaning-form pairs. Speakers were prompted to express atomic meanings (e.g. *BERTIE, SAY* or *GIVE*) 50% of the time, and simple or complex whole propositions (e.g. *HAPPY (CHESTER), LIKE(JO,PRUDENCE)* or *SAY(BERTIE,(HAPPY(JO)))* 50% of the time.

Given an atomic meaning, the inventor would select a possible syllable at random. Given a complex meaning (i.e. a whole proposition), the inventor would select a random syllable (for the whole meaning) 50% of the time, and otherwise would select a rule at random for expressing the particular type of meaning involved, by the process explained in the previous section.

At an early stage in this simulation (after 2 cycles), a typical individual had nothing more than a big lexicon, for both simple and complex meanings. There were no general syntactic rules. There was multiple synonymy. Table 19.1 gives a subset of such a typical individual's grammar. At a later stage, after 15 cycles, a typical speaker had adequate productive syntactic rules for the domain, some complex meanings were still looked up lexically, and there was still some synonymy, as shown in Table 19.2. Finally, after 30 cycles, a typical speaker had a maximally economical grammar[7] for this domain, with three adequate general syntactic rules, no 'idiomatic' rules expressing whole propositions as lexical items, and no redundancy (synonymy) in the lexicon, as shown in Table 19.3.

Table 19.1. *Experiment 1: Part of an early speaker's grammar, 28 rules given out of a total 107 (after 2 cycles)*

WEALTHY : lar

SAY(ETHEL,(SAY(FIONA,(LIKE(PRUDENCE,FIONA))))) : duz

SAY(ETHEL,(LIKE(CHESTER,CHESTER))) : bef

JO : raz

SAY(FIONA,(GIVE(BERTIE,PRUDENCE,CHESTER))) : bad

BERTIE : xux

JO : qux

GIVE(JO,FIONA,BERTIE) : qem

SAY(ETHEL,(SAY(BERTIE,(LOATHE(CHESTER,FIONA))))) : key

RUN : roj

FIONA : tiy

RUN : wuz

GIVE(ETHEL,ETHEL,CHESTER) : qom

LOATHE : laq

SAY(FIONA,(SAY(JO,(GIVE(FIONA,CHESTER, ETHEL))))) : qag

BERTIE : bew

BERTIE : gav

SAY(JO,(LIKE(FIONA,JO))) : xin

SAY(JO,(GIVE(JO,BERTIE,ETHEL))) : pic

PRUDENCE : ked

SAY(FIONA,(SAY(FIONA,(GIVE(ETHEL,JO,ETHEL))))) : qib

PRUDENCE : joc

RUN : muj

GIVE(ETHEL,FIONA,CHESTER) : hil

SAY(FIONA,(SAY(FIONA,(RUN,ETHEL)))) : roh

HOWL : tuq

SAY(JO,(LOATHE(JO,PRUDENCE))) : fek

SAY(JO,(GIVE(ETHEL,CHESTER,BERTIE))) : bop

Table 19.2. *Experiment 1: A later speaker's complete grammar (after 15 cycles)*

PRED(ARG1) → < F-ARG1, F-PRED >

PRED(ARG1,ARG2) → < F-PRED, F-ARG1, F-ARG2 >

PRED(ARG1,ARG2,ARG3) → < F-ARG3, F-PRED, F-ARG1, F-ARG2 >

SAY : feq

PRUDENCE : qej

LOATHE : kih

FIONA : qig

CHESTER : diw

JO : red

LIKE : veb

SAY : dus

LAUGH : woz

BERTIE : xux

ETHEL : kun

JO : nux

HAPPY : soh

WEALTHY : lar

SING : faq

GIVE : cic

GIVE(ETHEL,PRUDENCE,BERTIE) : com

SAY(FIONA,(GIVE(BERTIE,ETHEL,CHESTER))) : buz

GIVE(ETHEL,BERTIE,PRUDENCE) : lag

HAPPY : hel

RUN : roj

BERTIE : faq

SING : xux

RUN : wuz

PRUDENCE : soh

HAPPY : qej

JO : faq

SING : nux

HOWL : tuq

HAPPY : cuc

Table 19.3. *Experiment 1: A 'final' speaker's complete grammar (after 30 cycles)*

$PRED(ARG1) \rightarrow$ < F-ARG1, F-PRED >

$PRED(ARG1,ARG2) \rightarrow$ < F-PRED, F-ARG1, F-ARG2 >

$PRED(ARG1,ARG2,ARG3) \rightarrow$ < F-ARG1, F-PRED, F-ARG2, F-ARG3 >

SAY : dus

PRUDENCE : qej

JO : red

RUN : roj

CHESTER : diw

GIVE : cic

BERTIE : xux

ETHEL : qig

FIONA : qig

WEALTHY : lar

LOATHE : kih

HOWL : tuq

LIKE : veb

LAUGH : woz

SING : faq

HAPPY : soh

Comments on Experiment 1. Several things are shown in this experiment: social coordination, the elimination of synonymy, and the takeover by general rules.

Social coordination. At first, when no speaker has any learned meaning-form correspondences, such correspondences are randomly invented in a way that is not coordinated across the community. Thus the first hearer/acquirers hear a variety of different meaning-form correspondences, and they hear them with differing frequency. Hearer/acquirers do not, however, hear all possible forms corresponding to a given meaning (because, of course, not all possible meaning-form correspondences have been invented by the first generation). So, even in the second generation, there is a limited set of meaning-form correspondences circulating in the community. Hearer/acquirers in these simulations are affected by the frequency with which they have experienced particular meaning-form pairs. They internalise (i.e. acquire) all observed meaning-form pairings, but in their own spoken performance will only utter the form which they acquired first for a particular meaning, which was likely to have been one of the more frequent forms for that meaning in circulation. In this way, the set of form-meaning correspondences in circulation in the community is gradually reduced, resulting in a shared set across all members of the community.

Elimination of synonymy. It will be evident that the process just discussed also leads to the elimination of synonymy. If a speaker has several forms corresponding to one meaning, but only actually uses one of them when speaking, the next generation will only hear a single form for that meaning from this speaker. Taken together with the social coordination just discussed, this clearly results in the elimination of synonymy from the community's language.

Comparing the two mini-grammars in Tables 19.2 and 19.3, note that the 'later' speaker's and the 'final' speaker's respective grammars had different rules for the expression of three-place predications. This reflects and illustrates the random origin of the rules. Which of the 24 possible three-place predication rules comes out on top is a matter of chance, as equally valid alternative forms die out (with their individual owners), and the population converges on the only remaining form.

Generality of syntactic rules. Early generations of speakers in these simulations acquired idiosyncratic, noncompositional rules for particular whole propositions. Speakers in the final stages of the simulations only acquired general syntactic rules, each applying to a whole class of propositions (one-place, two-place, three-place). This is also a consequence of the social coordination taking place in the simulated community. The first generation of speaker/inventors invent various different constituent orders for expressing the propositions they are prompted to express. They invent inconsistently, even within individuals. For instance, a speaker prompted with *LOATHE(BERTIE,FIONA)* might invent an 'SVO' ordering for it, but later, when prompted for another (or even the same!) two-place predication, might invent a 'VOS' ordering for it. At this stage, too, the community will not have settled on a coordinated vocabulary for the basic predicate and argument terms.

A hearer/acquirer can only acquire one rule at a time from any particular observation of a meaning-form pair. In early stages of the simulation, then, it is likely that the observed meaning-form pairs will have inconsistent constituent ordering and also use unfamiliar (i.e. not yet acquired) lexical items. At this stage, because of the limitation to acquiring only one rule per observation, acquirers cannot decompose an observed string into elements corresponding to constituents of the simultaneously observed meaning. For instance, a hearer/acquirer might be given the meaning *LOATHE(BERTIE,FIONA)* and the syllable string *<gem, due, mix>*. At an early stage, the learner is unlikely to have acquired lexical entries linking any of these particular meanings with any of these particular forms, and will not be able to make any generalisation about the ordering of form-elements corresponding to elements of the proposition. In this circumstance, no learning occurs.

As the meaning-form pairs used by speakers may consist of simple term-syllable correspondences (e.g. *ETHEL: faf*), acquirers after a few generations will begin to acquire a coordinated basic vocabulary. Given such a stock of basic vocabulary items, it will now be possible for hearer/acquirers to acquire the constituent-ordering rules that they are able to generalise from their observation of string-proposition pairs. For instance, now a hearer is likely to have acquired, say, the lexical pairings *LOATHE* : *duc*, *BERTIE* : *gem*, and *FIONA* : *mix*. If hearer/acquirers now observe the complex pair *LOATHE(BERTIE,FIONA)* : *<gem, duc, mix>*, they will be able to infer the general rule that two-place predications are expressed in SVO order.

An individual who has acquired a general rule will be prompted, as a speaker, to express a variety of propositions. For some of these propositions the speaker may happen to have, and may use, an idiosyncratic, holistic rule. But for other propositions the speaker will have no such idiosyncratic rule; if such a speaker has a general rule for expressing all propositions of that type (e.g. two-place), it will be used. For the cases where the general rule is applied, the community of learners in the next generation will be presented with a consistent set of exemplars. There will thus be an increasing tendency, as the simulation progresses, for speakers to converge on a common set of meaning-form patterns.

Experiment 2: Frequent Meanings Attract Idioms

In the previous experiment, we saw how idiosyncratic, holistic meaning-form pairings are eliminated from the community language in favour of general rules. This was an effect of the greater generality of general (i.e. nonholistic) rules. By definition, a general rule applies to a larger proportion of the meaning space than does a single holistic rule. In all the experiments described here, the meaning space was restricted for practical purposes, by arbitrarily limiting the depth of recursion, to 4,137 possible meanings. In the first experiment (and in the third and fourth) these meanings were roughly equiprobable, but it is possible to manipulate the meaning space in such a way that a particular meaning occupies a disproportionate share of it. If some particular meaning is expressed with greatly enhanced frequency in the community, we can expect an original holistic form-meaning pairing to persist in the language, regardless of the existence, alongside it, of general rules which could also be used to express this meaning. This is indeed what happens in these simulations, as shown in the current experiment.

In this second experiment, speakers 'choose' to express a particular meaning, *SAY(JO,(HAPPY,FIONA))*, with artificially high probability. In this case, a grammar with three general syntactic rules, plus one idiomatic rule for the particularly frequent meaning emerges, as shown in Table 19.4.

Comments on Experiment 2. Because of the artificially inflated frequency of one proposition, a learner is likely to acquire the idiosyncratic rule involving it before acquiring the two general rules required to express this meaning in a regular way.

Given the meaning space used in these simulations, it was possible to identify a critical frequency band above which a proposition tended to retain an idiomatic, holistic expression. Runs were carried out with the probability of the meaning *SAY(JO,(HAPPY(FIONA)))* being expressed set at various values between 0.01 and 0.09. That is, on an arbitrary occasion of a speaker being prompted to express some meaning, the probability of that meaning being *SAY(JO,(HAPPY(FIONA)))* would have been, say, 0.03, and the probability of the speaker being prompted for any other meaning in the meaning space was, accordingly in this case, 0.97. These results are shown in Figure 19.1.

Experiment 3: Even Limited 'Rule Making' Makes Regular E-Language

The previous experiments have shown the emergence of languages conforming to generalisations that the language acquirers are disposed to make. In these experiments, acquirers had a strong disposition to generalise from observation. That is, if an acquirer could assimilate a particular observed meaning-form pair at the 'cost' of internalising just one general rule, then that general rule would immediately become part of the acquirer's grammar. This can be seen as a strong influence of innate language-forming dispositions on the emerging shape of the community's language. In the next experiment, it will be shown that if individual acquirers' dispositions are considerably weakened, then, although the individuals' grammars will contain many nongeneral rules, the common E-language shared by the community is nevertheless shaped to conform to a small set of general rules.

Table 19.4. *Experiment 2: Final grammar with three general rules and one idiosyncratic, holistic rule for a common meaning*

PRED(ARG1) → < F-PRED, F-ARG1 >

PRED(ARG1,ARG2) → < F-ARG1, F-PRED, F-ARG2 >

PRED(ARG1,ARG2,ARG3) → < F-PRED, F-ARG1, F-ARG2, F-ARG3 >

SAY(JO,(HAPPY,FIONA)) : noz

HOWL : jad

PRUDENCE : laz

FIONA : qaf

JO : vow

LIKE : viz

ETHEL : doy

HAPPY : hal

SING : wuv

SAY : tan

LAUGH : sug

BERTIE : jep

LOATHE : rey

WEALTHY : mey

CHESTER : cam

GIVE : his

RUN : voh

In this experiment, acquirers were disposed to generalise from experience (i.e. to induce general rules) with a probability of only 0.25. Otherwise, acquirers simply rote-memorized the form-meaning correspondences they experienced. The resulting internalised grammars are redundant, as will be discussed. The emergent community E-language generated by such redundant grammars can be described fully by the general rules and the lexicon, without use of the redundant idiosyncratic rules. That is, all the idiosyncratic rote-learnt correspondences conform to the general rules anyway. Some acquirers even acquire no general

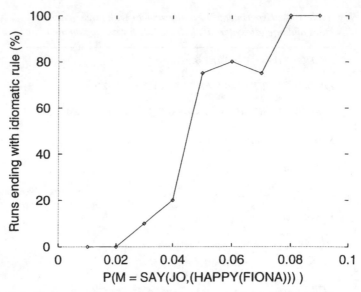

Figure 19.1. These runs showed that when the frequency of the prompt for the meaning *SAY(JO,(HAPPY(FIONA)))* was 2% or below of all meaning prompts, this meaning was not expressed idiomatically. When the frequency of the prompt for this meaning was 8% or above, it was always expressed idiomatically. Between 2% and 8%, results were mixed, with idiomatic expression tending to increase with frequency.

rules at all, but their rote-learnt sequences still conform to the rule-generated community language.

Comments on Experiment 3. We have become accustomed, in the Chomskyan era, to assuming that regularities observed in the language behaviour of a community will be represented economically, as regularities, in speakers' heads. And, further, we have assumed that it is the regularities in speakers' heads that in fact determine the regular observed behaviour. This experiment shows (again) the reverse effect, the effect of social coordination on the grammars of individuals. The individuals in this experiment all internalised many nongeneral rules, rote-learnt facts about particular meaning-form pairs. But these holistically memorised meaning-form pairs all conformed to the general constituent-ordering rules which had become established in the community as a result of a quite weak (25%) tendency to generalise from observation. If 'the language' is taken to be the abstract system, described in the most economical way, apparent in the behaviour (including intuitive judgments of form-meaning correspondence) of the community, we are dealing with E-language. The economising generalisations made by the descriptive linguist are, then, statements about the E-language, and not about any individual's I-language.

Table 19.5. *Experiment 3: Final grammar with three general rules, a lexicon and a set of rote-learned holistic rules, which nevertheless conform to the general rules*

GENERAL RULES

$PRED(ARG1) \rightarrow$ < F-ARG1, F-PRED >

$PRED(ARG1,ARG2) \rightarrow$ < F-ARG1, F-ARG2, F-PRED>

$PRED(ARG1,ARG2,ARG3) \rightarrow$ < F-PRED, F-ARG1, F-ARG2, F-ARG3 >

LEXICON

BERTIE : sud	*CHESTER* : qot	*ETHEL* : lef	*FIONA* : def
GIVE : xiy	*HAPPY* : soy	*HOWL* : juq	*JO* : qaq
LAUGH : sal	*LIKE* : hoc	*LOATHE* : qow	*PRUDENCE* : lef
RUN : fur	*SAY* : xuh	*SING* : juq	*WEALTHY* : mug

ROTE-LEARNED CORRESPONDENCES

HAPPY(CHESTER) : < qot, soy >

RUN(CHESTER) : < qot, fur >

GIVE(JO,JO,BERTIE) : < xiy, qaq, qaq, sud >

GIVE(JO,ETHEL,PRUDENCE) : < xiy, qaq, lef, lef >

SAY(JO,(HAPPY(FIONA))) : < qaq, < def, soy >, xuh>

SAY(JO,(LOATHE(FIONA,CHESTER))) : < qaq, < def, qot, qow >, xuh >

SAY(ETHEL,(LIKE(FIONA,FIONA))) : < lef, < def, def, hoc >, xuh >

SAY(BERTIE,(GIVE(ETHEL,CHESTER, BERTIE))) : < sud, < xiy, lef, qot, sud >, xuh >

SAY(FIONA,(GIVE(ETHEL,FIONA,BERTIE))) : < def, < xiy, lef, def, sud >, xuh >

SAY(FIONA,(SAY(JO,(LOATHE(JO,FIONA))))) : < def, < qaq, < qaq, def, qow > xuh > xuh >

SAY(JO,(SAY(JO,(LOATHE(BERTIE,FIONA))))) : < qaq, < qaq, < sud, def, qow >, xuh >, xuh >

SAY(FIONA,(SAY(BERTIE,(GIVE(JO,ETHEL,CHESTER))))) : < def, < sud, < xiy, qaq, lef, qot >, xuh >, xuh >

Experiment 4: A Binary Rule Supersedes Nonbinary Rules

The grammars arrived at in the three previous experiments missed a kind of generalisation that one normally finds in real languages. These simple grammars all had three separate general rules for each of the three types of predication: one-place, two-place, and three-place. In natural languages, of course, one typically finds consistent constituent orders for intransitive, monotransitive and ditransitive clauses. The previous experiments reached these unnatural grammars because the generalising principles available to speaker/inventors and hearer/acquirers were limited to generalisations over constituent order based on the elements of the given meaning representations. For example, an inventor inventing a rule to express a two-place predication shuffled the three terms involved *(PRED, ARG1, ARG2)* into some random order. In parallel, all that an acquirer noted when internalising a general rule on the basis of an observation was the order of the constituents. This ordering was the only permitted operation on meaning representations. There was no linkage between the orderings 'chosen' for one-place, two-place and three-place predications.

In the final experiment, speaker/inventors and hearer/acquirers were allowed a further operation on meaning representations, namely restructuring into binary bracketed structures. For example,

LOATHE(BERTIE,FIONA)

would be restructured as

[LOATHE,[BERTIE,FIONA]]

And

GIVE(JO,CHESTER,BERTIE)

would be restructured as

[GIVE,[JO,[CHESTER,BERTIE]]].

The restructuring operation thus reduces all meaning representations (one-place, two-place, three-place) to uniformly binary (often recursively nested) structures. Such binary structures could be input to the same (re)ordering and lexical lookup operations as were used by speaker/inventors and hearer/acquirers in the previous experiments.

The binary restructuring rule can apply to predications of any degree (one-place, two-place, three-place), and so is more general than any of the 'semi-general' rules we have seen emerging in the previous experiments.

In this experiment, individuals were permitted to invent /learn either (1) semi-general rules for each type of proposition (one-place, two-place, three-place), as before, or (2) to break any proposition into a binary-branching structure, and invent/learn a general rule for expressing any such binary-branching structure. The (1) and (2) possibilities here were chosen at random on each occasion of use, but with equal probability.

In this experiment, instead of three separate rules for one-place, two-place and three-place predications, the community converged on a language in which all types of propositions were expressed with uniformly right-branching binary structures. The internalised binary restructuring rule cannot be represented in the same format as the constituent-ordering rules given in the grammars of previous experiments, and so will not be given here (in fact, of course, it was a piece of computer code). Rather, a set of example sentences produced in the evolved community language is given in Table 19.6, along with the lexicon of the language.

Comments on Experiment 4. The single binary rule covers more data than any of the semi-general rules specific to particular degrees of predication. The less productive rules were permitted throughout to speakers/inventors and hearers/acquirers, and were indeed present earlier in the simulation. But they were superseded by the single more general binary structure–inducing rule.

(The fact that this particular run of the experiment ended with right-branching, rather than left-branching, structures is not significant. It was an artefact of this particular implementation, deriving from an 'innate' behaviour of the individuals, who 'discovered' right-branching structures before happening on left-branching ones.)

Comments and Conclusions

Summary

In brief, the four experiments have shown the following.

Experiment 1. For each type of proposition (one-place, two-place, three-place predication), a general rule specifying the ordering of the forms expressing their constituent terms is favoured over a set of specific rules, each specifying how to express a particular proposition. Individual learners are capable of acquiring either the specific or the general type of rule. The effect is due to the general rules having a greater 'yield' in the performance data produced by speakers.

Table 19.6. *Experiment 4: Final language, which expresses all propositions as binary right-branching structures*

LEXICON

SING : xax

RUN : xap

GIVE : bul

CHESTER : caz

ETHEL : ner

SAY : rih

JO : wom

HOWL : pin

WEALTHY : hoq

HAPPY : luq

FIONA : caz

LIKE : xuc

BERTIE : mub

PRUDENCE : xuc

LOATHE : xok

LAUGH : *wup*

SOME EXAMPLE SENTENCES

MEANING	SENTENCE
HAPPY(FIONA)	< luq, caz >
LOATHE(FIONA,BERTIE)	< xok,< caz, mub >>
GIVE(FIONA,ETHEL,CHESTER)	< bul,< caz,< ner, caz >>>
SAY(JO,(LOATHE(FIONA,BERTIE)))	< rih,< wom,< xok, < caz, mub >>>>
SAY(BERTIE,(SAY(ETHEL,(RUN(JO)))))	< rih,< mub,< rih,< ner,< xap, wom >>>>>

Experiment 2. In a language evolving from nothing, as in these experiments, if a particular meaning is used with disproportionate frequency, that meaning will tend to retain a nongeneral (idiomatic) expression in the history of a language. This is an effect of the evolution of the language from original sets of expressions specific to particular meanings toward sets of expressions falling under general rules. The idiomatic expression of a commonly used meaning is a conservative feature, reflecting an earlier stage of the language. In the simple scenarios of these experiments, if a community is 'seeded' with a 'mature' grammar having only general rules and no idiosyncratic rules, an idiosyncratic rule will not 'grow' for a commonly expressed meaning. This is because systems with completely general rules can be securely transmitted from one generation to the next. (However, a more complex and more realistic model might postulate that more frequent expressions are more prone to phonetic erosion in the cycle of language transmission; this could lead to the introduction of idiosyncratic forms for the more common meanings.)

Experiment 3. Even when individuals are biased against acquiring general rules, rather than specific rules for particular meanings, the language that emerges in the community will conform to general rules. Individuals acquire large sets of rules specific to particular meanings, alongside a few general rules. The grammars of such speakers are redundant. The general rules that (some) speakers do acquire are sufficient to impose a convergent pressure on the language data produced as exemplars for the next generation of learners. In this experiment, the learners were biased 25:75 against internalising general rules, yet the population still converged on general rules. I hypothesise that this bias could be taken much further (say to 1:99) with the same eventual effect, although it would take longer for populations to converge on languages conforming to general rules.

Experiment 4. A very general type of rule capable of being applied to all types of proposition (one-place, two-place, three-place predications) is favoured over the rather less general types of rule which only apply to one type of proposition each. This is because the more general type of rule, once introduced into the community, has a greater 'yield' in the performance data presented by the next generation of learners than the somewhat less general rules specific to each type of proposition.

Biocultural Coevolution

The model used here incorporates neither Darwinian natural selection nor rewards for successful communication. Throughout a given experiment, the generalising dispositions attributed to individuals remain constant. And although the individuals speak and hear, there is no modelling of real communication, since the hearers are always given both the full form and the full meaning for the form-meaning pairs uttered by speakers. A more sophisticated simulation would attempt to model the coevolution of innate generalising dispositions and of languages as cultural objects created, transmitted and maintained by communities.

It has been shown here that more general linguistic rules are favoured by a completely nonbiological mechanism, namely the social transmission of language from one generation to the next. But this does not mean that natural selection is necessarily neutral with regard to degrees of linguistic generalisation. To the extent that the social process leads to grammars with particular types of generalisations, there will be evolutionary pressure to produce individuals capable of acquiring such grammars with facility. In a coevolutionary scenario, the individuals' innate, biologically determined, dispositions to make certain kinds of linguistic generalisation are the source of the learning behaviours from which the social transmission process selects to produce communal grammars of greater generalisation. But in turn, the evolved, more general communal grammars provide a humanmade environment which selects for individuals with greater aptitude for learning just such languages.[8]

Limits to the Favouring of General Rules

What are the limits to the kind of generality towards which languages will apparently tend, according to the tendencies shown in these experiments? The kinds of generalisation attributed to speaker/inventors and hearer/acquirers in this study have all been relatively sensible. More extreme and far less sensible kinds of generalisation are theoretically possible. For example, on hearing a particular syllable used to express a particular atomic meaning, an acquirer might in theory make the absurd overgeneralisation that any syllable can be used to express any meaning. Human learners don't do that – why not?

Any tendency to make overgeneralisations of such an absurd kind would presumably be eliminated by natural selection based on success in correctly divining a speaker's meaning and/or successfully signalling one's own meaning. Any mutants displaying any tendency to generalise from the primary linguistic data in ways which will lead to speakers' being misunderstood, as they would be if they used any form to convey any meaning, will be at a disadvantage.

How This Model Relates to Others

I will give here a few brief notes on the more significant differences between the simulations reported here and similar current work by Kirby (this volume) and Batali (in press). (A much fuller survey and comparison of models of this general type is to be found in Hurford (in press).)

Compositionality. Kirby's model claims to explain the emergence of compositionality in language. In my model, the availability of compositional principles is assumed. This is apparent in both the invention and the acquisition behaviours. The essence of compositionality in a broad sense is not peculiar to language. Any deliberate behaviour that can be analyzed into parts will work according to the principle that the outcome of the whole behaviour is a function of the separate outcomes of the parts of the behaviour. For example, the chimpanzee behaviour of picking up a stick, breaking it to an appropriate length, inserting it into an anthill, withdrawing it and licking off the ants depends for its overall success on the success of each constituent action. Vision certainly works on a compositional principle, with a complex picture being built up from a host of sensory inputs. (This is not to deny the existence of some differences between the compositionality of language and of other behaviours.)

Speed. The simulations reported here converge on coordinated languages with syntactic rules much faster than those described by Kirby (this volume) and Batali (in press). This is due to the far greater power attributed to individuals in this simulation, inherent especially in their invention capacity. The goal of this chapter has been to show an effect of social transmission on the kinds of generalisations that may be hypothesised to be innately available to individuals. For this purpose, generalisations of a certain power had to be introduced, in order to be compared. Exactly what generalisations humans are in fact disposed to make in their language acquisition is an empirical matter.

From vocabulary to grammar: analysis versus synthesis. Both the simulations described here and those of Kirby (this volume) go through an early stage of 'one-word' communication. At this stage, speakers have no general grammar rules, but only lexical items.

In Kirby's model, at the one-word stage, the single utterances memorised by speakers express whole propositions. Kirby's simulation thus follows an 'analytic' route from vocabulary to grammar. In the analytic route, preexisting unitary signals with conventionalised, but complex, meanings become decomposed into segments, to each of which is assigned some subpart of the original complex meaning; the decomposition and assignment of meaning is such that the (original) complex meaning is a function of the (new) meanings of the parts.

In my model, the early memorised utterances can also stand for atomic subparts of meanings, such as names and predicates. These simulations follow a 'synthetic' route from vocabulary to grammar. In the synthetic route, preexisting unitary signals with conventionalised meanings are concatenated into strings; these strings then become organised to convey meanings composed of the original meanings of the units.

It is not a priori obvious whether language evolution had to take just one of these routes, or whether it was a mosaic of both routes. See Wray (1998) for some relevant arguments.

The Last Word

Contrasting the empirical claims implicit in various possible formalisms which capture different types of generalisation over linguistic data, Chomsky presents two sets of conceivable data over which generalisations of two different types are respectively possible: he numbers these examples (16) and (17), and writes of

the empirical hypothesis that regularities of the type exemplified in (16) are those found in natural languages, and are of the type that children learning a language will expect; whereas cyclic regularities of the type exemplified in (17), though perfectly genuine, abstractly, are not characteristic of natural language, are not of the type for which children will intuitively search in language materials, and are much more difficult for the language-learner to construct on the basis of scattered data. (Chomsky 1965: 43)

Note the strong implication that 'found in natural languages' equates to 'what the language learner will construct'. This chapter accepts the contribution to the shape of languages made by the natural generalising dispositions of language learners. What it shows is that the mechanism of social transmission of language adds an extra filter, or selection principle, to the processes giving rise to the generalisations that are characteristic of natural languages.

Notes

1. This work was inspired by the work reported in Kirby (this volume), but diverges from it in significant ways. The seeds for these ideas germinated during a Fellowship at the Collegium Budapest Institute for Advanced Study; the work was also supported by a research grant (R000 237551) from the UK Economic and Social Research Council. I thank Simon Kirby, Michael Studdert-Kennedy, Ted Briscoe and Mike Oliphant for stimulation and advice.
2. The terms 'E-language' and 'I-language' were introduced by Chomsky (1986); the 'Arena of Use' is discussed by Hurford (1987, 1991).
3. This is not always simple random selection from a list, as will be explained later.
4. In the fourth experiment, there was an additional kind of rule, to be described later.

5. See Wray (1998) for arguments that holistic expressions played a crucial role in the evolution of language from protolanguage.
6. Of course, at the very beginning of a simulation run, conditions are somewhat different from the situation at any later time. For example, at the end of the first complete simulation cycle (steps 1–3), we have three of the original adults who still have no language, one adult who began as a child and so has acquired some language, and one new child without language. So it takes four complete cycles through the simulation program to get four adults who have learned some language.
7. That is, maximally economical in terms of number of rules. The economy referred to here is not a matter of processing, or function.
8. For some other work on the coevolution of languages as social objects and of brains as hosts to linguistic competence, see the later chapters of Deacon (1997) and Hurford and Kirby (1999).

References

Batali, J. 1998. Computational simulations of the emergence of grammar. In J. R. Hurford, M. Studdert-Kennedy and C. Knight (eds), *Approaches to the Evolution of Language: Social and cognitive bases*. Cambridge: Cambridge University Press, pp. 405–426.

Batali, J. In press. The negotiation and acquisition of recursive grammars as a result of competition among exemplars. In E. J. Briscoe (ed), *Linguistic Evolution through Language Acquisition: Formal and computational models*. Cambridge: Cambridge University Press.

Cann, R. 1993. *Formal Semantics*. Cambridge: Cambridge University Press.

Chomsky, N. 1965. *Aspects of the Theory of Syntax*. Cambridge, MA: MIT Press.

Chomsky, N. 1986. *Knowledge of Language: Its nature, origin, and use*. New York: Praeger.

Deacon, T. 1997. *The Symbolic Species: The co-evolution of language and the human brain*. London: Penguin.

Hurford, J. R. 1987. *Language and Number: The emergence of a cognitive system*. Oxford: Blackwell.

Hurford, J. R. 1991. Nativist and functional explanations in language acquisition. In I. Roca (ed), *Logical Issues in Language Acquisition*. Dordrecht: Foris, pp. 85–136.

Hurford, J. R. In press. Expression /induction models of language evolution: dimensions and issues. In E. J. Briscoe (ed), *Linguistic Evolution through Language Acquisition: Formal and computational models*. Cambridge: Cambridge University Press.

Hurford, J. R. and S. Kirby. 1999. Co-evolution of language-size and the critical period. In D. Birdsong (ed), *The Critical Period Hypothesis and Second Language Acquisition*. Hillsdale, NJ: Erlbaum, pp. 39–63.

Oliphant, M. 1997. *Formal Approaches to Innate and Learned Communication: Laying the foundation for language*. Doctoral dissertation, University of California, San Diego.

Steels, L. 1996a. A self-organizing spatial vocabulary. *Artificial Life Journal* 2: 319–332.

Steels, L. 1996b. Emergent adaptive lexicons. In P. Maes, M. Mataric, J.-A. Meyer, J. Pollack and S. W. Wilson (eds), *From Animals to Animats 4: Proceedings of the*

Fourth International Conference on Simulation of Adaptive Behavior. Cambridge, MA: MIT Press, pp. 562–567.

Steels, L. 1997. Self-organizing vocabularies. In C. G. Langton and K. Shimohara (eds), *Artificial Life V: Proceedings of the Fifth International Workshop on the Synthesis and Simulation of Living Systems*. Cambridge, MA: MIT Press.

Steels, L. In press. The spontaneous self-organization of an adaptive language. In S. Muggleton (ed), *Machine Intelligence 15*. Oxford: Oxford University Press.

Wray, A. 1998. Protolanguage as a holistic system for social interaction. *Language and Communication* **18**: 47–67.

20

Words, Memes and Language Evolution

ROBERT P. WORDEN

Summary

This chapter describes a precise sense in which language change can be regarded as a form of evolution – not of the language itself, but of the individual words which constitute the language. Many prominent features of language can be understood as the result of this evolution.

In a unification-based theory of language, each word sense is represented in the brain by a reentrant feature structure, which embodies the syntax, semantics and phonology of the word. When understanding or generating a sentence, we unify the feature structures of the words in the sentence to form a derivation structure. The feature structure for any word can then be learnt by feature structure generalisation, which complements unification to replicate the word feature structure precisely in a new mind. By this replication, word feature structures propagate precisely from one generation to the next, just as DNA propagates precisely in cell replication. Words are memes.

The precision and transparency of DNA replication underlies the structure and diversity of life. Similarly, the precise and transparent replication of word memes underlies the structure and diversity of language. As word feature structures propagate from generation to generation, they undergo slow changes from selection pressures which cause many types of language regularities.

In this analogy, each language is an ecology, and each word is one species in the ecology. In language as in nature, different species exert selection pressures on one another. The pressures on a word are those factors which cause people to use it more or less often, and to learn it more or less easily – useful meaning, distinctive sound, lack of ambiguities, syntactic fit with other words, learnability, social acceptability and economy of expression. I illustrate by examples how these selection pressures act on words, creating many prominent features of language such as the Greenberg-Hawkins universals.

There are two alternative explanations of language structure – that it reflects genetic evolution of the human brain, or that it arises from the evolution of word memes. Evolution of word memes proceeds much faster than evolution of brains, and so actually removes the selection pressures which might lead to genetic evolution of language structures in brains. For many features of language, there is no need to suppose that they reflect any innate structure in the brain.

Words as Memes

The idea that language change is somehow analogous to evolution has a long and chequered history. Pre-Darwinian evolution, Lamarckian evolution and teleology have all been invoked in dubious explanations, which have given the idea of language evolution a bad name – but nevertheless, some kind of Darwinian evolution of languages is now regarded as a valid tool for thinking about language change (McMahon 1994). Other chapters in this volume (Hurford, this volume; Kirby, this volume) report on computer simulations of such an evolutionary process.

One form of this idea goes as follows: each word is represented in the brain by a package of information that embodies that word's sound, syntax and meaning. When people speak to one another, they combine the word packages to make sentence packages. A child, observing the sentence packages passing between adults, can somehow extract the component word packages, and thus learn the words. Thus the word packages propagate from generation to generation. Over many generations, as word packages reproduce via the speaking/learning mechanism, some words are more successful than others – more commonly used or easier to learn – and there is competition between the different 'species' of words. This competition leads to changes in the balance of word species in a language, and so leads to language change.

In this model, words are a form of Dawkins's (1976) 'memes' – culturally transmitted replicators that propagate through a population. Dawkins (1982: 290) defines a meme as 'a unit of cultural inheritance, hypothesised as analogous to the particulate gene, and as naturally selected by virtue of its 'phenotypic' consequences on its own survival and reproduction in the cultural environment'. As words are culturally inherited by learning, and are in some sense particulate like genes, it is clear that words might act as memes.

Such a picture is quite appealing, and could be used to model aspects of language change. However, as it stands it is unsatisfactory because of its looseness. Just what are these packages of information – what is in a word package and what is not? What is the mechanism of reproduction and what information can it propagate? Such a theory is like the theory of Darwinian evolution before the discovery of DNA replication – it is quite plausible, but fundamental questions remain about how it really works. Until we find the answers to these questions, the idea remains an appealing story rather than a predictive theory.

When the structure and replication mechanism of DNA was discovered, Darwinian evolution could be put on a much firmer footing. Core questions, such as the relation between Mendelian discrete inheritance and continuously variable traits, could begin to be answered.

DNA replication is done by a sequence of chemical analysis (splitting the DNA helix in two) and synthesis (accumulating new bases from the surrounding cell) – precisely matched to preserve the information in the order of the base pairs. The DNA molecule may be many millions of base pairs long, but can still replicate precisely with very few transcription errors. Any sequence of legal base pairs can be replicated; in this sense the replication is completely transparent to any sequence, and so can transmit any genetic information.

It is this extreme precision and transparency of DNA replication which underlies the huge diversity of life. Because each DNA molecule can carry a large amount of information, and can propagate it faithfully from generation to generation, this information can be used for the design of living things. Crossing and mutation create diversity – but without the precise DNA replication, that diversity would never be preserved long enough for selection to act on it.

We now see the challenge faced by a 'words as memes' theory of language evolution. If the word packages do not carry enough information, or cannot be reproduced faithfully enough, they cannot serve as the DNA of language; changes introduced by selection of word memes might be wiped out by any imprecision of the replication mechanism. From what we have said so far, word replication (by a child observing the words used by its parents) might well be 'sloppy' enough to wipe out subtle changes.

Is there a mechanism of word replication precise enough to serve as a basis for evolution of word memes? There is such a mechanism – a theory of language learning which I have developed within the framework of unification-based grammars such as Categorial Grammars (Oehrle, Bach and Wheeler 1988), HPSG (Pollard and Sag 1993) or LFG (Kaplan and Bresnan 1982). The theory is described in Worden (1997). I shall give enough detail here to show how word replication, like DNA replication, works by a process of analysis and synthesis – and how it propagates information precisely from one generation to the next.

In this theory, each word is described by a feature structure or 'script' – a treelike information structure in the brain, with information stored on the nodes of the tree. The feature structure for each word embodies the sound of the word, its meaning and the syntax associated with it. In this respect, the theory is fully lexicalised – all the syntax of a language is embodied in the feature structures of its words, not in any separate phrase structure rules or parameters. If you can learn the feature structures of the words, then you can learn the whole language.

Two simple word feature structures for the words 'Fred' and 'sleeps' are shown on the left of Figure 20.1. The treelike form, with information encoded in slot values such as 'cla:human' (meaning the class of this entity is human) on the nodes, is evident. The curved lines are reentrant links, which imply that any subtrees beneath the two ends of the link must be identical. The key operation on feature structures is called unification (Shieber 1986), and has been extensively studied mathematically (Siekmann 1989; Carpenter 1992). It is like a form of chemical synthesis – to unify two feature structures, you overlay them where they have structure in common, and include all the structure of each in the result. In Figure 20.1, the feature structures F for 'Fred' and S for 'sleeps' are unified to understand the sentence 'Fred sleeps'. The sentence meaning is the right-hand branch of the result, written as $F \cup S$.

In unification-based grammars such as HPSG, LFG and categorial grammars, unification is the central operation for both sentence understanding and generation. This gives a very powerful model of language performance, which can account for many intricate syntactic and semantic features of language, and has been tested against many languages. Mature adult languages can be well described by unification-based grammars (e.g. Pollard and Sag 1993).

In the unification-based grammar which I shall use here, if a sentence consists of words w, x, y... with feature structures W, X, Y..., then the sentence is understood by unifying the feature structures of all its words. The result of this unification is a feature structure called the derivation $D = W \cup X \cup Y...$, and always contains the meaning of the sentence in one of its branches. D also contains the feature structure for every word in the sentence amongst its substructures, because it is made by unifying them. Within these feature structures are the sounds of all the words of the sentence – which was the starting point for sentence understanding. Figure 20.1 shows a simple example for the sentence 'Fred sleeps', where the derivation $F \cup S$ contains feature structures for both words within it.

How do these word feature structures replicate, as a child learns a language? There is another operation on feature structures, called generalisation (Shieber 1986). This is the complementary operation to unification – and as unification is like chemical synthesis, so generalisation is like chemical analysis. The generalisation of two feature structures A and B is written as $A \cap B$, and is

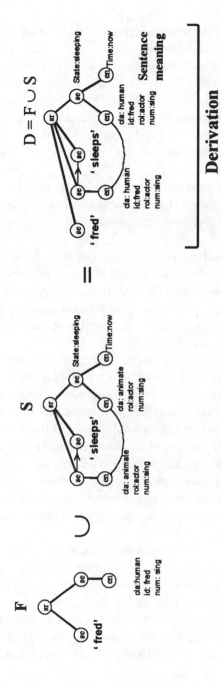

Figure 20.1. Word feature structures and their unification in a unification-based model of language.

357

formed by placing the two structures one on top of the other and only retaining the parts they both have in common.

Suppose there are several derivations D_1, D_2, D_3 ... for sentences all containing some word W. Since D_1, D_2, D_3... all have the feature structure for W within them, their generalisation $(D_1 \cap D_2 \cap D_3 ...)$ will also contain W as a substructure – and if there are several distinct derivations, their generalisation contains little else, so that to a very good approximation $(D_1 \cap D_2 \cap D_3 ...) = W$. By generalising the derivations, we can recover the original feature structure W.

In this sense, unification and generalisation play complementary roles in word replication, like chemical synthesis and analysis. Unification combines W with other feature structures, and generalisation recovers it from the results.

Suppose a child learning a language does not know the word W, but knows other words. Hearing sentences containing W and the other words, it can often infer the intended meaning from the context. In this way, it can reconstruct the derivations D_1, D_2, D_3 ..., even though it does not know W. By generalising them, it recovers the feature structure, and thus learns a new word. That is how children learn their native language.

The learning process is illustrated in Figure 20.2, where a child observes two distinct uses of the word 'sleeps'. In each case the child can infer the intended meaning nonlinguistically from the context, enabling construction of the whole derivation D. Generalising these derivations, the child learns the feature structure for the previously unknown word 'sleeps'. This learning mechanism is embedded in a Bayesian learning theory, which defines how many examples are needed to learn a word. Typically, in order to learn the word feature structure, a child requires about six good examples of the use of any word (where the other words in a sentence are known, and the intended meaning of the sentence can be inferred). The learning mechanism is very robust against poorly understood or misheard examples.

The learning process of unification and generalisation is the language equivalent of DNA replication. It works for any word feature structure – no matter how complex or what part of speech – and given a few examples of each word, it works reliably to reconstruct the original feature structure. That is the faithful and transparent replication of word feature structures on which the evolution of words is built. I have built a program which replicates word feature structures by just this process, and it can learn faithfully all parts of speech in a representative fragment of English.

The resulting model of language evolution, by replication of word feature structures, is shown in Figure 20.3.

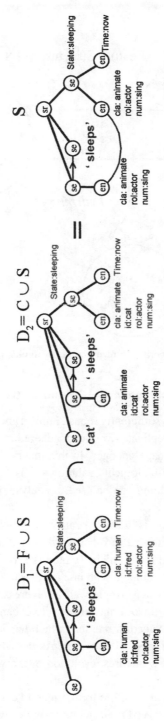

Figure 20.2. The word 'sleeps' is incorporated in two derivations by unification, and is recovered from them by generalisation.

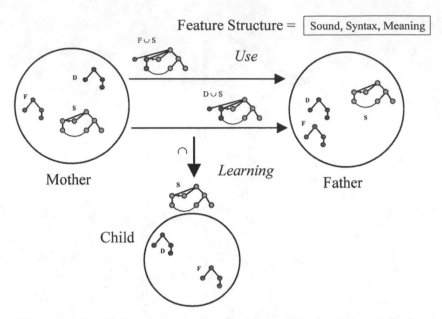

Figure 20.3. Replication of word feature structures by unification and generalisation.

Language Change by Evolution of Word Feature Structures

This learning mechanism is sufficiently robust, faithful and transparent to allow word feature structures to replicate over many generations, and thus to evolve. As words evolve, the language changes. In this theory, 'evolution of words' is not just an analogy with biological evolution – it is a precise evolutionary theory of language change, and can be used to analyse directly the observed forms of language change.

In this analogy, each word is like a separate species – not mixing its 'geno-type' (feature structure) with that of other words – and a language is like an entire ecology. Every word has a 'niche' which is a part of meaning space; different word species may compete with one another to occupy useful niches in the space of meanings which people want to express. By combining pro-ductively with other words, a word may effectively expand its meaning niche, and so prosper; this is the selection pressure which has led to the unbounded productivity of language, and to all of syntax. As the whole of a language is defined by its word feature structures, evolution of the words constitutes the whole of language change.

Each word species is a parasitic life form, much like a virus. A virus needs a living cell to host it, and a word needs a human brain. As I write, I have fifty thousand separate species of word parasite in my head, and I am spreading them into this document. You in turn are absorbing them, because you have virtually the same fifty thousand parasites already in your head. Some of these species are thousands of years old, and some are much younger.

To see how word feature structures evolve over generations, we need to understand the selection pressures which shape their evolution. 'Fitness' of a word species depends on how frequently it is used by speakers, and on how easy it is for children to learn the word when they hear it. There are six main factors which determine the fitness of a word feature structure:

Useful meaning: A word will tend to be used frequently if it expresses a meaning which people find useful, and need to express often.

Productivity: The use of a word depends not just on its own meaning, but also on how it combines with other words to express useful compound meanings – on the productivity of the constructs in which it figures. Evolution of word species is essentially symbiotic; the fitness of a word species depends on how well it cooperates with other species.

Economy: If a meaning can be expressed in two ways, and one is quicker and more economical than the other, then the quicker construct will tend to be used more, and therefore learnt more.

Lack of ambiguity: As language grows in productivity and complexity of sentences, the scope for ambiguity multiplies. The mind performs prodigious feats in resolving ambiguities on the fly; but any word feature structure which tends to cause ambiguity will be avoided, and be selected against.

Ease of learning: The learning mechanism is unconscious and automatic; to learn a word, a child needs to collect about six examples of its use, in unambiguous sentences where the child knows all the other words in the sentence, and can infer the intended meaning nonlinguistically. Ease of learning requires frequent use in unambiguous constructs, where the intended meaning can be inferred. Regular constructs can also reduce the amount of learning required, so making learning easier.

Social identification: We judge people by their language, and know that we are judged by our own language. Wherever people wish to identify themselves with some social group, they will tend to adopt the language of the group. Word evolution is continually shaped by peoples' social aspirations.

These six selection pressures act in different ways at different times to shape the words of a language.

Examples of Word Evolution

I shall use four examples to illustrate how word evolution creates language structure:

> *Semantic role selection*: how languages distinguish between agents, patients, actors and themes;
>
> *Verbs of motion*: what meanings are packaged with the verb, and what is expressed in other ways;
>
> *Language universals*: such as the Greenberg-Hawkins universals, leading to broad generalisations such as the Head Parameter;
>
> *Regularity and irregularity*: the mixture of the two seen in most languages.

For each example, I shall describe which of the six main selection pressures have given rise to the language features we see.

Semantic Role Selection

In a sentence such as 'Fred punched Tony' it is important to know who ended up with a bloody nose – who took the agent role, and who was the patient, in the punching event. Languages use a variety of devices to signal this information (Andrews 1985).

There are three main roles to distinguish – agent and patient of a transitive verb, and actor (or theme) of an intransitive verb. As there are at most two main semantic roles for any verb, languages only need to convey a binary distinction. They typically do so in one of three ways – by word order, by nominative/accusative case marking on nouns, or by ergative/absolutive case marking.

In languages which use word ordering to define roles (e.g. English SVO ordering), this ordering constraint is built into the feature structure for each verb. In such languages, case marking of the nouns tends to be redundant, and so is not used – a selection pressure for economy acting on noun feature structures. If a few common verbs have role determination by word order, this reduces the need for case marking on all nouns. This in turn implies that all verbs need to use word order to determine semantic roles. Thus a symbiotic selection pressure acts back and forth between nouns and verbs to create a regularity in the language.

In a more weakly ordered language such as Latin, where verb feature structures do not define semantic role by position, the nouns needs case markings to distinguish agents from patients. There are two main case-marking systems – nominative/accusative and ergative/absolutive. In both systems, the more commonly occurring case (the one which occurs in two out of the three semantic roles) tends to be unmarked, with fewer phonemes – a result of selection for economy.

For case-marked languages, the same verb feature structures work unchanged with either form of noun case marking – nominative/accusative or ergative/absolutive. So there is no mutual verb-noun selection pressure to line up all nouns along the nominative/accusative or ergative/absolutive axis, and mixed-ergative languages (which have both systems of case marking) are known, though rare. What is the selection pressure which disfavours such mixtures, and drives most languages to one axis or the other?

In weakly ordered languages, adjective-noun agreement is important in matching each adjective with the right noun, which may be separated from it. If nouns have mixed nominative/accusative and ergative/absolutive case marking, the cases for adjectives will be more complex and harder to learn. So the selection pressure for unambiguous matching of adjectives with nouns will drive languages towards pure nominative/accusative or pure ergative/absolutive case-marking systems. This is a weaker selection pressure than the pressure to fix semantic roles, and so acts more slowly. Mixed-ergative languages may be long-lived remnants of a collision between languages with opposite case-marking schemes, where the adjective-matching selection pressure has not yet extinguished either form of case marking.

Verbs of Motion

The elements of meaning which can be directly encoded in verbs of motion, rather than being expressed by other particles or phrases nearby, are the following:

The *motion* itself;
The *path* relative to the ground of motion (into, under, over, . . .);
The *manner* of motion (rolling, staggering, . . .);
The *form* of the moving thing (round, long, . . .).

Talmy (1985) noted that every language encodes just two of these – the fact of motion and one of the last three properties. Languages such as English directly encode the motion and the manner of motion, Spanish encodes the motion and its relation to the ground, and some American languages such as Atsugewi encode just the motion and the form of the moving thing.

Why does no language encode more or less than two of the attributes of the motion, and why is it the same two uniformly across any language? We can understand why, in terms of the selection pressures on the verb feature structures.

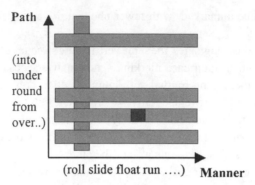

Figure 20.4. Portions of meaning space occupied by words describing one and two aspects of the motion.

The need to encode some of these aspects of the motion arises from the selection pressure to express useful meanings. The choice then is between expressing those meanings intrinsically in the verb itself, and expressing them in nearby particles and phrases. This choice is determined by a tradeoff between economy (for which you might tend to express everything in the verb itself) and ease of learning.

Consider a language where the verbs encode not two, but three or four of the possible elements of meaning. Suppose each optional element of meaning (relation to ground, manner, form of figure) has around ten distinct values. To encode motion plus one optional element, you require ten verbs of motion. Those encoding just the path are shown as horizontal bars on Figure 20.4. But to encode motion plus two optional elements, you would require a hundred verbs – like the small square in Figure 20.4 – which requires much more learning to master the system. Also each such verb will occur ten times less frequently in the child's learning data, and so will take ten times longer to learn. Going from one optional element to two imposes a massive extra learning load.

Why is the choice of optional element a languagewide choice? One answer comes from niche sizes. Consider a language that already has several verbs encoding motion and path of motion, like the horizontal bars in Figure 20.4. If a new verb arises which encodes just motion and manner of motion (the vertical bar), its meaning cuts across the meanings of path-encoding verbs, so half of its meaning niche is already occupied by them – so it will not be used so frequently, and will therefore not reproduce strongly. By contrast, there are empty niches for the remaining 'path' verbs. So, in a self-reinforcing process, a majority of path verbs will tend to drive out manner verbs. The same arguments apply for three dimensions, adding the dimension 'form of moving object'. In every language, one dimension will come to dominate.

Language Universals

Greenberg (1966), Hawkins (1994) and others have discovered universals of language structure, some of which hold with high statistical reliability over all known languages, and which have been interpreted as evidence of language-specific structures in the human brain. Typical of these is Greenberg's (1966) Universal 2:

In languages with prepositions, the genitive almost always follows the governing noun, while in languages with postpositions it almost always precedes.

Many of these universals can be understood not as a reflection of any structure in the brain, but as the result of evolution of word feature structures. The key selective forces responsible for Universal 2, and others like it, are the forces of reducing ambiguity while retaining productivity.

English is a language with prepositions rather than postpositions ('fiddler on the roof' refers to a fiddler, not a roof) and the genitive follows the governing noun ('man of action' is a man, not an action). In languages such as Japanese both go the other way round; Universal says that in essentially all languages the genitives and adpositions are similarly linked. Why are the English feature structures for 'on' and 'of' linked in this way?

One answer lies in the handling of structural ambiguities. Consider a compound phrase like 'the lid of the box on the table' which can be read in two ways:

((the lid of the box) on the table)
(the lid of (the box on the table))

Because English genitives and prepositions branch the same way, both of these readings refer to some kind of lid. In Japanese, both readings would refer to a kind of table. However, in a language which did not obey Greenberg's Universal 2, the two readings might be radically different (e.g. one reading would refer to a kind of lid, the other reading to a kind of table). This is shown in Table 20.1.

Table 20.1. *Ambiguity and Greenberg's Universal Number 2*

	← ← on of	→ → on of	← → on of	→ ← on of
(the lid of (the box on the table))	lid	table	box	lid
((the lid of the box) on the table)	lid	table	box	table

Greenberg   Anti-Greenberg

If the two readings have nothing in common (as in the last column, where one refers to a lid and the other refers to a table), then the structural ambiguity is a 'hard' ambiguity which will severely affect any later processing of the sentence. Either it needs to be resolved immediately before further processing, or the two distinct meanings need to be carried forward in parallel, at a large extra processing cost. If the two readings are rather similar (both referring to a kind of lid) then this is a 'soft' ambiguity, and we can use just their shared meaning to carry on processing one sentence meaning, coming back to resolve the ambiguity later when we have more information. So it is much easier to handle the soft structural ambiguities which arise in a language obeying Greenberg's Universal 2.

Similar accounts apply to many of the structural universals discovered by Greenberg and others. For instance, the structural ambiguity in 'I saw the man near the steps' would be hard to handle in a language with VO order and postpositions; so VO order is generally linked with prepositions, OV order with postpositions. VO/OV order must also be consistent with genitive order to avoid other similar hard ambiguities; the three features of VO/OV order, pre/postpositions, and genitive binding direction all exert selection pressures on each other to be mutually consistent, and so to avoid hard ambiguities. The ordering of relative clauses before or after a noun is similarly constrained.

The only way to obey these constraints simultaneously is to clearly be a head-first or head-last language – to have a well-defined Head Parameter. Feature structures for verbs, prepositions, genitives and relative pronouns are mutually selected to line up in this way. Therefore the Head Parameter, which has been taken as evidence for innate language-specific structure in the brain, and is central to the 'Principles and Parameters' model of language acquisition (Chomsky 1988), is not evidence for any innate structure in the brain; it can be just as well explained by the evolution of word feature structures in historic time.

Regularity and Irregularity

The word evolution picture gives an account of one of the most puzzling features of language – the mixture of regularity and irregularity observed in every language.

The theory of language use and learning outlined earlier can support languages of arbitrary irregularity. The theory is fully lexicalised, so the syntax associated with every word is packaged in the feature structure for that word; a language would still be viable if every word had different syntax packaged with it. However, because of the selection pressures on words, such a language would not stay completely irregular for long. Its word species would soon be driven towards regularity by three selection pressures:

Productivity: If many word feature structures have shared common 'shapes', they are easily interchangeable like Lego bricks in common patterns, giving a rapid combinatorial explosion of possible meanings. In contrast, if each word had its own idiosyncratic shape, finding patterns which fit properly together would be a new challenge for each sentence, limiting the productivity of the language.

Ambiguity: The examples of semantic roles and language universals illustrate how the need to avoid ambiguities can force different words of a language into a common mould of regularity.

Ease of learning: Regular syntax and morphology can be learnt by a secondary learning process which reduces the amount of learning required – so that for instance the inflectional morphology of every new verb or noun need not be learned.

On this basis, therefore, we might expect every language to continually converge to a state of greater and greater regularity. However, two main selective forces prevent this, leading to a mixture of regularity and irregularity.

The first of these can be understood from the analogy of a ferromagnetic crystal, in which neighbouring atoms, through their magnetic moments, tend to line each other up along a common axis of magnetism. The mutual selective forces exerted by words on one another are of this form – tending to line up the verbs of motion along a certain meaning 'axis' or to line up many parts of speech along a head-first or head-last axis, and so on.

However, in ferromagnetic solids, all atoms do not take the same alignment. Once the atoms in a certain region have become lined up in one direction, they stabilise each other in that direction – so it then becomes more difficult for any influence from neighbouring regions to realign them. So the solid splits up into a number of domains, each of which has a regular alignment, but irregular borders.

I suggest that words in a language show similar behaviour – words of similar meanings form 'domains of regularity', stabilising each other in those patterns and resisting change from other domains. Each new word is drawn into some domain of regularity – but the domains have irregular and unpredictable boundaries.

The second major force leading to irregularity is language mixing – typically caused by conquest or invasion. Here the conquering group brings its own language, which the conquered emulate and absorb (i.e. the word feature structures propagate like viruses from conquerors to conquered), producing an irregular mixture from two (possibly more regular) antecedent languages. This social/political force is the main initial agent of irregularity. The resulting irregularity may take a variety of long-lasting knock-on forms as the many new small domains of regularity – created and intermingled by the language collision – jostle to re-form their boundaries.

So the mixture of regularity and irregularity which we find in all languages – and which can be problematic for theories based on regularity – emerges naturally from the theory of word evolution.

Biological and Cultural Evolution

This chapter has argued that the mechanisms supporting language in the brain are actually quite general-purpose – for constructing feature structures, unifying them, and generalising to learn; and that many specific features of languages we see today arise from the evolution of word memes, not from biological evolution of the brain. In this section I discuss some general issues concerning this viewpoint.

Feature structures can be used for more than language. In a paper at the previous conference in this series (Worden 1998) I argued that language evolved from primate social intelligence, which uses the same feature structures. This theme has been taken up by Bickerton (this volume), who focuses on a 'cheater detection mechanism', one facet of social intelligence. I proposed more generally that all primate social intelligence uses a feature-structure internal representation of social situations which I called 'scripts' (Worden 1996), after Schank and Abelson (1977), and that scripts are the underlying meaning representation for language. I proposed that specific computations (such as unification) evolved for social intelligence, and are also used for language. The feature structures of this theory are the same as the scripts used in Worden (1998), and it is still proposed that these feature structures arose in primate social intelligence. The learning mechanisms are the same for language and for social intelligence.

This account of language use and language learning can apply equally well to gestural language as to spoken language. It is consistent with an account of the evolution of language where complex gestural language evolved first, before the evolution of physical features favouring spoken language. Feature structures can link gestures to meaning, and define a syntax for gestures – just as they can for sounds. The theory is consistent with a continual transition from gestural language to spoken language, either before or after the emergence of complex syntax.

There are two alternative accounts of the structure of language – that it reflects language-specific structures in the human brain (i.e. that it arises from biological evolution), or that it reflects just the functional requirements for language. This chapter espouses the latter kind, because it is the functional requirements for language which create selection pressures for the evolution of words.

If a particular feature of universal grammar (say, the Head Parameter) can arise from two distinct mechanisms, how do we decide which mechanism is responsible? One relevant piece of information is the relative speed of the two mechanisms. The speed of any evolutionary process depends on three factors (Worden 1995):

- The intergeneration time for replication
- The maximum number of offspring from one successful replicator in one generation
- The strength of the selection pressures (difference in fitness between least and most fit)

From each of these three factors, words are expected to evolve much faster than people. While children learn some words from their parents (with a generation time of twenty years) they can learn many words from their peers with a generation time of one year or less. While a reproductively successful person may have up to ten children, a successful word can spawn hundreds of copies of itself. And finally, while intelligence and loquacity certainly contribute to the fitness of people, other noncognitive selection pressures are equally important; and the linguistic selection pressure on people for ability to handle particular parts of syntax is probably rather weak. By contrast, if a word feature structure is a misfit, or is supplanted by another word, its outlook for replication is very bleak; linguistic selection pressures on words can be very strong.

Because these drivers of selection are all so much stronger for words than for peoples' language device in the brain, we would expect words to evolve much faster – by a factor of 1,000 or more. This expectation is borne out by the rapid evolution of languages over historic time, compared to the very small changes in human intellect for at least the last ten thousand years.

If two competing explanations of some change both seem to fit the facts, you should believe the faster one – the faster mechanism will get there first and make the change, even if the slower one might have done so in time. In fact, the faster mechanism will probably remove any selection pressure which could have driven the slower mechanism. If the words of our languages naturally line themselves up to be head-first or head-last, over hundreds of years, then our brains are under no selection pressure to evolve a Head Parameter (i.e. to force the words into line) over millions of years.

Deacon (1997) has similarly argued that selection pressures for specific features of language – such as the Head Parameter – are unlikely to have shaped the neural structures in our brains, because of the diversity of languages and their rapid rate of change compared to evolutionary timescales.

The idea that languages evolve has always seemed an attractive idea, but has been hard to cash out into a predictive theory. This is because the basic mechanism of language replication – in effect the 'DNA' of language – has been unknown; and without it, the language evolution story lacks crucial detail. Constraints on language replication might prevent or divert evolutionary changes. However, there is now a simple working theory of language learning, formulated in the framework of categorial grammars, which enables us to understand how words replicate, and so how they evolve.

In this theory, the basic mechanisms of language use and language acquisition are not highly language-specific or restrictive; they are built on more general operations of unification and generalisation. Each word in a language is a feature structure, with few restrictions on its form. Any one of these word feature structures will be faithfully transmitted across generations by the learning mechanism, and over many generations word species evolve.

I have illustrated how this picture of word evolution can account simply for a few prominent features of languages – such as the diverse syntactic means used to define semantic roles, the domains of syntactic regularity and irregularity seen in languages, and some language universals. It seems likely that a similar word evolution account can be given for many other features of language.

In this picture, therefore, many language features arise not from the restrictions of an innate language apparatus of the brain (cf. Chomsky 1988), but from the evolution of word feature structures (memes) under the selection pressures of use. Language tells us less about the structure of the mind than we thought it did.

To those who want to learn about the mind, this result may seem a disappointment. However, it need not be – because in a scientific theory, less is more. We need not assume that the mind has a whole range of complex language-specific devices; just that we have a few general and powerful mechanisms for learning and using feature structures, evolved from our primate social intelligence. These mechanisms place few constraints on the word feature structures, which then evolve freely as we use them, giving the structure of modern languages. As long as this model fits the data, a simpler theory of the human mind is a better one.

References

Andrews, A. 1985. The major functions of the noun phrase. In T. Shopen (ed), *Language Typology and Syntactic Description*, Vols. I–III. Cambridge: Cambridge University Press.

Carpenter, B. 1992. *The Logic of Typed Feature Structures*. Cambridge: Cambridge University Press.

Chomsky, N. 1988. *Language and Problems of Knowledge: The Managua lectures.* Cambridge, MA: MIT Press.

Dawkins, R. 1976. *The Selfish Gene.* Oxford: Oxford University Press.

Dawkins, R. 1982. *The Extended Phenotype.* Oxford: Oxford University Press.

Deacon, T. 1997. *The Symbolic Species: The co-evolution of language and the human brain.* London: Penguin.

Greenberg, J. H. 1966. Some universals of grammar with particular reference to the order of meaningful elements. In J. H. Greenberg (ed), *Universals of Language.* Second edition. Cambridge, MA: MIT Press, pp. 73–113.

Hawkins, J. A. 1994. *A Performance Theory of Order and Constituency.* Cambridge: Cambridge University Press.

Kaplan, R. M. and J. Bresnan. 1981. *Lexical Functional Grammar: A formal system for grammatical representation.* Cambridge, MA: MIT Press.

McMahon, A. M. S. 1994. *Understanding Language Change.* Cambridge: Cambridge University Press.

Oehrle, R. T., E. Bach and D. Wheeler (eds). 1988. *Categorial Grammars and Natural Language Structures.* Dordrecht: Reidel.

Pollard, C. and I. Sag. 1993. *Head-Driven Phrase Structure Grammar.* Chicago: University of Chicago Press.

Schank, R. C. and R. P. Abelson. 1977. *Scripts, Plans, Goals and Understanding: An inquiry into human knowledge structures.* Hillside, NJ: Erlbaum.

Shieber, S. 1986. *An Introduction to Unification-Based Approaches to Grammar.* Stanford, CA: CSLI.

Siekmann, J. H. 1989. Unification theory. *Journal of Symbolic Computation* 7: 207–274.

Talmy, L. 1985. Lexicalisation patterns: semantic structure in lexical forms. In T. Shopen (ed), *Language Typology and Syntactic Description*, Vols. I–III. Cambridge: Cambridge University Press.

Worden, R. P. 1995. A speed limit for evolution. *Journal of Theoretical Biology* **176**: 137–152.

Worden, R. P. 1996. Primate social intelligence. *Cognitive Science* **20**: 579–616.

Worden, R. P. 1997. A theory of language learning. Manuscript, http://dspace.dial.pipex.com/jcollie/.

Worden, R. P. 1998. The evolution of language from primate social intelligence. In J. R. Hurford, M. Studdert-Kennedy and C. Knight (eds), *Approaches to the Evolution of Language: Social and cognitive bases.* Cambridge: Cambridge University Press, pp. 148–166.

21

On the Reconstruction of 'Proto-World' Word Order

FREDERICK J. NEWMEYER

Motivating a 'Proto-World' Word Order of SOV

It is a truism that hypotheses about the evolution of cognitive faculties are problematic in ways that those about purely physical features are not. The language faculty, as an evolutionary emergent trait, multiplies such problems by an order of magnitude. As a result, claims about the origins and evolutionary history of this faculty tend to be underlain by a host of assumptions, any or all of which could well turn out to be ill-founded. This chapter is no exception. It takes as a starting point a half dozen or so underlying assumptions drawn from the fields of language typology and language evolution, and ranging from quite well accepted to highly controversial. Its purpose is to argue that if these assumptions are correct, then this conclusion follows:

> (1) The earliest human language had rigid SOV (i.e. subject-object-verb) word order.[1]

The first assumption is the following:

> (2) SOV order predominates among the world's languages today.

Earlier studies (e.g. Tomlin 1986) posited a roughly equal percentage of SOV and SVO languages. However, Dryer (1989) showed that such conclusions arise from a faulty sampling method. It is true, as Dryer noted, that if one simply counts languages, one does arrive at the conclusion that the two structural types are equally common. But accidents of human history conspire to underplay the predominance of SOV. For example, the great majority of languages in sub-Saharan Africa belong to a single family – the Niger-Kordofanian – and the great majority of these languages are SVO. Furthermore, every island in the Pacific has its own language (most belonging to a single family), and the majority of these languages are verb-initial. Dryer corrected for such skewing

Table 21.1. *Breakdown of genera in terms of basic word order, by area*

	Africa	Eurasia	Australia-New Guinea	NAmerica	SAmerica	Total
SOV	22	26	19	26	18	111
SVO	21	19	6	6	5	57
VSO	5	3	0	12	2	22

Source: Dryer 1989.

by dividing the languages of the world into units, each with the approximate time depth of a subfamily of Indo-European. These units, or 'genera', show a preference for SOV word order in all six continental groupings, and a strong preference everywhere but in Africa (see Table 21.1).

The second assumption (or, more properly, pair of assumptions) pertains to changes between OV and VO order:

(3) The historical change OV > VO is both more common than the change VO > OV and more 'natural'.

Changes in both directions have been both attested and reconstructed. However, far more word order changes of OV to VO than the reverse fall into both categories.[2] Indeed, Charles Li has remarked that, 'with the exception of the Chinese case which has developed certain verb-final constructions while the language is still SVO, ... the only documented types of word order changes that are not due to language contact are SOV to (VSO) to SVO' (Li 1977: xii–xiii). And that one putative 'uninfluenced' change to OV, which was argued for in Li and Thompson (1974), has since been called into question. Light (1979) and Sun and Givón (1985) show that there has been no recent diachronic trend toward verb-finality in Chinese, an order which, in any event, is far rarer in actual discourse than Li and Thompson imply. Furthermore, based on the comparative evidence provided by the related Tibeto-Burman languages, many scholars have concluded that the earliest stage of Chinese was SOV, not SVO.[3]

Several researchers have attempted to explain why verb-final order is more likely to give way to verb-medial order than the reverse. Vennemann (1973) points to the loss of case endings in SOV languages through phonological attrition. In such an eventuality, the shift of the verb to the middle serves to demarcate more saliently the subject from the object. A parsing-based argument for a drift to verb-mediality can be derived from the findings of Hawkins (1994). SOV languages with 'heavy' objects create considerable parsing difficulty. Process-ing efficiency is maximally improved by preposing the object to initial position, creating OSV order. Such a gain in efficiency is reflected cross-linguistically. As Greenberg (1963: 79) noted, 'in a substantial proportion, possibly a majority, of [SOV] languages ... if any other basic order is allowed, it is OSV'. However, efficiency is also increased (though not as greatly) by postposing the object, creating SVO order. And as it turns out, a substantial minority of SOV languages allow SVO an an alternative order. Thus there is a ready parsing-based mecha-nism for 'leakage' from SOV to SVO. Now, it is never advantageous from the point of view of parsing for an SVO language to prepose a heavy object to a position between the subject and the object. And hence, there is nothing based in language processing that would create 'leakage' from SVO to SOV.

More recently, Aske (1998) has put forward a rather complex information content–based argument for the greater naturalness of the move from OV to VO than from VO to OV. Very briefly, he points to discourse-based pressure for the development of a focus position after V in OV languages, leading ultimately to VO order. However, there is no corresponding mechanism for the loss of an NP after V in VO languages. Thus he posits a long-term drift to VO.

Supporting evidence for the greater stability of SVO than SOV is provided in Steele (1978). She has calculated that SOV languages are more likely to have alternate orderings of S, V, and O than do languages with other basic orderings (see Table 21.2). Indeed, SVO languages, in general, have no common alternate orders at all.

The conjunction of assumptions (2) and (3) is very curious. On the one hand, OV order predominates today. But on the other hand, there has been a drift away

Table 21.2. *Alternate orderings for basic orders*

	VOS	VSO	SOV	SVO
very common	VSO SVO	VOS	OSV	------
common	------	SVO	SVO	-------

Source: Steele 1978.

from OV order. Hence, the following interim conclusion seems inescapable:

(4) SOV order was once much more typologically predominant than it is now.

Now let us approach the matter from the opposite direction. I assume with Bickerton (1990) that the evolutionary antecedent to true human language was 'protolanguage', a pared-down system of communication devoid of argument structure (i.e. principles linking thematic roles and syntactic positions) and principles of recursion. Along with Bickerton, I make the following assumption:

(5) Protolanguage had thematic structure.

As Bickerton has observed, the ability to recognise and utilise the distinction between agents, patients, instruments and so on has to antedate by far the emergence of true human language. It stands to reason, then, that such arguments were marked overtly in protolanguage, whether by inflectional morphology or some other device.[4] Following Bickerton, there is no reason to assume that these arguments occurred in any fixed order. Pragmatic considerations would have been the only determinants of their positioning in any particular utterance.

Based purely on what strikes me as having a high degree of plausibility, I make an additional assumption about protolanguage:

(6) Protolanguage lacked quantificational structure.

I know of no evidence that higher apes can master the subtleties of quantifier scope or that of other logical operators. It seems reasonable to speculate that this ability was absent from the repertoire of *Homo erectus*, the species communicating by means of protolanguage.

Now let us make a new observation that will tie together all of the above. This observation concerns the typological properties associated with typical SVO and SOV languages. They are encapsulated in (7):

(7) a. SVO languages are 'good at' representing quantification directly, but 'bad at' representing thematic structure directly.
    b. SOV languages are 'good at' representing thematic structure directly, but 'bad at' representing quantification directly.

What might I mean by that? An old observation about the typological differences between SVO and SOV languages is that the former tend to be far more permissive than the latter in allowing grammatical elements to occur displaced from their subcategorised position or, put in more theory-dependent terminology, the former have more 'movement rules' than the latter. Dryer (1991), for example, has found that 71% of verb-final languages are 'Wh-in situ' (that is, they lack a rule of Wh-movement), while only 42% of SVO languages lack such a rule, and even fewer – 16% – of verb-initial languages are without Wh-movement. In other words, in this respect, SOV languages manifest a more direct matchup between overt syntactic position and thematic role than do SVO and VSO languages.

Along the same lines, rules that move elements to argument position are far more difficult to motivate for rigid verb-final languages than for other types of languages (for discussion, see Müller-Gotama 1994). The best motivated A-movement for Japanese is Passive, but this rule in Japanese (as in other languages) morphologically marks its subcategorisationally displaced argument, and thereby betrays its original thematic role (see Miyagawa 1989 for discussion). Other NP movements might well be completely absent in that language. Indeed, it is by no means out of the question that rigid SOV languages have no overt (i.e. non-LF) instantiations of Move-α at all. Even the 'scrambling' of the subject, object, and verb into nonbasic orders, which is common in SOV languages, is not necessarily the result of movement. A number of linguists have put forward arguments, quite strong ones in my opinion, that the repositioning that we find in scrambling lacks many of the hallmarks of a transformational rule (see Lee 1992; Bayer and Kornfilt 1994; Kiss 1994; Neeleman 1994).[5]

Furthermore, SOV languages tend to have a more restricted range of basic grammatical relations than do SVO languages. By that I mean that the argument structure of heads in SOV languages is 'simpler' than that in SVO languages in that a smaller range of thematic relations is associated with particular syntactic positions. So, in English, a typical SVO language in this respect, the verb *find*, say, can take an agent, a theme or a locative as a subject:

(8) a. Mary found what she was looking for.
    b. My old sofa found a home in the departmental lounge.
    c. Noon found Bill eating lunch in the Student Union.

Such a one-many mapping between grammatical and thematic roles is much rarer in SOV languages.

Hawkins (1995) has conveniently illustrated the strict grammatical role–thematic role match up in SOV languages by the following comparison between English and German, a nonrigid SOV language:

(9)   English (SVO) vs. German (SOV)
    a. Subject-to-Subject Raising
        E: The noise ceased to get on his nerves.
        G: ?Der Lärm hörte auf, ihn aufzuregen.

    b. Tough Movement
       E: Literature is boring to study.
       G: *Die Literatur ist langweilig zu studieren.
    c. Exceptional Case Marking (formerly known as 'Subject-to-Object
       Raising')
       E: I believe the farmer to have killed the cow.
       G: *Ich glaube den Bauern, die Kuh geschlachtet zu haben.
    d. Out-of-clause Wh-movement
       E: What did you assume that we would not bring?
       G: *Was hast du angenommen, dass wir nicht mitbringen würden?
    e. Semantic diversity of grammatical relations
       E: My guitar broke a string.
       G: *Meine Gitarre hat eine Saite zerrissen.
    f. Breadth of subcategorisation possibilities
       E: This door will open.
           This door will open new possibilities.
       G: Diese Tür wird sich öffnen.
          *Diese Tür wird neue Möglichkeiten öffnen.

Note that German does allow a restricted form of Wh-movement. Müller-Gotama (1994) demonstrates that rigid SOV languages like Japanese, Korean, and Malayalam not only prohibit Wh-movement outright, but are even fussier than German in demanding a strict matchup between thematic and grammatical relations.

    Another illustration of the fact that SOV languages reveal the thematic role of syntactic positions more directly than do SVO languages comes from the fact that the former are much more likely to have rich case marking than the latter. This, again, is uncontroversial. In the pioneering typological work of Greenberg (1963), such a correlation was presented as a universal of language:

    (10) Universal 41 (Greenberg 1963: 113)
        If in a language the verb follows both the nominal subject and
        nominal object as the dominant order, the language almost always
        has a case system.

In the sample of 237 languages presented in Siewierska and Bakker (1994), 64% of SOV languages have explicit case, but only 30% and 42% of SVO and VSO languages, respectively.

    Why should SOV languages force their arguments to toe the line in ways that SVO languages do not? Hawkins (1995) puts forward a reasonable parsing explanation for this typological difference. Heads, in general, are the best identifiers of their subcategorised arguments. If one hears the verb *give*, for example, one is primed to expect two associated internal arguments, one representing a recipient and the other an object undergoing transfer. On the other hand, a human NP might or might not be a recipient, and an inanimate NP might or not be an object undergoing transfer. Hence, if arguments precede their heads, as they do in SOV languages, extra cues are useful to identify their thematic status. This can be accomplished by keeping them contiguous to the head (that is, by restricting their movement possibilities) and/or by endowing them with case marking that uniquely identifies their thematic role or helps to narrow down the possibilities.

The rather direct representation of thematic structure in SOV languages leads to a less direct means of representing the scope of some logical operators. In English and other SVO languages the positioning of the moved wh-phrase acts as a scope marker. Hence from an underlying structure like (11a) can be derived (11b) and (11c), where the surface position of *who* uniquely identifies the former as an indirect question and the latter as a direct question:

(11) a. He was wondering [you saw who]
     b. He was wondering who you saw
     c. Who was he wondering that you saw?

But with no movement of the wh-operator, an SOV underlying structure like (12a) represents the order of elements both in the indirect and the direct question:

(12) a. he [you saw who] were wondering =
     b. He was wondering who you saw, or
     c. Who is he wondering that you saw?

While languages without Wh-movement have mechanisms for resolving scope ambiguities (the placement of special question particles, intonational cues and so on), such languages have far more indirect means for signalling scope than do SVO languages with Wh-movement.

So consider where we are now. Working backward in time from the present, we have postulated an increasing percentage of SOV languages. Furthermore, we have concluded that protolanguage marked thematic roles directly. Now, let us adopt Bickerton's hypothesis that the central feature of the transition from protolanguage to true language was the imposition of thematic structure onto syntactic structure, that is, the creation of argument structure. What would have been the most processing-efficient implementation of this imposition? I would argue for the following reasons that it would be to delay the appearance of the verb as long as possible. While heads do help to specify the thematic role of their complements, they rarely pick out a unique complement. Most verbs are ambiguous with respect to the argument types that they allow. Again, drawing on examples provided in Hawkins (1995), note that the English verbs *break* and *believe* occur in a number of different frames:

(13) *break*

    Frame 1. NP – V – NP   *John broke my guitar*
          [Agent] [Patient]
        2. NP – V   *My guitar broke*
          [Patient]
        3. NP – V – PP   *A string broke on my guitar*
          [Patient] [Locative]
        4. NP – V – NP   *My guitar broke a string*
          [Locative] [Patient]
        5. NP – V – NP   *My guitar broke a world record*
          [Instrument] [Patient]

(14) *believe*

    Frame 1. NP – V – NP   *I believe the farmer*
          [Agent] [Dative]
        2. NP – V – NP   *I believe this report*
          [Agent] [Patient]
        3. NP – V – S′   *I believe that the farmer killed*
          [Agent] [Object of belief] *the cow*
        4. NP – V – NP – VP   *I believe the farmer to have*
          [Agent] [Agent]   *killed the cow*

If thematic roles were (more or less) uniquely identified by inflection, as we have posited, it would actually have been less efficient to have the heads precede their subcategorised arguments than to follow them. The former option creates temporary ambiguity, the latter option does not. So from the point of view of processing the ideal solution would have been to delay the appearance of the verbal head until after the appearance of its complements. Put another way, we have arrived at the following conclusion: [6]

(15) The earliest human language had rigid SOV order.

It is occasionally suggested that there is something more 'basic' about SVO order than SOV. For example, Kayne (1994) argues, largely on theory-internal grounds, that all languages are underlyingly SVO. And, while I know of nothing in print to this effect, the fact that creole languages are largely SVO has been taken to mean that such ordering reflects an evolutionarily early stage of language. This is not the place to evaluate Kayne's hypothesis, whose correctness is far from established and, if correct, whose implication for language origins is obscure. However, I see no creole-based arguments for SVO as a proto-order for true human language. Creoles, by definition, derive from pidgins, and pidgins by definition are created by people who already have a language (indeed, different languages). In such a contact situation, inflectional morphology would be expected to be the first grammatical feature to disappear. And there are obvious functional reasons, already mentioned, why SVO is a better order than SOV when thematic roles are not overtly marked. Hence I see no creole-based arguments for early human language having a basic order of SVO.

Interestingly, Goldin-Meadow and Mylander (1998) have recently shown that home signs, the spontaneous signed languages created by deaf children in the absence of any prior linguistic input, are OV.

SOV Proto-Order and UG Constraints

The second half of this chapter will discuss the implications of conclusion (15) for the origins of the constraints that, by hypothesis, form part of our innately specified Universal Grammar (UG). Broadly speaking, there are three evolutionary scenarios regarding their origins:

(16)   Three theories of the origin of UG constraints
   a. Big-bang theories
   b. Genetic assimilation theories
   c. Constraints-as-epiphenomena theories

Under big-bang theories (16a), the evolutionary 'event' responsible for human language brought full-blown UG constraints along with it. In other words, the constraints are contemporaneous with the birth of true human language. In very different ways, Chomsky (1988, 1991) and Bickerton (1990) have taken such a position. Chomsky, for example, has speculated that UG might be an epiphenomenal by-product of brain evolution:

Perhaps these [properties of language] are simply emergent physical properties of a brain that reaches a certain level of complexity under the specific conditions of human evolution. (Chomsky 1991: 50)

That is, when a brain gets big enough or complex enough, UG follows as a consequence. For Bickerton, a single mutation turned protolanguage into full human language, complete with all UG principles intact. While more recently, Bickerton has abandoned the single-mutation approach to the origins of language, he still advocates a 'catastrophic', rather than a gradualist scenario for the origins of UG principles (Bickerton 1998).

Genetic assimilation theories (16b) posit that UG constraints resulted from the nativisation of parsing (and other performance?) principles via the Baldwin Effect (Baldwin 1896; Hinton and Nowlan 1987). In other words, such constraints have an ultimate functional motivation. Under conditions of a rapidly fluctuating environment and pressure to acquire common features of the speech community as early as possible, they were 'assimilated' into the genome. Berwick and Weinberg (1984) present an early version of this scenario in arguing that the UG principle of Subjacency had its roots in parsing efficiency. A genetic assimilation account for this principle is elaborated and modelled formally in Kirby and Hurford (1997).

Under constraints-as-epiphenomena theories (16c), what might be taken to be innate 'UG constraints' are argued to be epiphenomenal by-products of mechanisms not particular to grammar (Deane 1992; Kluender 1992). That is, their effects are claimed to be derivable synchronically from the interaction of principles from the domain of parsing, predication and so on. If (16c) is correct, then there is no issue for the evolution of grammar per se, though it would raise issues for the evolution of other aspects of cognition.

I will now argue that if the conclusions of the first part of this chapter are correct, then (16b), genetic assimilation theories, must be incorrect. It is a striking fact that in rigid OV languages such as Japanese and Korean, few of the UG principles put forward within the Government-Binding theory are manifest.[7] Let us begin with Subjacency. Since Japanese has no overt long-distance movement, the question of the applicability of Subjacency to this language arises only for LF movements. Such movements are not subject to this constraint, as (17) and (18) demonstrate:

(17) e_i osiete-ita   seito-ga rakudaisita sensei$_i$
       teaching-was student flunked   teacher
       'the teacher who the student that (he) was teaching flunked'

(18) John-wa Mary-ga nani-o katta   kadooka siritagat-te-iru   no
       John   Mary   what bought whether know-want-PROG NOM
       'John wants to know whether Mary bought what'

In (17) we have one relative clause embedded inside another. The gap inside the lower clause can be interpreted as coreferential to the head noun of the higher clause. In other words, there is a Subjacency-violating link between filler and gap. (19) illustrates:

(19)

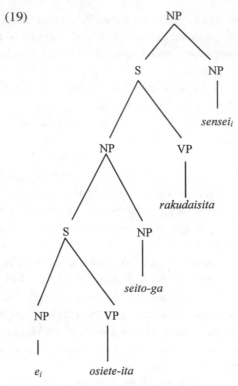

(18) can be interpreted with *nani* 'what' having widest scope, again illustrating that Subjacency does not regulate LF movements in that language.

The classic Binding Theory, developed on the basis of English and other VO languages, does not hold in rigid OV languages. Korean, for example, has two types of locally bound anaphors, *cakicasin* and a compound formed of a pronoun and *casin*. As (20) illustrates, such anaphors are not subject to Principle A of the binding theory.[8] Here we see an object binding a reflexive inside a subject:

(20) cakicasin$_i$ / ku-casin$_i$ -ui emeni-ga   John$_i$ -ul paeshin haess-ta
      himself's   mother   John   betrayed
      'Himself's mother betrayed John.'

Along the same lines, there is no subject-object asymmetry in negative polarity licensing in Korean and Japanese (Choe 1988; Suh 1990).

What does seem particularly relevant for rigid OV languages is the thematic role borne by the relevant element. For a first example, in an interesting study of Korean long-distance anaphors (LDA) within the framework of Optimality

Theory, Moon (1995) argued that the thematic role of the antecedent and anaphor is the major factor determining binding possibilities. The c-command relation is a distant fourth:

> (21) Ranked constraints in the binding of Korean long distance anaphors
>
>   a. Thematic Hierarchy Constraint (LDA must be bound by a thematically higher NP)
>
>   b. Larger Domain Preference Constraint (given potential antecedents for LDA in different domains, the more distant the domain, the stronger the preference)
>
>   c. Subject-Orientation Constraint (LDA must be bound by a subject NP)
>
>   d. C-Command Constraint (LDA must be bound by a c-commanding NP)
>
>   e. Discourse Binding Constraint (LDA must be bound by a prominent discourse NP if no antecedent is available within the sentence)

Second, the Case Filter appears to have no independent motivation in Japanese and Korean. Put another way, there is no sentence whose ungrammaticality might be attributed to that principle that could not be explained by a requirement that the NP in question bear a thematic role.

Finally, consider the Empty Category Principle (ECP). It is certainly true that LF movements of adjuncts are blocked in Japanese, which is a classic ECP effect. In (22) it is impossible to interpret *naze* 'why' with wide scope:

(22) *John-wa Mary-ga naze sore-o katta   kadooka siritagat-te-iru   no?
    John   Mary   why that   buy-PAST whether know-want-PROG Q
    'John wants to know [whether [Mary bought it why]]?'

However, the impossibility of this interpretation is easily reinterpretable as a thematic effect – empty adjuncts are not visible to the parser by virtue of not being theta-marked.

These facts would seem to rule out genetic assimilation theories (alternative (16b)) as the source of UG constraints. Under this scenario, the nativisation of parsing (and perhaps other) principles took place essentially to speed the process of language acquisition. But, as we have seen, the major UG constraints are not particularly evident in rigid SOV languages. If the first human language manifested this ordering, then there would have been no pressure driving them to nativise. That would have happened later as VO languages developed. But it is a truism that any normal child can learn any human language. And in particular, given exposure and nothing more, Japanese and Korean children can learn English. Thus we conclude that UG constraints must have appeared contemporaneously with the appearance of true human language, or they cannot be innate at all.

An Important Caution

There is the danger that the conclusions of this chapter might be misunderstood or endowed with implications that are neither implied nor intended. While I am happy to posit a long-term drift from OV to VO order, there is no coherent sense that a change to verb-medial order represents any kind of a progressive 'improvement' in language. Even at the level of parsing, there is no evidence that SVO has an edge over SOV (for discussion, see Hawkins 1994). To reinforce this point, let me give an analogy from phonology. There are good functional reasons for devoicing final stops, and many more languages have been known to devoice such stops than to voice them. Yet for all that, German and Russian are in no sense 'better' languages than are English and French because they have added a devoicing rule in the course of their histories. The same point can be made for the change from OV to VO order. I know of no objective measure that would rank English 'over' Japanese because the former, but not the latter, has undergone a change from OV to VO.

Unfortunately, there are scholars who, based on an exclusive investigation of changes within the Indo-European family, have written of SVO languages as being more 'functional' or 'efficient' than SOV languages or in some other way being more adequate modes of communication (Bichakjian 1991; Bauer 1995; Beaken 1996). Such a view is pure nonsense, and requires no further discussion.

The unquestioned ability of any normal child to learn any human language leads one to conclude that every possible human language dates from the evolutionary 'event' that created true language out of protolanguage. All that has happened over time is a change in the typological distribution of existing languages.

Conclusion

Based on the results of research in language typology and on conclusions reached by language evolutionists, I have argued that the earliest human language had rigid SOV order. Such a hypothesis, if correct, would seem to invalidate the idea that the constraints of Universal Grammar arose via the genetic assimilation of processing principles. We are left with the possibility that UG constraints must have appeared contemporaneously with the appearance of true human language, or they cannot be innate at all.

Acknowledgement

I would like to thank Julia Herschensohn for her helpful comments on an earlier version of this chapter.

Notes

1. I follow Greenberg (1963) in characterising a proper subset of SOV languages as 'rigid'. Japanese and Korean are modern examples. A hallmark of such languages is their (nearly) exceptionless instantiation of the word order correlations first noted by Greenberg, and then further elaborated in a series of papers by Matthew Dryer (see especially Dryer 1991, 1992). Among such correlations are postpositionality, relative clauses preceding the head noun, manner adverbs preceding the verb, auxiliaries following the verb, and lack of overt Wh-movement. I assume that nonrigid SOV languages were a historically later development.

2. The claim in Givón (1979) that an original SOV order can literally be reconstructed for all language families is certainly too strong, however (see Lightfoot 1979 and Van Valin 1981, for discussion). Claudi (1994) argues that the languages of the Mande branch of Niger-Congo have undergone a change from SVO to SOV as the result of a chain of events triggered by the grammaticalisation of tense-aspect constructions. While I am incapable of evaluating her claim, it is worth pointing out that other Africanists (Givón 1975; Hyman 1975; Williamson 1986) have argued that the SOV order of these languages can be traced back to Proto-Niger-Congo.

3. On the other hand, Peyraube (1996, 1997) presents evidence that Chinese was predominantly VO as far back as the 14th century BC. However, he too rejects the hypothesis that it is drifting to OV.

4. Bickerton's insight about the availability of thematic relations to prehumans did not lead him to posit that such relations were overtly 'tagged' in protolanguage, however. Quite the contrary, in fact; he maintains that 'protolanguage will seldom if ever have any kind of inflection' (Bickerton 1990: 126). But his conclusion is based in part on an identification of the structural properties of protolanguage with those of modern-day pidgins – an identification that I reject. Interestingly, based on computational modelling, Batali (1998) concludes that inflectional morphology appeared very early in evolutionary terms.

5. In particular, the change in position of the 'scrambled' elements does not lead to changes in binding relations or negative polarity interpretation, as one would expect if scrambling were an instantiation of Move-α.

6. Strictly speaking, the argumentation presented leads equally to the possibility of OSV order. I assume that OSV was excluded by a general principle of iconicity, which leads, all other things being equal, to conceptually close elements being co-constituents. It is uncontroversial, I believe, that verbs and objects together form the conceptual category of 'predicate'. For example, this generalisation is captured in the Montague tradition by the category IV corresponding to both the lexical category 'verb' and the nonlexical category 'verb phrase'.

7. I assume that what follows can be translated into the Minimalist Program, though I leave it for others to do so. I would like to thank Soowon Kim, Yongkil Jeong, Hideo Makihara and Toshiyuki Ogihara for help with the Korean and Japanese examples.

8. The claim that c-command is not relevant for local binding in rigid SOV languages is not equivalent to the claim that such languages are 'nonconfigurational' (Hale 1980; Farmer 1984). As shown in Saito and Hoji (1983), there is an asymmetric (i.e. c-command) relationship between subject and object in Japanese.

References

Aske, J. 1998. *Basque Word Order and Disorder: Principles, variation, and prospects*. Amsterdam: Benjamins.

Baldwin, J. M. 1896. A new factor in evolution. *American Naturalist* **30**: 441–451.

Batali, J. 1998. Computational simulations of the emergence of grammar. In J. R. Hurford, M. Studdert-Kennedy and C. Knight (eds), *Approaches to the Evolution of Language: Social and cognitive bases*. Cambridge: Cambridge University Press, pp. 405–426.

Bauer, B. L. M. 1995. *The Emergence and Development of SVO Patterning in Latin and French*. Oxford: Oxford University Press.

Bayer, J. and J. Kornfilt. 1994. Against scrambling as an instance of Move-α. In N. Corver and H. van Riemsdijk (eds), *Studies on Scrambling*. Berlin: Mouton de Gruyter, pp. 17–60.

Beaken, M. 1996. *The Making of Language*. Edinburgh: Edinburgh University Press.

Berwick, R. C. and A. Weinberg. 1984. *The Grammatical Basis of Linguistic Performance*. Cambridge, MA: MIT Press.

Bichakjian, B. H. 1991. Evolutionary patterns in linguistics. In W. von Raffler-Engel and J. Wind (eds), *Studies in Language Origins II*. Amsterdam: Benjamins, pp. 187–224.

Bickerton, D. 1990. *Language and Species*. Chicago: University of Chicago Press.

Bickerton, D. 1998. Catastrophic evolution: the case for a single step from protolanguage to full human language. In J. R. Hurford, M. Studdert-Kennedy and C. Knight (eds), *Approaches to the Evolution of Language: Social and cognitive bases*. Cambridge: Cambridge University Press, pp. 341–358.

Choe, H.-S. 1988. *Restructuring Parameters and Complex Predicates: A transformational approach*. Doctoral dissertation, M.I.T.

Chomsky, N. 1988. *Language and Problems of Knowledge: The Managua lectures*. Current Studies in Linguistics 16. Cambridge, MA: MIT Press.

Chomsky, N. 1991. Linguistics and cognitive science: problems and mysteries. In A. Kasher (ed), *The Chomskyan Turn: Generative linguistics, philosophy, mathematics, and psychology*. Oxford: Blackwell, pp. 26–55.

Claudi, U. 1994. Word order change as category change: the Mande case. In W. Pagliuca (ed.) *Perspectives on Grammaticalization*. Amsterdam: Benjamins, pp. 191–232.

Deane, P. D. 1992. *Grammar in Mind and Brain: Explorations in cognitive syntax*. Cognitive Linguistics Research 2. The Hague: Mouton de Gruyter.

Dryer, M. S. 1989. Large linguistic areas and language sampling. *Studies in Language* **13**: 257–292.

Dryer, M. S. 1991. SVO languages and the OV:VO typology. *Journal of Linguistics* **27**: 443–482.

Dryer, M. S. 1992. The Greenbergian word order correlations. *Language* **68**: 81–138.

Farmer, A. K. 1984. *Modularity in Syntax: A study of Japanese and English.* Cambridge, MA: MIT Press.

Givón, T. 1975. Serial verbs and syntactic change: Niger-Congo. In C. N. Li (ed), *Word Order and Word Order Change.* Austin, TX: University of Texas Press, pp. 47–112.

Givón, T. 1979. *On Understanding Grammar.* New York: Academic.

Goldin-Meadow, S. and C. Mylander. 1998. Spontaneous sign systems created by deaf children in two cultures. *Nature* **391**: 279–281.

Greenberg, J. H. 1963. Some universals of language with special reference to the order of meaningful elements. In J. H. Greenberg (ed), *Universals of Language.* Cambridge, MA: MIT Press, pp. 73–113.

Hale, K. 1980. Remarks on Japanese phrase structure: comments on the papers on Japanese syntax. In Y. Otsu and A. Farmer (eds), *Theoretical Issues in Japanese Linguistics.* Cambridge, MA: Department of Linguistics and Philosophy, MIT, pp. 185–203.

Hawkins, J. A. 1994. *A Performance Theory of Order and Constituency.* Cambridge Studies in Linguistics 73. Cambridge: Cambridge University Press.

Hawkins, J. A. 1995. Argument-predicate structure in grammar and performance: a comparison of English and German. In I. Rauch and G. F. Carr (eds), *Insights in Germanic Linguistics I.* Berlin: Mouton de Gruyter, pp. 127–144.

Hinton, G. and S. Nowlan. 1987. How learning can guide evolution. *Complex Systems* **1**: 495–502.

Hyman, L. M. 1975. On the change from SOV to SVO: evidence from Niger-Congo. In C. N. Li (ed), *Word Order and Word Order Change.* Austin, TX: University of Texas Press, pp. 113–147.

Kayne, R. S. 1994. *The Antisymmetry of Syntax.* Cambridge, MA: MIT Press.

Kirby, S. and J. R. Hurford. 1997. Learning, culture, and evolution in the origin of linguistic constraints. In P. Husbands and H. Inman (eds), *Proceedings of the Fourth European Conference on Artificial Life.* Cambridge, MA: MIT Press, pp. 493–502.

Kiss, K. É. 1994. Scrambling as the base-generation of random complement order. In N. Corver and H. van Riemsdijk (eds), *Studies on Scrambling.* Berlin: Mouton de Gruyter, pp. 221–256.

Kluender, R. 1992. Deriving island constraints from principles of predication. In H. Goodluck and M. Rochemont (eds), *Island Constraints: Theory, acquisition, and processing.* Dordrecht: Kluwer, pp. 223–258.

Lee, Y.-S. 1992. Case and word order variations in nominal clauses. *Language Research* **6**: 359–380.

Li, C. N. (ed) 1977. *Mechanisms of Syntactic Change.* Austin, TX: University of Texas Press.

Li, C. N. and S. A. Thompson. 1974. An explanation of word order change SVO → SOV. *Foundations of Language* **12**: 201–214.

Light, T. 1979. Word order and word order change in Mandarin. *Journal of Chinese Linguistics* **7**: 149–180.

Lightfoot, D. W. 1979. Review of *Mechanisms of Syntactic Change* by C. Li (ed). *Language* **55**: 381–395.

Miyagawa, S. (ed) 1989. *Syntax and Semantics, Vol. 22: Structure and case marking in Japanese*. San Diego, CA: Academic.

Moon, S. C. 1995. *An Optimality Approach to Long Distance Anaphors*. Doctoral dissertation, University of Washington.

Müller-Gotama, F. 1994. *Grammatical Relations: A cross-linguistic perspective on their syntax and semantics*. Berlin: Mouton de Gruyter.

Neeleman, A. 1994. Scrambling as a D-structure phenomenon. In N. Corver and H. van Riemsdijk (eds), *Studies on Scrambling*. Berlin: Mouton de Gruyter, pp. 387–430.

Peyraube, A. 1996. On word order and word order change in pre-archaic Chinese. *Chinese Languages and Linguistics* **4**, 241–263.

Peyraube, A. 1997. On word order in archaic Chinese. *Cahiers de Linguistique Asie Orientale* **26**: 3–20.

Saito, M. and H. Hoji. 1983. Weak crossover and Move-α in Japanese. *Natural Language and Linguistic Theory* **1**: 245–259.

Siewierska, A. and D. Bakker. 1994. The distribution of subject and object agreement and word order type. In A. Siewierska (ed) *Constituent Order Working Paper 6*. Strasbourg: ESF Eurotype Project, pp. 83–126.

Steele, S. 1978. Word order variation: A typological study. In J. H. Greenberg, C. A. Ferguson and E. A. Moravcsik (eds), *Universals of Human Language, Vol. 4: Syntax*. Stanford, CA: Stanford University Press, pp. 585–623.

Suh, J.-H. 1990. *Scope Phenomena and Aspects of Korean Syntax*. Doctoral dissertation, University of Southern California.

Sun, C.-F. and T. Givón. 1985. On the so-called SOV word order in Mandarin Chinese: a quantified text study and its implications. *Language* **61**: 329–351.

Tomlin, R. S. 1986. *Basic Word Order: Functional principles*. London: Croom Helm.

Van Valin, R. D. 1981. Toward understanding grammar: form, function, evolution (review of T. Givón, *On Understanding Grammar*). *Lingua* **54**: 47–85.

Vennemann, T. 1973. Explanation in syntax. In J. Kimball (ed), *Syntax and Semantics, Vol. 2*. New York: Seminar, pp. 1–50.

Williamson, K. 1986. Niger-Congo: SVO or SOV? *Journal of African Languages and Linguistics* **16**: 5–14.

EPILOGUE

22

The History, Rate and Pattern of World Linguistic Evolution

MARK PAGEL

Seven thousand or more different languages may currently be spoken around the world (Grimes 1988; Ruhlen 1991). This is more different languages spoken by a single mammalian species than there are mammalian species. Seven thousand different languages translate into up to seven thousand different ways of saying 'Good morning' or seven thousand different ways of saying 'It looks like it's going to rain'. Contrast humans' remarkable capacity for language with that of the chimpanzee, a species often touted as able to learn language. Only after years of almost continual Skinnerian training (harassment?) do chimpanzees show a limited facility with sign language word use, and even then, little or no concept of grammar. Humans, on the other hand, effortlessly acquire language, use grammar in inventive ways and require no prodding or incentives. New and fully fledged sign languages have been observed to emerge spontaneously among groups of deaf children (Kegl and Lopez 1990). Language use and linguistic diversity distinguish our species, which might more aptly be called *Homo sapiens loquens*.

Language diversity is not evenly distributed around the world. As many as 700 to 1,000 different languages, or approximately 10 to 15% of the total, are found on the island of New Guinea (Moseley and Asher 1994), which at a relatively small 310,000 square miles deserves the moniker of the World's Tower of Babel. In regions of northeast Papua New Guinean coastal rain forest one encounters a new language every few miles, or less. By comparison, even though China can boast perhaps a fifth of the world's population in an area twelve times the size of New Guinea, only about ninety different languages are recognised. What causes these wide variations in linguistic density? In addition to obvious homogenising influences on language, such as the European conquest of the Americas or the rapid spread of agriculture across Europe, ecological factors such as latitude, habitat and proximity to coastlines may also influence language diversity and language evolution (Austerlitz 1980; Nichols 1990, 1995; Mace and Pagel 1995). Quantitative investigation of the factors that influence the rate and patterns of language evolution promises more than just insights into language. If different language groups are roughly synonymous with different cultural groups, then 'linguistic ecology' (Pagel 1994; Mace and Pagel 1995) or the study of factors promoting language diversity may yield insights into cultural evolution.

The contributors to this volume have discussed the many ideas that have been put forward in an attempt to understand why language evolved in humans. I will develop ideas about the history and ecology of linguistic diversity, that is, how languages evolved once the capacity to form them was in place, and the factors that influence rates and patterns of language evolution. A theme I wish to return to throughout the chapter is the often close analogies between the concepts and methods that can be used to investigate linguistic and biological evolution. Like genetic systems, languages have discrete units, they have mechanisms for replication and inheritance and they experience mutation and selection (Table 22.1). Languages do, of course, differ from biological species in the extent of 'horizontal transmission': they borrow words and other linguistic features readily. And yet, horizontal transmission of genetic material is more common than imagined, with viruses, insects and transposable elements being the principal vectors.

Table 22.1. *Selected similarities between languages and genetic systems*

Attribute	Genetic systems	Languages
discrete units	nucleotides, genes, individuals	words and other linguistic elements
replication	transcription	teaching, learning, imitation
dominant mode(s) of inheritance	parent-offspring	parent-offspring, generational (including teaching)
horizontal transmission	many mechanisms (e.g., hybridisation, viruses, transposons, insects)	borrowing
mutation	many mechanisms (e.g., slippage, unequal crossing over, point mutations and faulty repair)	mistakes, vowel shifts, innovation
selection of favoured variants	fitness differences among alleles	societal trends

A Brief History of Language Diversity

Extant Linguistic Diversity

The number of different extant human languages can be used to trace different scenarios of the history of linguistic diversity since humans began talking. This exercise reveals that the current diversity of seven thousand or so languages may be little more than a faint echo of the linguistic diversity that has ever existed, and that under at least some plausible scenarios wide linguistic diversity may be a recent event on the planet.

The gradual accumulation of species resulting from the biological processes of speciation and extinction can be modelled by a simple form of mathematics known as the birth-death process. As a first approximation, this same mathematics can be applied to languages: like species, languages give rise to new languages, some of which go extinct, and others of which survive. Assuming that the first language or languages arose at time $t = 0$, and since that time languages have evolved and gone extinct at a more or less constant rate, the equation

$$n_t = n_0 e^{(\lambda - \mu)t} \tag{1}$$

returns the total number of languages extant at time t, where n_0 is the number of original or founder languages, λ is the birth rate and μ the death rate of languages per unit time, and t is the time elapsed since the origin of language.

By making some assumptions about the peak diversity of extant languages and the birth rate of new languages, it is possible to trace the rise of linguistic diversity since humans first began to speak. The assumptions may in some cases be only guesses, but the qualitative conclusions turn out not to be strongly dependent upon them. The peak of worldwide linguistic diversity may have been about ten thousand years ago, a time just prior to the development and spread of agriculture. Agriculturists, owing to their demographic success relative to hunter-gatherers and nomadic pastoralists, fanned out rapidly enough that they very likely replaced with their own languages many of the indigenous languages in their path (Renfrew 1987). Renfrew speculates that this may be one reason why Europe has a relatively homogeneous and small number of languages (approximately fifty) for its geographical size.

Figure 22.1a plots n_t, the number of extant languages, for three different values of times of the origin of language in humans, on the assumptions that the peak of linguistic diversity was 12,000 languages, just prior to the spread of agriculture, and that all languages originate from a single common ancestral language. Whether or to what extent the explosive phase of language evolution

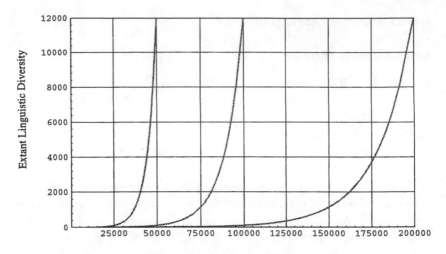

Number of Years Humans Have Spoken

Figure 22.1a. The number of extant human languages at various times after the origin of language, based upon Equation (1). The three curves correspond to the assumption that humans began speaking 50,000 (left curve), 100,000 (middle), or 200,000 (right) years ago, and that the peak of linguistic diversity was 12,000 languages. Each curve assumes that humans began talking at (arbitrary) time $t = 0$, and the x-axis shows for a given curve the number of years since $t = 0$. If language evolved 50,000 years ago, linguistic diversity is a relatively recent phenomenon. Choice of the net birth rate (Equation (1)) does not affect these curves.

evidenced by all three curves merely reflects languages carried along by the rapid expansion of the human population or whether languages in some way catalysed this growth is simply unknown, but must remain one of the more interesting questions of culture and the adaptiveness of language.

No one knows exactly when humans began talking. If it were as recently as 50,000 years ago, roughly coinciding with the appearance of modern humans in Europe, then there may have been fewer than 300 to 400 different languages spoken on the planet as recently as 20,000 years ago (Figure 22.1a). Clear evidence of very old linguistic diversity, then, could lead to the rejection of the 50,000-year figure. Another implication of this curve is that quite independently of whether languages evolve rapidly or slowly, one should not expect to find much time depth in language taxonomies if humans began to talk 50,000 years ago. This is not the same as saying that it is impossible to find time depths beyond about 5,000 to 6,000 years in comparisons among languages, a controversial point to which I shall return in a later section.

By comparison, substantial linguistic diversity would have been present by 20,000 to 50,000 years ago if humans began talking 100,000 to 200,000 years before the present. An estimate of 200,000 years ago may not be unreasonable based upon mitochondrial DNA evidence suggesting that the common ancestors to modern humans may have lived in Africa around that time (Stoneking 1993). Cavalli-Sforza and colleagues (Cavalli-Sforza et al. 1988) find that linguistic phyla tend to evolve within the major human genetic groups, so dating the nodes of the human gene tree could give upper estimates of the age of the linguistic phyla. They suggest that the deep nodes of their phylogenetic tree may correspond to 60,000 to 100,000 years ago. Choosing amongst these various scenarios for when humans began to talk must await better dating of the human phylogenetic tree, and independent linguistic or archaeological evidence for the timing of the emergence of major linguistic groups. It should not be difficult to garner support for one of these starting dates over the others. At the interesting time of about 20,000 years ago, the three curves make predictions about the standing level of diversity that differ by factors of five or more.

The Total Number of Languages Ever Spoken

The integral of Equation (1) can be used to investigate the total number of languages ever spoken on Earth.

$$n_{total} = \int_0^t \lambda n_t \, dt = \frac{\lambda}{\lambda - \mu} n_0 e^{(\lambda - \mu)t} \tag{2}$$

All of the terms are defined as before, and n_{total} is the total number of languages at time t. The total number of languages ever spoken dramatically exceeds the number of extant languages, and increasingly so as time passes (Figure 22.1b). If humans began talking 200,000 years ago and languages evolved at a rate of one per 500 years (a common estimate deriving from glottochronological investigations), then perhaps over 500,000 different languages have ever been heard on Earth. Choosing the middle estimates of 100,000 years ago for the origin and one language per 1,000 years still yields a figure of about 130,000 different languages ever spoken. Throughout history, the overwhelming majority (80–99%) of the languages humans have invented have gone extinct, never to be heard again, having been replaced either by a descendant language or by some other language. These figures are intriguingly similar to estimates of the fraction of biological species that have gone extinct. Raup (1991) estimates that up to 99% of all species that have ever lived are extinct. The extant stock of human languages is but a fraction of the languages that humans are capable of producing. Dr Seuss's 'On Beyond Zebra' may not be so farfetched after all (Seuss 1955).

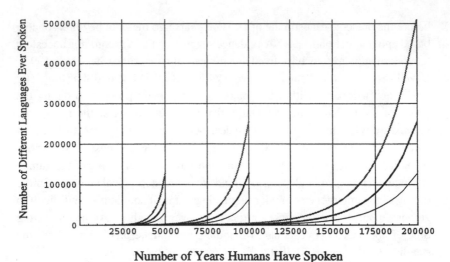

Number of Years Humans Have Spoken

Figure 22.1b. The total number of languages ever spoken as a function of time since the origin of language, and three different assumptions about the rate of language evolution. The top curve of each set of three corresponds to a rate of 0.002 per annum (one new language per 500 years), the middle curve to 0.001, and the lower curve to 0.0005. Choice of this rate determines the death rate.

Evolutionary Forces Producing Language Change

Rates of Language Evolution

The historical diversity of human languages can be breathtaking when viewed from the present, and questions naturally arise as to whence the diversity comes. In this section I will discuss some of the evidence for intrinsic or evolutionary forces producing language change. These forces yield what might be termed the linguistic clock or the regular evolution of languages analogous to the molecular clock of DNA (Li and Graur 1991).

The American linguist Morris Swadesh invented the branch of comparative linguistics known as glottochronology to investigate whether languages diverge from one another at a regular and constant rate (Swadesh 1952). Swadesh's method was to record, for pairs of languages, the proportion of shared cognate words from a standard list he called his 'fundamental vocabulary'. He then plotted that proportion against the number of years the two languages had been separated. The fundamental vocabulary consists of words likely to be common to all languages, such as the names of body parts, the seasons, and cosmological terms. He reasoned that such words would be much more resistant to borrowing than words outside of the fundamental vocabulary. He proved correct: owing to borrowing on a large scale following the Norman invasion of England, roughly 50% of English words are of Romance origin, whereas only 5% are in the fundamental vocabulary. The fundamental vocabulary, like a conserved gene sequence in biology, is less buffeted by evolutionary forces.

If Swadesh is correct that languages diverge at a constant rate, then the proportion of cognate words that two languages share will decline over time as a smooth curve. Theory predicts that the curve will follow $p_c = e^{-srt}$, where p_c is the proportion of shared cognates, t is the time the two languages have had to diverge, r is the rate at which the languages diverge per unit time, s is a coefficient that takes the value of 1 if the comparison is between an ancestor and descendant, or 2 if it is two sister languages that have diverged, and e is the base of the natural logarithm.

In Swadesh's original study, the pairs included Old and Modern English, Old High German and Modern German, and Middle Egyptian and Coptic, the last pair representing a time span of 23 centuries (Figure 22.2). Each of these pairs contains an ancestral language and its descendant language. Fitting $p_c = e^{-srt}$ to these data yields a value of 0.00019 for r, and the line explains 87% of the variance. This value for r corresponds to divergence of about 20% per 1,000 years in the fundamental vocabulary between ancestor-descendant pairs or 20% per 500 years between two sister languages ($2r = 0.00038$). Swadesh and others reported similar values for r (Swadesh 1952, Lees 1953). The comparison of Old English to Modern English fits the 20% per millennium prediction well, and is one of the reasons why Chaucer is more difficult than Shakespeare. Considering how often the figure of 15 to 20% per 1,000 years (or per 500 years for sister languages) figure is cited, it should be referred to as 'Swadesh's rule' for linguistic divergence.

Swadesh's early successes were later tarnished by studies finding that his rule could give inaccurate results. Some glottochronological calculations made Latin older than Greek (Rea 1958). Glottochronology fell into disfavour in the 1960s, and despite recent attempts at modernisation (e.g. Dobson 1978) is still treated with scepticism by many linguists. Such scepticism is appropriate if glottochronology is interpreted literally and simplistically as a means of estimating absolute times of divergence of languages. However, a little-known piece of work by Kruskal, Dyer and Black (1971) produced evidence suggesting that Swadesh's idea of a regular linguistic clock might have more than a kernel of truth.

Kruskal and co-workers scored the percent similarity in Swadesh's fundamental vocabulary for all 4,465 possible pairs of 95 Indo-European languages and dialects. Whereas Swadesh estimated a single rate constant (as in Figure 22.2), Kruskal et al. estimated a value of r for each word in Swadesh's list.

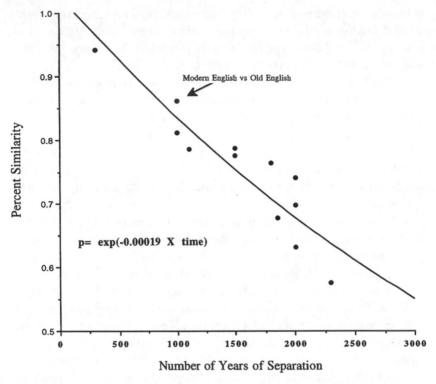

Figure 22.2. Percentage of shared cognate words in Swadesh's fundamental vocabulary between pairs of ancestor-descendant languages. Data are from Swadesh (1952). Curve fitted by least squares accounts for 87% of the variance. Exponent of 0.00019 corresponds to a rate of approximately 20% divergence per millennium, or Swadesh's Rule (see text).

Moreover, unlike in Swadesh's original work, the times of divergence of the Indo-European languages are largely unknown. So Kruskal et al. also estimated the 4,465 separation times, one for each pair of languages. They then repeated this procedure on data for 371 Malayo-Polynesian languages, necessitating a colossal 68,635 pairwise comparisons.

Under the $p_c = e^{-srt}$ model described earlier, the probability that the two languages are cognate for a given word is $p_m = e^{-2rt}$, and that they are not cognate is $p_m = 1 - e^{-2rt}$, where the subscript m denotes a given 'meaning' or 'word'. Treating words as independent, the probability of observing the set is the product of their individual probabilities. This is then repeated for all pairs of languages. The product over all words and languages is denoted the 'likelihood'. For the Indo-European languages it is given by

$$L = \prod_{ij=1}^{4,465} \prod_{1}^{m} p_{mij},$$

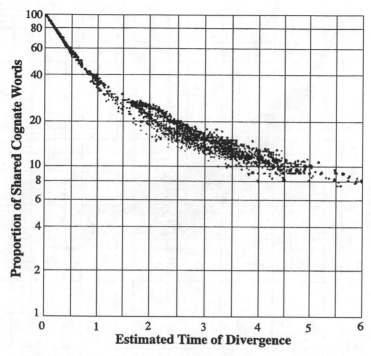

Figure 22.3a. Proportion of shared cognate words in Swadesh's fundamental vocabulary among 4,465 pairs of Indo-European languages and dialects as a function of separation time. Estimated time of separation is measured on an arbitrary scale of 0 to 6. The *y*-axis is in logarithmic form. For separation times of 5 or more the curve is nearly flat, and a range of separation times is possible for a given proportion of shared cognates. After Kruskal, Dyer and Black (1971).

where the *m* subscript is as described earlier, and the *ij* subscript represents the *ij*-th pairwise comparison. The rates of word substitution and the separation times were simultaneously estimated using the statistical technique of maximum likelihood. The values of *r* and the set of separation times that make *L* the largest are the maximum likelihood values.

Figure 22.3a displays the results of this remarkable study for the Indo-European languages, and Figure 22.3b for the Malayo-Polynesian languages. The observed proportion of shared cognates between each pair is plotted on the *y*-axis, against the maximum likelihood estimates of the separation times on the *x*-axis. The striking feature of both graphs is that most of the area is empty. Languages that have only recently separated are always very similar, and languages that have separated thousands of years ago are always very different. Languages never evolve too fast – presumably because of the need for communication among generations – and yet languages always spontaneously and predictably evolve.

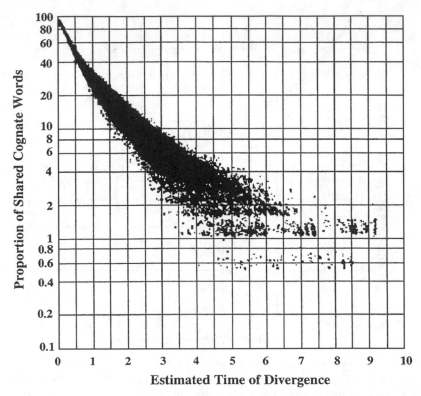

Figure 22.3b. Proportion of shared cognate words in Swadesh's fundamental vocabulary among 68,635 pairs of Malayo-Polynesian languages and dialects as a function of separation time. Estimated time of separation is measured on an arbitrary scale of 0 to 10. The *y*-axis is in logarithmic form. For long separation times the curve is nearly flat, and a range of separation times is possible for a given proportion of shared cognates. After Kruskal, Dyer and Black (1971). The word rate–variation model cannot explain the fanlike shape of these data. Instead these data indicate an up to threefold difference in the rate of evolution of the different Malayo-Polynesian languages.

The narrow band of points for the Indo-European languages and dialects suggests that to a rough first approximation, they diverge at a regular rate. The curve becomes nearly flat at very long separation times, indicating that there appears to be a limiting similarity of about 8 to 10% within which a range of separation times is possible. Swadesh (1952) estimated 8 to 10% to be the similarity that might be expected between two languages purely on the basis of chance and onomatopoeic words. In contrast to the Indo-European languages, the glottochronological results for the 371 Malayo-Polynesian languages show a much more fanlike pattern (Figure 22.3b), indicating significant variation in rates of evolution among these languages.

The shapes of the collection of points on these two graphs are signatures of underlying evolutionary forces that govern linguistic divergence. Figures 22.3a and 22.3b plot divergence on a logarithmic scale (unlike Figure 22.2). A constant rate of divergence should appear on this scale as a straight descending line with slope $-rt$. Instead, for both language groups, the divergence is linear early on, and then slows, producing the concave upwards curve of the figures. What causes this? One possibility is that different words may have substantially different rates of replacement (Cavalli-Sforza and Feldman 1981). Another possibility is that entire languages may diverge rapidly or slowly compared to others. Yet another possibility is that languages diverge more rapidly initially owing to a process of what I shall call 'cultural displacement'.

These ideas can be formalised and tested. The possibility that the rate parameter r varies for different words, but that these rates are constant across languages can be explored by fitting the observed similarities between languages to the basic e^{-2rt} model, integrating over all possible values of r for the different words. Write

$$p_{obs} = \int_0^\infty f(r)e^{-2r_i t}\, dr, \tag{3}$$

where $f(r)$ specifies the probability distribution of r for values of r between zero and infinity, where zero corresponds to a word that never changes. A particularly useful and general form of $f(r)$ is the gamma distribution, given by

$$f(r) = \frac{1}{\alpha\Gamma(\beta)}(r/\alpha)^{\beta-1}e^{-r/\alpha},$$

where α and β are parameters of the gamma distribution that determine its shape. The product $\alpha\beta$ is the mean rate of word substitution. The gamma distribution can take a variety of shapes including the negative exponential, a chi-squared and normal-like distributions, and has the relevant property for modelling rates of not including values less than zero.

Substituting the gamma distribution into (4) and solving the integral yields the prediction that, if rates of evolution vary among individual words, then the observed proportion of shared cognates between two languages will decline with time according to

$$p_{obs} = 1/(1 + \alpha t)^\beta \tag{4}$$

Call this the 'word rate–variation' model.

If words all evolve at the same rate, but different languages diverge at fundamentally different rates, then p_{obs} will for a given language follow

$$p_{obs} = e^{-r_i t}\int_0^\infty f(r)e^{-r_j t}\, dr, \tag{5}$$

where now we assume that language i has some fixed rate of change, and that it is being compared to each of the other j languages in the sample whose r values can vary between zero and infinity. If we again allow $f(r)$ to follow a gamma distribution (here the distribution of rates of whole-language evolution), Equation (6) simplifies to $e^{-r_i t}/(1 + \alpha t)^\beta$. This result gives the shape of the curve relating p_{obs} to time for a given language averaged over all of the other languages in the sample. If we repeat this for each of the languages in the sample, the integral over all of the individual p_{obs} will be given by

$$\bar{p}_{obs} = 1/(1 + \alpha t)^{-2\beta}, \tag{6}$$

which is just the square of the result for words having different rates of evolution (Equation (4)). Call this the 'language rate variation' model.

The cultural displacement model supposes that more change will occur in a given unit of time early on than later. This is easily modelled as $p_{obs} = e^{-2rt^\lambda}$, where it is presumed that $\lambda < 1$.

I estimated the parameters α, β and λ for the three models by finding the values that minimise the squared difference between the data of Figures 22.3a and 22.3b, and the predicted values derived from the relevant equation. These are reported in Table 22.2. For the Indo-European data the cultural displacement model improves upon the Swadesh model of simple exponential decay. The word rate–variation model (allowing variation in the rates of evolution for different words) substantially improves on both of these. It also provides a surprisingly good fit to the data (Figure 22.4). The language rate–variation model fits the data identically to the word rate–variation model, as it must given that they differ only by the parameter β being multiplied by two in one case, but not in the other. However, the language rate–variation model is rejected for the Indo-European data by considering that were there significant variation among languages, the data would appear as a spreading fan shape as time increases. This pattern is not observed: the data tend to be tightly clumped, and all of it curves concave upwards. Indo-European languages appear to evolve at broadly similar rates, even though different words within the languages evolve at different rates.

In contrast to the Indo-European languages, the glottochronological results for the Malayo-Polynesian languages indicate significant variation in the overall rates of evolution among these languages. Fitting the language rate–variation model to these data significantly improves upon the fits of either the Swadesh or the cultural displacement models (Table 22.1). The lower edge of the fanlike cloud represents the fastest-evolving languages, and the upper edge the slowest. The midpoints of the cloud are described by a rate parameter of 0.00025. The lower edge of the fanlike cloud corresponds to a rate of approximately 0.00036

Table 22.2. *Models of linguistic evolution fitted to Indo-European and Malayo-Polynesian data sets*

Model	$\sum\left(p_{obs}-p_{pred}\right)^2$	Parameters	F-test	p-value
Indo-European Languages				
1) e^{-2rt}: Swadesh model	0.0448	r=0.00018		
2) $e^{-2rt^{\lambda}}$: cultural displacement	0.00412	r=0.0036 λ=0.632	2 vs. 1 = 10.87	<0.001
3) $(1+\alpha t)^{-\beta}$: word rate differences	0.00069	α=0.00044 β=1.390	3 vs 2=5.97	<0.005
4) $(1+\alpha t)^{-2\beta}$: language rate differences	0.00069	α=0.00044 β=0.695	4 vs. 2=5.97	<0.005
Malayo-Polynesian Languages				
1) e^{-2rt}: Swadesh model	0.00916	r=0.00053		
2) $e^{-2rt^{\lambda}}$: cultural displacement	0.000542	r=0.0036 λ=0.755	2 vs. 1 = 16.90	<0.001
3) $(1+\alpha t)^{-\beta}$: word rate differences	0.0000951	α=0.00025 β=2.811	3 vs 2=5.70	<0.005
4) $(1+\alpha t)^{-2\beta}$: language rate differences	0.0000951	α=0.00025 β=1.405	4 vs 2=5.70	<0.005

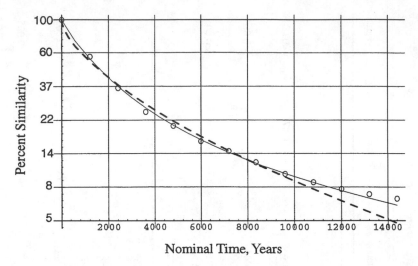

Figure 22.4. Goodness of fit of the word rate–variation model (solid curve) and the 'cultural displacement' model (dashed curve) to estimated midpoint values of the data in Figure 22.3a. The word rate–variation model significantly improves upon the model of cultural displacement.

and the upper to roughly 0.00012, or an approximately threefold difference in rates of evolution among the Malayo-Polynesian languages. The word rate–variation model has no explanation for the spreading fan shape of Figure 22.3b.

The Malayo-Polynesian languages appear on islands of varying sizes and distances from one another. Renfrew (1987) documents how the Polynesian subgroup of the Malayo-Polynesian languages is characterised by significant 'founder effects' as people spread across Oceania inhabiting new islands. Each of these factors – small population sizes, founder effects and geographical isolation – is expected to contribute to varying rates of evolution among the Malayo-Polynesian languages.

The results of these modelling exercises reveal a striking regularity in data on percentages of shared cognate words as a function of time. Phylogenetic trees of languages (e.g. Dyen, Kruskal and Black 1992) could be used to highlight individual languages that evolve more or less rapidly, but the overall Indo-European picture is one of uniformity compared to the Malayo-Polynesian languages.

Rates of Word Evolution in the Fundamental Vocabulary

The parameters of the gamma distribution for the word rate–variation model fitted to the Indo-European data (Table 22.2) predict the frequency distribution

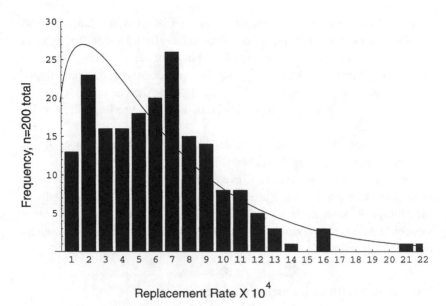

Figure 22.5. Predicted and actual frequency distributions of rates of word substitution in the Indo-European sample.

of the actual rates of word substitution. The estimated parameters predict a unimodal distribution skewed to the right with a mean of $\alpha\beta = 6.1 \times 10^{-4}$ and a variance of $\alpha^2\beta = 2.7 \times 10^{-7}$. These compare well to the actual values of 5.8×10^{-4} and 1.53×10^{-7} that can be calculated from the Kruskal et al. (1971) investigation. The theoretical gamma distribution is plotted in Figure 22.5 against the actual frequency distribution of word rates. The fit is far from perfect, but it should be borne in mind that the theoretical curve was derived solely from the shape of the plotted data in Figure 22.3a. What this reveals is that deep evolutionary processes (like variation in rates of word substitution) leave behind detectable and interpretable traces in the differences among languages (see also Pagel 1997).

The existence of individual words that evolve at very slow rates, where $r \ll 5.8 \times 10^{-4}$ (Figure 22.5), shows that word comparisons can in principle resolve even very old relationships among languages. A word that evolved at a rate of 0.0002 per year would have a 50% chance of being shared between two languages that had been separated 3,500 years, a 25% chance at 7,000, and a 14% chance at 10,000 years. A word with a rate of evolution of 0.000014 per year would have a 50% chance of not having changed in 50,000 years and could thereby be a serious candidate for a universal word, that is, a word that is cognate to all languages. Merritt Ruhlen has recently restated his arguments for a single Mother Tongue or Eve language that is ancestral to all extant languages (Ruhlen 1994). One piece of evidence Ruhlen cites for a Mother Tongue is the existence of glosses that, he avers, are found in all or nearly all languages. The best known of these is 'tok', which variously represents the word 'one', 'finger' or 'toe' among diverse languages. Intriguingly, 'one' had an estimated rate of replacement in the Kruskal et al. study of 0.000033, giving a linguistic half-life of 21,000 years.

Investigation of the classes of words likely to evolve at faster or slower rates could parallel the highly successful research in differential rates of gene sequence evolution. Some genes and even parts of genes evolve rapidly, whereas other genes or regions of them are highly conserved. Alongside knowledge of the ecological or other forces producing variation in overall rates of evolution this could do much to advance our understanding of the processes of language evolution generally.

Patterns of Variation in Linguistic Diversity

The previous sections have traced the inevitable rise of languages and of linguistic diversity, given that there are intrinsic forces of change that operate on languages, similar to the way that genes accumulate mutations over time. In the following sections I explore some of the extrinsic, or ecological, factors that may speed up or slow down the intrinsic rates of change.

Variation in the Density of Languages

Table 22.3 lists estimates of the number of languages per unit area for several well-known language groups. These numbers are only approximations because both the counts of the numbers of languages and the areas over which the languages are found are subject to error. The table displays a remarkable range of densities spanning over three orders of magnitude. The extraordinary diversity of languages in New Guinea is usually explained by reference to the richness of the tropical rainforest habitat. An alternative is that variations in density around the world reflect the amount of time the languages have had to diversify. Some regions of lower density may simply have not yet reached their linguistic 'carrying capacity'. Comparisons among language groups that have reached carrying capacity can provide direct evidence for different regions supporting different densities of languages, whereas language groups that have not reached this point cannot, their numbers being largely a function of elapsed time. Not enough is known with certainty about timings of occupation to make reliable tests of these ideas.

Table 22.3. *Variation in linguistic density around the world*

Language Group	No. of Languages (approx)	Area (millions of sq. miles)	Languages per million sq. miles
Amerind	583	13.3	55
Na Dene	34	1.7	18.5
Eskimo-Aleut (including Chukchi -Kamchatkan)	14	1.5	7.6
Indo-European	50	4.0	13.5
Polynesian	28-38	0.13	245
Bantu	510	5.5	86
Indo-Pacific	700-1000	0.31	2741
Australian	500	2.9	172

Sources: Data principally from Moseley and Asher (1994); Ruhlen (1991, 1994).

Ecological Forces Producing Language Change

Birdsell (1953) discovered that the density of Australian aboriginal language groups was higher in wetter areas, which were usually those nearer to the coast. Nichols (1995) documents the numerically greater diversity of major language groups in coastal areas, in equatorial areas as opposed to temperate or polar regions, and in areas of ecological abundance such as New Guinea. These patterns seem plausible: where the environment is richer and more diverse it is reasonable to expect more self-sufficient groups. But as Nichols and others allow, it may be that human groups migrate first to the richer areas, leaving the less bountiful areas for later immigrants. Table 22.3 makes clear that this phenomenon could present problems for interpreting measures of linguistic diversity.

Recently, Ruth Mace and I undertook an investigation of latitudinal gradients in language diversity in North America (Mace and Pagel 1995), in which we attempted to control for some of the confounding influences on linguistic diversity, including amount of time in a region. We recorded the number of different languages found along a line of latitude for two-degree latitudinal steps between the equator and the North Pole in North America. Latitudinal gradients in animal species diversity have been demonstrated in many animal

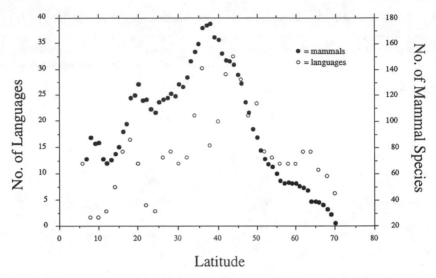

Figure 22.6a. Mammalian species diversity and human language diversity in North America as a function of latitude. Data from Mace and Pagel (1995) and Pagel, May and Collie (1991).

groups including mammals, birds and even undersea invertebrates (Trevelyan and Pagel 1995). The common finding is that species diversity increases from the poles to the equator.

We found that the diversity of human language groups at different latitudes surprisingly closely mirrors the diversity of mammals in North America: both have their peak diversity at or around 40 degrees North latitude and fall off sharply on either side (Figure 22.6a). The shape of this curve may reflect the shape of North America, and so we calculated linguistic density by dividing each measure of diversity by the area of the continent at that latitude. These data reveal that, like mammals, human language groups show a pronounced latitudinal gradient (Figure 22.6b).

The similarity of geographical variation in human linguistic diversity to geographical variation in mammalian species diversity is striking. It suggests that there may be much to learn about the origin and maintenance of human cultures from studying biological speciation and the ecological factors that promote it. Environmental factors may lead to a generalised increase in the rate at which new cultures form, or equivalently to a decrease in the rate at which cultures go extinct. Many ecological factors vary with latitude, and so Mace and I attempted to unravel the latitudinal effect by investigating the diversity of the habitat, a factor that had been shown in an earlier investigation (Pagel, May and Collie 1991) to be associated with mammalian species diversity.

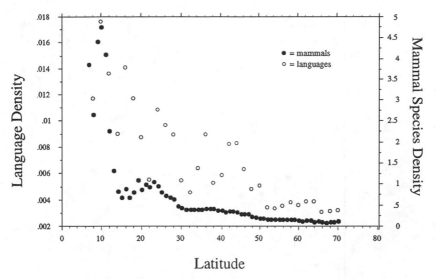

Figure 22.6b. Densities of mammalian species and human languages in North America as a function of latitude.

We recorded the number of different major habitat zones at each line of latitude, and found that a greater diversity of languages is found in regions of greater habitat diversity (Figure 22.7a). This relationship may arise simply because language diversity and habitat diversity both vary with latitude, and so we statistically removed its effects. Figure 22.7b shows that even within a given line of latitude, language diversity increases with increasing habitat diversity. But what of the charge that there may be greater diversity of languages in southern latitudes simply because people have been there longer? The charge can be ruled out for these data because the three major language groups of North America (Amerind, Na Dene, Eskimo-Aleut) migrated from the north, and thus the area of longest habitation (the north) is where the least diversity is found.

Habitat diversity seems either to allow or promote human cultural-linguistic diversity in a manner similar to the way it promotes biological species diversity. A complex and structured habitat may promote speciation in animals by allowing animals to specialise or by increasing the likelihood that populations will live allopatrically. Humans on the other hand are characterised as a species by extreme generality and the ability to overcome the vagaries of the environment. Humans also regularly trade with each other, migrate through each others' territories, wage war and are capable of interbreeding throughout their entire worldwide range. In the light of this, the simple answer that there are more language groups in southern latitudes because the environment supports a

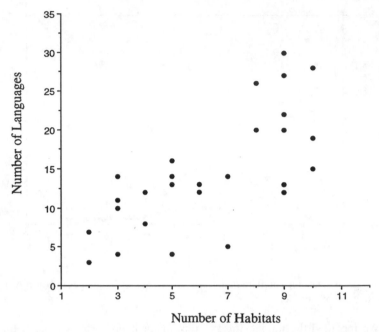

Figure 22.7a. Number of different languages as a function of habitat diversity in North America. Data from Mace and Pagel (1995) and Pagel, May and Collie (1991).

larger number of people begs the question as to why higher densities of people per se lead to more languages and cultures. This must be one of the fundamental questions of human cultural evolution.

One possibility is what might be termed the 'territory defence hypothesis'. Other things equal, if people must traverse large areas simply to find enough food to eat, language and culture will tend to be homogenised because it may be impossible to exclude others from such a large area. This may account in part for the low density of languages in northern latitudes. On the other hand, where it is possible to make a living in a smaller area, it may pay to actively exclude others from one's territory, but at the same time not pay to exclude them from too large an area, especially if the terrain is mountainous or difficult to defend. This sort of process may provide the explanation for the extreme linguistic diversity of coastal regions and New Guinea.

The geographical distribution of language groups can help to understand the geographical distribution of key genetic markers. Sokal et al. (1990) found over 30 areas of Europe characterised by zones of sharp changes in gene frequencies over short geographical distances. Most could be easily explained by geographical features such as mountain ranges and large bodies of water. Seven of the zones could not be explained on the basis of any obvious geographical

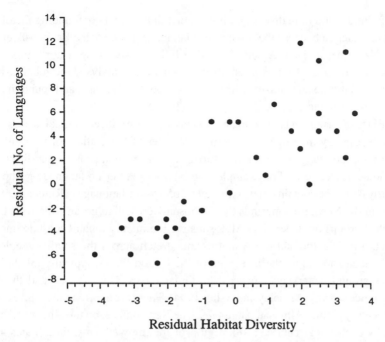

Figure 22.7b. Number of different languages versus habitat diversity in North America after statistical removal of the association of each with latitude.

feature or political boundaries, but all seven were zones of linguistic change. It seems that language differences act as barriers to gene flow, and so an understanding of the factors that promote linguistic heterogeneity goes hand in hand with understanding genetic differentiation.

Phylogenetic Trends, Linguistic Diversity and Rates of Culturogenesis

A feature of linguistic data that is often overlooked in comparative investigations of cross-cultural variation is that languages evolve predominantly within hierarchically nested groupings, or phylogenies. This means that closely related species or closely related cultures cannot be treated as having independently evolved their features: two cultures may possess a common character not because both have independently acquired it, but because both inherited it from a common ancestor (Mace and Pagel 1994; Pagel in press).

This has implications for interpreting the patterns in Figures 22.6 and 22.7. There may be more language groups in southern latitudes simply because it happens that the dominant linguistic groups in the north and south intrinsically differ in their tendency to form new groups. The chance placement in the south of the group with a greater tendency to form new groups could produce the latitudinal gradient in diversity. This is potentially a real confounding factor in North America because the three major language groups – the Eskimo-Aleuts, the Na Dene, and the Amerinds – also fall roughly along a north-to-south gradient. To allow for this possibility we separately analysed the relationship between latitude and density within each of the three groups, and found that it was positive in each case.

Rates of change of languages and their association with ecological factors can also be directly investigated by comparing rates of 'speciation' or what might more appropriately be termed 'culturogenesis' between groups that differ on some ecological trait. For example, the Northern Amerind language group of North America contains approximately 165 extant languages (Ruhlen 1991). Within the Northern Amerinds the Almosan-Keresouian group comprises two 'sister' groups or clades. The Almosans predominantly inhabit coastal regions of both the Pacific and the Atlantic, and stretch across the southern regions of Canada and the northern regions of the United States, typically inhabiting areas around waterways, such as the Great Lakes, Hudson Bay and the St. Lawrence seaway (Moseley and Asher 1994). There are approximately 82 extant or recently extinct Almosan languages. The Keresouians, on the other hand, are nearly exclusively confined to a region of the midwestern United States and the prairies of Canada, and comprise fewer than half as many languages with 38 extant or recently extinct languages. Does this more than twofold difference provide evidence for a higher net rate of production of languages among the coastal and waterway-inhabiting Almosans?

Figure 22.8 portrays these two sister clades, showing the implicit assumption that they are a 'monophyletic' group, that is, that all of the members of both groups uniquely share a common ancestor. This means that the number of languages in each sister group measures the net rate of production of new cultures, because time is the same for both groups. The null hypothesis is that both groups have the same net rate, and that new groups have appeared (or not gone extinct)

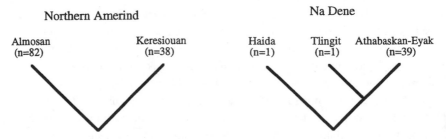

Figure 22.8. Partial phylogenies of the Northern Amerind and the Na Dene language groups. Number of languages in parentheses. Data from Ruhlen (1991).

at the same rate in both clades. Under this null hypothesis, all configurations of branching patterns are equally likely (Slowinski and Guyer 1989), and the two-tailed probability of observing this result or more extreme is given by

$$p = \frac{2(n - k)}{n - 1}, \tag{7}$$

where k is the number of languages in the larger group, and n is the total number of languages.

For the Almosan-Keresouians the value for p is 0.64. Allowing for stochastic variability, the greater than twofold difference observed in the net rate of culturogenesis in this group is no evidence at all that the Almosans split off new language-culture groups at a higher rate (if additional information were available on the lengths of the branches in the phylogeny of these two groups, a potentially more powerful test could be applied; see Pagel 1997).

If the phylogenetic perspective is salutary in this instance it can in other instances point the way towards groups that demand explanation. The Na Dene consist of two principal groups, the Haida and the Continental Na Dene. Within the Continental Na Dene linguists describe two further groups, the Tlingit and the Athabaskan-Eyak (Ruhlen 1991). The relationships among these groups and the number of extant or recently extinct languages are shown in Figure 22.8. The Haida and the Tlingit are each isolated languages. The Haida are confined almost exclusively to the Queen Charlotte islands off the west coast of Canada. The Tlingit are found almost exclusively in a narrow strip of coastal territory along the same west coast region of Canada. The Athabaskan-Eyaks in contrast occupy large regions of Canada's interior and a pocket of the southwestern United States. Applying the test of Equation (7) reveals that there are fewer Haida languages than would be expected by chance ($p = 0.050$) compared to the others, and that within the Continental Na Dene, there are fewer Tlingits than expected by chance ($p = 0.051$). What is the explanation for this?

Without adopting a phylogenetic perspective there would have been no reason even to ask this question. Once we know that these groups are sister clades, the distribution of languages compels us to ask why there are so few Haida and Tlingit languages? Along with the phylogenetic perspective, the geographic clustering of these two languages may suggest that they were systematically displaced, perhaps even pushed to the sea, by Athabaskan-Eyak peoples.

Epilogue

I hope to have shown how linguistic diversity can be studied in its own right and in concert with ecological features to gain insight into the forces that act on rates of linguistic and cultural evolution. Indo-European languages reveal evidence of variation in the rates at which different words are replaced in their fundamental vocabularies, but comparatively little evidence that overall rates of evolution vary from language to language. Cultural displacement may give rise to languages diverging faster when they are closely related. Malayo-Polynesian languages on the other hand appear to evolve at different rates, varying perhaps threefold from slowest to fastest. Ecological factors also play an important role. Habitat diversity emerges as a clear correlate of language diversity. A phylogenetic perspective can help to control for important but often subtle factors that may confound investigations of linguistic diversity.

Widespread linguistic diversity may be a relatively recent phenomenon on the planet. Lamentably, the remarkable Babel of linguistic diversity that arose

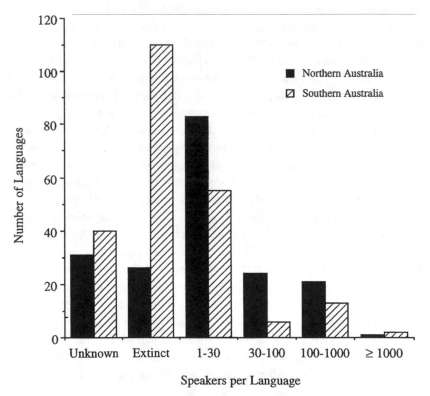

Figure 22.9. Number of speakers per language for Aboriginal languages of Australia. Southern Australian Aboriginal languages predominantly have fewer than 30 speakers, a property often used by linguists to categorise a language as moribund. Southern Australia is the region of greater European settlement. Data from Moseley and Asher (1994).

perhaps as recently as fifteen to twenty thousand years ago is disappearing rapidly. Some linguists estimate that up to three thousand of the languages currently spoken will not survive the next century. The reasons are obvious. A few languages, some owing to trade, others to colonialism and historical accident, are rapidly achieving linguistic hegemony. Where English is spoken, typically between 80 and 90% of the native languages have been lost. In Russia some 70% of the indigenous languages are moribund. As a result of these forces, thirty or so languages per year are witnessing their last speakers die, or are no longer being taught to the young.

The rate of language extinction is two to eight times higher than the expected worldwide rate of production of new languages. The process can be observed in Australia where most of the aboriginal languages are either now extinct or teetering on the verge of extinction (Figure 22.9). The languages in southern Australia tend to have fewer speakers, and it is probably no accident that this is the area of greatest European settlement of the country. Because of forces like these, the more pessimistic linguists estimate that as few as five hundred languages will survive the twenty-first century. Languages are suffering a mass extinction comparable to that of biological species, and the linguistic landscape is, like parts of Australia itself, rapidly coming to resemble a desert.

References

Austerlitz, R. 1980. Language family density in America and North Eurasia. *Ural-Altaische Jahrbücher* **52**: 1–10.

Birdsell, J. 1953. Some environmental and cultural factors influencing the structuring of Australian aboriginal populations. *American Naturalist* **87**: 171–207.

Cavalli-Sforza, L. L. and M. W. Feldman. 1981. *Cultural Transmission and Evolution: A quantitative approach*. Princeton: Princeton University Press.

Cavalli-Sforza, L. L., A. Piazza, P. Menozzi and J. Mountain. 1988. Reconstruction of human evolution: bringing together genetic, archaeological, and linguistic data. *Proceedings of the National Academy of Sciences* **85**: 6002–6006.

Dobson, A. J. 1978. Evolution times of languages. *Journal of the American Statistical Association* **73**: 58–64.

Dyen, I., J. B. Kruskal and P. Black. 1992. An Indo-European classification: a lexicostatistical experiment. *Transactions of the American Philosophical Society* **82**: 1–132.

Grimes, B. F. 1988. *Ethnologue: Languages of the world*. Dallas, TX: Summer Institute of Linguistics.

Kegl, J. and A. Lopez. 1990. The deaf community in Nicaragua and their sign language(s). Unpublished manuscript, Department of Molecular and Behavioral Neuroscience, Rutgers University.

Kruskal, J., I. Dyer and P. Black. 1971. The vocabulary method of reconstructing family trees: innovations and large scale applications. In F. R. Hodson, D. G. Kendall and

P. Tautu (eds), *Mathematics in the Archaeological and Historical Sciences*. Edinburgh: Edinburgh University Press, pp. 30–55.

Lees, R. B. 1953. The basis of glottochronology. *Language* **29**: 113–125.

Li, W.-H. and D. Graur. 1991. *Fundamentals of Molecular Evolution*. Sunderland, MA: Sinauer.

Mace, R. and M. Pagel. 1994. The comparative method in anthropology. *Current Anthropology* **35**: 549–564.

Mace, R. and M. Pagel. 1995. A latitudinal gradient in the density of human languages in North America. *Proceedings of the Royal Society of London (B)* **261**: 117–121.

Moseley, C. and R. E. Asher (eds). 1994. *Atlas of the World's Languages*. London: Routledge.

Nichols, J. 1990. Linguistic diversity and the first settlement of the New World. *Language* **66**: 475–521.

Nichols, J. 1995. The spread of language around the Pacific Rim. *Evolutionary Anthropology* **3**: 206–215.

Pagel, M. 1994. Linguistic geography (review of Atlas of the World's Languages – Moseley and Asher). *Nature* **368**: 361–362.

Pagel, M. 1997. Inferring evolutionary processes from phylogenies. *Zoologica Scripta* **26**: 331–348.

Pagel, M. In press. Maximum likelihood models for glottochronology and reconstructing linguistic phylogenies. In C. Renfrew (ed), *Time-Depth in Historical Linguistics*. Cambridge: The McDonald Institute for Archaeological Research.

Pagel, M., R. May and A. Collie. 1991. Ecological aspects of the geographical distribution and diversity of mammalian species. *American Naturalist* **137**: 791–815.

Raup, D. M. 1991. *Extinction: Bad genes or bad luck?* Oxford: Oxford University Press.

Rea, J. A. 1958. Concerning the validity of lexicostatistics. *International Journal of Applied Linguistics* **24**: 145–150.

Renfrew, C. 1987. *Archaeology and Language: The puzzle of Indo-European origins*. London: Penguin.

Ruhlen, M. 1991. *A Guide to the World's Languages, Vol. 1: Classification*. London: Arnold.

Ruhlen, M. 1994. *The Origin of Language: Tracing the evolution of the Mother Tongue*. New York: Wiley.

Seuss, Dr. 1955. *On Beyond Zebra!* New York: Random House.

Slowinski, J. B. and C. Guyer. 1989. Testing the stochasticity of patterns of organismal diversity: an improved null model. *American Naturalist* **134**: 907–921.

Sokal, R., N. L. Oden, P. Legendre, M.-J. Fortin, J. Kim, B. A. Thomson, A. Vaudor, R. Harding and G. Barbujani. 1990. Genetics and language in European populations. *American Naturalist* **135**: 157–175.

Stoneking, M. 1993. DNA and recent human evolution. *Evolutionary Anthropology* **2**: 60–73.

Swadesh, M. 1952. Lexico-statistic dating of prehistoric ethnic contacts. *Proceedings of the American Philosophical Society* **96**: 452–463.

Trevelyan, R. and M. Pagel. 1995. Species diversity. In W. Nierenberg (ed), *The Encyclopedia of Environmental Biology*. San Diego, CA: Academic.

Author Index

417

Subject Index